Sporting Gentlemen

Men's Tennis from the
Age of Honor
to the
Cult of the Superstar

E. Digby Baltzell

To Clark Sterlings, Tennis Player!
Jim

THE FREE PRESS

New York · London · Toronto · Sydney · Tokyo · Singapore

The Free Press
A Division of Simon & Schuster Inc.
1230 Avenue of the Americas, New York, NY 10020

Printed in the United States of America

Text design by Carla Bolte

printing number

1 2 3 4 5 6 7 8 9 10

Library of Congress Cataloging-in-Publication Data

Baltzell, E. Digby (Edward Digby)
    Sporting gentlemen: men's tennis from the golden age of amateurism to the cult of the superstar / E. Digby Baltzell.
        p.   cm.
    Includes bibliographical references and index.
    ISBN 0-02-901315-1
    1. Tennis—History.   2. Tennis—Social aspects.   3. Tennis players—Conduct of life.   I. Title.
GV992. B35   1995
796.342   de20   94-41401
                                             CIP

The author wishes to thank the following for permission to reprint material included in this book:
    Simon & Schuster Inc., for quotations from *Covering the Court;* copyright © 1968 by Al Laney.
    Sterling Lord Literistic, Inc., for quotations from *Don Budge: A Tennis Memoir;* copyright © 1969 by Frank Deford.
    McIntosh and Otis, Inc., for quotations from *The Scandalous Mr. Bennett,* by Richard O'Connor; copyright © 1962 by Richard O'Connor; copyright renewed 1990 by Olga O'Connor.
    The Economist, for excerpts from the article "Different Ballgames," published September 25, 1993; copyright © 1993 by The Economist Newspaper, Inc.
    Tennis Week, for quotations from "King Borg Reigns for Fifth Year at Wimbledon," by Richard Evans, published July 17, 1980; copyright © 1980 by Tennis Week, Inc.
    William F. Talbert, for quotations from *Playing for Life;* copyright © 1958 by William F. Talbert.
    Frank Deford, for quotations from *The Game,* by Jack Kramer; copyright © 1979 by Frank Deford.

For my darling wife, Jocelyn,
and my tennis friends, living and dead, among them:
Butch Greene, Princeton jock and my teenage idol at the
Mantoloking Yacht Club, Bill Clothier, Al Sulloway, Mac Muir,
Haven Waters, Charlie Dick, Cal Chapin, Arthur Stanwood Pier,
Donald Unger-Donaldson, John Rummery, Freddie Godley,
Tom Rutledge, Bob Miller, Vince Hopkins, Robert Strausz-Hupé,
Jim Cox, Bill DeWitt, Howard Fussell, John Thomas, Frank Koniecho,
David Lavin, Chris Busa, Fred Roll, Max Silverstein, Jack Appel, Ed Thayer,
Howard York, Tom Townsend, John Clark; and Nancy Ritchie,
Hope Knowles, and Nori Delamos.

Thus, to comprise all my meaning in a single proposition, the dissimilarities and inequalities of men gave rise to the notion of honor; that notion is weakened in proportion as these differences are obliterated, and with them it would disappear.

—Alexis de Tocqueville

Certain values and standards that had bonded players in my earlier years as a professional—certain codes of honor and a spirit of cooperation and camaraderie—disappeared. In some ways, the youngest players arrived in a world in which the very concept of values and standards was unknown or quaint and obsolete, like wooden racquets or white tennis balls on which Wimbledon insisted long after the superiority of color had been demonstrated.

—Arthur Ashe

Contents

Figures

Acknowledgments

THIS BOOK IS THE PRODUCT OF OVER HALF A CENTURY OF PLAYING AND LOVING tennis and a decade spent in writing and research. Along the way I have been helped and encouraged by the following persons, who have my thanks:

Bill Clothier, whose fine tennis library was invaluable.

The late Carl Fischer, a Tilden protégé, who encouraged me in the beginning and gave me a copy of Tilden's great classic, *Match Play and the Spin of the Ball*, signed by the author.

Fred Roll, who encouraged a trip to the West Coast where I met and talked to tennis enthusiasts, including the tennis dean of the San Francisco Bay area, Edward "Bud" Chandler, Intercollegiate Champion (1925–26), who played regularly with Helen Wills in his youth and is her legal advisor today.

John W. Sears, who supplied me with a tennis genealogy of his family as well as copies of letters written by his grandfather, Richard D. Sears, first U.S. Tennis Champion.

Mrs. R. Norris (Sue) Williams II, who shared many delightful stories about her husband, winner of the last tennis championship to be played at Newport (1914); also her son, Quincy Williams, who supplied me with some pictures taken by his father.

Donald Budge, who lingered over a two-hour breakfast to share stories of his illustrious tennis career.

Jan Armstrong, Librarian at the International Tennis Hall of Fame in Newport, Rhode Island, who was a constant help over many years, as has been her recent successor, Mark S. Young.

Alan Little and the helpful staff of the Wimbledon Museum Library.

The wonderfully helpful staff of the Van Pelt Library of the University of

Pennsylvania, especially Hilda Pring and David Azzelina. The same should be said of the staff at the Free Library of Philadelphia, especially William Lang and his colleagues in the Art Department.

Peter Bodo, of *Tennis Magazine*; Cindy Smerler, of *World Tennis*; Edwin Fabricus, of the USTA staff; and Edward T. Chase, of Charles Scribner's Sons, all of whom helped bring me closer to the tennis world.

Frank V. Phelps, Richard Geiger, Richard Miller, Harold Bershady, Marvin Wachman, Loretta Denner, Norman Filzman, and Haines Stockton, who were also helpful.

Finally, I have been inspired over many years of squash and tennis at Penn by my old friends, Al Molloy and Hunter Lott.

Above all, I am indebted to Bruce Nichols, my editor, for his solid judgment and dedication to his craft.

Prologue

I BEGAN THIS BOOK IN 1984, THE YEAR JIMMY CONNORS AND JOHN McEnroe disgraced themselves and their country by their crude and rude behavior in the course of losing to Sweden in the Davis Cup Final Round matches held in Göteborg. In spring 1994, while I was making final revisions in preparing the book for publication, two articles in the popular press suggested that professional tennis was in a very bad way indeed.

First, the May 9 issue of *Sports Illustrated* had a coverline asking the question: "Is Tennis Dying?" and featured an article by Sally Jenkins entitled "The Sorry State of Tennis." "Fans are bored, TV ratings are down, equipment sales are soft, and most pros seem to be prima donnas who don't care about anything but money. What can be done about this sinking sport?"

At the end of the month, the May 30 issue of *People* magazine featured Jennifer Capriati in the coverline, asking "What Went Wrong?" "At 13, she was a bubbly kid with a booming forehand. At 18, she's burned out, partying hard and facing a drug charge. Is this payback for a stolen childhood?"

One of the purposes of historical sociology is to help us understand the causes of current problems through historical analysis. This book should shed some light on the plight of pro tennis as of May 1994, for as Oliver Wendell Holmes, Jr., once put it, "A page of history is worth a volume of logic."

CHAPTER 1

Introduction:
Leveling Upwards and Leveling Downwards

There is in fact a manly and lawful passion for equality which incites men to wish all to be powerful and honored. This passion tends to raise the humble to the rank of the great; but there exists also in the human heart a depraved taste for equality which impels the weak to attempt to lower the powerful to their own level.

—Tocqueville

JUST ABOUT A DECADE BEFORE THE END OF AMATEUR TENNIS AT WIMBLE-
don, I spent a sabbatical year (1958–59) in southern Spain. In November, I went up to London where I spent two weeks doing research at the
British Museum before taking a five-day car trip with a criminologist
friend, Norman Johnston, to see some sights in Southwestern England,
including, for my colleague's sake, a visit to the famous Dartmoor Prison,
in Devonshire, where he had a luncheon appointment with the warden.

Before lunch, the warden showed us around the prison. My colleague
was on his way to becoming a world authority on prison architecture; but
we had both taught the popular introductory course in criminology at our
university, so that I knew enough to be amazed at how the warden
opened all the doors with the same antique door key (in the style of my
grandfather's day). A far cry from the dynamite-proof doors and locks at
the Eastern States Penitentiary in Philadelphia, where I often visited with
my students. But the highlight of the Dartmoor visit was our passing
through the working section of the prison: "You see that man over there,
Dr. Johnston," the warden said to my friend. "He squealed on a break
last month." "Why?" we asked. "One of his friends was going to use a
gun," the warden replied, "and he knew that was *not cricket*." I could
hardly believe my ears. Ever since, and especially while writing this book,
I have thought about how a class code of conduct, mythically developed
on the playing fields of Eton before the Battle of Waterloo, could have
penetrated the British social structure so deeply that it bound even an inmate of Britain's maximum security prison in the second half of our increasingly anarchic century.

Back before the First World War, this class code had penetrated to the
four corners of the earth. "It isn't cricket" and "Keep a straight bat" had
become part of a metaphorical code of the Victorian British Empire,
which then ruled about a fifth of the world's population. And it permeated the values of one of the most loyal members of a black cricket club in
the little village of Tunapuna, eight miles outside Port of Spain, the capital of Trinidad. C. L. R. James was born the year Victoria died (1901) and
grew up with the wicket of the Tunapuna Cricket Club in his backyard.
The son of a schoolteacher, he attended the island's major secondary
school, where he later taught for a time in the twenties. He went to
England in 1932, where he made his mark as an historian, novelist, cultural and political critic and activist—a Marxian black-nationalist. In

3

1963, he published a brilliantly idiosyncratic book, *Beyond a Boundary*, which has come to be recognized as a classic in the sociology of sport.

Young James was a passionate sportsman and scholar; when he went to the library, he spent his time browsing through old cricket magazines and parsing Virgil. "I was brought up in the public school code," he wrote. "It came doctrinally from the masters, who for two generations, from the foundation of the school, had been Oxford and Cambridge men."[1]

"We were a motley crew," James wrote of his schoolmates.

The children of some white officials and white businessmen, middle-class blacks and mulattos, Chinese boys, some of whose parents still spoke broken English, Indian boys, some of whose parents spoke no English at all, and some poor black boys who had won exhibitions or whose parents had starved and toiled on plots of agricultural land and were spending their hard-earned money on giving the eldest boy an education. Yet rapidly we learned to obey the umpire's decision without question, however irrational it was. We learned to play with the team. . . . We kept a stiff upper lip. . . . We did not denounce failures, but "Well tried" or "Hard luck" came easily to our lips. We were generous to opponents and congratulated them on victories, even when we knew they did not deserve it. . . . Eton and Harrow had nothing on us.

What a stunning example of an age and culture that still believed in *leveling upwards*!

From the playing fields of the Tunapuna Cricket Club and the government school, James developed a lifelong set of values which he so beautifully summed up as follows:

Before long I acquired a discipline for which the only name is Puritan. I never cheated, I never appealed for a decision unless I thought the batsman was out, I never argued with the umpire, I never jeered at a defeated opponent, I never gave to a friend a vote or a place which by any stretch of the imagination could be seen as belonging to an enemy or to a stranger. My defeats and disappointments I took as stoically as I could. If I caught myself complaining or making excuses I pulled up. If afterwards I remembered doing it I took an inward decision to try not to do it again. From the eight years of school life this code became the moral framework of my existence.

It has never left me. I learnt it as a boy, I have obeyed it as a man and now I can no longer laugh at it. I failed to live up to it at times, but when I did I knew and that is what matters. I had a clue and I cared, I couldn't care more.

After five years in England—where he wrote articles for the Manchester *Guardian* on cricket, became a Marxist, a Trotskyite, and published "large books and small articles" on politics and other subjects, James came to America in 1938, where he was shocked to realize how deeply loyal he still was to the cricket code of his youth: "At that time," he wrote in *Beyond a Boundary*,

> especially after the debunking autobiographies of the twenties of Robert Graves, Siegfried Sassoon and others, and, later, Labour politics in England, my attitude to the code was not merely critical. It was, if anything, contemptuous. I had said good-bye to all that. I didn't know how deeply the early attitudes had been ingrained in me and how foreign they were to other peoples until I sat at baseball matches with friends, some of them university men, and saw and heard the howls of anger and rage and denunciations which they hurled at the players as a matter of course. I could not understand them and they could not understand me either—they asked anxiously if I were enjoying the game. I was enjoying the game; it was they who were disturbing me. And not only they. Managers and players protested against adverse decisions as a matter of course, and sometimes, after bitter quarrels, were ordered off the field, fined and punished in other ways.

James finally realized that what was strange to him was quite natural to his friends and he dismissed the differences as just a matter of national character.

"Then in 1950," he wrote, "came a series of events which I could not ignore. Day after day there appeared in the Press authenticated reports that university basketball teams had sold out games or played for results arranged beforehand, in return for money from bookmakers. The reports continued. . . . that young men playing for school or university should behave in this way on such a scale was utterly shocking to me."

James's friends and associates in America were largely political people on the left. "Some of them, young university graduates or students themselves," he wrote,

had demonstrated that they could not be shifted from their political and social principles by threats of gaol or promise of any material benefit. Some of
them had rejected all the bribes offered by wealthy parents to return to the
fold of Democrats or Republicans. But to my outburst they shrugged their
shoulders. . . . The boys were wrong in being caught, that was all. The
school? Why should they put 'the school' above what they wanted?

"I didn't press the matter," James concluded. "I merely record the im-
mensity of the gulf that suddenly opened between me and the people to
whom I was so closely bound, speaking the same language, reading the
same books and both of us ready when we had nothing better to do to
make our jokes at the expense of the old-school tie."

Perhaps James was overly sensitive to the seeming lack of ethics in American sports because he had been so disillusioned by the recent decline of the
cricket code in England. In a late chapter in *Beyond a Boundary*, significant-
ly entitled "The Decline of the West," he wrote: "The blow from which 'It
isn't cricket' has never recovered came from within and it came in 1932.
This was body-line." Body-line, in brief, is a form of fast bowling in which
the bowler deliberately attempts to intimidate, if not severely injure, the
batsman; it is the cricket counterpart of the deliberate beanball in baseball.
Baseball batters have always been unintentionally injured and intimidated
by wild pitches as have cricket batsmen. What was new in the Test matches
in Australia in 1932 was the fact that the British captain (a "gentleman"
graduate of Winchester and Cambridge) ordered his two fast bowlers (who
were coal miners) to deliberately intimidate the "enemy." The British team
received a hearty welcome when they arrived in Australia; when they left,
not a single member of the Australian team came to see them off. When
Douglas Jardine was selected as the British captain that year, the coach at
his old school, Winchester, was reported to have said: "Well, we shall win
the Ashes—but we may lose a dominion."

James's discussion of the various and increasing abuses of his beloved
game after 1932 hauntingly anticipated the decline of manners in American tennis after 1968. "Body-line was not an incident, it was not an accident, it was not a temporary aberration. It was the violence and ferocity
of our age expressing itself in cricket." And he concludes with the idea
that the final Decline of the West will come when "It isn't cricket" is replaced for good and all by the cynical phrase: "Why isn't it cricket?"

I have begun this chapter with an anecdote about an inmate of Dartmoor Prison in the ancient days of 1958, and, above all, with excerpts from the memoirs of a brilliant black intellectual and activist who refused to betray his white flannel origins, because both men held on to a set of values which help to clarify our own.

Ever since my visit to Dartmoor Prison in 1958, I have seen civility in America slowly but steadily decline, especially after President Kennedy's shocking assassination in 1963. This slow decline, however, took a quantum leap in 1968, the tragic year which witnessed the assassinations of Martin Luther King, Jr. and Senator Robert Kennedy; the My Lai and *Pueblo* incidents which tarnished the honor of our army and navy; the street fighting at the Democratic Convention in Chicago; and the student rebellions at Columbia and elsewhere across the nation at the very best private schools and elite colleges. Almost overnight, as it were, our democratic traditions of *discussion* were replaced by the new age of the bullet and the bullhorn. At my own and other universities since 1968, civility and tolerance have steadily declined, as a growing minority of undergraduates and younger faculty members came to look upon persons whose values differ from their own as no longer *opponents* to be argued with, but *enemies* to be forbidden from speaking on the campus, or booed off the stage when the still-tolerant majority of students successfully asserted their rights to hear both sides of various issues.

Until 1968, it was the mannerly majority of tolerant students who set the tone of political discussion on the campus; after 1968, it was a minority of bright but intolerant and ideological egalitarians who set the new tone of bullhorn and demonstration democracy. As one clever but cynical member of this new elite said to me after a lecture on the nature of cricket and class authority in the Anglo-American political traditions: "All that playing-fields-of-Eton bullshit is totally irrelevant to my lifestyle." For his kind, "why isn't it cricket?" has already won the day.

Open tennis was born in that anarchic year of 1968. Until then, all major tennis tournaments were limited to amateurs. ("Open" originally meant that a tournament was open to both professionals and amateurs, though today these tournaments, such as the U.S. Open, are played entirely by professionals.)

In March Lyndon Johnson announced his decision not to run for re-election; in April Martin Luther King was assassinated and the first open tennis tournament was held at Bournemouth, England; Robert Kennedy was assassinated in early June and the first Open Wimbledon started at the end of the month; at the end of August the tragic Democratic Convention was held in Chicago at the same time that the first U.S. Open was being played at Forest Hills and won by Arthur Ashe, an amateur.

In his *Levels of the Game*, a gem of a book, John McPhee describes, point by point, Ashe's semifinal match at Forest Hills that year with Clark Graebner, at the same time drawing, between the points, as it were, detailed character portraits of Graebner—the white middle-class, meticulous, and spoiled son of a Cleveland dentist, and Ashe—a black lieutenant in the Army Reserves stationed at West Point, who, by natural instinct, parental training, and education was a Virginia gentleman in the very best moral and mannerly meaning of that term.[2] McPhee devoted almost three pages to Ashe's genealogy, which, on his father's side, went back to a Colonial Governor of North Carolina, Samuel Ashe. A kinswoman of Ashe's in Washington, D.C., has produced a family tree with fifteen hundred leaves, one of which—Arthur Ashe, Jr.—is painted in gold. The tree has since been the center of family reunions, in Washington, Philadelphia, Pittsburgh, and so forth, which have attracted as many as three hundred at a single meeting. With an artist's sense of irony, McPhee closed the last paragraph of his lengthy discussion of Ashe's genealogy with the following sentence: "Graebner has no idea whatever when his forebears first came to this country."

Arthur Ashe, Jr., was brought up in Richmond, Virginia, by his widower father, whose wife died not long after teaching Arthur to read at the age of four. Mr. Ashe was a rigid disciplinarian with high aspirations for his children. "I kept the children home pretty close," he told McPhee.

> A regular schedule is very important. A parent has got to hurt his own child, discipline him, hold him back from things you know aren't good for him. I don't believe in arguing and fussing, I can't stand it and never could. I don't believe in speaking two or three times, neither. . . . I told Arthur I wanted him to get an education and get himself qualified so people could respect him as a human being. I wanted him to be a gentleman that everybody could recognize, and that's what he is right now.

Ashe was an "A" student all the way through school. He was and remained an omnivorous reader, never "wasting time" as a child on "detective stories, Westerns or comic books." Always a good all-around athlete, his tennis education began in earnest when his father took him to stay with Dr. Robert Walter Johnson, in Lynchburg, whose hobby was developing black tennis players. Even more important than the techniques of tennis were the set of moral and mannerly standards which Dr. Johnson insisted on. Supreme among these was self-control: "No racquet throwing, no hollering, no indication of discontent with officials' calls. . . . We don't want anybody to be accused of cheating. There will *be* some cheating, but we aren't going to do it." Much like his similarly disciplined hero, Jackie Robinson, Ashe was well prepared to conquer the white world of tennis. He was most proud of his demeanor on the court: "I always strive to cultivate it. . . . You must expect four or five bad calls a match. A match can be won or lost on a bad call." He once lost in the finals of the Australian National Championship when a foot fault was called against him on the last point of the match. He kept his cool, as few others would have done.

Dr. Johnson's dream of producing a first-class black tennis player began to come true when Ashe became the first black to win the National Interscholastic Championship in 1961. In the meantime, J. D. Morgan, tennis coach at UCLA, who was to become a powerful and trusted influence on Ashe, called Richmond and offered him a tennis scholarship. In the fall of 1962, Arthur entered UCLA as a freshman and graduated four years later, winning the Intercollegiate Championship in 1965. His best friend and roommate was also a great tennis player, Charles Pasarell,* wealthy scion of one of the First Families of Puerto Rico. Ashe took ROTC all four years and graduated with a reserve commission. When he was stationed at West Point, Private Pasarell was stationed a few miles away, at Newburgh. They saw a lot of each other.

Lieutenant Ashe won the match with Graebner and then went on to win the first Open in five exhausting sets. His was a great amateur victory against a field that included many professionals—and it was a fitting end to the amateur era. He never won another U.S. Open, though his career was far from over. He had his finest hour at Wimbledon, in 1975, when he won the most coveted title in tennis, beating Jimmy Connors in a brilliantly conceived final match.

---

*In the first round in 1969, Pasarell played the longest match in Wimbledon history, against Pancho Gonzales (112 games in over five hours).

Arthur Ashe held fast all his life to a set of traditional values which were almost diametrically opposite to those of all too many of his white peers, both inside and outside the world of professional tennis. These values were revealed on almost every page of his three autobiographical volumes, especially in his inspiring posthumously published memoir, *Days of Grace*.[3] Above all, Ashe favored the old traditions of *leveling upwards* rather than the new bureaucratic traditions of *leveling downwards*. Thus in his second book, *Off the Court*, written after his heart attack, he had some keen observations to make on our leveling downwards age: "I like the English language and its nuances," he wrote, and "have no interest in learning how to be a master of Black English."

In the increasingly uncivil quarter-century between his victory at Forest Hills, in 1968, and his tragic death, in 1993, the moral life of Arthur Ashe has constantly renewed my faith in the staying power of the gentlemanly ideal. After all, he was still living by the same "cricket code" which had governed so many lives since the days of C. L. R. James.

━━━

The ten years following the tragic disruptions of 1968 were the most anarchic and antiauthoritarian in our history. Campus revolts continued, especially at Harvard and Cornell, in May 1969; four Kent State students were shot to death the following May (1970); ten days later two black students were killed at Jackson State College in Mississippi; some five hundred campuses across America were shut down or went on strike as a result of this violence.

At the height of the Watergate Affair, on September 20, 1973, exactly a month before Elliot Richardson and Archibald Cox resigned from the Justice Department, the great American public was absorbed in the most vulgar and most popular media event in the history of tennis. The largest crowd ever to watch a tennis match—30,472—gathered at the Houston Astrodome (courtside seats went for $100) to watch the Male Chauvinist Pig, Bobby Riggs, do battle with tennis's leading Female Chauvinist, Billie Jean King. It was right out of a Cecil B. DeMille movie; King wore a mint-green and royal-blue dress, covered with about two hundred rhinestones and almost as many sequins, especially designed at great cost by the late Ted Tinling, official clothing designer for the Virginia Slims Tennis Circuit, who was proud to learn from letters sent him from four continents that the "glittering rhinestones that outlined the Virginia Slims motif . . . showed clearly on the approximately 200 million color TV screens around the world."[4] King was borne into the arena on a red and gold litter adorned with a profusion of red and white ostrich feathers, all carried by four husky football players from Rice University; Riggs had a group of female escorts, or Bosom Buddies, carry him on the court in a rickshaw. He gave King a large red lollipop; she gave him a little live pig. The crowd loved every vulgar bit of it, as did some fifty million American TV viewers.

The next year (1974), when young James Scott Connors defeated the great Australian stylist, Kenneth Rosewall, in the finals of both Wimbledon and Forest Hills, the most vulgar decade in the history of men's tennis began. The only Americans to win our National Championship in that decade were Connors and John McEnroe, who last won it in 1984.

In the meantime, the new National Tennis Center, at Flushing Meadow, Long Island, held its first U.S. Open Championships, in 1978. Compared to the charm of Roland Garros, in Paris, or the dignity of Wimbledon, Flushing Meadow was, and still is, a noisy, tasteless place, set in positively uncivil surroundings. It is hard not to feel some sympathy with Kevin Curren, runner-up to Boris Becker at Wimbledon in 1985, when he made the following explosive remarks during the U.S. Open that year: "I hate New York. I hate the city. I hate the environment. I hate Flushing Meadow. They should drop an A-Bomb on it."[5]

=====

When thinking about the rise of professional tennis and the events of the tragic decade which witnessed its birth, it is well to be aware that, as C. L. R. James and all of those who are familiar with the classic civilizations of Greece and Rome have known, it has all happened before. The men who laid the intellectual and artistic foundations of Western civilization were enthusiastic organizers and players of games. The earliest recorded date in the history of the West was 776 B.C., the date of the first games held at Olympia, as part of the religious ceremonies honoring the shrine of Zeus, which was located in this remote place. For several centuries, the games were run and participated in by aristocratic amateurs who followed the Greek ideal of the whole man. Finally, however, after the Golden Age of Pericles, at about the time of Plato (who was usually found in a front seat at the games), democracy and professionalism began to assert themselves: "When athletes became out-and-out professionals, abandoning all other occupations, interest in the games began to abate," wrote a leading tennis journalist, John R. Tunis, in the *New Yorker* in 1928. "This was the beginning of their decline. The famous Olympics of Greece, conceived in the spirit of purity, became a victim of professionalism and, after a period of over seven hundred years of existence, came to an end in 293 A.D." The inner-barbarians had triumphed, and the Greco-Roman civilization lost its will and was soon overrun by the outer-barbarians.

The following pages will suggest how the tragic fate of the Olympic Games in the ancient world, after professionals finally replaced amateurs, may be repeating itself in modern tennis. The decline of amateur tennis is only a century-long story, as opposed to the seven centuries of amateurism in the ancient world. But, in the end, the same forces of dissolution may very well triumph.

Nothing in history is ever inevitable; I should like, however, to make one important point here: both in ancient and modern times, just as aristocratic, or upper-class, values tend to foster amateurism, so democracy fosters professionalism. While, for example, upper-class values still permeated the whole of their societies in the days of Winston Churchill and Franklin Roosevelt, this is no longer the case today, especially since the revolutionary days of 1968 and after. In this connection, finally, one must bear in mind that it was in the classless totalitarian societies that sport first became a profession wherein athletes devoted the whole of their time to *one sport*. Hence the astonishing post–World War II victories of the East Germans and Russians, first at the traditional, amateur rowing championships at Henley, in England, and later at the Olympic Games. Totalitarian, or mass, man, in other words, is one-dimensional, while the ideal man in class-led, liberal democracies was always multidimensional. The changing nature of sports is a fine measure of changing historical social structures and their varying values. And tennis may be the finest of all, as I hope to show in this book.

The Anglo-American Amateur Tradition, the Making of a National Upper Class, and a Gentlemanly Code of Honor in America, 1880–1914

At the beginning of this century, one-fifth of the inhabitants of the globe were British subjects, while the Royal Navy policed the seas of the world. Throughout this vast empire, the rulers, everywhere a tiny minority among the ruled, were men who modeled themselves on the tradition of the English gentleman ..., "Never since the heroic days of Greece has the world had such a sweet, just, boyish master," wrote George Santayana, of Harvard.
> —Philip Mason, *The English Gentleman*

The important thing in the Olympic games is not to win but to take part, the important thing in life is not to triumph but to struggle. The essential thing is not to have conquered but to have fought well. To spread these precepts is to build up a stronger and more valiant and, above all, more scrupulous and more generous humanity.
> —Baron Pierre de Coubertin

THE AMERICAN NATION WAS FOUNDED BY GENTLEMEN AMATEURS, OF whom the most indispensable was George Washington, Esquire, a Virginian by birth but also an honorary Roman. Like Cincinnatus, the noble Roman volunteer who returned to his plow when his duty was done, Washington agreed to leave his beloved acres to lead a revolutionary army on two conditions: that he receive *no pay*, and that he be allowed to *resign* after the war was won.

Unlike Caesar, the professional soldier, Washington never crossed the Rubicon. After the Yorktown victory, for instance, his as yet unpaid fellow officers threatened mutiny and a possible takeover of the weak central government; at a tension-filled meeting at winter headquarters in Newburgh, New York, Washington brilliantly persuaded his comrades at arms to abandon their proposed plans, and, henceforth, the amateur civilian has always stood above the professional soldier in American history. After the Newburgh meeting, Washington went down to Annapolis and resigned his commission. Giving up power only increased his authority.

Orphaned at an early age, Washington virtually brought himself up in the style of the class of Colonial British gentlemen into which he was born. He composed his own "Rules of Civility" at the age of 15; its 110 precepts were not too different from those in Richard Barthwart's *English Gentleman*, the standard guide among eighteenth-century Virginians. But he probably took his rules more seriously than most; though in private he had a violent temper, for instance, he rigidly disciplined himself in public. All his biographers, from Parson Weems to Douglas Southall Freeman, have stressed character and self-discipline as the qualities which set him apart and above his contemporaries, and made him so perfectly qualified to become the father of his country. And his authority reached monumental proportions when he stepped down from the power of the presidency after two terms and returned to his enlarged Mt. Vernon and some hundred thousand beloved acres. This two-term precedent became a traditional gentleman's agreement which lasted until Franklin Roosevelt's presidency; and it is still in force today, but only after being made a Constitutional Amendment, in the style of our mistrustful, bureaucratic age.

Washington's habit of authority and command, and his consummate aristocratic presence, were only outstanding examples of traits which were common to his whole class of Virginia planters. Like most of the tidewater First Families, Washington's ancestors were Royalist Cavaliers and thus on the losing side of the English Revolution of the 1640s. They came to America, not to escape English vices, but to perfect the traditional English virtues which were aristocratic and amateur. The members of this class of Virginia gentlemen were expected to serve without pay as vestrymen, justices of the peace, commanders of local militias, and delegates to the House of Burgesses. It was this class of planters, bred to the habit of authority, which produced the Virginia Dynasty—Washington, Jefferson, Madison, and Monroe—but also, if less well known, such presidents of similar breeding as William Henry Harrison, John Tyler, Zachary Taylor, and Benjamin Harrison, all of whom carried this Virginia gentleman's tradition down through the nineteenth century. In the twentieth century, the nearest thing to an heir of this class survived in the form of the Harvard-Yale-Princeton gentlemanly traditions of undergraduate education which prepared two Roosevelts, Taft, Wilson, and John F. Kennedy for the White House.

Contrary to conventional wisdom today, the class traditions of the gentleman-amateur have played a vital role in preserving America's republican political traditions in their Englishness, that is to say quite contrary to the bureaucratic-professional and elitist traditions of Continental Europe. In France after the Revolution it was Napoleon, the professional soldier, who further bureaucratized and professionalized his country's government. The state came to dominate society, as Tocqueville saw so clearly, and no societal ruling class developed as it did in England.

The aristocratic and amateur traditions in England survived the agricultural, urban, commercial, industrial, and political revolutions which ushered in the modern world for a variety of reasons. Some of these reasons were institutional: primogeniture, for example, limited the peers of the realm to eldest sons (three hundred in 1879), thus forcing the younger sons to maintain their aristocratic positions by achievement rather than inheritance alone. Protestantism and Parliamentarianism, too, encouraged moral leadership by amateurs. "To serve one's country without pay," wrote Trollope, "is the grandest work a man can do." Both he and Bagehot despised the "expert" and felt that bureaucracy tended to "undergovernment in point of quality and overgovernment in point of quantity."[1] Members of the House of Commons (which included the Prime Minister) received no pay at all until 1911, and attendance at the

House of Lords is voluntary, and rewarded with only *per diem* expenses, to this day. Honorable members feared the corruption of money, when professionals replace amateurs and tactics replace principles.

Beyond politics, Protestantism, and primogeniture, however, there were two other reasons for the strength of the amateur ideal which concern the origins of modern amateur tennis more directly: the *public school ethic*, and the *collegiate,* as against the *university,* emphasis at Oxford and Cambridge.

A Gentleman's Education

In 1828, Thomas Arnold, an Anglican clergyman and a graduate of Winchester and Oxford, took over as headmaster of Rugby School. It was a time when such schools as Eton, Harrow, Rugby, and Winchester were ripe for reform. Dr. Arnold, who favored the Reform Bill, deeply distrusted both reactionary Toryism, and the crude materialism of the new industrialism as well as the money values of the City. It was his aim to produce a class of educated, truth-telling, Christian gentlemen who would stand aloof from both the new materialism and the old ossifying Toryism. He saw the need for converting pampered boys of birth or wealth into a hardened band of platonic Guardians of moral merit and responsibility. In the segregated democracy of the public boarding school, moreover, sons of the nobility, the gentry, and the rising middle classes could be molded into one gentlemanly class.

Arnold's values stressed religious and moral principles first, gentlemanly conduct second, and intellectual achievement last. His vigorous, Christian character left a lasting impression on his pupils and masters, many of whom carried his principles into all the public schools of England (the original nine schools in 1800 grew to nearly three hundred by 1914). *Tom Brown's School Days*, written by his former pupil, Thomas Hughes, influenced several generations of schoolmasters and made Rugby School world famous.[2] Both Hughes and Arnold stressed character above intellect, but while Arnold stressed religion, Hughes, and later generations of public school leaders, placed more faith in the religion of games and sportsmanship. The aristocratic field sports—shooting, fishing, and fox hunting—which became a cult, almost a religion, in the early nineteenth century, now gave way to organized team sports like rugby and cricket at the public schools.

The game of rugby was founded at Rugby when a young student, frustrated with kicking the ball, picked it up and ran with it. Eventually the game was adopted at all the public schools as well as at Oxford and Cambridge. The first interscholastic rugby contest did not take place until 1873, when Westminster defeated Charterhouse. The following year, Harvard played its first "football" game against McGill, using the so-called Boston rules, a bastard form of rugby. By the 1880s, "muscular Christianity" was the religion of the public schools of England.

Character was to be developed by team games and hardship. Games demanded loyalty, self-discipline, and, for those with ability, a sense of command and accomplishment. Cold baths, cold dormitories, runs in the rain, and plain food all helped to build character. A housemaster, on hearing that one of his boys had taken two hot baths in a week, reprimanded him sternly: "That is the kind of thing that brought down the Roman Empire." Along with toughened character, the code of good sportsmanship stressed the amateur values of the all-rounder, and winning as less important than playing hard and fairly.

At the university level, Oxford and Cambridge, founded by the Church to educate poor boys for the clergy, became schools for gentlemen as early as the late sixteenth century—and have remained so well into the twentieth. "This notion of a gentleman's education," Samuel Eliot Morison wrote,

> has made the English and American college what it is today [1934]: the despair of educational reformers and logical pedagogues, the astonishment of Continental scholars, a place which is neither a house of learning nor a house of play, but a little of both; and withal a microcosm of the world in which we live. To this . . . tradition, we owe that common figure of the English-speaking world, "a gentleman and a scholar."[3]

The ideal toward which this gentleman's education aspired, at both the public schools and at Oxford and Cambridge, was the amateur all-rounder, educated in the classics and good at games. Anthony Wilding, later a Wimbledon Champion and captain of both the Trinity College and Cambridge University tennis clubs in 1905, wrote of Oxford and Cambridge in his day as follows: "To get a degree at either university entails little work, and interferes so little with games that any man ought to be ashamed to 'come down' without having defeated the examiners in at least a pass degree. . . . The fashion in vogue at Oxford and Cambridge of making every afternoon from two to four-thirty absolutely sacred to exercise is heartily to be commended."[4] Tennis had already become a major part of collegiate life. In his day Trinity College alone possessed fifty grass courts and "on a fine afternoon in the May term every court was occupied, and often by two successive doubles during the afternoon."

Sports have never been part of French or German formal education, either at the secondary or university levels; there are no rituals in either country to compare to the Eton-Harrow cricket matches, the Oxford-Cambridge boat races, or the Harvard-Yale football classic. Baron Pierre de Coubertin, the founder of the modern Olympic Games, was very aware of the differences between his beloved France and England. In 1875, he read a French translation of *Tom Brown's School Days*, and thereafter Dr. Thomas Arnold became the single most important influence on his life. Although he had an assured career in the army after his graduation from St. Cyr, he devoted his life to pedagogical reforms in France and the revival of the Olympics. His dogged determination finally paid off when the first modern games were held at Athens, in 1896.

The ideals of Thomas Arnold of Rugby, which became the public school ethic in England, not only influenced Baron de Coubertin to found the modern Olympic Games; they also had a great influence on the manners and morals of the members of a new upper class which took shape in America in the years between 1880 and the First World War. The Arnold ethic was especially influential through the New England boarding schools such as Groton which was founded by young Endicott Peabody who will be discussed below.

The Making of the American Upper Class

Up until the 1870s or so, a still largely rural (50 percent farmers) and decentralized American society was led by countless autonomous and local upper classes made up of old-stock lawyers, doctors, and clergymen, local merchants, prosperous farmers, and owners of family business firms. Members of these mansion families, as they were often called in small-town America, took the lead in local politics, in philanthropy, and in support of cultural and civic organizations. In New York City a deeply rooted provincial upper class reached its apogee in the downtown brownstone world described by Edith Wharton in her most well-known book, *The Age of Innocence*.

Gradually, however, in the course of the 1880s, the rapidly centralizing steel and railroad economy produced a new national upper class which increasingly centered in uptown Manhattan (by 1885 there were seven Vanderbilt mansions in the Forties and Fifties along Fifth Avenue), out on the North Shore of Long Island, at Tuxedo Park, up the Hudson River, and at such fashionable summer resorts as Newport, Southampton, Bar Harbor, and the Berkshires. The social competition in Manhattan between the old rich, brownstone families and the newly rich from all over the nation who were building their uptown, Fifth Avenue mansions was symbolized by the opening of the Metropolitan Opera House, at Broadway and Fortieth Streets, in 1883. The old rich had long dominated the ancient Academy of Music on 14th Street; after trying unsuccessfully to buy boxes in the old academy for some years (offering as much as thirty thousand dollars a box), the new breed decided to build their own house of music uptown. Edith Wharton's biographer, R. W. B. Lewis, describes the opening night at the Metropolitan in 1883 as follows:

> "All the nouveau riche were on hand," as one reporter wrote with some contempt. "The Goulds and Vanderbilts and people of that ilk perfumed the air with the odor of crisp greenbacks." Downtown that same evening, the writer continued, the people who truly represented New York Society, and who were "distinguished by their brilliant social altitude and by the identification of their names with Manhattan's history," crowded the Academy of Music. . . . Mrs. Paran Stevens, who owned boxes in both places, sized up the situation perfectly and divided her evening between them.[5]

Mrs. Paran Stevens was one of the most skillful social climbers of her era in New York and Newport; her efforts to mix with old and new money were soon imitated. The members of new and old rich families were amalgamated into one national upper class through marriage and the education of succeeding generations at various Episcopalian boarding schools in New England and at the originally Calvinist colleges of Harvard, Yale, and New Jersey (Princeton in the 1890s). It was thus highly appropriate that the first three presidents of the United States in the twentieth century were Theodore Roosevelt, of Harvard; William Howard Taft, of Yale; and Woodrow Wilson, of Princeton.

In the first year of the upper class-forming 1880s, William Howard Taft, who had graduated second in his class at Yale in 1878, graduated from the University of Cincinnati Law School; Woodrow Wilson, of the Princeton class of 1879, was studying law at the University of Virginia; and Theodore Roosevelt, who eventually became the first gentleman-sportsman in the White House, graduated from Harvard. In the same year, Walter Camp, the father of American football, graduated from Yale; and Endicott Peabody, the greatest American educator of upper-class boys, graduated from Trinity College in Cambridge, England. Edith Jones (later Wharton) made her debut in New York in the winter season of 1879–80 and then spent a very gay summer in Newport. Her heaviest beau at the time, Harry Stevens, son of the pushy Mrs. Paran Stevens, brought back enough tennis equipment from England (he had studied but took no degrees at St. Mark's School and Oxford) to lay out the first tennis court in Newport, on the lawn of his mother's mansion on Belle-vue Avenue. "In June and July," wrote Wharton's biographer, "Edith could watch Harry among other young gentlemen in tail coats playing tennis with young ladies in tight whalebone dresses." This was no mere fad, and lawn tennis soon replaced archery as the favorite pastime of the idle rich at Newport.

The next year, in 1881, the Newport Casino, designed by Stanford White for James Gordon Bennett, Jr., one of the leading American sportsmen of his day, was completed at its present site on Bellevue Avenue. In the meantime, the United States National Lawn Tennis Association was founded in New York under the leadership of James Dwight, of Boston and Clarence M. Clark, of Philadelphia. And the first National Championship was held at the new Casino in August and won by Richard D. Sears, of Brahmin Boston. Earlier, in June, William C. Renshaw, whose unmatched record at Wimbledon marked the turning of English lawn tennis from a pastime into a sport, won the first of his seven Men's Singles Championships at Wimbledon.

In many ways, the year 1882 was symbolic of upper-class confidence and dominance in the years between 1880 and 1914. As the year opened, the great and powerful gathered for a dinner at Delmonico's restaurant in New York City to honor the visiting British sociologist and Social Darwinist, Herbert Spencer, who allegedly had scientifically "proved" the Anglo-Saxon gentleman's Natural Fitness to rule the world. Spencer had been brought to America by his close friend and greatest admirer, Andrew Carnegie; the main speaker of the evening, Henry Ward Beecher, the most famous preacher in America, noted in the course of his speech that he had been a reader and admirer of Spencer for twenty years or so. Among the honored guests was William Graham Sumner, a Phi Beta Kappa and Skull and Bones man at Yale who, after graduate study abroad and ordination as an Episcopal priest, became one of the founders of American sociology and taught generations of Yale students to have faith in their Natural Fitness to rule.

While Social Darwinism provided the ideological rationale for the Anglo-American gentleman's right to rule, the *club*—both urban and suburban, and around the world from Calcutta, Kimberley, and London to New York, Boston, and Philadelphia—was becoming a major factor in creating and preserving class mores and class exclusiveness. In Brookline, Massachusetts, a suburb of Boston, The Country Club was founded in 1882. Just as members of the British aristocracy spent long weekends at the great country houses of rural England, so the families of the American business gentry spent their leisure hours at the hundreds of imitators of the original country club in Brookline. No wonder Henry James, the supreme novelist of the Anglo-American upper class of his day, found the country club to be "a deeply significant American symbol."

While The Country Club in Brookline was the first of its kind in America, "Tuxedo Park," up the Hudson from New York City and not far from the Harriman lands around Bear Mountain, was a veritable caricature of the Victorian millionaire's mania for exclusiveness. It was built by Pierre Lorillard II in 1885, on six thousand acres he had just inherited (when the first Pierre Lorillard, who had built an enormous snuff and tobacco fortune, died in 1843, the term "millionaire" was used for the first time in America). In less than a year Lorillard built an eight-foot fence around the whole property, graded some thirty miles of road, built a complete sewage and water system and a gatehouse which looked like a frontispiece to an English novel, a clubhouse staffed with English servants, and twenty-two turreted English "cottages" which were soon sold to club members. In addition to the clubhouse and the cottages, there were two

blocks of stores, a score of stables, four lawn tennis courts (and eventually a court tennis court), a bowling alley, a swimming tank, a boathouse, a
dam, a trout pond and hatchery, and so forth. All good Tuxedoites wore
ties, hatbands, socks, and other items of dress adorned in the club colors
of green and gold. Tuxedo was an immediate success. Each fall, from
1886 through the Second World War, the New York Social Season
opened with the Autumn Ball at Tuxedo, where a select group of debutantes were introduced to Society. At one of the early Autumn Balls,
Pierre Lorillard II cut off the tails of an old tailcoat and wore it with a
black tie. Hence the dinner jacket is known as a tuxedo to thousands
who have never heard of Tuxedo Park.

In March 1888, Ward McAllister told a reporter from James Gordon
Bennett's New York *Tribune* that "there were only about 400 people in
fashionable New York Society. If you go outside that number you strike
people who are either not at ease in a ballroom or else make other people
not at ease." Legend has it that he used the figure "400" because that
number was about the limit of Mrs. Astor's ballroom in her mansion on
Fifth Avenue where the Empire State Building now stands. McAllister,
who had spent several years in Europe preparing himself to become the
arbiter of American Society by observing the mores of court and aristocracy, was Mrs. Astor's close friend and chief mentor in her rise to become
Queen of New York and Newport Society in the Gilded Age.*

The American upper-class kinship system has always included both
celebrity socialites like Caroline Astor and aristocratic socialites such as
Nancy Astor, the first woman to sit in the British Parliament, or the two
Roosevelt presidents. Surely the greatest American aristocrat since
George Washington was Franklin Delano Roosevelt. Franklin's older
half-brother, James Roosevelt, married Caroline Astor's daughter; his
great-uncle on his mother's side, Franklin Delano, was the husband of
Caroline's sister-in-law, Laura Astor. As President, Franklin often escaped the cares of office when cruising with his Republican friend, Vincent Astor, Caroline's grandson. These connections, pushed a bit further,

---

*Mrs. Jay, wife of John Jay, our first Secretary of State, was the first Queen of New York Soci-
ety. Her "Dinner and Supper List of 1787 to 1788" was probably the first list of American "Socialites." While her list included a dozen doctors and clergymen, McAllister's list, a hundred
years later, included one doctor and no clergymen.

begin to suggest the class nature of amateur tennis. Everyone knew, or was related to, everyone else. Vincent's father (Caroline's son), John Jacob Astor IV, as we shall see in a later chapter, sailed aboard the *Titanic* in 1912 along with R. Norris Williams II who, two years later, won the last U.S. Singles Championship to be held at the Newport Casino. And Caroline's great-grandson, James H. Van Alen, was one of the last leaders of amateur lawn tennis. He took the initiative in saving the declining Casino by locating the Tennis Hall of Fame there in 1954. He also pioneered in developing the "tie break" which has contributed so much to American television's dominance of tennis moneymaking.

At the same time that McAllister was telling the *Tribune* reporter about the "400," a much younger New Yorker, Louis Keller, who had long been fascinated by the doings of the "400," came up with the idea of a *Social Register*, listing fashionable families rather than celebrity individuals: a volume for New York City was published in 1888; Philadelphia and Boston (1890); Baltimore (1892); Chicago (1893); Washington, D.C. (1900); St. Louis and Buffalo (1903); Pittsburgh (1904); San Francisco (1906); and Cleveland-Cincinnati-Dayton (1910).* Volumes for all these twelve cities continued down to 1976, when they were replaced by one large and bulky *Social Register* for the whole country, a tribute to increasing centralization and social mobility in America. Several things should be said about the *Social Register* as an index of a national, American, urban upper class: in the first place, Keller was wisely quite different from Ward McAllister in that he insisted that the *Register* keep a very low profile, there was from the first no publicity about who should or should not be included; it was, moreover, to include families and not individuals such as McAllister's list and various celebrity registers which have followed. It has always included both families of high achievement and descendants of high achievers; both wealthy and once wealthy families; both celebrities and aristocrats and just plain men and women of good manners and cultivated minds. Perhaps most revealing of all is the changing rate of growth: in 1988, for example, the *Social Register* included some 40,000 conjugal family units; in the first half-century, between 1888 and 1938, the twelve *Social Registers* grew to include some 38,000 fami-

---

*Actually, the first volume of the *Social Register* was published in 1887 for Newport but was never continued.

lies; in the next half-century—1938–88—only two thousand families were added. An upper class, of course, grows by natural increase (birth rate) and inclusion of new families of achievement; in the first fifty years the *Social Register* was a more or less accurate index of both the natural increase of its WASP families as well as inclusion of new families of power and wealth. In the second fifty years, however, two things probably happened. First, since the close of World War II, new families of power, talent, and wealth are more and more likely to be drawn from outside WASP ethnic pools; e.g., from Catholics, Jews, and blacks. I have the definite impression, in the second place, that more and more individuals whose families have been included in the *Social Register* from its early days consider it to be an elitist and undemocratic aspect of our egalitarian society and have insisted on not being listed.

Rising ruling classes have always encouraged great artists—especially authors, architects, and portrait painters—who have preserved for posterity the spirit of their ages. Tudor and Stuart England produced the portraits of Van Dyke; seventeenth-century Amsterdam, Rembrandt; Tory Boston before the Revolution, John Singleton Copley; and the founders of the new Republic, the portraits of Gilbert Stuart. And John Singer Sargent, between the time he first set up his London studio in 1885 and the end of the First World War, painted his elegant portraits of the famous, fashionable, and beautiful members of the new, Anglo-American class establishment which grew up in his day. The elegant confidence of this class was immortalized in his portraits of Lord Ribblesdale, the Wyndham Sisters, the Duchess of Marlborough, Consuelo Vanderbilt, and the Sitwell Family, in London, and of Mrs. Jack Gardner, Frederick Law Olmstead, Woodrow Wilson, Theodore Roosevelt, and Endicott Peabody, in America. On his first visit to America in 1887–88, he met Stanford White, who later commissioned him to paint the famous murals in the Boston Public Library, perhaps the finest example of the work of McKim, Mead, and White. The firm opened in 1879 and its first great building was the Newport Casino, to be followed by casinos at Narragansett Pier and at Rhinebeck, New York, where John Jacob Astor IV played tennis and swam. At the end of the 1880s, in 1889, the firm designed surely the finest tennis club building after the Casino, the new Germantown Cricket Club in Philadelphia. The great age of elegance in architecture was led by Stanford White and his firm between 1880 and 1916, when the firm's last masterpiece, the New York Racquet and Tennis Club, was completed. None of the three founders were still active members of the firm by this time, White having been dramatically assassinated from behind while attending an event at Madison Square Garden, which he had designed in 1889 for a group of his wealthy friends for their sporting and other pleasures.

The new, national upper class which took form in America during the 1880s was at the peak of its power and authority when Victoria died in 1901. In that year, the Anglo-American, White-Anglo-Saxon-Protestant (WASP) establishment, consolidated through family alliances between Mayfair and Murray Hill and involving many millions of dollars, authoritatively ran the world, as their ancestors had done since Queen Elizabeth's time. It was also the year when the Protestant patrician, Theodore Roosevelt, entered the White House and J. P. Morgan, leading layman of the Episcopal Church and unrivaled czar of our business civilization, formed the first billion-dollar trust, the United States Steel Corporation. Morgan's close friend, Bishop Henry Codman Potter, who five years earlier had blessed the most famous Anglo-American marriage of them all when Consuelo Vanderbilt brought her wealth to the House of Marlborough, was often called the "First Citizen of New York."*

This class of Protestant patricians not only held the vast majority of positions at the heart of the U.S. national power structure; it also set the styles in arts and letters, at the Big Three universities, in sports,[†] and in the more popular culture which governed the aspirations and values of the masses. In serious literature, Henry James was at the very height of his creative powers, publishing three great classics in the three years after 1901—*The Wings of the Dove* (1902), *The Ambassadors* (1903), and *The Golden Bowl* (1904). Edith Wharton, finally breaking away from the restricting patriarchal mores of her class, published a collection of short stories, *Crucial Instances*, in 1901 and her first novel, *The Valley of Decision*, in 1902. And Theodore Roosevelt's good friend and Porcellian club-

---

*The era of transatlantic marriages began when Jennie Jerome, the daughter of a New York broker and sportsman, married Winston Churchill's father, younger son of the Duke of Marlborough, in 1874. Between that date and 1909, more than five hundred rich American women married titled foreigners, an estimated $220 million following them to Europe.

[†]Harvard, Yale and Princeton men made up a majority of "first eleven" all-American football players, every year down to 1916.

mate from Philadelphia, Owen Wister, painted his classic portrait of the gentleman-cowboy in his novel *The Virginian*, which was the year's best-seller in 1902.

———

Fortunately, during the quarter-century preceding the First World War, the aspirations of the average, red-blooded American boy were being molded by the Proper-Protestant heroes of sport rather than the Ward McAllister values of the "400." By 1901, the chivalrous exploits of a wealthy, private-school boy at Yale, Frank Merriwell, made for far more popular reading than the Horatio Alger sagas of the dull, bootlicking bores from the hinterland who rose to wealth through keeping their eyes on the cash register and the boss's daughter. For each boy who read the Alger stories, more than five hundred read about the exploits of fabulous Frank of Fardale Academy and Yale. In those long-gone days of upper-class hegemony in America, Frank Merriwell, who looked like a Charles Dana Gibson blue blood, was the young god everybody wanted to be: gentlemanly, wealthy, educated, brave, a great athlete, adventurous, handsome, brilliant in the classroom, and almost unbearably clean-living; after knowing her for years, Frank finally kissed his truelove which, of course, led to marriage and the end of the Merriwell stories (in 1914). A journalist-historian and avid reader of the Merriwell sagas in his youth, Stewart H. Holbrook compared them with the Alger stories as follows: "Frank Merriwell was many cuts above the rags-to-riches hero. Even at birth, Frank already had it made—socially, financially, intellectually. He was instantly and wholly accepted by millions of boys, city or country, native or foreign-born, and to them he represented not only manliness and success, but the more admirable attitudes and characteristics of the Anglo-Saxon 'ruling class' of the period."[6]

Endicott Peabody, Theodore Roosevelt, and the American Ethic of Sportsmanship

Endicott Peabody and his good friend and kinsman-through-marriage, Theodore Roosevelt, did more to advance the gentlemanly values of sportsmanship in America than any other two men in the first half of the twentieth century. They were exact contemporaries, Roosevelt graduating from Harvard in 1880, the same year Peabody earned his First Class degree from Cambridge. What Peabody did for young boys, Roosevelt did for college-age and adult citizens. A detailed look at both men thus offers a capstone of the building of the amateur sportsman ideal.

The New England boarding schools, modeled on the British public school traditions, played an important role in forming a national upper class in America. They educated several generations of upper-class boys, from all over the nation if primarily from the Eastern Seaboard, in the Tom Brown-Frank Merriwell traditions of gentlemanly sportsmanship. The twelve leading schools, along with their founding dates, are listed below:

Old Academies Nondenominational	Episcopalian Boarding Schools	Nondenominational Preparatory Schools
Andover 1778	St. Paul's 1856	Taft 1890
Exeter 1783	St. Mark's 1865	Hotchkiss 1892
	Groton 1884	Choate 1896
	St. George's 1896	Middlesex 1901
	Kent 1906	Deerfield 1902

Endicott Peabody founded Groton School in 1884 and led it for fifty-six years before his retirement in 1940. From an upper-class point of view, he was the most distinguished headmaster of his era. Convinced that a vigorous democracy needed the leadership of a manly and moral aristocracy, he was proud of the fact that Groton was a class school which over the years became somewhat of an incestuous family surrogate. On the school's fiftieth anniversary, for example, of the thirty-six members of the class of 1934, no fewer than twenty-five—including Theodore Roosevelt's grandson and Franklin Roosevelt's son, such scions of old Eastern Seaboard families as Alsop, Coolidge, Gerard, Saltonstall, Welles, and Whitney, and a Deering McCormick and a McCormick Blair, of the Harvester families in Chicago—were sons of Old Grotonians. And in the first half of the twentieth century, Peabody produced far more distinguished national leaders per number of alumni than any of the other schools listed above.

Peabody spent his formative years at Cheltenham College, an English public school (private boarding school). His father, who had just been made a partner in Peabody and Morgan, the leading American investment banking firm in London, took his family abroad, and, in the spring of 1871, enrolled Endicott, along with his brother Francis, at Cheltenham. The Peabody brothers were contemporaries of the wealthy Renshaw twins who became famous as the first modern lawn tennis champions at Wimbledon.

Young Peabody was a healthy, tall, fair-haired and blue-eyed Adonis, with all the charm and grace of the born gentleman and natural athlete. He avidly absorbed the values of Thomas Arnold of Rugby and the public school code which he found at Cheltenham where he was a veritable Frank Merriwell, loving and excelling at all sports, especially cricket and rowing, at fives (the Irish and British origin of our handball) and racquets, all of which he must have played with Willie and Ernie Renshaw. He won the fives championship of the school, and a little, brown, wooden cup with a silver top adorned the mantelpiece of his Groton study for many years. Though Peabody made a sacrament of exercise all his life, he was an all-around leader at Cheltenham where he was a good student and a prefect.*

After five years at Cheltenham, Peabody went up to Trinity College, Cambridge, where he rowed, played cricket, and also took up the game of real, or court, tennis. Most of his intimate friends were serious about religion and he soon found his spiritual home in the Anglican traditions of Thomas Arnold, Frederick Dennison Maurice, and Charles Kingsley. He wanted a good law degree and came down from Cambridge with First Class honors.

Following Arnold of Rugby, Peabody educated his Groton boys to be Christians, gentlemen, and scholars, in that order. True to the traditions of muscular Christianity, he always seemed to favor the football captain over the top scholar; and he was proud when, among a graduating class of eighteen boys in 1898, three became Harvard captains, two of football and one of baseball. All told, moreover, between 1883 and 1983, Groton produced five football captains at Harvard and two at Yale. The last, a

---

*Prefects were sixth-form boys chosen to run the school during their senior year. This tradition began with Arnold at Rugby and was followed by Peabody at Groton. Franklin D. Roosevelt, Jr., was the Senior Prefect at Groton in 1933.

grandson, Endicott Davison, captained Yale in 1947; another grandson, Endicott Peabody, of Harvard, was the last (1941) All-American to be drawn from *Social Register* families.*

It has often been said that the status of the nonathlete at Groton was more or less inconsequential, as the author Louis Auchincloss (Groton, 1935), has nicely noted in his autobiographical writings. Though Peabody emphasized team sports as ideal builders of character, he surely encouraged excellence in scholarship, too. Of some one thousand boys graduating between 1890 and 1932, for example, many won high honors in college, including 72 winners of Phi Beta Kappas—thirty at Harvard, thirty-five at Yale, and seven at other colleges. Few if any schools have equaled that record.

In 1930, when Peabody was asked to discuss the differences between American and English schools, his talk was surely prophetic and must be briefly quoted here:

> Sports, as conducted in England, provide both health and moral education. The highest achievement of any game can be claimed for the national game of cricket which is used as a measure of moral quality. Of some fine action, they will say, "That's cricket!", while final condemnation is found in the criticism, "That's not cricket!"
>
> In America our first approach to a game is apt to be the quest for someone to beat. . . . Athletics are in many cases just plain business. . . . They come under the instruction of professionals whose positions depend in many cases on their success in "delivering the goods"—that is, achieving victory. . . . "That's cricket!" could not be applied to many plans pursued by professional coaches. . . . Worst of all, in consequence of the intense competition there has grown up in many schools the notion that any play is legitimate if it is not forbidden by the letter of the rules. In laying out athletic programs, a good deal of attention is given by us to considering the spectators, many of whom would be better off if they themselves were taking an active part in games elsewhere.[7]

---

*St. Paul's School, a Groton rival in social status, was more than twice as large but never produced a football captain at Harvard or Yale. It did produce Hobey Baker, Princeton (1913) captain of both football and ice hockey, who was surely the most gallant gentleman-athlete of his age.

Peabody, of course, always looked upon athletics as a means of moral training for later life. Though he appreciated the game of cricket as a moral mentor, his favorite sport was American football, largely because it was rough and hard and required courage, endurance, and discipline. He liked to win and hated to lose, but would not stand for poor sportsmanship; if there was any sign of it by a Groton team, he went on a rampage. For many years, one of his masters was the best schoolboy football coach in New England, but at Groton the coach was always subservient to the players, and football captains ran the traditional St. Mark's game without interference from the coaches. The rector himself coached the crew for many years, his oarsmen going on to produce thirty-two letter-winners (two captains) at Harvard, and twenty-two (five captains) at Yale.

Just as Peabody abhorred the all-too-prevalent American ethic of winning at any cost, so he looked with disdain at bigness and mediocrity in favor of the small and excellent. And he kept Groton small, less than two hundred boys. He and his great lady said good night to every boy every night; and Peabody kept in touch with his alumni long after they had left the school, marrying many of them, admonishing those who strayed from the straight and narrow, and praising those who were doing good, as well as well. At its fiftieth anniversary in 1934, Groton's most famous alumnus and the most distinguished American in the twentieth century, Franklin Delano Roosevelt, was in the White House. Peabody had married Franklin and Eleanor, and held a simple service in St. John's Church opposite the White House in March 1933, as he did each year thereafter, as well as at the beginning of each of Roosevelt's presidential terms.

The Chapel symbolized the spiritual core of the Groton Ethic, and the following lines from one of Peabody's favorite poems—"Clifton Chapel," by Henry Newbolt—would apply to both the British public schools and Groton, as well as most other New England boarding schools of the Peabody era:

This is the Chapel: here, my son,
Your father thought the thoughts of youth,
And heard the words that one by one
The touch of life has turned to truth. . . .

To set the cause above renown,
To love the game beyond the prize,

To honor as you strike him down,
The foe that comes with fearless eyes;
To count the life of battle good,
And dear the land that gave you birth,
And dearer yet the brotherhood
That binds the brave of all the earth.

Both Peabody and his friend and kinsman Theodore Roosevelt stressed the duties rather than the rights of privilege and believed that a successful democracy needed the leadership of an aristocracy. Roosevelt was a natural showman and public figure, while Peabody shunned publicity and was an intensely private person. In 1903, for example, Groton first came before the public eye when President Roosevelt, who had two sons there at the time, agreed to give the main address at the twentieth anniversary ceremonies the following spring. Quite naturally the press was curious about the President's speaking at such a small and little-known school and plagued the rector for information; he was hardly co-operative and defended his privacy: "It will be impossible," he wrote to one reporter, "for me to assist you with the article concerning Archie Roosevelt by allowing the school or the boy to be photographed."*[8]

Theodore Roosevelt returned from his well-publicized charge up San Juan Hill a national hero, went to Albany as Governor of New York, in 1898, and into the White House, after McKinley's assassination, three years later. He was surely the most widely read and broadly educated of our twentieth-century presidents; he published no less than seven books during the first ten years after graduating from Harvard, and knew personally most of the leading artists and writers of his age. At the same time, he was a vigorous sportsman and his effect on the growth of games in this country was greater than that of any other president. A veritable, real-life Frank Merriwell in the White House, he was the first public figure in America to use the phraseology of sport, especially football, for didactic purposes: "Don't Flinch, Don't Foul, Hit the Line Hard." As an

---

*Groton educated all four of Theodore Roosevelt's sons as well as Franklin Roosevelt and all four of his sons.

advocate of clean living he had no rival: he never used tobacco and drank only rarely, mostly to be polite at formal occasions. He abhorred the discussion of sex in public and hated foul language: he once noted that during the whole time that he led the Rough Riders, "there was never a foul or indecent word uttered at the officers' mess—I mean this literally; and there was very little swearing." Roosevelt once became quite uneasy when his good friend, Owen Wister, discussed his theories of the relationship between sexual potency and artistic creativity: "He might almost have been," wrote Wister, "a refined, nineteenth-century lady, to whom I was making risqué remarks."[9]

Roosevelt had the first tennis court built on the White House grounds, where he played with friends who came to be known as his "tennis cabinet." Roosevelt intimates included such cultivated public servants as Henry Cabot Lodge and Elihu Root; the famous sculptor Saint-Gaudens; the artist Frederic Remington; Owen Wister, the novelist; and historians like Henry Adams and James Ford Rhodes. As Wister wrote: "Distinguished civilized men and charming women came as a habit to the White House while Roosevelt was there. For once in our history, we had an American *salon.*"

The tennis court was enclosed with a twenty-foot-high canvas fence for purposes of privacy. The vigorous sporting life which Roosevelt wanted to encourage in the American people from his "bully pulpit" did not include tennis. He, for example, never allowed himself to be photographed in tennis clothes or while playing, preferring to project his exploits in more vigorous sports such as hiking, rowing, horseback-riding or big-game hunting. Actually, Roosevelt was a sportsman rather than an athlete: his mediocre tennis game was surprisingly good considering his very poor eyesight, overweight, and poor coordination. In spite of his lack of skill, however, he competed vigorously with his family and friends on the courts at Sagamore Hill, his Long Island estate, and at the White House: "When we were able to beat him at singles it was to have passed the entrance exams for college as far as tennis was concerned," his son, Theodore, once remarked.

Roosevelt, above all, believed in sport as a means of cultivating a vigor of body which, in turn, led to a vigor of mind and character. He was vitally against professionalism and the commercialization of sport: "When money comes in at the gate, the game goes out the window." He was against making sport "an end rather than a means, and especially permitting it to become the serious business of life."[10] Anticipating the boredom of the modern mass man of leisure, Roosevelt knew that too much fun becomes work of the most tedious sort: he abhorred both the professional athlete and the professional socialite: "Personally," he wrote, "the life of the Four Hundred, in its typical form, strikes me as being as flat as stale champagne. I do not think that anyone can permanently lead his or her life amid such surroundings and with such objects, save at the cost of degeneration in character."[11] And Theodore Roosevelt taught a whole generation of his fellow Americans to see the vigorous, athletic, and sporting life as a means of building character rather than making money.

No one has better summed up the influence of Roosevelt on the sporting mores of his age than the fine tennis journalist John R. Tunis, in the following lines taken from his essay on Roosevelt as "The First American Sportsman":

> Eighteen football players were killed and one hundred badly injured in the year 1905. So in 1906 T. R. called a conference of the representatives of Harvard-Yale-Princeton in the White House and told them to clean things up—or else. Consequently, new rules doing away with the mass pushing and fighting were made, freshmen were banned from competition, tramp athletes discouraged, and the game opened up for the introduction of the forward pass.
>
> Naturally, this had a tremendous effect upon our sports and upon the people of the United States. Teddy publicized athletics before the era of the sports page, made exercise fashionable, and, aided by the advice of Gifford Pinchot in his conservation policies, promoted and furthered outdoor life all over the nation. If you have ever camped, fished, hiked, or skied in our national parks or forests, you have these two men to thank for it.
>
> From his earliest days in Washington stemmed the start of the national interest in sport. The changes in our mores . . . the growing love of young America for games and sports were greatly influenced by a man who, for the first twenty years of this century, was constantly in the public gaze. Youngsters believed in him, loved him, and tried to follow his example.[12]

———

Both Teddy Roosevelt and Endicott Peabody talked far more of team sports like football as molders of a gentlemanly code of honor than they did of tennis. But the Anglo-American gentleman's code was not a code for any particular game, whether cricket, baseball, football, or tennis. Rather, it was an ethical ideal which guided the gentleman's total way of life, on the sporting field as well as in the courtroom or boardroom, on Wall Street or in the City, in Congress or in Parliament, on Park Avenue or Mayfair, indeed throughout the British gentleman's empire from Port of Spain to Singapore or New Delhi. The amateur sporting code, in short, was an aspect of a class code of honor which was uniquely characteristic of the Anglo-American social systems roughly in the years between the American Civil War and World War II.

Perry Anderson, a leading English Marxist, surely understood, though he hardly approved of, the virtues of the British social system which he grudgingly praised as follows: "English society today," he wrote, "can be most accurately described as an immensely elastic and all-embracing hegemonic order." Hegemony means, he continued,

> "the dominance of one social block over another, not simply by force or wealth, but by a total social authority whose ultimate sanction and expression is a profound cultural supremacy. . . . The hegemonic class is the primary determinant of consciousness, character, and customs throughout the society. This tranquil and unchallenged sovereignty is a relatively rare historical phenomenon. In England, however, the unparalleled temporal continuity of the dominant class produced a striking example of it."[13]

And it is our thesis that the national, WASP upper class was similarly hegemonic in America, if perhaps somewhat less tranquil.*

One final clarification needs to be made here, and that is the conceptual difference between a class and an elite: on the one hand, the term "upper class" refers to a morals- and manners-generating community at the top of the society where, in families, exclusive schools, and colleges, class codes are passed on from generation to generation. The Anglo-

---

*The great German sociologist, Max Weber, was the original and most perceptive sociologist of bureaucracy, as Karl Marx was of class. He clearly saw, following Tocqueville, that gentlemanly authority was the unique characteristic of the English class structure when he wrote as follows: "The Gentry maintained possession of all offices of local administration by taking them over *without compensation* in the interest of their own social power. *The gentry saved England from the bureaucratization which has been the fate of all continental states*" (my italics).[14]

American upper class was, in a very real sense, both a national and transnational community. The term "elite," on the other hand, refers to something quite different. Above all, it is not a community of families but a collection of the more successful individuals in any society. The elite is actually a collection of functional elites—legal, medical, and clerical (once known as the learned professions), and a multitude of others, such as the political, intellectual, scientific, and communications elites or, since 1968, the pro-tennis elite.

The hegemonic WASP upper class in America still dominated the most important elites, including lawn tennis, down to the Kennedy presidency. Among the younger generation, class hegemony got its first jolt when Kennedy was assassinated in 1963 and finally died a slow death during the revolutionary years after 1968. Today, no one would speak of the American medical profession as Sir William Osler, distinguished Anglo-American physician, did in pre–World War I Philadelphia: "Morgan, Shippen, Redman, Rush, Coxe, the elder Wood, the elder Pepper, and the elder Mitchell of Philadelphia—Brahmins all, in the language of the greatest Brahmin among them, Dr. Oliver Wendell Holmes—these and men like them have been the leaven which has raised our profession above the dead level of a business."[15] Almost from the beginning, especially since the age of McEnroe and Conners, pro tennis has remained at the "dead level of a business." One wonders if the high honor code in professional golf is not at least partly due to the fact that the golf tour is still played at the more exclusive golf clubs in the nation?

The Rise of Lawn Tennis:
The Harrow and Harvard Era, 1877–1887

> . . . If You can meet with Triumph and Disaster and treat those two impostors just the same.
> —Kipling

THE ORIGINS OF LAWN TENNIS, AND ALL OTHER RACQUET SPORTS, GO back to royal, or court, tennis, the game of kings which went through its Golden Age in Europe during the sixteenth and seventeenth centuries. In 1571, Charles IX of France noted that it was "one of the most honourable, worthy and healthy exercises which princes, peers, gentlemen and other distinguished persons can undertake."[1] Henry VIII was champion of England in his day, although it probably did not pay to beat him anyway. In 1519, the Venetian Ambassador wrote of young Henry as follows: "His Majesty is 29 years old and . . . much handsomer than any other sovereign in Christendom. . . . He is extremely fond of tennis, at which game it is the prettiest thing in the world to see him play, his fair skin glowing through a shirt of the finest texture."[2] Henry built a royal tennis court at his favorite palace, Hampton Court, in 1519; it is still in use today.

Royal, or court, tennis is today the most exclusive game of them all, there being some thirty courts and only about two thousand players in the entire world (about one-fourth in America). An audience of a hundred spectators is considered a huge crowd. Although there are courts at Oxford and Cambridge, court tennis in America is too expensive even for the Big Three universities (Harvard, Yale, and Princeton) though Richard Sears, the first U.S. Court Tennis Champion, was a Harvard man, and most champions since have been graduates of Harvard, Yale, or Princeton, or, as with the greatest champion of them all, Jay Gould, very rich men's sons who felt no need for college degrees. While Jay Gould won eighteen championships in a row, the next most frequent champion, Alastair B. Martin, a Princeton graduate, won it once before World War II and seven times in a row afterwards (he is enshrined in the Tennis Hall of Fame, in Newport). The first court tennis court in the United States was privately built in Boston, in 1876; courts were subsequently built at the racquet clubs of Boston, New York, Philadelphia, and Chicago, as well as at Tuxedo Park, New York, and at the Newport Casino.

When Nathaniel Thayer and Hollis Hunnewell built their private court in Boston, in 1876, they hired both a tennis pro and a young locker boy, Tom Pettit, from England. Pettit soon became the best professional player in America, also winning the world championship at Hampton Court, in 1885. When the Newport Casino was opened in 1880, Pettit was hired as the professional in both court and lawn tennis; he remained at the Casino for sixty-five years until his death in 1946; he was enshrined in the Tennis Hall of Fame in 1982.

In 1874, the year Benjamin Disraeli, a baptized Jew, began his great second ministry, a retired army cavalry officer, Major Walter Wingfield, patented a new game which he called Sphairistike, or Lawn Tennis. It immediately appealed to the Anglo-American leisured classes who were rapidly becoming rich beyond their wildest dreams of avarice. Though hard up for cash himself, Wingfield was proud of his ancient line whose family seat at Wingfield Castle, in Suffolk, was supposed to have been erected in 1362. He was therefore delighted that, during the first year, his sets were bought, according to Herbert Warren Wind, by such distinguished customers as "the Prince of Wales, the Crown Prince of Prussia, and Prince Louis of Hesse; by eight dukes, including the Duke of Edinburgh and the Duke of Devonshire; by fourteen marquises, including the Marquis of Lansdowne and the Marquis of Exeter; by forty-nine earls, including the Earl of Cadogan, the Earl of Leicester, and the Earl of Salisbury; and by eight viscounts, including Viscount Halifax and Viscount Bangor."[3] At the same time, an American lady, Miss Mary Outerbridge, saw the new game played in Bermuda and brought a set back to America, where the first game of tennis was probably played on a court that her brother, A. Emilius Outerbridge, helped her lay out on the lawns of the Staten Island Cricket and Baseball Club.

"The 1870's, with industry and agriculture booming and British prestige at its height," wrote Mark Girouard in his definitive study of *The Victorian Country House*, "were the golden age of Victorian country house building, as of most other aspects of Victorian life."[4] He also noted, moreover, that the boom reached its peak in the first four years of the decade. Thorstein Veblen might have gleefully noted (if he had written on the subject) that idle lawns, instead of productive crops, were excellent symbols of conspicuous waste. As the lawn mower gradually replaced the traditional scythe, more and more once-productive acres were converted into lawns where leisured ladies and gentlemen whiled away the hours playing croquet at longer and longer weekend house parties.

Prosperity, as it still has a way of doing, fostered the idea of sexual equality. In 1869, John Stuart Mill published his *Subjection of Women* and the first women's colleges were soon founded at Oxford and Cambridge.

In spite of this mild emancipation, as there were more than half a million more women than men in England, most of them, with the help of their mothers, were basically engaged in hunting husbands. On the smooth croquet lawns, as well as in the surrounding shrubbery looking for lost balls, proper, crinoline-clad Victorian ladies, with more or less cunning, sought to capture the hearts of clean-cut English gentlemen.

A year before the publication of Mill's famous book, the All-England Croquet Club was founded in the London suburb of Wimbledon. But gradually, even the ladies grew bored and impatient with croquet's leisurely lack of vigor. At the same time, the ancient Indian game of "Poona," which had been taken up by British officers in the 1860s, was officially launched in England at a garden party, in 1873, at the Duke of Beaufort's country house, "Badminton," in Gloucestershire. While bad-minton was far more vigorous than croquet, control of the feathered shuttlecock was almost impossible on windy days. Lawn tennis came to be seen as the ideal game in these respects, and it soon drove both cro-quet and badminton off the velvet lawns of the stately homes of En-gland.

The Marylebone Cricket Club, the Kremlin of that national game, watched the growth of lawn tennis with some apprehension. Not only had tennis players adopted the white shirt and white flannel uniform of cricket, but the new game was also threatening to cut into cricket's popu-larity. The MCC was already negotiating with Wingfield for control of the rules of the game when, in 1877, the All-England Croquet Club changed its name to the All-England Croquet and Lawn Tennis Club, and took control of the game by holding the first National Championship at Wim-bledon. To this day, in spite of the formation of the Lawn Tennis Associa-tion in 1887, the All-England Club has been the *de facto* ruler of British tennis, in much the same style as the MCC's rule of cricket.

As with the gentlemanly social games of cricket and tennis, political and financial hegemony in England and throughout the empire has been maintained since the Victorian era through the polite authority of The Club. Major decisions in both the City and at Whitehall, for instance, were made along Pall Mall, where Conservatives met at the Carleton Club and Liberals at the Reform. But perhaps the best illustration of the role of the club in the making of gentlemen and as an instrument of power, was a "gentlemanly agreement" that created the De Beers Diamond monopoly in the 1880s. And it is indeed symbolic that it should have been made in racialist South Africa by the great imperialist visionary, Cecil Rhodes—the only Englishman ever to have a nation named after him.

After a breakdown of his health at the age of seventeen, young Rhodes, an Anglican clergyman's son, was sent out to take a rest on his older brother's cotton plantation, in Natal. Almost immediately, however, he was off to seek his fortune among the diamond diggers in the Big Hole, at Kimberley. By 1877, the year of the first tennis championships at Wimbledon, he had complete control of the (then smaller) De Beers Diamond mines, had his first heart attack, and wrote the first of seven wills which envisioned the formation of a Nordic secret society, much like Loyola's in organization, and devoted to the English-speaking gentleman's rule of the world. In the meantime, he planned to monopolize control of diamond mining. His most important competitor was a Jew named Barney Barnato, son of a Whitechapel shopkeeper, who was possessed by a passionate desire to make his pile and, above all, to become a gentleman. By 1885, Rhodes was worth fifty thousand pounds a year, but Barnato was richer. Now Rhodes began his "subtle" and persistent dealings with Barnato in order to gain control of his Kimberley mines. Nearly every day he had him to lunch or dinner at the "unattainable" (at least for Barnato) Kimberley Club (Rhodes of course demanded that the club make an exception to its rule which limited the entertainment of a non-member to once a month). At last, Barnato agreed to sell out for a fabulous fortune, membership in the Kimberley Club (at Rhodes's command), and a secure place among the caste of gentlemanly imperialists. While Rhodes had perhaps used his club and his race with a somewhat ungentlemanly lack of subtlety, no American trust ever had such power over one commodity as Rhodes now had over diamonds.

In the meantime, Barney Barnato, having realized his dreams of becoming both a millionaire and a gentleman, eventually committed suicide by jumping into the sea on a trip home from Cape Town to Southampton. After Rhodes's own premature death in 1902, his lifelong dreams that "between two and three thousand Nordic gentlemen in the prime of life" should run the world became a partial reality in the Rhodes Scholarship Association. A large majority of the American scholars selected for polishing at Oxford fulfilled Rhodes's ideal of the clubable, WASP, scholar-athlete for the first four decades after 1904. Since the Second World War, however, the religious, racial, and even sexual criteria have gradually been abandoned. As we shall see, the abandonment of these taboos—so intimately a part of the Anglo-American, Victorian ideals in which amateur tennis had its roots—were partially responsible for the coming of open tennis at Wimbledon in 1968. It is perhaps symbolic that the only American Rhodes Scholar to reach world-class rank in tennis was among the last generation of amateur players: a Southern gentleman from Tulane University, Hamilton Richardson, was Intercollegiate Champion in 1953 and 1954, ranked eleven years in the First Ten (number one twice), and on five Davis Cup teams, before his retirement from competitive tennis in 1965. It is doubtful that any future Rhodes Scholar will be attracted by the values of today's tennis-brat millionaires.

=====

The twenty-two gentlemen who played in the first Wimbledon championship in 1877 quite naturally exhibited a wide variety of strokes as well as racquets. But, wrote Edward Clarkson Potter, Jr., a gentlemanly product of St. Paul's School and Harvard, and one of America's leading tennis writers for many decades preceding the end of amateur tennis, "they all had in common a code of ethics which seems absurd in these victory-mad days [1960s]. No one cared very much whether he won or lost as long as the match was well and fairly fought."[5] Instead of today's cursing of linesmen and bullying of umpires, "Jolly good stroke, old chap" echoed back and forth across the net. Almost all the players were public school men. The class nature of the event was further suggested by the fact that no matches were scheduled for Friday and Saturday of the first week in order that players and spectators would be free to attend the fashionable Eton-Harrow cricket match at Lords. The final round was scheduled for Monday (Victorians did not play on Sunday), but was further delayed because of rain. The Wimbledon scheduling was never again interrupted for another social or sporting event, and the tournament eventually came to rank almost equally in social and popular importance with Lords, Henley, and Ascot.

Spencer Gore, an old Harrovian racquets player, was the first Wimbledon Champion. He seemed to be the only player who really wanted to win, which he did by rushing up to the net and hitting the ball on-the-fly, or what we now call volleying. Losers of course took their beatings like gentlemen, but nevertheless lost no time afterwards in trying to outlaw the stroke that beat them; for weeks the columns of the *Field*, the leading British sporting journal of that day (and up to 1935), were filled with the pros and cons of the volleying controversy. As they have done so often since, official Wimbledon stubbornly refused to bow before crowd pressure and stuck to their rules. And they were proven right in doing so at the next year's Wimbledon championships.

At the second Wimbledon, Gore was allowed to "stand out" while thirty-four all-comers competed for the right to challenge him for the title. A young coffee planter home on leave from Ceylon, Frank Hadow, entered the tournament along with his older brother A. A. Hadow; both had been ardent racquets players at Harrow. The older brother was beaten in an early round, but Frank Hadow won through to the challenge round rather easily. Against Gore he used both his brains and his athletic ability: when the champion dashed for the net, he nicely lifted a lob over his head, a new and as yet unheard-of stroke; Gore was confused and Hadow won.

Since Frank Hadow went back to Ceylon after his victory and never returned to Wimbledon until the half-century celebrations in 1927, there was no defender in 1879 and the tournament was won by a Yorkshire clergyman, J. T. Hartley, who had been court tennis champion of Oxford as well as an old Harrovian cricketer. When he found himself still in the tournament on Saturday, the Vicar had to journey all the way up to Yorkshire to preach his Sunday sermon; preach he did and then turned around and came back to London, arriving at Wimbledon on Monday afternoon, just in time to change into his flannels and win the tournament from a wild Irish aristocrat, Vere Thomas St. Leger Gould. Some years later Gould's wildness got the better of him, and he was tried and convicted of murder, in Monte Carlo. He died on Devil's Island in 1909.

St. Leger Gould had won the first Irish championships in 1879, which anticipated the future by including not only men's singles and doubles, but also women's singles and mixed doubles. The first Scottish Championships were also held that year, and the first English Doubles Championship was held at Oxford.

In 1880, the Reverend Hartley again won Wimbledon by defeating Herbert Lawford, a baseliner whose powerful forehand became known as "The Lawford Stroke" and served as a model for other players taking up the game. Lawford eventually won the All-England Championship at Wimbledon in 1887 after being runner-up four times. The 1880 Wimbledon was of historic importance because it was the first to include the Renshaw twins, William and Ernest, who were both beaten in early rounds by O. E. Woodhouse, who soon sailed for a vacation in the United States where he won the first unofficial championship (see below).

The Renshaws transformed lawn tennis from a pastime into a great sport. Beginning in 1881, Willie won Wimbledon seven times, six years in a row, and then, after Lawford won in 1887 and Willie's twin, Ernest, in 1888, Willie won again and for the last time, in 1889. Willie also won the doubles seven times, all with his brother. His record has never been equaled.

The Renshaw twins were well-to-do boys who lived in Cheltenham and went as day-boys to Cheltenham College. The twins were excellent cricketers but early on turned to tennis, Cheltenham having one of the first covered courts in England. After they both lost at Wimbledon in 1880, they went south to the French Riviera where they built a later-famous tennis court at the Beau Site Hotel, in Cannes. They practiced every day on the hard-sand surface until it was time to go home for the 1881 tennis season. They won everything that year: Willie took the Irish championship at Dublin, and the brothers won the doubles; Ernest won the singles at Cheltenham; Willie won the Wimbledon singles for the first time, and the twins combined to take the Doubles Championship, still held at Oxford, for the second time. The Renshaw name became famous just as tennis was spreading round the world. And Willie won his first Wimbledon in 1881, the year the first U.S. Championship was held at Newport.

The game spread rapidly in the United States. By 1880, tennis was played in some thirty clubs, largely along the Eastern Seaboard but also in Chicago and New Orleans as well as out in San Francisco.

While Mary Outerbridge (who brought one of Major Wingfield's first sets) and her brother were laying out the tennis court on the lawns of the Staten Island Cricket and Baseball Club, James Dwight and his cousin and Beacon Street neighbor, Frederick R. Sears, Jr., set up the first court in the Boston area at the favorite Brahmin summer resort at Nahant, a narrow peninsula which juts out to sea about twenty miles north of

Boston. William Appleton was one of Nahant's most prominent resorters. His son-in-law, J. Arthur Beebe, had brought back one of Wingfield's sets from London, in 1874. Dwight and Sears laid out the first court on the Appleton's lawn that summer, and they and their cousins and friends soon became obsessed with the new game; and in 1876 they held their first handicap tournament. Among the fifteen entries were Dwight's cousins, Bill Appleton, Bob Grant, and young Billy Lawrence. Cabot Lodge, who was first elected from Nahant to the Massachusetts House in 1879, was three years ahead of Dwight at Harvard and one of the friends who played. To this day, an old-fashioned racquet hangs on the wall in a prominent place at The Country Club, in Brookline, under which is the following inscription: *Racquet used by Bishop Lawrence in the first tennis game in this country* (one of the first at best). This tournament was the first one on record ever held in America. The finals were between Dwight and Sears, and Dwight won it, 12–15, 15–7, 15–13 (the racquets and squash scoring system was used). The next summer, Fred Sears's younger half-brother, Richard D. Sears, became fascinated with the game at the age of fifteen. A natural athlete, he rapidly improved, banging the ball by the hour against a barn door.

In 1877, a group of twenty-five cricketers organized a club located on a corner of the six-hundred-acre Sears estate on the edge of Boston, at what is now Brookline and Longwood Avenues. In 1840, David Sears, whose father left him the largest fortune ever inherited in New England and was then the richest citizen of Boston, named his new country place "Longwood," after the dilapidated house where his hero Napoleon died on St. Helena. Sears's Napoleonic complex, as they would say today, is revealed to any guest at Boston's most patrician club, the Somerset, at 52 Beacon Street, which was originally Sears's town house. The flamboyant Empire style, down to the frequent Ns and Golden Eagles, is still very much in elegant evidence.

In 1878, a year after the founding of the cricket club, a tennis court was laid out; by 1890 Longwood was essentially a lawn tennis club; it remained at its original site for forty-six years before moving further out in the country to Chestnut Hill, not far from the old Lawrence ("Our Bishop") estate which is now Boston College. Like Symphony Hall or The Country Club, Longwood has become a Boston institution, and the hub of New England tennis. David Sears's two grandsons, Fred and Richard, pursued their tennis at Longwood as did their friend Jim Dwight. Dick Sears and his Harvard classmate from Philadelphia, Joe Clark, were in the habit of cycling over to Longwood several times a week in the spring term. In their junior year, incidentally, Clark beat Sears for the Harvard Singles Championship. The most well-known pictures of Dick Sears, first U.S. Singles Champion, and James Dwight, Father of American tennis, show them in the full cricket regalia of Longwood.

As of Longwood's hundredth anniversary in 1977, the following members had been enshrined in the International Tennis Hall of Fame at the Newport Casino: 1955—Richard D. Sears, Dr. James Dwight, Robert D. Wrenn, Malcolm D. Whitman, and Joseph S. Clark; 1956—William J. Clothier, Dwight F. Davis, Holcombe Ward, and Beals C. Wright; 1957—Hazel Hotchkiss Wightman and R. Norris Williams; 1958—Maude Barger-Wallach; 1963—Sarah Palfrey Danzig; 1968—Eleonora Sears; and 1974—Fred Hovey. And the foreword to the anniversary publication, *One Hundred Years of Longwood*, by Robert Minton, was written by Bud Collins, club member and distinguished tennis writer for the Boston *Globe*.

In 1877, the first issue of the *American Cricketer*, published in Philadelphia, noted that "lawn tennis is very popular in Germantown." The three pioneers of American tennis from Philadelphia—Clarence Monroe Clark (1859–1937), Joseph Sill Clark (1861–1956), and Frederick Winslow Taylor (1856–1915)—all lived in Germantown, a stone's throw from the famous Germantown Cricket Club, founded in 1854. (All three men then belonged to the Young America Cricket Club which was absorbed by Germantown in 1890.) "My brother Clarence and I," wrote Joseph Sill Clark in a privately circulated letter (95 pages) to his grandchildren at the celebration of his ninetieth birthday, in 1951, "became interested in the game of tennis in the year 1878, I think it was, and we laid out a tennis court on a part of our father's property located on the corner of School Lane and Township Line in Germantown. . . . A little later, Mr. Fred Taylor, a great friend of ours, built a much better court on his father's property on Ross Street, Germantown, on which my brother Clarence and I played a lot of tennis with Fred Taylor and others."[6]

Of the three pioneers of Philadelphia tennis, Clarence Clark was the natural organizer. In 1879, he formed the All-Philadelphia Lawn Tennis Committee in order to unify the local competition as to rules and regulations. The next year, he and his best friend, Fred Taylor, challenged

Emilius Outerbridge's team from Staten Island to an intercity doubles match. Philadelphia lost, and Clark was especially impressed by the wide differences in regulations and equipment between the two teams. At the same time, in late August, the Staten Island Cricket and Baseball Club held the first American tournament open to all. James Dwight and young Richard Dudley Sears came down for the Staten Island tournament. Though they planned to play in both the singles and the doubles, when they discovered that the balls to be used were lighter, softer, and much smaller than those used in Boston, they withdrew from the singles and were beaten in an early round of the doubles by a team from Morristown, New Jersey. An Englishman, O. E. Woodhouse, who had beaten both the Renshaw twins at Wimbledon earlier in the year, was crowned "Champion of America," beating a Canadian, J. F. Hellmuth, in the Staten Island finals.

After this first unofficial tournament, Clarence Clark, Outerbridge, and Dwight all agreed that some central organization was needed in order to regulate the growing game. Accordingly, Clark arranged for the *American Cricketer*, in the May 8 issue, to announce that all interested parties were invited to attend a New York convention on May 21, 1881, in order to settle differences and draw up uniform regulations. Representatives from thirty-three clubs came to New York, Dwight noting that "close to one hundred people were in the room" at this historic meeting at which the United States National Lawn Tennis Association was formed (it dropped the "National" in 1920 and the "Lawn" after the coming of professional tennis, in the 1970s). The Lawn Tennis Association (Great Britain) was not formed until 1887. The New York convention chose a General Oliver, from Albany, New York, as first president in order to have a neutral leader that first year. The executive committee consisted of Dwight from Boston, Outerbridge from Staten Island, and Clarence Clark from Philadelphia, who was made secretary. It was agreed that the first official championships in both men's singles and doubles were to be held in August, at the newly built Newport Casino.

The Newport Casino was built by a young millionaire whose immigrant father, James Gordon Bennett, had built the New York *Herald* from a four-page, penny paper (1835) into the largest, most prosperous and respected newspaper in America when he handed it on to his son and namesake, in the 1870s. Bennett the younger was brought up, largely abroad, by a doting mother, private tutors, and endless servants who spoiled him in three languages. Long before the era of permissive education, he somehow absorbed the ethic of instant gratification. And he grew up to be the most notorious and mannerless millionaire of his day in Newport and New York. In fact, the Newport Casino, the home of the sacred shrine of American tennis today, was originally conceived in a fit of rudeness. One fine day, a British houseguest at Bennett's Newport villa, presumably on a dare, suddenly veered his polo pony across the lawn and into the halls of Newport's most sedate and exclusive men's club, the Reading Room. After being censured by the Reading Room membership, Bennett commissioned the day's most distinguished architectural firm, McKim, Mead & White, to build him his own proper retreat, opposite his villa on Bellevue Avenue. And the new Casino soon became the tennis, both court and lawn, center of Newport.

Several years before he was censured by the Reading Room, Bennett's rudeness reached its heights at a New Year's Eve engagement party before his planned marriage to a beautiful daughter of the prominent May family of Washington, D.C.; the scholarly *Dictionary of American Biography* version of the affair reads as follows: "The engagement was abruptly broken off by the May family under mysterious circumstances; his fiancee's brother, Fred May, attacked Bennett with a horsewhip on Jan. 3, 1877, as the latter was emerging from the Union Club on Fifth Avenue; and a duel followed immediately on the Delaware-Maryland borderline, shots being exchanged harmlessly."[7] A less academic Bennett biographer described the horsewhipping and duel in more vivid detail and wrote of the engagement party as follows:

Jimmy Bennett, veteran of fleshpots, terror of polite society, naked coachman, reckless polo player, high-living and free-spending clubman, was about to be tamed by domesticity; was there some half-hidden motive behind the conduct which, in less than an hour, was to horrify Miss May, enrage her family, and scandalize New York society? Lurching slightly, he was ushered into the drawing room. . . . He moved around the room, whacking his male friends on the back and loudly making bawdy remarks which the ladies pretended not to hear. . . .

Happily roaming the crowded drawing room with its cheery fire blazing and everyone in high spirits, he suddenly felt the need to relieve himself.

The bathroom was a long lonely march away, down chill and drafty corridors. It was ridiculous to have to leave such jolly company simply because of what the Nice Nellies described as a "call of nature." Since childhood, though "permissive" methods of childrearing had not yet been formulated, he had done exactly what he pleased. Right now he had to pump out the bilge, and he damn well wasn't going to walk half a block for the purpose.

So Bennett unbuttoned, unburdened himself . . . into the roaring fireplace. . . . Several ladies pretended to faint . . . a number of their menfolk quickly surrounded the preoccupied Bennett until he finished his indelicate task and turned around to inquire where the hell everyone was running off to. . . . Hardly a minute elapsed before he was deposited in his sleigh and his coachman was ordered to drive him away rapidly—anywhere—preferably to some remote and savage corner of the world where he was always sending other men.[8]*

It must be said for Bennett that he was one of the pioneer sportsmen of his day. Along with Winston Churchill's grandfather, Leonard Jerome, he was among the first members of the Jockey Club and a leading sponsor of horse racing in Metropolitan New York; he was an enthusiastic four-in-hand driver both in Newport and New York, once recklessly upsetting his coach while trying to impress the dark-eyed Jennie Jerome (Winston Churchill's mother), who, fortunately for all of us in World War II, lived through the accident. After witnessing the first games of polo in England, Bennett brought the game to Newport, where he built the first polo field and organized the first international match there in 1886 (the British won). He was a pioneer in international yacht racing and a one-time commodore of the New York Yacht Club. At any rate, were it not for his rudeness and sportsmanship, the famous Newport Casino, seat of American lawn tennis and the Tennis Hall of Fame, would not exist as we know it.

Bennett eventually used up his welcome in genteel American society and moved to France where he divided his time between his house in Paris, a shooting lodge at Versailles, a villa at Beaulieu, and one of the largest steam yachts in the world. He autocratically ran the *Herald* by

---

*On a famous hunch, Bennett had once sent one of the *Herald*'s roving reporters, Henry M. Stanley, into the heart of unmapped and unexplored Central Africa, on the chance of his finding a celebrated Scottish missionary-doctor-explorer named Livingstone, who had not been heard from for over three years. They met and the *Herald* had the scoop.

cable and occasional hasty visits to his homeland. In 1887, he founded the Paris edition of the New York *Herald*, and, ever since, American tennis players, especially in our jetting age, have been grateful for the Paris *Herald** wherever they happen to be playing in Europe.

The saga of James Gordon Bennett, who left us such a charming tennis shrine, suggests that vulgarity and self-indulgence have been abroad in every age. Some ages suppress it while others, like our own, tend to foster it. Perhaps our present crop of mannerless American tennis players have been infected, in some subliminally historical way, by the values of their indirect Founding Father.

═══

At the end of August 1881, twenty-five gentlemen, largely Bostonians and Philadelphians, came to Newport, by boat, train, and carriage, to compete for the first official championships of the United States. The players were largely undergraduates or alumni of Harvard, Yale, Princeton, and the University of Pennsylvania. Richard D. Sears, a Harvard sophomore, won the singles; he and his older friend, James Dwight, entered the doubles and were beaten in the third round by Clarence Clark and Frederick W. Taylor, from Philadelphia. The doubles final was an all-Philadelphia, Penn-Princeton affair, in which Clarence Clark (Penn) and Fred Taylor, who did not go to college, beat Alexander Van Rensselaer (Princeton) and Arthur Emlen Newbold (Penn). The tone of the first championship was nicely caught in the following lines written by Dick Sears for a little volume celebrating the first *Fifty Years of Lawn Tennis in the United States* (1931):

> All of the players came from the East, and most of the doubles teams were made up on the spur of the moment with the result that there was little teamwork and the partners were constantly interfering with each other. . . .
>
> A large number of the players wore knickerbockers, with blazers, belts, cravats, and woolen stockings in their club colors. . . .
>
> None of their sleeves were cut off, and while a large majority rolled them up, a few left them at full length.
>
> They all wore caps or round hats with a rolling brim that could be turned down in front to ward off the glare of the sun.[9]

---

*In my judgment, the best edited American newspaper, the Paris *Herald*, now the *Herald Tribune*, is run jointly by the *New York Times* and the *Washington Post*.

Dick Sears won the second of his seven straight National Singles Championships in 1882, beating Philadelphia's Clarence Clark in the finals: 6–1, 6–4, 6–0. He and Dwight won the doubles for the first of five times. In the meantime, Dwight had been made president of the United States National Lawn Tennis Association, a post which he held for twenty-one of the first thirty-one years of American tennis.

The year 1883 was a critical one for the game's development in America. First, Dwight, as president of the USNLTA, went to Joe Clark who, after graduating from Penn, was completing the two years he needed for a Harvard B.A., and discussed ways of stimulating intercity tennis; as a result, Sears and Dwight, National Doubles Champions, went down to Philadelphia and played a match with the Clark brothers (young Joe substituting for Fred Taylor who was too busy at the Midvale Steel Company to play any more serious tennis). The Clarks won the match. In the meantime, they were planning a bicycle trip through England that summer, and Dwight gave them official permission to challenge the Renshaw brothers to a match at Wimbledon. The Clarks thus became the first Americans to play on the Center Court at Wimbledon, although they were soundly beaten by the British twins. In the meantime, before the Clarks departed for England, the first National Intercollegiate Championships were held at Hartford, Connecticut, Joe Clark winning the singles as well as the doubles with a Harvard freshman, Howard A. Taylor, as his partner. At the end of August, Sears again won the singles at Newport and teamed with Dwight to win the doubles. In the singles final, Dwight lost in three straight sets, 6–2, 6–0, 9–7. Up to that time, Dwight had won more matches from Sears than he had lost; afterwards, the younger man by ten years won pretty regularly.

After losing the American singles final, Dwight went abroad, determined to see for himself just how good the Renshaws really were. He was soundly beaten by Willie in a specially arranged match at the Maida Vale Club in London. He had to admit that the great Englishman was a tennis genius and in a class by himself. Ever the devoted tennis student, Dwight befriended the Renshaw brothers and arranged to spend the next winter (1884) on the Riviera, playing with them often on their court at the Beau Site Hotel, in Cannes. He persuaded his friend Sears to join him there in the late winter; they then played through the English spring circuit, doing only fairly well; they had the distinction, however, of being the first

James Dwight (left) and Richard Sears were lifelong friends and Beacon Street neighbors in Boston. Dwight was a founder of the United States National Lawn Tennis Association, serving as its president for 21 of its first 31 years. Sears won the first U.S. Singles Championship, in 1881, and the next 6 years in a row (an unmatched record). Dwight and Sears won the U.S. Doubles 5 times between 1882 and 1887. Both gents, as pictured, are dressed in the cricket garb of the Longwood Cricket Club, Brookline, Massachusetts. (International Tennis Hall of Fame Library, Newport, R.I.)

The Newport Casino, home of the U.S. Men's Singles Championships between 1881 and 1914, today serves as the home of both the International Tennis Hall of Fame and an annual men's grass court tournament, as well as a ladies' tournament later in July. (International Tennis Hall of Fame Library, Newport, R.I.)

Endicott Peabody, educated in England at Cheltenham College (a private boarding school) and Cambridge University, founded Groton School in 1884. During 56 years as Headmaster, Peabody instilled the values of the Anglo-American, upper-class sports theology in a select group of boys from some of the most distinguished families in the WASP establishment, including President Theodore Roosevelt's four sons, and Franklin D. Roosevelt and his four sons. (John Singer Sargent portrait, now in the Groton School Collection)

Theodore Roosevelt graduated from Harvard the same year (1880) that his lifelong friend and kinsman-through-marriage graduated from Cambridge. While Peabody preached the gospel of muscular Christianity to a small group of privileged boys, Roosevelt spread the same gospel to the boys of the whole nation. As the sociologist David Riesman once wrote, "Roosevelt was the first president of the United States who was a self-conscious patron of youth, sport, and the arts." Roosevelt built the first tennis court on the White House grounds. His small group of intimate friends, including Owen Wister and Henry Cabot Lodge, was called his "Tennis Cabinet." (John Singer Sargent portrait, now part of the White House collection)

The First International Tennis Match at Wimbledon, in 1883: William and Ernest Renshaw of England vs. Clarence and Joseph Clark of Philadelphia. Clarence Clark won the first U.S. Doubles Championship (1881) with Fred Taylor (later the founder of Scientific Management); his brother, Joseph, won the first Intercollegiate Singles and Doubles championships (1883) and the U.S. Doubles Championship in 1885 with Dick Sears. The Renshaws won this first international match and easily beat the Americans again five days later. *(American Lawn Tennis)*

William (left) and Ernest Renshaw. Wealthy schoolmates of Endicott Peabody at Cheltenham College, the Renshaw twins are known as the first modern tennis champions. William's Wimbledon record—7 singles and 5 doubles (with Ernest) titles between 1881 and 1889—has never been equalled. Ernest won the Wimbledon singles title once, in 1888. (David Rudkin)

The Doherty brothers, R.F. or Reggie (left) and H.L. or Laurie (right). The Doherty Gates at Wimbledon memorialize the brothers as the greatest British tennis players ever. Many think that Reggie was the better of the two, but he was a sickly man and Laurie had a slightly better record: they won the doubles at Wimbledon eight times as a team. No other man has ever won eight Wimbledon doubles titles. Reggie won singles four times in a row (1897–1900); Laurie won the singles five times in a row (1902–1906). No man equalled Laurie's record until Bjorn Borg (1976–1980). The brothers visited America in 1902 and 1903. In the latter year, Laurie won the U.S. Singles title at Newport and the brothers won the Davis Cup 4–1, Laurie winning both singles and the doubles with Reggie, who defaulted his singles match on the first day and won the last match on the final day. (Brown Brothers)

Arthur Balfour (left) and Anthony Wilding talking between matches at Wimbledon (circa 1910). Balfour, philosopher-statesman and the most brilliant Englishman of his generation, was the last unpaid Prime Minister (1902–1905). He coined the term "lawn tennis" to differentiate the new outdoor game from "real" or "court" tennis, which was played indoors. Between 1907 and 1914, Tony Wilding won four singles and four doubles titles at Wimbledon. He was the idol of teenage girls at Wimbledon and of the idle rich along the Riviera, where he often played with Balfour. (*American Lawn Tennis*)

Arthur Gore was the "Iron Man" of Wimbledon: he played in every Wimbledon (except in 1895 and the war years) between 1888 and 1927 (39 years). He won his first singles title in 1901 at the age of 33; he won again in 1908 and 1909. Gore was the last Englishman to win the singles at Wimbledon until Fred Perry won it in 1934. *(American Lawn Tennis)*

Fred Perry was the last great English tennis player and the best player in the world in 1934, 1935, and 1936. Born a short time before Wimbledon in 1909, Perry was 25 when he first won the Wimbledon singles title. The son of a Labor M.P., Perry was an outsider and a determined winner rather than a "good loser." He won the singles championships of the U.S. in 1933, 1934, and 1936, of France in 1935, and of Australia in 1934. He was the first man to win all four of the major championships but was not a Grand Slam winner because he did not win the titles in one year. In recent years the Perry Gates have been added to the Doherty Gates at Wimbledon. *(American Lawn Tennis)*

Thomas C. Bundy's new Cadillac. The owner is at the wheel with Maurice McLoughlin beside him, Karl H. Behr sitting on the floor, and Richard Norris Williams II standing beside the car. The picture was taken in August 1914 at the Longwood Cricket Club. Williams had won the last U.S. Singles championship at Newport, and Bundy and McLoughlin had won the doubles. (Quincy N. Williams)

Davis Cup between Australasia and the United States at the West Side Tennis Club, Forest Hills, in 1914. The score was 1–all (Williams lost to Wilding, and McLoughlin beat Brooks on the first day) when this doubles match started: Norman Brookes, hitting, and Anthony Wilding won from McLoughlin and Bundy (left side: left to right). Australasia won the tie 3–2 and took the cup Down Under as the German army marched. (*American Lawn Tennis*)

William T. Tilden II, of Philadelphia—in my considered judgment, the best player of all time. *(Sport and General)*

At the West Side Tennis Club, Forest Hills, in 1924; this was the first year the championships were played in the new concrete stadium. William T. Tilden II and Vincent Richards are walking down the steps from the Marquee. Note that Tilden has thrown his Top-Flight racquet down first, forcing Richards to choose "rough" or "smooth." Also note the two famous lines from Kipling on the sign behind them—put there by Julian (Mike) Myrick, tennis Czar of the time. (*American Lawn Tennis*)

The Germantown Cricket Club, Tilden's home club, in 1922, when the U.S. Championships were held there. Thenceforth this picture was above the table of contents of *American Lawn Tennis* for many years. The exquisite Georgian clubhouse, built in 1891, was designed by McKim, Mead and White. (*American Lawn Tennis*)

Americans to play in the Wimbledon championships. Sears never played abroad again, but Dwight spent the next two winters playing on the Riviera, often with the Renshaws in Cannes.*

Richard Dudley Sears won his last championships at Newport in 1887, taking the singles and also the doubles with Dwight. He won the first three championships in singles without losing a set; he stood out the next four years in which he lost only two sets in four challenge round matches. His toughest challenge round was played in 1886 when he beat R. L. Beekman, a native Rhode Islander, who later became governor of the state. Sears was not only our first lawn tennis genius, but also the first tennis champion of the United States. The Sears family, moreover, became our first and still-greatest tennis dynasty, winning twenty-seven National Championships in all (see Figure 1). Dick's younger brother, Philip S. Sears, won the Intercollegiate Singles Championship for Harvard, in 1887 and 1888, and the doubles with his cousin, Quincy Adams Shaw, Jr., in 1887; Dwight's classmate and pioneer on the Appleton court at Nahant, Frederick Richard Sears (a

---

*Between the battles of Waterloo and the Marne, the French Riviera became the most fashionable winter watering place in Europe. Napoleon had improved the roads to such an extent that the English could reach Nice in less than a fortnight. All the royal families of Europe, especially the Russians, turned up for the season each year, including such statesmen as Talleyrand and Metternich. The first train ran from Paris to Nice in the 1860s. But the big change came in the 1880s: there were ten hotels, including the Promenade, the Victoria, and the Hôtel des Anglais, in Nice by 1880; Victoria preferred to stay in a quiet suburb of Cannes, but her son Edward VII, under the incognito of Baron Renfrew, stayed on the Promenade. After 1883, when the "Blue Train"— the Calais-Paris-Nice express—made its first trip in December, the English, including members of the increasingly affluent and powerful middle classes, came in larger and larger numbers each winter. No wonder all foreigners were referred to as "Les Anglais." Or that an Englishman was heard to say to a friend: "This would be a perfect place to spend the winter if there were not so damned many Frenchmen about." Perhaps it was prophetic of our age that Friedrich Nietzsche, a professor at Basel, spent parts of five winters in Nice, 1883–88, writing his book *Beyond Good and Evil*.

And tennis, of course, thrived on the Riviera long after the days of James Dwight and the Renshaws. As we shall see, R. Norris Williams won a famous postwar tournament there in 1919, and the Wills-Lenglen match was played at the Carleton, in Cannes, in 1926. It makes for a sense of historical continuity to know that the beautiful young Helen Wills and her mother came to Cannes on the Blue Train; and that by far the most interesting eyewitness account of the match is to be found in a book called *Love and Faults*, by the late Ted Tinling, who witnessed more great tennis matches than anyone in his day (1911–90) and was the Pro era's First Statesman and aristocratic democrat.[10]

half-brother of Dick's) did not win any championships himself but his daughter, the handsome, eccentric, and incredible Eleo (Eleonora Randolph Sears) won the National Women's Doubles four times in 1911, 1915, 1916, and 1917 (she was also runner-up in the singles in 1911, 1912, and 1916); Evelyn Georgianna Sears, Dick's distant cousin, won the U.S. Singles in 1907; and finally, the daughter of Albertina (Dick's sister) Sears mar-

FIGURE 1

The Sears Family: A Tennis Genealogy

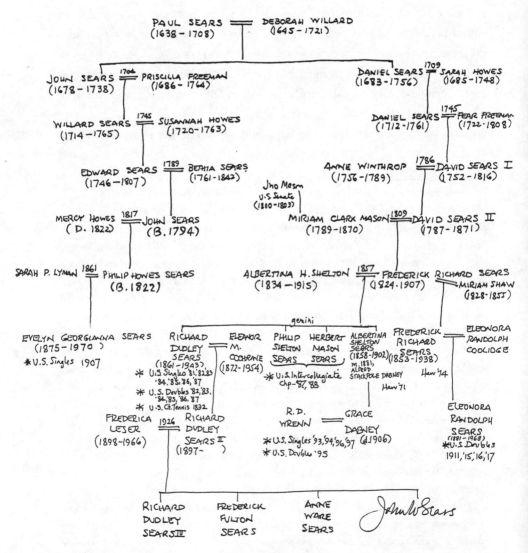

John W. Sears kindly drew this genealogy for the author.

ried R. D. Wrenn, winner of the U.S. singles, in 1893–94 and 1896–97, and the U.S. doubles, in 1895.

═══

A brief look at the four families, Sears and Dwight in New England and Clark and Taylor in Germantown, Pennsylvania, whose sons founded American tennis, should indicate the historical and sociological roots of the values of the amateur game in America, especially up to the First World War but also, if to a lesser extent, in the years between the wars. In the first place, James Dwight and Richard Sears were cousins bred at the very heart of Brahmin Boston, which was, along with the Virginia planters, one of the two greatest ruling classes in American history, playing a leading role in the writing of the Declaration of Independence, in the Revolution, and in the writing of the Constitution.

The first Sears in America was "Richard the Pilgrim," who settled in the town of Yarmouth, on Cape Cod, in 1637–38; Squire Daniel Sears, his great-grandson, was a Town Clerk of nearby Chatham, and his son, David, was an enterprising young man who came to Boston to seek his fortune; as ambitious men usually do, he married well, taking as his bride in 1786 Anne Winthrop, a direct descendant, in the fifth generation, of the Great Governor. At the time of his marriage, David was already well on his way to wealth as a merchant in the India and China trades. He was also a leading land speculator in Boston and elsewhere in New England, in 1806 becoming one of the main owners of a tract of land thirty miles square, embracing all the islands at the mouth of the Penobscot River, as well as the present town of Searsport at the head of the river, which was named in his honor. In the years before the Civil War, David Sears and Peter Chardon Brooks (Henry Adams's grandfather) were the two wealthiest men in New England. And as we have seen, Richard Dudley Sears's grandfather, David, inherited this fortune, and was both a Beacon Street Brahmin and one of the first summer residents of Nahant. Just as the Adamses were primarily known for politics, history, and letters, so the Searses, since the first David, have been primarily known for their money.*

---

*While eight members of the Adams line, including two presidents, were included in the *Dictionary of American Biography*, Richard, the tennis champion, was the only one of his line to be included. Americans may worship money, but their most famous heroes have rarely been moneymakers.

The Dwights were deeply rooted in New England. The best-known branch moved to the western part of Massachusetts and produced the two Timothys, the first, president of Yale at the end of the eighteenth century, the second becoming president of Yale in 1886. James Dwight's mother, however, was a Warren, undoubtedly Boston's (and surely America's, too) First Family of medicine. Her children and grandchildren were brought up on the Warren genealogy, which included seven generations of physicians who taught and studied at the Harvard Medical School: John Warren (1753–1815) was a physician in the Continental Army and, in 1782, was appointed the first Professor of Anatomy and Surgery, at Harvard. His older brother, Joseph Warren, a physician in the Continental Army, was appointed a Major-General two days before he was killed leading his men in the Battle of Bunker Hill. Later generations of Warren doctors took the lead in almost every branch of Boston medicine, as founders of the Massachusetts General and Peter Brent Brigham hospitals, and as pioneers in the use of anesthesia and plastic surgery. James Dwight followed in the Warren tradition by graduating from the Harvard Medical School. For obscure health reasons, he never practiced medicine. His older brother by ten years, however, had succeeded Oliver Wendell Holmes as Parkman Professor of Anatomy at Harvard.

Jim Dwight and Dick Sears were not only deeply rooted in the history of New England; they were also intimately related to upper-class Boston of their own day. As boys they were neighbors on Beacon Street (the Dwights at 70 Beacon and the Searses at 51), as well as at Nahant in their summers. After their marriages, they settled down almost opposite one another on Beacon Street in the Back Bay (numbers 225 and 232, respectively). Dwight spent his whole married life at 225 Beacon, serving as the USNLTA's president from 1894 through 1911, taking up golf in his forties, and playing all sorts of games on his daily visits to the Somerset Club (always with a bachelor's button placed in his lapel by one of his four servants).

Richard Dudley Sears was a solid Brahmin of the highest order, not that he was stuffy or without charm. Like Dwight, he almost invariably wore a bachelor's button in his lapel and carried a handsome ivory cigar holder; he had been one of the Porcellian gay blades at Harvard, playing several musical instruments and taking active roles in the Hasty Pudding shows, much like his older friend and Porcellian clubmate, Henry Cabot

Lodge, the "U.S. Senator from Nahant." He was a natural at all ball games (which, incidentally, I have found is often accompanied by an ear for music)*; he won the first U.S. Court Tennis Championship, in New York in 1892; he originated the so-called "railroad" serve which is still used by leading players today; he was a first-rate but not outstanding squash racquets player; and he was a founder of the Boston Tennis and Racquet Club and carefully supervised its construction, especially the Court Tennis court. He was also one of the founders of Boston's most patrician hunt club, the Myopia.†

The Searses spent many summers at Dark Harbor, in Maine. Richard built a tennis court there about 1897 and held an invitation tournament every summer for his friends. He was always guided by a rigid code of sportsmanship and, one summer, when he found out that the two finalists had tossed a racquet rather than playing out the final match, he was so enraged that they were unwelcome in later years. He also built the local golf course and was for years in the habit of playing in the same daily foursome, which included two famous Philadelphia doctors, Biddle and Cadwalader.

Sears was a State Street trustee in the very proper George Apley mold; worth in the seven figures in 1929, he had a bad time in the Crash. But perhaps his married life is most revealing of the values of this gifted sportsman and deeply rooted Bostonian. He celebrated his golden wedding anniversary at 232 Beacon Street where he had taken his bride a half a century earlier. The stability and continuity of their lives is also indicated in their faithful servants, a Swedish cook and an English chauffeur, who remained with the family for fifty-three and fifty-one years, respectively. Surely the openings and closings for the four letters written by Sears to his fiancée and wife, shown in Figure 2, are most revealing of the contrast in values between his age and our own. How different from our age of instant intimacy were the subtle closings of the intimacy gap in Sears's two letters to Miss Cochane in 1889 and 1890. Sears simply could not have imagined a time when, as with John McEnroe and later

---

*Like Sears, Spencer Gore, first Wimbledon Champion, was a naturally gifted instrumentalist. John McEnroe also has a gift for music.

†According to Sears's grandson, John Winthrop Sears, it was not until the late sixties that the golf or tennis pros were ever seen sitting on the club's porch while members were present.

Pete Sampras, the fiancée (girlfriend) of the Tennis Champion of the United States would be subject to a public discussion of her pregnancy, even before the announcement of a wedding date or place. In Sears's generation, and even up to the eve of World War II, a lady would have her name in the papers only three times in her lifetime: at birth, at her marriage, and at her death. Not only was the Sears marriage a long one; it was surely full of affection, as witness the loving letters of 1928 and 1936 in Figure 2. It is my own impression that, while there may today be more sexual intimacy before marriage than in Sears's day, there is probably less afterwards. There is, after all, hardly time in the busy two-career marriages of short duration which are surely the fashion among today's bright and beautiful people.

The Clark brothers, and their good friend Fred Taylor, were brought up in a more, or, less New England enclave in Philadelphia. Germantown in the 1880s, according to Taylor's biographer, "was in all respects a vivid bit of essential New England."[11] The Clarks' grandfather, Enoch W. Clark, after severe financial reverses in New England, came down to Philadelphia and opened an investment banking firm, E. W. Clark and Company, in 1837, amid the panic brought on by President Jackson's defeat of Philadelphia's great banker, Nicholas Biddle. In that same year, Francis Drexel, an itinerant Austrian portrait painter, founded his own banking firm; and the Drexels and Clarks became the leading banking families in the city. Though solid New Englanders since the seventeenth century, the Clarks were still considered newly rich by all too many pedigree-proud Proper Philadelphians.

The Taylor family had solid Quaker roots in the Delaware Valley ever since Penn's time, while Fred's mother was a Winslow of Mayflower stock. The important point about the two families was that they were Unitarians, driven by the intellectual and reforming values of New England rather than the usual conforming values of Philadelphia's Episcopalian gentry. Their local Unitarian Church was led by two sons of New England, Samuel Longfellow (the poet's brother), and Charles Gordon Ames. And they were often visited by Dr. William Howard Furness, Minister of the First Unitarian Church in Center City and Emerson's Har-

FIGURE 2
Terms of Endearment, Victorian Style

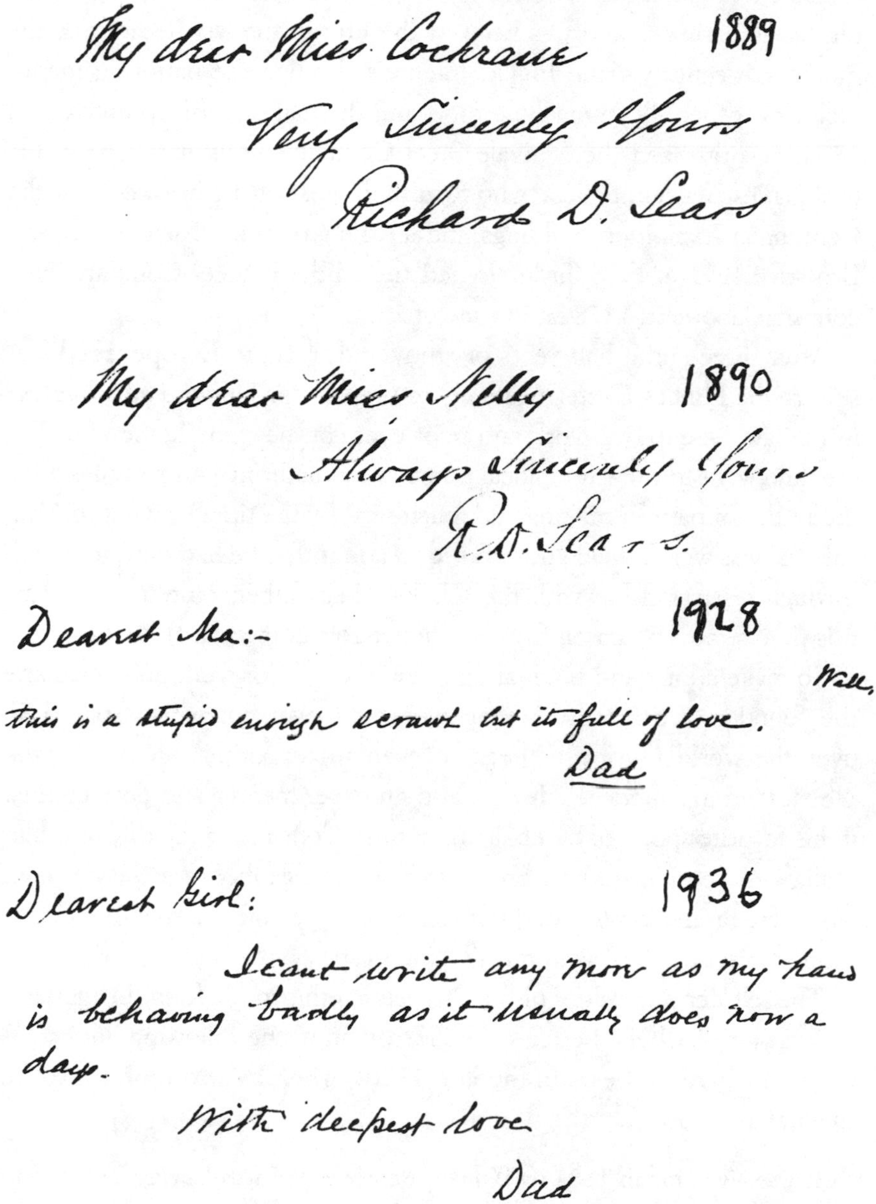

My dear Miss Cochrane   1889

Very Sincerely Yours

Richard D. Sears

My dear Miss Nelly   1890

Always Sincerely Yours

R. D. Sears.

Dearest Ma:-   1928

Well,

this is a stupid enough scrawl but its full of love.

Dad

Dearest Girl: 1936

I cant write any more as my hand
is behaving badly as it usually does now a
days.

With deepest love

Dad

vard classmate, who led the abolitionist movement (along with Lucretia Mott, a close friend of Fred Taylor's mother).*

Enoch W. Clark died relatively young and his son Edward succeeded him at an early age and was head of the firm in the last decades of the nineteenth century when Philadelphia was leading the nation in manufacturing, especially in machine tools and the making of locomotives. In 1873, he organized the Midvale Steel Company along with a machine tool genius, William Sellers, who furnished most of the ironwork for the Centennial Exhibition buildings and all the structural ironwork for the Brooklyn Bridge. Fred Taylor joined the Midvale Steel Company as a common laborer in 1878, at the age of 22.

After three and a half years of study and travel in Europe, Fred was sent to the Phillips Exeter Academy to prepare for Harvard and a career in the law. Due to overwork and poor eyesight, he came home after Exeter and went to work for a local pump manufacturing company, learning the trades of pattern-making and machinist. By the time he went to Midvale, he was well trained and refused to admit that he had gotten the job through his friendship with the Clarks (their father, moreover, had by this time removed himself from any active role at the plant).

To make a long and fascinating story brief, Taylor went on to become the founder of Scientific Management, a movement which spread all over the world (Taylorism became even more popular in the former USSR than in America). He was also an experimenter and perfectionist in his favorite sports of baseball and tennis. Contrary to the now-popular malign image of Taylorism, Fred was a sterling symbol of a class of men who were far more interested in the means of production than the purely money prizes in both economic life and in sport.

The self-denying values of the Protestant ethic in the founding generation have never been better symbolized than in the following lines written by Richard D. Sears in the late 1920s, when he wrote of a favorite racquet as follows:

> It was given me in 1884 by William Renshaw as I was leaving England to defend my championship at home. Much to my surprise and delight he gave this to me with best wishes for my success, saying that it was the best

---

*Dr. Furness's son, Frank, was the architect for the present Merion Cricket Club.

racket [*sic*] that he had ever had in his hand. It was made by James J. Tate, by far the best racket maker in England at that time. Renshaw had won the Irish and English singles and doubles championships with it in this year and it was still as good as when new, except for the need of restringing. The balance was perfect. When I got home I had it carefully restrung, won the singles with it, and for precaution, only used it in the finals of the doubles, winning again.

I then cut out the stringing, gave the frame a slight oiling, placed it very carefully in a press and put it away. When the 1885 championship came around it was restrung, holding its shape wonderfully, and I won both the singles and doubles with it again. All told it won eight championships![12]

"In those days," wrote Fred Hovey, National Singles Champion in 1895, "a bat lasted weeks and a player who came on the court with more than one racket would have been thought to be putting on 'some dog.'"[13]

The Expansion of Lawn Tennis
in an Age of Innocence, 1887–1912

The old world in its sunset was fair to see.
—Churchill

AFTER SEARS RETIRED IN 1887, HENRY W. SLOCUM, JR., WON THE SINGLES at Newport in 1888 and 1889. He had played football with Walter Camp at Yale, and they were doubles partners, representing Yale in the first Intercollegiate Championships played in Hartford, Connecticut, in 1883. He was a practicing lawyer by the time he won his first championship, and his father did not approve of his wasting his time on a game: "The old gentleman had an early vision of what has been known in modern times as a 'tennis bum' and had become distinctly stern in his opposition to the game," wrote Slocum. "It is my recollection that we then changed from one court to the other only at the end of a set, and it was while making one of these changes that I spied the face of the stern parent peering into the court from the last row of spectators. I found him, after the match was finished, plainly a little ashamed at having come from New York to Newport to see me play, and trying quite hard to conceal his pleasure that I had gained the championship. . . . This story had a happy ending, too, for immediately afterwards I started to work hard at my profession."[1]

Slocum, always in fine physical condition, came up to Newport the following August and successfully defended his title against Quincy Adams Shaw, Jr., who had won the all-comers that year. As he had been critical of Sears's failure to defend his title in 1888, Slocum defended again in 1890, when he was beaten by Oliver S. Campbell, of Columbia University. Campbell was the most aggressive net-rusher in the nineteenth century; unfortunately, all too many Americans copied his style. He lost the title in 1893 to Robert D. Wrenn, one of Harvard's greatest all-around athletes, a football, ice hockey, and baseball star who relied almost entirely on his natural athletic ability and an agile defensive game. Wrenn won again in 1894, and, after losing to Frederick H. Hovey in 1895, won two more titles, in 1896–97. Hovey was a graduate (A.B.) of Brown and the Harvard Law School. The Wrenn-Hovey rivalry at the top of American tennis between 1893 and 1897, much like the Renshaw-Lawford duels at Wimbledon in the 1880s, greatly increased the popularity of the game.

In 1898, Bob Wrenn did not defend his title because he and Bill Larned had joined Teddy Roosevelt's Rough Riders and were off fighting the war in Cuba. Malcolm D. Whitman, a young Harvard student, took over the vacant throne, beating another Harvard student, Dwight Filley

Davis, in the final round. Whitman's tennis career was brief but brilliant: "In three glorious years," wrote the well-known tennis critic and author, Edward Potter, Jr., "he reached heights which place him among the most complete and illustrious players of all time. He was a beautiful figure on the courts, a tall, blond, Grecian hero. He was blessed with a studious, inquiring mind, was utterly lacking in the desire for transitory fame, and approached tennis in a detached, curious spirit.[2]" His book, *Tennis Origins and Mysteries* (1932), is now a classic in the tennis literature.

Whitman's father was a native of Canada who went to work in a local dry-goods store before coming down to Boston at the age of 14 to seek his fortune. He became one of the most successful and largest textile manufacturers in New England. Young Malcolm learned to play tennis at an early age and in the spring of his freshman year at Harvard won the Intercollegiate Singles Championship; that summer he beat Holcombe Ward in the quarterfinals at Newport and lost to Larned in the semifinals. In his sophomore year, he won the Intercollegiate doubles for Harvard (with Leonard Ware) and reached the semifinals at Newport once more; in the first round he beat a young schoolboy from Philadelphia, William J. Clothier, and then in the second round, he beat the Irishman, Harold Mahony, who had won Wimbledon in 1896 and was runner-up to Reginald Doherty in 1897. He was beaten in the semis by a visiting Englishman, H. A. Nisbet. Whitman won the championship in 1898, and successfully defended the title in 1899 and 1900. His most successful year was 1899, his senior year at Harvard: he won at Longwood, the Middle States at the Orange Lawn Tennis Club, at Southampton, and the Canadian championship, in addition to the Nationals at Newport in August.

That same year, 1899, two Harvard students in the class behind Whitman, Dwight Filley Davis and Holcombe Ward, won the doubles championship for the first of three times. Both boys were born in comfortable circumstances and were members of the Fly Club at Harvard (the club of Franklin Roosevelt as well as of countless Philadelphia Clarks, including Joe Clark's son and namesake who became the greatest reform mayor in Philadelphia history). Davis, born to one of St. Louis's most prominent and wealthy families, was endowed from youth with a strong sense of *noblesse oblige* and an itch for public service. Later in life, he served on the boards of almost every cultural institution of importance in St. Louis and on many at the national level; he went with the Missouri National Guard to France in the First World War, winning the Distinguished Service Cross for "extraordinary heroism in action." Calvin Coolidge appointed Davis Secretary of War, and Herbert Hoover made him Governor-General of the Philippines. He married a Proper Bostonian and they had four children: their daughter, Cynthia, married William McChesney Martin, Jr., Chairman of the Federal Reserve Board from 1951 to 1970 and President of the National Tennis Foundation and Hall of Fame from 1979 to 1982. Holcombe Ward came of a wealthy family of textile manufacturers in New Jersey.

Right after the Newport tournament, according to Dwight Davis, "the national champions in singles and doubles Malcolm Whitman, Holcombe Ward and I, and the national interscholastic champion, Beals Wright, with that splendid veteran sportsman George Wright* as guide, philosopher, and friend," went out to Monterey, California, to play a series of exhibition matches with local players, as well as taking part in the Pacific Coast Championships held at the famous Del Monte Hotel. The experiment in Monterey was so successful that the group also played in Portland, Seattle, Tacoma, and Victoria, B.C.: "Young boys just beginning to take up the game became enthusiastic players," continued Davis. "Young 'Maurie' McLoughlin, then a boy in his teens, volunteered as a ball-boy and other boys who later became great players and national champions gained inspiration and ambition from the matches."[3][†]

On the way home from the matches, Davis envisioned the idea of a trophy to stimulate international competition which he described as follows:

Just as the team reluctantly started eastward, the International Cup races for the America's Cup were being sailed; the newspapers were full of accounts of the preliminary tryouts and then of the races themselves. Putting two and two together . . . this thought occurred to me: "If team matches between different parts of the same country arouse such great interest and

---

*George Wright was a famous baseball player and a founder of the sporting goods firm, Wright & Ditson, whose tennis ball was the official ball of the USLTA and used in our National Championships for over half a century after 1893 when it was first officially used at Newport.

[†]Davis was in error here: McLoughlin did not come to California until 1903, at the age of 13.

promote such good feeling, would not similar international contests have even wider and far-reaching consequences?"[4]

Almost immediately after returning to Boston, Davis went to see Dr. James Dwight, still president of the USNLTA. Dwight was enthusiastic about young Davis's idea of a trophy for international team competition in lawn tennis. A Boston silversmithing firm designed a handsome trophy, soon known as the Davis Cup, and the first challenge round,* between the United States and Great Britain, was planned for early August 1900, at the Longwood Cricket Club. In that first year, the American team was composed of Whitman, Ward, and Davis. England was engaged in the Boer War and many first-class players had enlisted; for other reasons the famous Doherty brothers could not come. Finally the British team was made up of Arthur Wentworth Gore, who had been runner-up to Reginald Doherty at Wimbledon the previous year, Herbert Roper Barrett, and Ernest Black, Scottish Champion. It was a good group, but far from Britain's best possible team. The United States defeated Great Britain 3–0: on the first day, Whitman defeated Gore in three straight sets, and Davis defeated Black in four. In the doubles, Ward and Davis defeated Black and H. Roper Barrett in three sets. On the third day, Davis was leading Gore when the match was called because of rain; the Whitman-Black match was never played.

H. Roper Barrett was in the top circles of British lawn tennis for the first four decades of the twentieth century. He played on the British Davis Cup team again in 1907, 1912, 1913, and 1914, and after the war in 1919; and he was nonplaying captain of the team in the great Perry years when Britain won the cup four times 1933–36. He narrowly missed winning Wimbledon twice, in 1908 when he lost to Gore in five long sets, after winning the first two sets; and in 1911, in a final played in the broiling heat, he had to default (because of the heat) to Anthony Wilding, at two sets all, in the fifth set. He did win the Wimbledon Doubles Championship three times, in 1909, paired with Gore, and again in 1912 and 1913, partnered by Charles P. Dixon.

He has fortunately left us his impressions of Niagara Falls, Boston,

---

*The "challenge round" is the last Davis Cup tie (match) of the year. After that first year, when only Great Britain and the United States took part, the previous year's winner was challenged by this year's winner.

Longwood, and American tennis players and playing conditions generally. These recollections give a hint of the sporting character of the early
tennis greats, as well as the British sense of superiority:

> The *Carpathia* landed us at New York on a Saturday morning. . . . Having had
> no particular facilities offered us for practice, it was unanimously decided . . .
> that we should forthwith visit Niagara. . . . Having inspected this bewildering
> sight, we journeyed back to Boston. Here we were heartily welcomed by
> Palmer Presbrey, M. D. Whitman . . . and many others famous in the lawn ten-
> nis world of America. Palmer Presbrey looked after us right royally, made us
> members of all the leading clubs and had us put up at the University Club. . . .
>
> Now as to the conditions of play at Longwood, the venue of the interna-
> tional matches. The grounds were abominable. The grass was long. Picture
> to yourself a court in England where the grass has been the longest you ever
> encountered; double the length of that grass and you have the courts at
> Longwood at that time. The net was a disgrace to civilized lawn tennis, held
> up by guy ropes which were continually sagging. . . . As for the balls. . . .
> They were awful—soft and motherly—and when served with the American
> twist came at you like an animated egg-plum. . . . We had never experi-
> enced this service before and it quite nonplused us. The spectators were
> most impartial and the female portion thereof not at all unpleasant to gaze
> upon. . . . The umpires, who sat on chairs perched on tables, and the lines-
> men discharged their duties most satisfactorily. Indeed, we had nothing to
> complain about in regard to American sportsmanship and hospitality. . . .
>
> I was only in America a week, and I often laugh to myself over the fact
> that I journeyed some 6800 miles to play thirty games. I still do not grum-
> ble. There was no one else to represent England and I felt I had to go de-
> spite the inconvenience and personal expense to which we were put.
>
> Whitman, let me conclude, was one of the finest singles players I ever saw . . .[5]

After the Davis Cup at Longwood, Malcolm Whitman defended his
national title at Newport for the last time, defeating William A. Larned in
the challenge round. Whitman was now in Law School and his stern father, much like Henry Slocum's father seventeen years earlier, insisted
that he get down to serious business, forever quoting the biblical admonition: "When I was a child I spake as a child . . . when I became a man I
put away childish things." Though these parental attitudes may have
been unusually harsh, they accurately reflect the skewed understanding

of amateur sports in those decades. The well-rounded gentleman should play team sports as a youth, in order to build character—but sports were never to be a profession. Who, in 1900, would have predicted that hundreds of grown men in America today, especially tennis players, would be earning many millions of dollars playing at "childish things"?

William A. Larned was 29 years of age when he won his first National Championship in 1901. He had competed at Newport since 1891. He first achieved notice in 1892 when he won the Intercollegiate Championship for Cornell, reached the finals at Newport where he was beaten by Hovey, and was ranked sixth. He ranked in the First Ten for twenty years, except for 1898 when he and Bob Wrenn went to Cuba with the Rough Riders. He ranked first eight times; second five times; third four times; fifth once; and sixth, his first year. Larned had an aggressive, all-around game, with probably the best backhand ever seen, at least until Donald Budge. He was always on the attack if possible, possessing great concentration and a tenacious competitive instinct. On occasion, however, he would be upset by small annoyances and bad line calls.

In 1902, Larned successfully defended his title at Newport, defeating R. F. (Reggie) Doherty in the Challenge Round. It was an especially sweet victory as Reggie had beaten him earlier in the summer in the first match of the Davis Cup challenge round, which that year was held at the Crescent Athletic Club, in Brooklyn, New York. The United States barely won 3–2, Larned winning his second singles match against the charming Irishman, Dr. Joshua Pim, and Whitman, coming out of his proposed retirement, winning both his singles matches; the Doherty brothers won their doubles match for the first of five Davis Cups in a row (1902, 1903, 1904, 1905, and 1906).

In 1903, the younger Doherty brother, H. L. (Laurie), defeated Larned in the challenge round at Newport, thus becoming the only non-American to win our National Championship until René Lacoste did so in 1926. Laurie Doherty also won two singles and one doubles match in the Davis Cup challenge round which was held that year at the Longwood Cricket Club. On the third day of the tie, he beat Larned in a very close (6–3, 6–8, 6–0, 2–6, 7–5) match in which he won a very crucial point at four–all in the fifth set, after Larned had thought he had won it: "Laurie was serving with the score 15–40," wrote E. C. Potter, Jr., who witnessed the match. "He came to the net and was passed down the line. The score was called 5–4 for Larned. Laurie asked the umpire if his service had been good. The official looked to where a linesman should have been. The chair was empty. Dwight was referee. He was appealed to for a ruling. He canceled the point and called a let. Larned, on his way to victory, was halted in his stride. Laurie won the replayed point, the game, set, match and Cup."[6] There were no arguments on the court at the time, but much discussion afterward. Although it would be decades before John McEnroe made a practice of disputing line calls, it was astonishing in these early decades how *absolutely* unquestioned were the decisions of umpires and line judges, even when they clearly missed a call.

The British, who won the cup 4–1 and took it back to England for the first time, could only feel justified after the fact when Laurie Doherty easily beat Larned for the National Championship in three straight sets, thus firmly establishing his superiority.

Following Laurie Doherty's unique victory at Newport, in 1903, three Harvard men—Holcombe Ward (1904), Beals C. Wright (1905), and William J. Clothier (1906)—won the U.S. Singles Championship. Larned then came back and won it five years in a row (1907–11). Clothier, who had a bad case of water-on-the-knee, did not defend in 1907; some felt that, had he played and won, he would have defended successfully for the four years following, as Larned did. At any rate, Larned played through and won in 1907. In 1912, the tennis authorities decided to eliminate the challenge round, and Larned, refusing to play through, retired undefeated. In the dozen years between the first Davis Cup matches in 1900 and the winning of the U.S. Championship at Newport by Maurice McLoughlin in 1912, a small group of boys from the Big Three colleges and solid upper-class families won most of the important matches of the period (see Figure 3).

The great Doherty brothers, Reggie (R. F.) and Laurie (H. L.), were almost exact contemporaries of Larned. Born in Wimbledon, they were sent to Westminster School before going up to Trinity College, Cambridge, where they were both good athletes and outstanding blues. (At Oxford and Cambridge, to win a "blue" (blazer) is like winning a letter at American schools and colleges.) Their older brother had captained the Oxford tennis team in 1892 but gave up serious tennis in favor of theology.* Although Reggie and Laurie were leaders of tennis at Cambridge in

---

*In 1931, the Doherty gate at Wimbledon was given by the Reverend William Doherty, in memory of his two famous, younger brothers.

FIGURE 3
American Tennis Stars, 1900–1912:
U.S. Singles Champions and Davis Cup Challenge Round Participants

Davis Cup Challenge Rounds American Teams	U.S. Singles Champions
1900 U.S. d. England 3–0 Malcolm Whitman, Dwight Davis, and Holcombe Ward	1900 Malcolm Whitman
1901 No Match	1901 William A. Larned
1902 U.S. d. England 3–2 Whitman, Ward, Davis, and William A. Larned	1902 William A. Larned
1903 England d. U.S. 4–1 Larned, Robert Wrenn, and George Wrenn	1903 H. Laurie Doherty
1904 England d. Belgium	1904 Holcombe Ward
1905 England d. U.S. 5–0 Larned, Ward, William J. Clothier, and Beals C. Wright	1905 Beals C. Wright
1906 England d. U.S. 5–0 Ward, Raymond D. Little	1906 William J. Clothier
1907 Australasia d. England	1907 William A. Larned
1908 Australasia d. U.S. 3–2 Wright and Fred B. Alexander	1908 William A. Larned
1909 Australasia d. U.S. 5–0 Maurice E. McLoughlin and Melville H. Long	1909 William A. Larned
1910 No Competition	1910 William A. Larned
1911 Australasia d. U.S. 5–0 Wright, Larned, and McLoughlin	1911 William A. Larned
1912 England d. Australasia 3–2	1912 Maurice E. McLoughlin

During these first thirteen years of Davis Cup history, twelve American tennis stars and one Englishman, Laurie Doherty, either played on our Davis Cup teams, won our National Championship, or both. Of the twelve Americans, ten were young college boys: seven from Harvard—Whitman, Davis, Ward, Wright, Clothier, and Bob and George Wrenn; two were Princetonians—Alexander and Little; and one, the greatest of them all, Larned, went to Cornell. McLoughlin and Long were outsiders from California.

1896 (Laurie's first year there) they were both beaten in the first round at Wimbledon. Like the Renshaws before them, they spent the next winter playing the Riviera circuit, Reggie winning the first of his six Monte Carlo singles titles. In June, the brothers won the doubles title at Wimbledon, and Reggie played through to the singles title without losing a set.

While the Renshaw twins laid the foundations of modern lawn tennis at Wimbledon in the 1880s, the Doherty brothers made Wimbledon world-famous in the years between 1897, when Reginald Frank (Reggie) won the singles for the first time, and 1906, when his younger brother, Hugh Lawrence (Laurie), won his last Singles Championship. In fact, the first thirty years of Wimbledon were dominated by the Renshaw and Baddeley twins* and the Doherty brothers, who between them won twenty Singles Championships: Willie Renshaw won the singles eight times, his brother Ernie once; Wilfred Baddeley won the title three times, Reggie Doherty four times, and Laurie five. With the exceptions of Laurie Doherty and Fred Perry, the British over the years have probably been better at doubles than at singles. Of the twenty-five Doubles Championships, the Renshaws won seven titles, the Baddeleys four, and the Dohertys eight.

While the Renshaws dominated Wimbledon in the 1880s, and the Dohertys between 1897 and 1906, the first years of the 1890s were lean ones: three Irish invaders won the singles four times between them; the utterly charming and beautiful natural athlete, Dr. Joshua Pim, won in 1893–94 before retiring to devote himself to his profession. Wilfred Baddeley won in 1891–92 and 1895. In the meantime, interest in Wimbledon almost died out in those years: Pim was far more interested in perfecting his beautiful form than in winning, and Wilfred Baddeley was of such an unemotional and perfectionist temperament that he was a bit of a bore to watch. The mannerist age had temporarily triumphed, and the number of entries fell to twenty-two in 1891, and the first and only financial loss in Wimbledon history occurred in 1895, when the tournament ended up thirty-three pounds in the red.

Wimbledon became an international tournament for the first time in 1905: the determined Californian, May Sutton (actually born in En-

---

*The Renshaws were fraternal twins and the Baddeleys identical.

gland) was the first American, and overseas, winner at Wimbledon. At the same time, the record entry of seventy-one gentlemen in the singles included three Australasians*—Norman Brookes, Anthony Wilding (both future champions), and A. W. Dunlap—and four top Americans— Beals Wright, Bill Clothier, Bill Larned, and Holcombe Ward—all of whom had been or were to become U.S. Singles Champions. Belgium, Denmark, Sweden, and South Africa also sent players that year. Wilding and Larned reached the last eight, while Brookes was beaten by Laurie Doherty in the challenge round in what many at that time believed to be the finest singles match yet played on the Center Court.

Laurie Doherty won his last Wimbledon singles title in 1906 and also played in his last Davis Cup challenge round when the British trounced the Americans 5–0, Laurie winning two singles and one doubles match to complete a still unequaled Davis Cup record of seven singles and five doubles victories without losing a match in five challenge rounds.

Laurie Doherty's last two glorious years as Amateur Lawn Tennis Champion of the World coincided with the famous British election of December 1905, when Arthur Balfour and the Tories suffered an igno- minious defeat at the hands of the Liberals, symbolizing the final passing of political power in England from the aristocracy to the middle classes (even young Winston Churchill "ratted" on his Tory peers and crossed the aisle to take his seat with the Liberals). The makeup of the Members of Parliament in the two parties was as follows:

	Percent Tories	*Percent Liberals*
Gentlemen	30	18
Businessmen	25	40
Officers	20	6
Barristers & Solicitors		22
Others	25	14
	100	100

It is important to the general theme of this book that, just as the pass- ing of the Tory aristocracy in 1905 marked the decline of the amateur and the rise of the professional in British politics, so the reign of the Do-

---

*Australia and New Zealand made up one Davis Cup team in those days.

herty brothers at Wimbledon symbolized the end of thirty years' rule of world tennis by the British amateur gentleman. While it was Sir Henry Campbell-Bannerman, wealthy heir to a Scottish mercantile fortune, who defeated Balfour in 1905, the two leading members of the Liberal Party at the time were Herbert H. Asquith and David Lloyd George, both of whom made their way up in the law. As Tocqueville had predicted of America, it is the professional lawyers who fulfill the role of previous aristocracies in modern democratic societies; thus, while Campbell-Bannerman held the prime ministership for only three years, Asquith and Lloyd George ruled England in its critical years of transition, from 1908 to 1922 (Asquith was Prime Minister from 1908 to 1916, and Lloyd George from 1916 to 1922). It was under Asquith's rule that, in 1911, Members of Parliament were paid for the first time.

It is indeed fitting that the two main entrances to Wimbledon are now called the Doherty and Perry gates. Laurie Doherty and Fred Perry were perhaps the greatest of English amateur lawn tennis players: they were the only Englishmen to have won the U.S. Singles Championship. Although Perry may have been the better player, Laurie Doherty surely had the better official record. At Wimbledon, he won the singles five times to Perry's three; while Perry never won the doubles title, the Doherty brothers won it eight times, a record never equaled. In Davis Cup competition, Laurie Doherty holds the only undefeated record:* twelve victories and no defeats, while Perry won nine singles victories with one defeat (no doubles wins). It is important to note that while Laurie has the best amateur record of any Englishman, his older brother, Reggie, had the second-best record (four singles titles at Wimbledon and eight doubles titles with his brother). Contemporary observers thought that the older brother had the more beautiful and better game, and, as a matter of private record, Laurie never beat Reggie in the many informal matches played for fun on private courts. This was partly due to the fact that Reggie suffered from constant bouts of acute indigestion and could interrupt or cancel these informal matches! At any rate, the Dohertys were the greatest pair of brothers ever to compete at Wimbledon, as well as the last strictly amateur Englishmen of the very top rank.

---

*John McEnroe was on his way to equaling the great Doherty record in 1984, when he lost his first Davis Cup matches in Sweden and coincidentally disgraced himself and his country.

Although Arthur Wentworth Gore never played tennis in a class with the Dohertys or Fred Perry, he surely established a unique and very British sporting-gentleman's record at Wimbledon, which he entered thirty-five times between 1888 and 1927. Win or lose, Gore played for the love of the game: he won sixty-four of his ninety singles matches, and 1,729 of 3,071 games; he won the singles title three times: in 1901, at the age of 33, ending Reggie Doherty's four-year winning streak; in 1908, at the age of 40, he won again with a finals victory over his good friend and longtime doubles partner, H. Roper Barrett; and finally in 1909, at the age of 41, he won in a long-drawn-out final of five sets. He still holds the record as the oldest singles titleholder in Wimbledon history. He went on playing year after year, winning his last singles match in 1920 when he was 52. He was put out of the doubles (with his old partner, Roper Barrett) in the first round, in 1927, at the age of 59, and died the following December (1928). Gore, a hard-working businessman all his life, was the quintessential English gentleman-amateur who surely met with Triumph and Disaster, treating those two impostors just the same. His breed has never again won at Wimbledon.

After 1906, the singles title, which had never left the British Isles for thirty years, was destined to go overseas each year for the next seventy, with five exceptions—when Gore won it in 1908–9, and when Fred Perry won it in 1934, 1935, and 1936. The Australasians turned the tennis world upside down when Norman Brookes, born the year of the first Wimbledon tournament in 1877, won the Singles, Doubles, and Mixed Doubles Championships in 1907. Brookes beat Gore for the singles title, and with Anthony Wilding, of New Zealand, defeated the Americans Beals Wright and Karl Behr in the doubles; Brookes and Wilding, in fact, completely dominated the doubles, not losing a set in five rounds. Brookes and Wilding also won the right to take the Davis Cup "down under" for the first time: nine days after Wimbledon, they won a close victory over the Americans, 3–2; four days later, they beat the British team of Gore and Barrett, 3–2.

Both Norman Brookes, of Melbourne, Australia, and Anthony Wilding, of Christchurch, New Zealand, were born in comfortable circumstances, very much a part of the colonial aristocracies of their respective countries. The Brookeses eventually became one of the first families of Melbourne, in the state of Victoria, where the first lawn tennis championship tournament in Australia was held in 1880. Norman Brookes was knighted in 1939 and his wife was made a DBE (Dame of the British Empire) in 1953. Dame Mabel fortunately has left us a chatty and informative autobiography, *Crowded Galleries*.[7]

Norman's father, William Brookes, arrived in Melbourne from Northamptonshire in 1852, an orphan of 18 with nine pounds in his pocket. In the best traditions of the success sagas of our own Horatio Alger and England's Samuel Smiles, he soon made a place for himself in the sun, methodically building up a fortune in railways, bridge building, shipping, paper milling, and sheep ranching. A religious man of simple faith, plain tastes, and absolute integrity, he insisted that Norman earn his own living and treat tennis and his other games as secondary pastimes. Just as Norman was about to enter Melbourne University, for example, his father put him to work in one of his paper mills, where he began as a clerk licking stamps and ended up as chairman. At the same time he became one of Victoria's business, civic, and sporting leaders. Already in his thirties, Brookes was attracted by a young lady of 17 who was a member of one of Melbourne's distinguished families of far older wealth than his own. Her great-grandfather had come out to Sydney in 1824, after belonging to the British civil service stationed on St. Helena in Napoleon's day.

Norman Brookes, having had his smashing success at the 1907 Wimbledon, was a national hero when he met his future bride. The style of life among Melbourne's gentry before the First World War is nicely revealed in the following description of their wedding in 1911: "When we married there was great interest in the wedding," wrote Dame Mabel in *Crowded Galleries*.

> Melbourne was the home of both families; so barricades went up along the streets by St. Paul's Cathedral. Buzzard's, the cake-makers, sent from England a monster wedding-cake with silver nets, tennis-rackets and tennis-balls on it. There were ten bridesmaids, and mother had the lace of my veil made in Venice. . . .
>
> While waiting at Raveloe to depart to the Cathedral, with mother already gone and father fidgeting with his white carnation buttonhole at the door, I picked up my train and went into the ballroom, empty save for the perfume of the bridal arch and massed lilies in the fireplace. It was a sub-

conscious act. Some part of me was saying "good-bye" to the place of many parties and much fun and carefree youth. Beyond was the great marquee with its white lining spread over the tennis lawn where chairs and tables awaited the guests. The cake stood before the bridal table. The maids came flocking to see my dress. The flower-massed vases were being sprayed by Miss Kemp. There was the wedding-bell! I had everyone's good wishes. The future lay unwritten.[8]

Throughout their married life, both Sir Norman and Dame Mabel dedicated themselves to the best interests of lawn tennis. In 1926, Brookes was made president of the Lawn Tennis Association of Australia, a post he held for 29 years before retirement in 1955. Brookes came back to Europe and America in 1914, winning at Wimbledon in June and taking the Davis Cup back to Australia in August. After the war, he devoted his time to business and tennis administration. But he was still playing first-class tennis in his forties: in 1919, he won the U.S. Doubles Championship (at the age of 42) with his pupil, Gerald Patterson; and in 1924 (at 47) he won the Australian Doubles Championship with John Anderson, who also won the singles that year.

Norman Brookes was an extremely gifted, all-around athlete, often called "The Wizard" by his contemporaries. As a left-hander possessed of consummate concentration, a tenacious will to win, uncanny anticipation, and a deft touch at the net, he was apparently quite like our own John McEnroe. They both were great doubles players and, incidentally, very outspoken and direct in manner; but unlike McEnroe, Brookes was always a great gentleman, impeccably dressed on the court; while McEnroe, moreover, first won Wimbledon at the age of 22, Brookes was 30 when he first won it in 1907; finally, Brookes was slightly built and of average height, his sallow complexion indicating his always-delicate health. He was a remarkable man from a remarkable family, as his friend, Anthony Wilding, wrote in his fascinating memoirs:

> A more versatile games man I have seldom met. He can make his hundred break at billiards fairly regularly. He is on or near the plus mark at golf. He was one of the finest left-hand schoolboy bowlers in Australia, and if he had stuck to cricket his appearance in test matches must only have been a question of time. I remember staying with Brookes at his home in Melbourne when the croquet championship of Australia happened to be taking place.

Brookes invited the winner to play him a match on Sunday, and a dreadful act of sacrilege was committed—the tennis court was marked out for croquet. The champion came, saw and was badly defeated. . . . As a [doubles] partner Brookes is not always tranquil. He occasionally does things you don't expect him to do and leaves undone others which you anticipate. But once understand him and no man can wish for finer support.[9]

Unlike the wizened and often sickly Brookes, Anthony Wilding was a six-foot-three Adonis, always a picture of perfect health. If perhaps less naturally gifted than Brookes, he was nevertheless a fine all-around athlete and a keen and systematic student of lawn tennis, constantly experimenting and perfecting his strokes. In several surviving photographs, Wilding's classic British looks resembled Fred Perry's to an unusual degree; like Perry, too, he was a fitness fanatic and always counted on being the stronger player in the fifth set. (At Wimbledon he beat two great Harvard players who were also friends and national champions, Beals Wright and Bill Clothier, in the fifth set after losing the first two.)

Wilding's father was a West Country English gentleman. At Shrewsbury School, he was a fine athlete who held the public school broad-jumping record in his day. When he migrated to New Zealand in the 1870s, he bought a great country estate near Christchurch, on the South Island. He soon had tennis courts of asphalt and grass, a cricket pitch, a swimming pool, and riding stables. Tony and his brothers and sisters went barefoot until they were 7. The boy Tony was constantly on horseback from the age of 4; quite naturally he preferred cricket and football to tennis in his school days. When he came of age, his father sent him back to Cambridge to be schooled in the gentlemanly values of the classics and cricket. As he expected young Tony to win a cricket blue at Cambridge and perhaps a Wimbledon title, he made sure he was qualified to pass the Trinity entrance exams by sending him home to England on a freighter rather than a passenger ship, thus allowing him six uninterrupted weeks to polish his Greek verbs. After arriving in England, Wilding spent six months at a well-known cram school.

Like Harvard in America, Cambridge was the nursery of British tennis at the turn of the century. Following the paths of the Dohertys, Tony Wilding enrolled at Trinity. His first summer was spent playing cricket for Trinity, whose team included seven blues and easily swept the college championships that year Wilding soon switched to lawn tennis, however, and, in 1905, was the captain of both the Trinity and University clubs. He also reached the quarterfinals at Wimbledon. In 1906, he lost to Gore in the semifinals; in an earlier round he played the longest match of his life against William J. Clothier of Philadelphia; Clothier had him two sets up, five games to two and 40–15, in the third set; Wilding won that third set and finally won the match at 12–10, in the fifth set.

The next year, Wilding won the Wimbledon doubles and the Davis Cup along with Brookes. He and Brookes successfully defended the cup in 1908 and 1909 against the United States. In the meantime Wilding had been called to the New Zealand bar. Afterwards, in January 1909, he sailed again for Europe by way of South Africa, an eight-week trip. He met everyone who seemed to matter there and won the national championship at Johannesburg: "My stay in Johannesburg was absolutely delightful," he wrote in his memoirs, "and I never wish to meet a finer school of sportsmen than those with whom I came in contact." At Wimbledon he won both the singles and doubles titles; he beat Beals Wright in the all-comers final in five long sets and then beat Gore in the challenge round. "I consider Beals Wright," Wilding wrote, "one of the finest sportsmen it has been my good fortune to be defeated by (a five-setter in Australia) and in turn defeat. A tryer from first to last, invariably keen, he takes victory and defeat with the same smiling grace."[10]

While at Cambridge and afterwards, Tony Wilding liked to spend as much time as possible each winter playing along the Riviera. And he won many tournaments at Monte Carlo (following the Dohertys), at San Remo, in Italy, at Cannes, and at Nice, where he retired the cup after winning it three years in a row without losing a set.* He of course met many prominent persons, including King Gustav of Sweden and Lord Balfour, with whom he played often and whom he got to know quite well. He spent a lot of time with the Craig Biddles of Philadelphia and Newport. His most frequent doubles partner, Biddle, who inherited a Drexel fortune, was a first-rate player of not quite top rank who, along with his stylish wife, was for many years both a leader of Newport Society

---

*There was an old tradition in amateur tennis which allowed anyone who won a tournament three years in a row to take permanent possession of the cup or trophy. Otherwise only his name appeared on the cup with the year of victory.

and an official of the National Championships at the Casino. Wilding's delightful memoirs not only cover his years on the Riviera but also his playing throughout Europe—in Norway and Sweden, in Germany and Austria, in Hungary and Czechoslovakia, and at many fashionable spas such as Baden-Baden and Marienbad. All the tennis world was his oyster as he traveled around at his own expense, in these last truly amateur days before the First World War.

Class Complacency Challenged in 1912: The Sinking of the Titanic and the First California Invasion of the Eastern Grass Court Circuit

The *Titanic* was the last stand of wealth and society in the center of public affection. In 1912 there were no movie, radio, or television stars; sports figures were still beyond the pale; and cafe society was completely unknown. The public depended on socially prominent people for all the vicarious glamour that enriches their drab lives.

—Walter Lord, *A Night to Remember*

The dramatic figure of McLoughlin had come storming out of the West with dynamic service and overhead smashes to electrify the small enclosed tennis world of the Eastern Seaboard and drew non-tennis crowds to a game theretofore largely ignored and faintly dispised by the public. The whole circumstances of McLoughlin's unheralded arrival on the sports scene was immensely exciting, and he quickly became the chief hero to a group of boys who had dared to play tennis publicly when it was still considered by many people a sissy game. . . . We knew his record at Wimbledon, Newport, and elsewhere as we knew Ty Cobb's exact batting average and how many times the villainous Three Finger Brown of the Cubs had beaten our Giants.

—Al Laney, *Covering the Court*

In the year 1912, a complacent and confident Eastern Seaboard upper class which had ruled American society as well as lawn tennis ever since the first championship was held at the Newport Casino in 1881, was challenged by two symbolic events: the sinking of the *Titanic*, in April, and the winning of the Men's Tennis Championship, in late August, by Maurice E. McLoughlin, a simple California boy with flaming-red hair. The son of a Scotch-Irish immigrant, he learned his tennis on the public courts of San Francisco. While prominent members of the Eastern Society crowd sank to the bottom of the sea, as it were, a burst of new energy and talent came East from a distant coast to take all the marbles.* While these two events were coincidental at most, I find them interesting omens of changes to come in the American class system and the world of lawn tennis.

The leaders of the gossiping Society crowd who promenaded around the Casino Courts during Tennis Week were also in the habit of bumping into each other abroad at such fashionable places as the Pyramids, in Egypt, along the French Riviera, at Baden-Baden, in Germany, or at Marienbad, outside Vienna, and finally in England during the London Season when many went to Henley, Wimbledon, Lords, or Cowes, and the more Anglophilic families had their daughters presented at the Court of St. James's (along with the British debutantes and dignitaries of the year)†. In those days of Anglo-American, upper-class dominance, *Social Register* listings often included the arrivals and departures of prominent families on a series of hierarchically rated ocean liners such as the *Lusitania* or *Mauritania*. The in-crowd usually booked passage with their favorite captain rather than any particular ship. For this reason, when the International Merchant Marine, a trust formed in 1902 by J. P. Morgan and his British associates of the White Star Line, decided to build the largest (four blocks long) and most luxurious (including a special suite for Mr. Morgan) ocean liner in the world, they assigned a Captain Smith, a "400" favorite, to take command of the ship on its maiden voyage. J. P.

---

*McLoughlin and Tom Bundy took the doubles; Mary K. Browne took the women's singles and doubles, as well as the mixed doubles with Dick Williams.

†Miss Helen Wills was the only American tennis champion to be presented at the Court of St. James. The invitation for debutantes has died out in our time—for both British and American young women.

Morgan, a truly transatlantic colossus, did not make the trip due to ill health; he died in Rome the following March.

When the RMS *Titanic* set sail from Southampton on April 12, 1912, the front page of the *New York Times* listed the more prominent First Class passengers, including such leaders of Newport Society as "Colonel" J. J. Astor and his new wife (with manservant and maid) and Mr. and Mrs. George D. Widener (with manservant and maid) and their son, Harry, an ardent bibliophile who carried a recently purchased and priceless copy of Bacon's *Essays* (1569) in his pocket.* Colonel Astor, who somehow got his title from the Spanish-American War, was the son of The Mrs. Astor who ruled Newport Society with an iron hand for two decades before her death in 1908. He had been married to the most beautiful woman in the Four Hundred for almost twenty years when, in 1910, he arranged a carefully hushed-up divorce and soon married a 19-year-old lady from Brooklyn. To avoid the vicious gossip surrounding both the divorce and the remarriage, he took his bride abroad and was bringing her back on the *Titanic*, five months pregnant with J. J. Astor VI.

Scientifically guaranteed to be unsinkable, the *Titanic* brushed the tip of an iceberg in the North Atlantic at 11:45 on Sunday evening, April 14; two hours and 40 minutes later she slipped silently to the bottom of the sea; only 705 of the 2235 passengers and crew were picked up, most from half-filled lifeboats and others from debris to which they clung as they floated on the glassy-calm sea. Aboard the *Titanic* that terrifying Monday morning, class turned out to be a matter of life or death: while 60 percent of the First Class passengers survived, only 36 percent of the Second Class and 24 percent of the Steerage passengers survived.

While hardly anyone at the time, especially the press, seemed to question these differences in life chances, they also took great differences in luxury for granted: there seemed to be nothing unusual about the fact that the combined wealth of the First Class passengers was in the neighborhood of half a billion dollars, that the Ryersons (steel fortune) were traveling with no less than sixteen trunks, or that the 190 First Class fam-

---

*Harry went down with the ship. Eventually, Mrs. Widener went up to Cambridge and offered his valuable, rare-book collection to Harvard, his *alma mater*. President Lowell accepted her gift and enlarged it to include the whole Widener Library. Harry never learned to swim, but thereafter all Harvard students had to learn to swim before graduating.

ilies were served by twenty-three private maids, eight valets, numerous governesses and nannies, and hundreds of the ship's stewards and stewardesses (many of whom had served them on previous voyages). And perhaps most indicative of the age was the fact that, according to Walter Lord, "Even the Third Class (Steerage) passengers weren't bothered. They expected class distinction as part of the game . . . never since that night have Third Class passengers been so philosophical."[1]

The inequalities of class and sex have tended to vary together in history. In our egalitarian age when the chivalrous male has been transformed into the chauvinist pig by the likes of Billy Jean King, it is worth noting that a great majority of the prominent males, including J. J. Astor, George D. Widener, John B. Thayer, Arthur Ryerson, Washington Roebling, Benjamin Guggenheim, Martin Rothschild, and Isadore Straus, stayed with the ship in accord with the *sexist* norm: "women and children first." All of the First Class children, and all except four (three voluntarily) of the 143 First Class women were saved. While blatant class injustices were ignored, gentlemanly honor and wifely devotion were highly valued virtues in that long-departed Edwardian age. Thus Colonel Astor "stood on the deck," a survivor wrote, "and fought off man after man until his wife was in the lifeboat. Then he remained on deck."[2] (Of course there have always been men who have followed the egalitarian ethic of "every man for himself.") At the same time, Benjamin Guggenheim, a philo-WASP, went down with the ship dressed in his finest evening clothes: "Tell my wife," he told a survivor, "I played the game out straight and to the end . . ."

One of the *Titanic* legends originated when a romantic Canadian lady, whose husband remained on board, told a reporter: "What we remember was that as the ship sank, we could hear the band playing 'Nearer My God to Thee.' We looked back and could see the men standing on the deck, absolutely quiet and waiting for the end." The facts about what the band was playing were probably false, according to the best historical opinion; yet the legend served as a romantic rallying point at the time when this age of confident calm had plunged, over one Sunday night, into chaos and doubt.

At any rate, in most Protestant churches, on Sunday April 21, services began with "Nearer My God to Thee," after which preachers went on to extol the virtues of the self-sacrificing gentlemen. Many churches "draped together the flags of the United States and Great Britain in mournful caress," especially such Episcopal churches as fashionable St. Bartholomews's, on Park Avenue, where the Reverend Leighton Parks's sermon reflected the values of his class and sect. After noting that in another age of anxiety and transition "the Son of Man came into a world that was lost," he went on to say that "the men on the *Titanic* sacrificed themselves for the women and children. The women did not ask for the sacrifice, but it was made. Those women who go about shrieking for their rights want something very different."

Radical suffragettes, indeed, knew exactly what they wanted, and the ideal of male chivalry was a barrier to their ideal of sexual equality. A suffragette demonstration, the first of its kind in America, was planned for May 4. It was ill-timed, and while sixteen thousand were expected for the march down Fifth Avenue led by women on horseback, only eight thousand showed up. At the same time, antisuffragettes mounted a campaign to raise money to build a monument to "the everlasting memory of male chivalry." The President's wife, Nellie Taft, gave the first dollar and over twenty-five thousand other women followed suit (only women were to give). Wyn Craig Wade, whose book, *The Titanic*, is far and away the best one on the American public's reactions to the disaster, wrote of this monument to the chivalrous ideal as follows:

> The resulting monument, sculpted by Gertrude Vanderbilt Whitney, was unveiled in Washington, D.C. and can still be seen across from East Potomac Park. It consists of an eighteen-foot classic statue of a half-clad male, his arms outstretched in the form of a cross. This stunning figure is posed on a thirty-foot pedestal which is engraved in homage "to the brave men" of the *Titanic* "who gave their lives that women and children might be saved." The inscription also records that the monument was "Erected by the women of America."[3]

Who in that innocent age would have predicted in 1976 that the traditional "man of the year" cover of *Time* magazine would have been replaced, on the two hundredth anniversary of our nation's founding, by twelve women, including Billie Jean King; or that the winners at Flushing Meadow, both male and female, would be rewarded with an equal amount of green dollars?

At all events, both sides of the sexual battle line were touched by the

Straus Legend (a true one) which will surely live as long as the *Titanic* disaster is remembered. Mrs. Isadore Straus, wife of the founder of Macy's, resisted all orders from the authorities and went down at her husband's side; after all, they had come a long way together, from "the ashes of the Confederacy . . . the small china business in Philadelphia . . . to the building of Macy's into a national institution . . ." In an era of blatant anti-Semitism, the almost universal adulation of Mrs. Straus's bravery and devotion may have relieved the guilty consciences of many gentiles. At a memorial service at a Broadway theatre, William Jennings Bryan, equating Mrs. Straus with Ruth in the Old Testament, found her womanliness to be "in the best American traditions." And Wyn Craig Wade finished his book as follows:

> For the *Titanic* was the incarnation of man's arrogance in equating size with security; his blindness to the consequences of wasteful extravagance; and his technology. . . . As long as this self-same Hubris is with us, the *Titanic* will continue to be not just a haunting memory of the recurrent past but a portent of things to come; a Western apocalypse, perhaps, wherein the world, as Western man has known and shaped it, is undermined from within, not overcome from without; and ends not in a holocaust but with a quiet slip into oblivion.[4]

Among the First Class *Titanic* passengers was a rather close-knit group of Proper Philadelphians who, in addition to the Wideners, heirs to the city's greatest traction fortune, included John B. Thayer, a vice president of the Pennsylvania Railroad, his wife, her maid, and son, John B., Jr., as well as Duane Williams, a wealthy patron of tennis on the Continent, who was living in Switzerland for reasons of health. Williams was bringing his son, Richard Norris II, back home to enter Harvard in the fall.

Dick had won the men's tennis championships of Switzerland, both in singles and doubles, the previous October. On the boat train between Paris and Cherbourg where they were to board the *Titanic*, young Dick noted that Karl Behr, well-known international tennis star, was in the same car. Along with the rest of the *Titanic* survivors on the dawn of April 15, Dick Williams was picked up by the *Carpathia* in an almost frozen state; he had remained with the ship along with his father and his friends, and only jumped into the icy Atlantic moments before the gigantic hulk plunged, bow first, down to the ocean depths, and just after his father was killed instantly before his eyes when one of the four huge funnels came crashing down upon him. We shall have more to say below about the tennis career of R. Norris Williams II, but, because it nicely suggests the romantic and gentlemanly style of this last American aristocrat to win our National Championship, I quote his observations (in his privately typed memoirs) on the shipboard romance between Karl Behr and his future wife:

> The story on the *Carpathia* was to the effect that they became engaged in a life boat. Although I have often seen them and played tennis a great deal with him since, I never dared ask him if the story were true. It would be such a shame to spoil a beautiful story.

Immediately after landing, young Williams went directly to Philadelphia where he stayed with his uncle, R. Norris Williams, in the suburb of Chestnut Hill. He was soon playing number one on the Philadelphia Cricket Club tennis team; he won all his interclub matches, even though the Merion Cricket Club team won the championship that year. On June 3, he entered his first American tournament, the Pennsylvania State Championships, at the Merion Cricket Club. He won, beating, in the following order, Craig Biddle, William Tatum Tilden, Jr., Alexander Dixon Thayer, Herbert Marmaduke Tilden, and Wallace Ford Johnson (all Proper Philadelphians and top tennis players). The next week, he watched the Ladies National Championships at the Philadelphia Cricket Club, and won the mixed doubles with the new Ladies Champion, Mary K. Browne, of California. He then went out to Pittsburgh and won the U.S. Clay Court Championship. "Not for many years," *American Lawn Tennis* magazine noted in its June 15, 1912 issue, "has a player leaped into fame so quickly as Richard Norris William, Jr., of Philadelphia."

═══

While Dick Williams was starting out on a brilliant but erratic tennis career in Philadelphia, Maurice McLoughlin was winning everything on the West Coast, in preparation for a complete conquest of the Eastern establishment in July and August. In his first Eastern Circuit tournament at the Longwood Cricket Club, he won the singles. Williams, incidentally, was defeated in the third round by his fellow *Titanic* survivor, Karl Behr, after winning the first two sets (the first set at love). McLoughlin and Williams first met in the finals of the New York State Championships, at the Crescent Athletic Club, Brooklyn, New York; McLoughlin won in five hard-fought sets and with his partner from Los Angeles, Tom Bundy, won the doubles. The week preceding the nationals, at the Meadow Club, Southampton, McLoughlin and Bundy won the doubles but did not compete in the singles. At Newport in late August, McLoughlin became the first Californian (and the first non-Ivy League American) to win the Men's Singles Championship, beating three Philadelphians on his way to victory: Williams in the quarterfinals, Clothier in the semifinals, and Wallace Johnson in the finals. He and Bundy won the Doubles Championship. When the First Ten rankings for the year 1912 were published, McLoughlin was ranked number one and Williams number two.

Maurice Evans McLoughlin was born in Carson City, Nevada, in 1890; his father was born in Ireland and his mother in Portland, Maine. Until Maurice was 8 years old, the family resided in Carson City, when the local branch of the U.S. Mint was closed, and Mr. McLoughlin was made superintendent of machinery at the U.S. Mint in Philadelphia.* When Maurice was 13, his father was transferred to San Francisco; along with his three older brothers, Maurice took up tennis at the public courts of the Golden Gate Park; one older brother, Ralph, was the better natural talent, but Maurice persisted and soon became the best young player on the park courts. He graduated from Lowell High School in San Francisco and qualified for the University of California, though he never entered. He played in many junior tournaments and began his adult career when he won the San Francisco City Championships in 1907 (at age 17).

Richard Norris Williams II was born of wealthy Philadelphia parents in Geneva, Switzerland in 1891.† Williams was formally known as R. Norris or Norris, but as Dick to his close friends and tennis partners. He was not a "Junior" but used the "II" to distinguish himself from his uncle of the same name. His father, C. Duane Williams, was directly descended from Benjamin Franklin, through William Duane who married Franklin's granddaughter. He was also descended from Richard Norris, one of the ten richest men in Philadelphia by the time of the Civil War, when his locomo-

---

*Ezra Pound's father worked at the mint at the same time. The Pounds and the McLoughlins lived in the same Philadelphia suburb of Jenkintown.

†Williams's widow, Francis "Sue" Williams, was most helpful in her husband's life and tennis career.

tive company had become world-famous, building locomotives for railroads all over the United States as well as some hundred or so for railroads in France, Austria, Prussia, Italy, Belgium, South America, and Cuba. Norris Williams's mother, born Lydia Biddle White, was a direct descendant of William White, first Protestant Episcopal Bishop of Pennsylvania, and Philadelphia's First Citizen for several decades after the death of Franklin.

Williams was educated by private tutors and at a strict, Swiss boarding school before coming to America and entering Harvard in 1912. He started playing tennis at 12, largely under the expert guidance of his father. In 1906, the family spent the winter in Pasadena, California, where Dick met and played with Ward Dawson, who later won the Championship of Southern California several times and often played doubles with McLoughlin. In 1911, Dick won the Swiss Championship and took a set from Wilding in the Cannes tournament. He spoke French and German fluently, which prepared him to act as unofficial interpreter for the German Davis Cup team when it played in America in the summer of 1914. It also allowed him to rise to a high staff position in the AEF during the First World War.

McLoughlin and Williams came from opposite coasts of America and almost opposite ends of the social scale; yet they immediately became close friends after their first meeting at the Crescent Athletic Club in 1912. It is difficult for today's dogmatic democrats to understand how an aristocrat in a more stable age could be far less status-conscious than they, but so it was. In the 1912 final at Newport between McLoughlin and Wallace Johnson, for instance, the former champion, William J. Clothier, volunteered to act as a line judge and impressed the spectators by calling out decisions "in the dignified voice of a Senator," as they put it at the time. One could hardly imagine the likes of Connors or McEnroe volunteering to act as linesmen at Flushing Meadow. Just as R. Norris Williams II of Philadelphia was a classic example of the old-stock, Eastern Seaboard roots of American lawn tennis, so his redheaded friend from the Golden West, often called the "California Comet," was an ideal symbol of the new men who have added the "Big Game" and California zest to the Eastern amateur circuit, in each generation up until the end of the amateur era in 1968.

═══

Although this is a history of men's tennis, when it comes to discussing California tennis something must be said about the women's game, especially about two of the greatest ladies in the early history of world tennis, May Sutton of Southern California, and Hazel Hotchkiss of the San Francisco Bay Area.

Stable and traditional societies have tended to be patriarchal; in new, more open, and egalitarian societies, women come to the fore. It is consequently highly appropriate that women from the open society of California should have become leaders in women's tennis before the men did. Thus Maurice McLoughlin and Hazel Hotchkiss first came East from the San Francisco Bay Area in 1909. While McLoughlin did well and was ranked sixth that year, Hazel Hotchkiss swept the women's field, winning the Ladies Championships in singles and doubles, as well as winning the mixed doubles with Wallace Johnson.* Moreover, she totally dominated her Eastern Seaboard opponents. In the challenge round of the singles, for example, she defeated the defending champion, Mrs. M. Barger-Wallach of Newport and New York, in less than half an hour, winning the first set 6–0 (losing only seven points) in ten minutes and the second 6–1 in less than twenty minutes (her opponent served underhand, as many Eastern women still did at that time). The following two years, Miss Hotchkiss also won all three National Championships; she easily defended her singles title the next year, 6–4, 6–2; only in 1911 did she have any trouble winning when she was extended to three sets by a fellow Californian, Miss Florence Sutton. Herbert Warren Wind perfectly caught the spirit and style of the California pioneers of women's tennis when he wrote of that day at the Philadelphia Cricket Club: "Hazel first took the court at three o'clock for the singles final against Florence Sutton," he wrote in the *New Yorker* in 1952.

> With the sets at one-all, Hazel was trailing 6–5 in games and 40–30 on Florence's service, one point from defeat, when she killed a lob, drew up to deuce, pulled the game out of the fire, and went on to win the set and

---

*While California society, in the Hotchkiss-McLoughlin era, was more open than Eastern Seaboard society, it was not by any means similar to the permissive society which has taken over California since World War II. And it is important to note here that, after decades of dominating world tennis, California boys and girls of today apparently are no longer willing to make the effort or just lack the necessary discipline. Billie Jean King and Stan Smith, both born during the war (1943 and 1946), are the last *native* Californians to have reached the top ranks in world tennis.

match, 8–10, 6–1, 9–7. The final of the mixed doubles followed immediately; Hazel and Wallace Johnson took this, 6–4, 6–4. A sudden squall forced her to sit down and rest until the turf dried out, but at six o'clock she was back in action in the women's doubles final, which she and Eleonora Sears, the original Boston glamour girl, won by the scores of 6–4, 4–6, 6–2. Between three o'clock and seven forty-two, the triple champion played eighty-nine games, a feat the more remarkable when one considers that the women players lugged around several layers of undergarments beneath their starched linen shirts and ankle-length white duck skirts.[5]

═══

The game of lawn tennis was played in California as early as the 1880s. After the defeat of Mexico in 1848, California was ceded to the United States and taken into the Union in 1850. The "Forty-Niners" made the early city of San Francisco; the Big Four capitalists, Leland Stanford, Colis P. Huntington, Mark Hopkins, and Charles Crocker, brought the first transcontinental railroad to the city in 1869, and fifteen years later, in 1884, the frontier city had its first tennis club—the California Lawn Tennis Club. The California Lawn Tennis Association was organized in the city in the same year. In 1889 the association was officially recognized by the USNLTA and awarded the Pacific Coast Championships which were played for many years on the courts of the Del Monte Hotel in Monterey, down the peninsula from San Francisco. The famous Del Monte, built by Charles Crocker in 1880, was the center of fashionable society in California when Dwight Davis, Holcombe Ward, Malcolm Whitman, Beals Wright, and George Wright played there in 1889. Incidentally, the National Doubles Champions, Davis and Ward, were beaten in the Pacific Coast finals that year by two pioneers of California tennis, Sumner and Sam Hardy.

Among the founders of the California Lawn Tennis Club (which had five asphalt courts by 1895) was Walter MacGavin, a peripatetic Scotsman who came to San Francisco from Bombay, India. Known as the "Father of Tennis" in Northern California, he was president of the club in 1899–1903 and won the Pacific Coast Doubles Championship when it was first held in 1890. Two years later the Championship was won by Samuel and Sumner Hardy. Their father and his seven sons were introduced to tennis when Walter MacGavin suggested that they turn their croquet lawn into a tennis court. Sam Hardy won the Pacific Coast singles in 1894, at the age of 17, and again in 1895 and 1896. Sumner also won the singles title in his teens, in 1898.

Dr. Sumner Hardy was president of both the California Lawn Tennis Association and the California Lawn Tennis Club for over twenty years. While Sumner was the unofficial dean of Northern California tennis and one of San Francisco's First Citizens for a half-century before his death in 1949, Sam went East, where he captained the Davis Cup teams in 1920 and again in 1930 and edited the *A. G. Spalding Lawn Tennis Annual* for many years.

Members of the California Tennis Club (as it is now known) competed in the East as early as the 1890s. The first club member to rank in the First Ten was C. P. Hubbard, who ranked tenth in 1892. Carr Neal was next, ranking sixth in 1895 and moving up to third in 1896 when he and his brother, Samuel, won the national doubles title at Newport (the first Californians to win a National Championship). Two famous members of the California Tennis Club, Maurice McLoughlin and Melville Long, came East in 1909; they were ranked sixth and seventh and were chosen to represent the United States that year in the Davis Cup matches which were held in Sydney, Australia; they were soundly beaten by Norman Brookes and Anthony Wilding (5–0).

Although Maurice McLoughlin represented the California Tennis Club when he stormed the East in 1909, he first learned the game on the public courts of the Golden Gate Park where he began to play at the age of 13, in 1903. He was the most famous member, along with little Billy Johnston later on, of the Golden Gate Park Junior Tennis Club which was founded, supported, and run by Dr. Sydney R. Marvin, a leading San Francisco capitalist and estate manager. An Englishman and an Oxford graduate, Dr. Marvin was no tennis player but took great pride in character building. As a contemporary wrote: "Perhaps it would be fairer to Dr. Marvin to state that he formed a club for these boys more because he loved to work with them, than to make only expert tennis players out of them. In any case he has practiced character building, and no youngster who couldn't be a little gentleman ever got far in his good graces."[6] For many years, the Golden Gate courts were the best in the city. As the best players often played there, the juniors under Dr. Marvin had a chance to watch and learn from them. The main point, however, is not that some of the best players in the world were developed there; it is rather that Dr. Marvin produced mature and honorable gentlemen. How else explain the fact that McLoughlin and Long were not only accepted by their Eastern peers, but were deemed worthy of representing their country in the Davis Cup matches in far-off Australia after their very first year in the East? To have chosen McLoughlin as playing-captain when he was only 19 years of age was unprecedented then and never equaled since. In such a class-dominated world of trust, no wonder Maury McLoughlin and Dick Williams quite naturally became close friends.

Tennis writers, usually with Eastern backgrounds, have always stressed the fact that McLoughlin was the first national champion to come from *across the tracks*, having been bred on the courts of a public park rather than a private club. But the class structures of California and the Eastern Seaboard, at that time and since, were quite different. Thus McLoughlin, as soon as he reached the maximum age (19) for membership in Dr. Marvin's Junior Club, moved easily into the California Lawn Tennis Club, as did Billy Johnston. Similarly, in later years, both Margaret Osborne and Alice Marble, who were equally broke in their younger days, learned to play on the Golden Gate courts before becoming members of the California Tennis Club as they rose to world fame. On the other hand, in Philadelphia, which was more or less typical of the Eastern establishment, public park players lived in entirely different worlds from the players at the cricket clubs. The Woodford Tennis Club, in the Strawberry Mansion section of the city's famous Fairmount Park, founded in 1894, was the oldest of its kind in the East, and no first-rate young players there were ever taken into membership at the Merion or Germantown cricket clubs.

While McLoughlin learned his tennis in San Francisco's Golden Gate Park, Hazel Hotchkiss learned to play across the Bay, in Berkeley, where the only tennis court in town belonged to the University of California. She and her four brothers were born of Virginia covered wagon stock and bred on a one-thousand-five-hundred-acre ranch, in Healdsburg, California. In 1900, the family moved to Berkeley where Hazel's two older brothers, Homer and Marius, took up tennis and soon won their first tournament. In 1902, they took their sister to watch the Pacific Coast Championships; she fell in love with tennis at first sight and later wrote of that first tournament as follows:

The way girls played singles in those days, there was no net game at all. They didn't budge from the baseline. The ball passed over the net as many as fifty times in a single rally before someone made an error or finally won the point on a placement. Doubles like Sam and Sumner Hardy played it—now that appealed to me. They were awfully quick up at the net, and even a green horn like myself could appreciate the precision with which they volleyed and smashed and their split-second maneuvers for drawing their opponents out of position and setting up their openings. I decided that afternoon that I'd go in for tennis and model my game on the Hardys'.[7]

Necessity is the mother of invention. Thus Hazel Hotchkiss's volleying genius was not only modeled on the Hardy brothers but was also a product of playing conditions at the time. As the one asphalt court in Berkeley allowed women to play only before 8 A.M., Hazel and her brothers were up at five every morning for a game before the zero hour for women. They also played a great deal at home on a gravel driveway where the bounces were so erratic that they soon got used to coming to the net (a rope strung between the house and a cluster of rosebushes) and taking the ball on the fly.

The third great center for developing champions from the Bay Area, the Berkeley Tennis Club, was founded in 1906. The first president of the new club was Vernon Hardy, of the Hardy clan, and the Hotchkiss brothers and their sister now had a fine tennis home. Soon after the club was organized with five courts and a fine backboard for practicing, an interclub series of matches took place between the Berkeley, Alameda, California, and Golden Gate Park tennis clubs (and how those Golden Gate youngsters could eat!). "Transportation for those events," wrote Gail Baxter, historian of the Berkeley Tennis Club, "was by public conveyance except when members were fortunate enough to ride in one of the members' Model T Fords or, perhaps, the Electric Carriage owned by Hazel Hotchkiss's mother."[8]

The Berkeley Tennis Club moved in 1917 to its present site on the grounds of the beautiful and impressive Hotel Claremont, at the foot of the Berkeley Hills. The land was leased from the hotel for many years but is now owned by the club. The Pacific Coast Championships were held alternately at the California Tennis Club in San Francisco, and at the Berkeley Tennis Club from 1920 until after the Second World War. Between 1951 and 1971 the tournament (since 1962, the Pacific Coast International Championships) was held at Berkeley because the facilities at the California Club were too small to hold the ever-increasing crowds.

After 1969, the tournament became "open." In 1970 the open tournament was managed by Barry MacKay and sponsored by the Redwood Bank, offering the then princely sum of $15,000 in prize money. Due to spiraling prize money and ever-increasing crowds and costs, the last championships were held at the club in 1971. The Cow Palace was surely a more appropriate place for the new commercial game whose values, as a club member put it, "were not in keeping with the traditions of the Berkeley Tennis Club." Or, as the club historian summed it up: "The best years of the Pacific Coast Tournament at Berkeley are generally considered by the Club members as those when the enthusiasm of members to work the tournament, house the players, and enjoy the matches in an aura of non-commercial competition was at its highest."[9]

While the Hotchkisses and Hardys were the two most distinguished tennis families at the club in the pre–World War I days, many fine players, including the two Helens (Wills and Jacobs), have learned the game there since, among them Edward "Bud" Chandler, winner of the National Intercollegiates in 1925 and 1926 (singles and doubles) and many national senior titles. A Harvard-bred lawyer, he is today the grand old man of Bay Area tennis (member of both the California and Berkeley clubs) and the legal advisor to his old friend, Helen Wills Moody Roark, with whom he played two or three times a week on the Berkeley courts in the 1920s.

Hazel Hotchkiss of Berkeley, and May Sutton of Pasadena, surely did more to popularize the game of lawn tennis in California than any other players. Their rivalry eventually developed into a kind of family and sectional feud. May won their first match rather easily at Del Monte, in 1908. They next met on July 5, 1909, in the California State Championships, playing on the courts of the Hotel Rafael, in San Rafael. May beat her sister, Florence, in the final 6–0, 6–0, and then went on to beat Hazel Hotchkiss in the challenge round. "The greatest crowd in the history of the game in California," it was reported at the time, "gathered to see the match between Miss Hotchkiss and Miss Sutton. In as much as Miss Hotchkiss had just returned from Philadelphia, after winning the national title, the match was doubly interesting."[10] The first set was keenly fought before Miss Sutton won it at 6–4; she took the second set and the match easily at 6–1. May won again rather easily in the finals of the Pacific Coast Championships, at the Del Monte, in September.

Hazel Hotchkiss won her first victory over May Sutton in April 1910, in the finals of the Ojai Valley Championships; it was a hard-fought match (2–6, 6–4, 6–0), with an enthusiastic crowd which soon realized that the impossible was taking place; the World Champion was being beaten. May offered no handshake at the end of the match.* The intensity of the Sutton-Hotchkiss rivalry became so heated that the Pacific Lawn Tennis Association decided to hold a small invitation tournament over the Memorial Day weekend on the courts at the top of Mt. Washington in East Los Angeles. "The fame of the match," wrote a reporter for *American Lawn Tennis*,

> had been rumored far beyond the one thousand five hundred announcement cards of the tennis managers. The grandstand of one thousand two hundred capacity was crowded beyond standing room. Society was there in full force; automobiles filling every available inch of ground and attentive rooters expressing their excitement in their respective feminine or masculine manners. Even the moving picture photographers were present, recording the progress, in their incessantly whirling machines.[11]

The most famous of the Sutton-Hotchkiss tennis duels in California took place in the finals of the Del Monte tournament in September. "May took the first set 7–5 by running around her backhand," wrote Herbert Warren Wind.

> Hazel fought back to take the second set at 6–4 with a mixture of dropshots and smashes. Feeling that she had May on the run, she was waiting on the baseline, eager to get on with the crucial third set, when May sauntered off the court without a word, announced regally to the umpire that she felt like a cup of tea, deposited herself on a wicker chair, and sat in silence until the waiter appeared from the hotel carrying her tea on a tray. Twenty minutes later, May was ready to resume play, and she pulled out the final set, 6–4. After this controversial episode—the Southern Californians consid-

---

*May Sutton was a supreme winner but Hazel Hotchkiss was probably the finest sportswoman in American tennis.

ered it the resourcefulness of a true champion, the Northern Californians, shocking sportsmanship—there was seldom an empty seat in the stands when the two rivals clashed.[12]

‗‗‗

While Hazel Hotchkiss went on to become one of the finest ladies doubles players of all time and a great benefactor and super-mother of women's tennis in America for more than five decades, May Sutton— U.S. Champion in 1904 and All-England Champion in 1905 and 1907— was the top women's tennis player in the world in 1912; she had beaten each of her two closest rivals, Hazel Hotchkiss and Dorothy Douglas Chambers (seven times All-England Champion) in a majority of their meetings. May was, of course, the first Californian to win a U.S. Singles Championship and the first American to win Wimbledon.

May was the star of the First Family of Southern California tennis. She and her three older sisters—Violet, Florence, and Ethel—won the Southern California Tennis Association (founded 1887) Ladies Singles Championship *every year* between 1899, when Violet first won it, and 1915 when May took the title (May won it again in 1928, four children and 28 years after her first victory in 1900). Not only that. Violet's son, John Hope Doeg, won the Southern California Singles Championship in 1929 and the National Championship at Forest Hills in 1930. May's daughter, Dorothy (Dodo) Bundy, ranked in the First Ten every year except one between 1936 and 1946. As Dorothy Bundy Cheney, moreover, she has had an unmatched record of championships in the various senior divisions.

Three other landmark events in tennis history took place in that *Titanic* year: James Dwight, the father of American lawn tennis, resigned from the presidency of the USNLTA, and May Sutton and Hazel Hotchkiss got married. In June, Hazel Hotchkiss symbolically sealed the new geographical and stylistic diversity of tennis by marrying George Wightman of Boston. He had been a member of the Harvard tennis team in college, was a top-flight court tennis player, and became president of the USLTA in 1924. The young couple settled down near Coolidge Corner and next door to the original Longwood Cricket Club. Mrs. Wightman soon became a do-gooder in the best Boston Brahmin style. She will be most remembered as a promoter of Anglo-American ladies tennis competition.

In 1920, she donated a cup which, much like the Davis Cup, was to promote international tennis among women. The only nation to challenge was England, in 1923, after which the Wightman Cup was competed for by only English and American teams.

In December 1912, May Sutton married Thomas C. Bundy, at Christ Episcopal Church in Los Angeles, in one of the most distinguished Society weddings of the year. Tom Bundy was Southern California's leading player at the time. In 1910 he won the all-comers at Newport and carried William A. Larned to five sets before losing in the challenge round. He and McLoughlin won the men's doubles in 1912, 1913, and 1914. When the famous Los Angeles Tennis Club, which, as will be shown below, produced more world-class tennis champions than any other club in the world under the leadership of Perry Jones, was founded in 1920, Tom Bundy was the first president.

If the Proper Boston Searses produced our first tennis dynasty, the Sutton women of Southern California produced our second. If increasing individualism and the decline of the family continue, tennis dynasties may very well have ended in America with the Searses and the Suttons. As yet there have been no dynasties since. The only family to possibly qualify are the Philadelphia Clothiers who will be discussed below (Chapter 7).*

---

*In Catholic Spain, where the family has not yet been eroded by modernity, the Sanchez family of Barcelona has produced world tennis's latest dynasty. Two brothers, Emilio and Javier, attained high pro rankings in the 1990s (Emilio #8 in 1990 and Javier #32 in 1991). Ever since their younger sister, Arantxa, won the French Open in 1989, she has been at the very top, just a notch behind Steffi Graf of Germany.

The Old Order Changes: Amateurism Becomes an Issue, the Davis Cup Goes Down Under in 1914, and the Championships Are Moved from Newport to Forest Hills

More than any of the great players, Richard Norris Williams views lawn tennis as a game rather than a serious pursuit. Both in strokes and outlook he is the Chevalier Bayard of lawn tennis, preserving a chivalry which, while it may appear old-fashioned in these days of intensive competition, commands the respect of all who know him. He carries the attitude to the point of refusing to lob to an opponent facing the sun or, as a persistent tactic, to one whose smash is weak or off color.

By his perfect example of court manners, unquestioning acceptance of doubtful decisions, and generosity to opponents, he has done as great service to the fair name of American sportsmanship as the Dohertys did for England in earlier years.

—B. H. Liddell Hart, *Lawn Tennis Masters*

WHILE MAURICE MCLOUGHLIN AND OTHER LEADING CALIFORNIANS were revolutionizing the game of tennis, on the lawns of the Eastern Seaboard, the officers of the United States National Lawn Tennis Association (USNLTA) were reacting to changing conditions at their annual February meetings in the transition years of 1912, 1913, 1914, and 1915. The first rule change in 1912 was the abolition of the challenge round in the Men's Singles Championship; the change was made more easily because Larned, having been ranked in the First Ten 19 times since 1892 and having won the Championship seven times, the last five in a row (1907 through 1911), was more than ready to retire from championship tennis; and McLoughlin became the first playthrough winner of the Championship.*

While the elimination of the champion's privilege of standing out was a liberalizing move, it created other problems. The standing-out champion had been in effect the *only* seeded player. Now there were *no* seeded players, and it was theoretically possible for all of the top-ranking players to be in the upper half of the draw and even for the two best players in the tournament to meet in the first or second round. In the first California invasion of the East in 1909, two top Californians, McLoughlin and Melville Long, met in the fourth round, McLoughlin winning in five long sets. At the same time, five of the First Ten (including the first four in rank) were in the upper half of the draw, while only three, including Long and McLoughlin, were in the lower half (two did not compete). It is hard to believe that seeding had rarely come up or had been voted down when it did. Two factors were at least partly responsible. First, the Society crowd at Newport liked the luck-of-the-draw idea because it meant they might see excellent matches, such as the McLoughlin-Long battle, in the early rounds (the Society crowd dictated tennis mores then at Newport somewhat as the TV-money-crowd does today at Flushing Meadow).† Secondly, the United States was much in the

---

*The challenge round was kept in the doubles: traditionally, the doubles were played elsewhere, mostly at Longwood, the playthrough winners coming to Newport where the challenge round was played each year.

†Society values had led to another abuse of pure tennis values at Newport. Many less-than-first-rate players of social standing formally entered the tournament in order to have the privileges of the Casino during this fashionable season. They then often defaulted. The abuse was particularly glaring in 1909, when 156 gentlemen were officially entered, 41 of whom subsequently defaulted.

habit of following the lead of the British, and their LTA had brought up the question of both seeding and the abolition of the challenge round at their annual meeting in 1911. Both had been voted down.*

It should be noted at this point that, while the United States eliminated the challenge round in 1912, the British did not do so until 1922, in their first Championship at the new Wimbledon, on Church Road (Tilden, who won the last championships at Marple Road, stayed in America and was not available to defend). In that same year, at the Germantown Cricket Club, in Philadelphia, our National Championship was seeded for the first time; Wimbledon followed suit in 1924.

In the course of human history, unwritten customs and traditions tend to rule until they are questioned or become suspect and the enactment of written laws becomes necessary; thus Papal infallibility was assumed for generations before the Vatican Council felt the need to institute it by decree in 1870. The British, with their famous unwritten constitution, have always preferred tradition to legislation; we Americans, who have always been weak in tradition, have felt safer with clearly written laws. In the same way British lawn tennis had never felt any need for a written definition of amateurism until 1910, when the Olympic Council asked the Lawn Tennis Association for a definition of the amateur lawn tennis player. That same year some amateurs had been suspended by the LTA because they exchanged tournament prizes for "consumable goods."† At the annual meeting of the LTA in 1911, a rather severe definition of amateurism was drawn up. In America, as early as 1882, the USNLTA ruled that "none but amateurs should be allowed to enter for any match play by this association." At the same time, the by-laws included a rather loose

---

*Tony Wilding, Wimbledon Champion in 1911, was strongly in favor of abolishing the Challenge Round, should the LTA authorize a change in the rule. At the same time, he was against seeding and in favor of the luck-of-the-draw.

†It is of interest that in the days of assumed amateurism, a sporting goods industry in tennis began when the Bancroft brothers started their racket factory in Pawtucket, Rhode Island, in 1882. Soon they were naming their rackets after famous champions whose pictures, along with those of professional baseball stars, appeared on cards advertising smoking tobacco. Champions like Richard Sears and Henry Slocum, aristocrats of unquestionable amateur status, were opening the door for professional endorsements, which practice is now running wild, decorating (or desecrating) the clothes of the better players on the pro circuit.

definition of amateurism until 1913 when a new and draconian code was proposed at the annual meeting of the association in February.

The main business of the annual meeting that year was the discussion and ratification of a new constitution and by-laws which were published ahead of time in the January (1913) issue of *American Lawn Tennis* magazine, the official organ of the association. Since the definition of amateurism, included in Article II of the revised by-laws, proved to be the major issue at the February meetings, the entire article is shown in Figure 4.

The main issue proved to be centered on items 4 and 5 of section 4, as S. W. Merrihew, the publisher and editor of *American Lawn Tennis*, revealed in the following editorial in the January issue:

FIGURE 4

USNLTA Definition of Amateurism, 1913

ARTICLE II.

Sec. 1. All clubs represented in this Association shall be governed by the laws of Lawn Tennis as laid down by this association.

Sec. 2. Laws of Matches, etc.—All matches played by clubs represented in this association shall be played under all the rules adopted by it.

Sec. 3. None but amateurs shall be allowed to enter for any match or matches played under the auspices of this association.

Section 4. An amateur is one who

1. Has never entered a competition open only to professionals nor played for a money prize, public or admission money, or entrance fee.

2. Has not played, instructed, pursued or assisted in the pursuit of tennis or other athletic exercise as a means of livelihood or for gain or any emolument.

3. Did not obtain and does not retain membership in any tennis or athletic club of any kind because of any mutual understanding, express or implied, whereby such membership would be of any pecuniary benefit to the member or the club.

4. Is not connected with the sale of tennis goods, nor with a firm manufacturing or selling tennis goods, except when such connection shall be of a general nature in a firm manufacturing or selling general athletic goods and the person so connected has to do with tennis goods to no greater extent than with any other line of goods.

5. Has never accepted, from any hotel, club, or similar organization, at which or in connection with which a tennis tournament is being held, transportation or money for transportation or board, lodging or other general living accommodations, or money to cover any or all of the same, or any secret or exceptional reduced rate in connection with such tournament. The interpretation of this rule shall not prevent a player from taking advantage of a reasonable special rate from such hotel, club or similar organization, if such special rate is properly announced and is open to any one entering the tennis tournament.

6. Has never sold, pledged or otherwise converted into money any prize won in a tennis tournament, or converted any prize so won into any article or articles, commonly known as necessities, such as food, ordinary clothing, etc., or accepted as a prize any such article.

7. After doing or committing any of the foregoing acts has been reinstated as an amateur by the Executive Committee of the U. S. N. L. T. A.

The Executive Committee of the U. S. N. L. T. A. shall be the tribunal to decide whether a player is a professional or an amateur.

Note: Any infraction of the above rules previous to February 14th, 1913, shall not constitute a player a professional unless such action would also have been an infraction of the laws in force prior to that date.

Sec. 5.—No player shall be allowed to enter for any match given by this Association unless he is a member of a club belonging either directly to this association, or indirectly as specified in Article II, Section 2, of the Constitution, or has played in an interscholastic tournament of the same year. But the Executive Committee is empowered, at its discretion, to permit, for special cause, any foreigners or other players to enter for any match given under the auspices of this association.

The adoption of a new constitution and by-laws by the U.S.N.L.T.A. is a step of great importance. . . . It is unquestionably a great improvement over the present antiquated constitution and by-laws, and as to its main provisions there will be little difference of opinion. Its most important changes are a slight increase in the dues of both the principal classes of membership, and increase in the executive committee and the districting of the country to provide for this increase, and the putting forth of a Draconian amateur rule. It is the last named that will be most criticized and discussed. It has been very carefully framed and with full knowledge of its revolutionary character; and presumably, therefore, it has very strong backing. But that it will be strongly opposed we have not the slightest doubt. We do not believe that it is needed or that it will, if adopted, work to the interests of the game. It reminds us of the man who was so anxious to walk erect that he leaned backwards. We do not see why, for example, the head of a firm making or selling *tennis goods* should be denied amateurship while a competitor who makes or sells tennis *and* general athletic goods is granted it. Nor do we see why a club should be prohibited from "putting up" players, as the Meadow Club of Southampton does; or even from furnishing them transportation. There may be abuses of these practices, but in such case regulation would be vastly better than prohibition.[1]

The annual meeting of the USNLTA was called to order at four o'clock on Friday, February 14. Former champion Robert D. Wrenn, who had followed James Dwight in the presidency, was in the chair. Routine business as well as matters which come before the meetings every year were rapidly taken care of in order to allow the maximum time for a thorough discussion of the revisions of the constitution and the by-laws. Former champion and vice president Henry W. Slocum, chairman of the Revision Committee, opened the discussion. As it turned out, the revised constitution was passed without much discussion, as were all of the by-laws except items 4 and 5 of Article II, section 4, on the definition of amateurism. While the revision of an item on players' connections to sporting goods houses was passed surprisingly quickly, a second item on expenses took up most of the rest of the meeting. As might be expected, the Californians were the most affected by this rule which was also objected to by many delegates at the meeting, as well as in letters from such leaders in California as Dr. Sumner Hardy who immediately saw how the revised rule would virtually stop the California invasion of the Eastern establishment. A sympathetic delegate from Pittsburgh read a letter from a leading California player who, wishing to remain anonymous, wrote:

> Those who are familiar with the conditions governing tennis in California know full well that the passing of this amateur rule will prevent a California invasion, despite the statement of the revision committee to the contrary. . . . Almost, if not nearly all, of the matches which will decide which California players are to come East each year are played in Los Angeles or thereabouts. The players from other parts of the state are invited to Southern California and their entertainment and transportation provided for by the Southern California clubs and hotels. The gate derived from the attendance at these matches provides the funds for these expenses, and also for sending the winning team in doubles and the champion in singles to the Eastern tournaments, where they have so far been successful in establishing themselves as champions, and incidentally, swelling the gate receipts at Longwood and Newport. If Los Angeles is to be prevented from extending this courtesy to the other California players, it may easily be seen what becomes of one, at least, of our present champions, in both singles and doubles. Few of the Eastern tournament holders have so far seen fit to tender any courtesies in this direction, and under the new laws would not be allowed to do so, even though the desire were apparent at any time.[2]

The delegates were unable to agree on an appropriate resolution of the travel and expenses issue, and a committee was duly appointed to come up with a new proposal at the annual meeting in February 1914. The facsimile of the editorial page of *American Lawn Tennis* nicely sums up the climate of opinion in this amateur age of innocence, in the winter of 1913 (see Figure 5).

The problem of amateurism was one of the main reasons for forming some sort of official organization to regulate the game internationally. Although the British and American lawn tennis associations, as well as similar associations in other countries, had been formed in the nineteenth century, the British LTA had always been unofficially recognized as the parent body with rights to make up the rules of the game until 1913. In that year, at a meeting in Paris on March 1, the International Lawn Tennis Federation was organized. Since the USNLTA had not yet agreed on

FIGURE 5
Definition of Amateurism, 1913

AMERICAN LAWN TENNIS

Official Organ of United States
National Lawn Tennis Association

Vol. VI   FEBRUARY 15, 1913   No. 14

Published monthly, October to June; semi-monthly, July, August and September

Publishing Office: Singer Building, 149 Broadway, New York City
Tel. Cortlandt 6941

S. W. MERRIHEW . . . . Publisher and Editor

Entered at the New York Post Office as Second Class Matter

TERMS OF SUBSCRIPTION

United States, per Year...$2.00
Foreign, per Year...2.60
Single Copies..15
American Lawn Tennis can be ordered through the American News Company

THE NEXT ISSUE WILL BE THAT OF MARCH 15.

Productive to a marked degree was the annual meeting of the lawn tennis governing body last week. Furthermore there was practical unanimity on nearly all subjects discussed or acted upon, and the delegates were clearly earnest, intelligent and thoroughly representative of the best there is in lawn tennis taken as a whole. There were, as is natural, marked differences of opinion regarding some matters, and few of the delegates hesitated to express their views or to set forth their arguments with vigor. There were tense periods, and on a few occasions personalities were dealt in. But in spite of the strong feelings aroused everybody kept within bounds and the bitterness that some expected to develop did not materialize. Subjects which in former years had afforded grounds for controversy—such as the selection of Newport for the Championship and the report of the Ranking Committee—were disposed of with dispatch and with practically no differences of opinion. In short, the delegates were a deliberate body, seriously inclined and anxious to accelerate matters wherever possible.

A Productive Body

We are in hearty sympathy with the efforts of the revision committee and the executive committee to retain the amateur spirit in lawn tennis in all its pristine purity. We believe that the game should be confined to real amateurs—men who play the game for the love of it and without hope or desire of gain. We take pride in the fact that in all the years lawn tennis has been played the element of professionalism has either been entirely absent or has manifested itself timidly and been promptly scotched. We point to the almost entire absence of scandal in the history of the game in this country, and believe that there have been cases where a few players *could* have been proceeded against with the entire approval of the lawn tennis world. But we do not believe that it is either necessary or desirable to strike a blow at the tournaments of today that in some cases would be mortal and in nearly all severe. We believe that the game is destined to grow in popularity and that as the years pass thousands of men and women now ignorant of its healthfulness and general goodness will become possessed of knowledge and become as keen players as those of today. We believe furthermore that it is injudicious, if not actually wrong, to say to a club that it shall not entertain as its guests players who, at considerable inconvenience and expense, favor them with their presence. As long as lawn tennis players are gentlemen who play the game for the pure love of it, just so long will they be welcome at the tournaments of the future as they have been at those of the past. Finally, we do not think that it should be made impossible for players with moderate incomes (or no incomes at all, as in the case of very young men) to attend a few tournaments each season as the guests of clubs which are delighted to have them.

The Amateur Spirit

Source: American Lawn Tennis, January 15, 1913.

a definition of amateurism at their annual meeting a month earlier, they sent no official delegate to Paris. The USNLTA was, nevertheless, included among the founders as informal members without a vote. The definition of "amateurism" was to plague the ILTF for many years to come.

At the annual meeting of the USNLTA in February 1914, a debate arose as to the reimbursement of expenses, which produced an extensive discussion. The best speech of the evening was made by a young Texan who was teaching English literature at the College of the City of New York:

It seems to me that we would be directly opposed to the trend of the times in athletics were we to adopt any drastic rule [against expense reimbursement] for lawn tennis.

I have had to review the matter of amateur athletics a good deal in connection with school and college athletics, with which I have been somewhat connected, and I know that we are undergoing a gradual transition in regard to our ideas, at least so far as school and college athletics are concerned. The fact is that most of the modern amateur standards arose in England, where amateur athletics were of course the only athletics that counted in matters of this sort to a leisure class. Now, we have a very different society in this country, for in this country even wealthy men usually work. That makes a good deal of difference, for even if a man's traveling expenses and living expenses are paid, he is contributing his time, which has a money value in most cases exceeding by a good deal his traveling expenses and his living expenses, and we all know that even if those expenses are paid there are other incidental expenses. So, from the financial point of view, a man is still much out of pocket if he does take advantage of such payments. Even in England itself, owing to the gradual inroads of democracy, we begin to see some changes, and in this country it has been brought to a head in regard to the college and in regard to the matter of summer baseball.

As we all know, one of the knotty points of recent years has been in regard to the college boy going out and playing baseball for a little money during the summer months. Now, a few years ago there were very few persons who avowedly stood for pure amateur athletics who would countenance such a thing at all. I can well remember that when it was first proposed that any such thing be allowed, I thought that that was a terrible thing, but I know that my own ideas have been undergoing transformation. I know that many reputable institutions which have usually upheld high amateur standards are now at a point where they are ready to let the boys play for money on a baseball team during summer months, go back to college and play on the college teams, provided that they are bona fide students. That is where, so far as college athletics are concerned, England has recognized that this matter of amateur athletics is not a matter of laws and rules, but a matter of spirit. We are beginning to see that it is a very foolish thing to debar a boy from participating in college athletics because he once pitched a baseball game in Podunk and received five dollars for it.

In other words, I think the general opinion throughout our country is coming to be that a man is a professional who gets his livelihood, or any considerable part of it, by following athletics. If he does not do that, he is an amateur. Why, this proposed—the originally proposed amendment is far more drastic than that prevailing in any other branch of athletics in this country. What is there about the game of tennis that should set it apart from all other amateur athletics, and make it a thing apart, to make necessary a rule very much more drastic than that obtaining in every branch of sports? Take the Amateur Athletic Union. Why is there any doubt entertained there that a man has the right to expenses? (Applause)[3]

In the end, a looser standard of reimbursement won out in a proxy vote by the close margin of 82–79. While the 1914 meeting of the USNLTA had come to an agreement on the definition of amateurism, the issue was to plague the amateur game for over half a century. In many ways, as the proportion of independently wealthy players declined, amateurism may very well have been doomed. Never again could any American write, as S. W. Merrihew did in his *ALT* editorial of 1913, of "the almost entire absence of scandal in the history of the game in this country."

═══

Maurice McLoughlin was undoubtedly the most famous American tennis player in the world by the end of 1912. When he went to Wimbledon in the spring of 1913 his fame had preceded him and his first-round match, on the Center Court against Roper Barrett, drew an overflowing crowd. He won the match at 8–6 in the fifth set and then went on, without losing a set in his next four matches, to become the first American to play in the challenge round. The Center Court was packed, hundreds were turned away, and ticket scouts were asking ten pounds a seat. He was beaten by Tony Wilding in three close sets.

McLoughlin had come to London at the same time as both the American and Australasian Davis Cup teams. In early June, America played the Australasians at the West Side Tennis Club, in Van Cortlandt Park, New York. Since Brookes had remained in Melbourne and Wilding had stayed on in London, the Australasian team of Captain Stanley Doust, Horace Rice, and A. B. Jones was easily defeated (4–1) by McLoughlin, Williams, and Harold Hacket. Soon after Wimbledon, America defeated the German Davis Cup team at Nottingham (5–0).

At the end of July, on the Center Court at Wimbledon, the American team won a narrow (3–2) victory over the British in the challenge round. It was one of the closest matches in the history of the Davis Cup, with four of the five matches going to five sets. McLoughlin lost the first match to J. Cecil Parke in five sets, while Williams beat Charles Palmer Dixon in five on the second day, Hacket and McLoughlin won the doubles from Roper Barrett and Dixon in five. Finally, on the third day, McLoughlin defeated Dixon in three sets and Parke defeated Williams in five. The victory was especially sweet because the United States had not won the Davis Cup since 1902. After American victories in 1900 and 1902, Great Britain won it five times and Australasia four times in the next nine years of competition. When the team returned to New York a fine formal dinner was held at Delmonico's to celebrate the victory.

In late August, McLoughlin beat Williams in the finals of the National Championship at Newport. The most interesting match in the tournament came in the fourth round when Dick Williams defeated a future national champion from California, William M. Johnston. A product of the Golden Gate Park courts in San Francisco, little Billy Johnston was only 18 and weighed 122 pounds when he came East in July. In his first tournament, he defeated the old champion, William J. Clothier, in the finals of the Longwood Bowl, in five furious sets. He was defeated by Clothier a week later at Southampton in another five-set final. At the end of the 1913 season, Billy Johnston ranked number three. McLoughlin was ranked number one for the second year in a row (he and Bundy again won the doubles title), and the Californians reigned supreme at the top of American lawn tennis.

The last months of peace leading up to August 4, 1914, when the German armies crossed the Belgian frontier and Great Britain officially declared war, were surely symbolic and eventful ones in lawn tennis history. By the first Monday in March, Germany, France, Belgium, Canada, Australasia, and the British Isles had officially challenged for the Davis Cup. Tony Wilding dominated the last prewar Riviera Season, beating Norman Brookes the only two times they met. In the first week in June, Wilding won the World Hard Court Championship at St. Cloud near Paris, and, most astonishingly, a young French child of 13, Suzanne Lenglen, won the women's singles and doubles (with Elizabeth Ryan, of California).* At Wimbledon, the invincible Champion of four years, Tony Wilding, lost his title to his Davis Cup partner, Norman Brookes. Finally, as war was raging in Europe, the Australasian Davis Cup Team defeated the United States team at the new West Side Tennis Club in Forest Hills and took the historic trophy down under for the duration.

Early in 1914, both Norman Brookes and Anthony Wilding announced that they were to be available to play in the Davis Cup matches, wherever they might be held. They decided to train on the Riviera, where Tony had been the social lion for several seasons. Sometime in February, Brookes, with his young wife Mabel, a one-month-old baby in a basket, and a nurse, left Melbourne for the fourteen-thousand-mile voyage to Europe. After landing in Naples, the whole menage went straight to the Hotel Beau Site in Nice. While Norman was playing in every available tournament, Mabel was avidly absorbed in the beautiful people of that day, Greek syndicate gamblers, kings, Russian grand dukes, rich merchants, smart French types from Paris, all leavened by solid English families of more famous names and much more money.

If Mabel Brookes was impressed with the glitter and style of the Riviera world that last prewar winter, she was even more impressed with the simple ways of the aged Lord Balfour, the last aristocratic amateur (unpaid) Prime Minister of Britain. "He was a mixture of the very simple and the very great," she wrote in her memoirs. "Usually when alone in Cannes he sat for *déjeuner* at our table and ate a frugal meal. He was sincerely attached to Tony and Norman, and played both tennis and golf with them, basking in their physical youth and strength." Tony and Balfour won the doubles handicap tournament at Monte Carlo that winter. (It was Balfour, in fact, who coined the term "lawn tennis" to differentiate the new game from real or court tennis.)

After a winter on the red courts of the Riviera and the hard courts of Paris in the early spring, Norman and Tony were glad to get back to English grass

---

*The tournament was run by the newly founded ILTF and the winner of the ladies' singles was awarded the Coupe Duane Williams, in memory of Dick's father who had done so much to bring such a federation into being before his going down on the *Titanic*.

in the several county tournaments preceding the London Championship (at the Queens Club) and the Wimbledon fortnight. Norman won at Surbiton and Beckenham, adding two bowls to his trophy collection. He was now quite up to the final Wimbledon test which he passed in a final blaze of glory.

This last, prewar Wimbledon championship attracted an entry of 102 gentlemen. Brookes, who had not been to Wimbledon since his sweep of the singles, doubles, and mixed doubles in 1907, played in fine form from the beginning, winning his first three matches in straight sets, six of them at love. In the quarterfinals, he beat the former Wimbledon winner, Arthur Gore, and in the semis beat A. E. Beamish.

In the all-comers final, Brookes beat Otto Froitzheim, once Chief of Police at Wiesbaden, an officer on the Kaiser's staff, and the best player in Germany for almost twenty years. The German's game most resembled that of Lacoste in its patient precision. Brookes then beat Wilding in the challenge round. These two matches were among the greatest in Wimbledon history and have been written about, in *American Lawn Tennis*, by a great Australian sportswriter. While reading the lengthy but beautifully written, point-by-point description of the Brookes-Froitzheim match, I was struck, time and again, how very similar this match was to the famous Borg-McEnroe 1980 Wimbledon final. In native skill alone, Brookes and McEnroe, in my opinion, were more alike than any other two players in history.

———

In 1914, the main topic of conversation in American tennis circles was the Davis Cup. After Norman Brookes and Tony Wilding announced in January that they were planning to play, all looked forward to the challenge round when the four leading tennis players in the world, McLoughlin and Williams of the United States and Norman Brookes and Tony Wilding of Australasia would undoubtedly be facing each other.

The six challenging nations began their elimination matches in early July. Germany had earlier withdrawn from competition but had reconsidered after Froitzheim had done so well at Wimbledon. The British Isles first defeated the Belgians at Folkstone and then went on to defeat the French at Wimbledon. In the meantime, the Australasian team came to America and first defeated the Canadians at the Onwentsia Club, in Chicago's most fashionable suburb of Lake Forest. They next met the Germans at the Allegheny Country Club, in Sewickley, the iron and steel barons' favorite suburb of Pittsburgh. The matches were played on July 30, 31 and August 1. After the Austrian Archduke Ferdinand was assassinated at Sarajevo on June 28, and Austria declared war on Serbia on July 28, everyone knew that the outbreak of war was only a matter of hours; the Germans announced that they would at once cease play; the club managers and the spectators prayed that the last two matches would be finished before a German declaration of war. Brookes and Froitzheim met in the first match. The German, playing flawlessly, got off to a 5–2 start in the first set. The applause was tremendous, and wild cheering followed every winning German stroke. There was dead silence at each of the Australian's fabulous volleys. But after Froitzheim won the first set at 10–8, it was all Brookes; Froitzheim had nothing left. Wilding beat Kreutzer with the loss of only eight games, and on the second day, the Australasians won the doubles easily.

Though merely a formality, the third day's matches were to be played as planned. The club president feared interruption, and telephone lines were cut off and newspapermen excluded from the club. Sometime during the afternoon, while both Wilding and Brookes were easily winning their matches, news reached the club that Germany had declared war on Imperial Russia. As the last ball was played, a megaphone announced the sad news to a silent crowd. The German team hurried to board a ship for home. They were taken off their boat by a British warship, interned in Gibraltar, and later taken to England where they spent the rest of the war. The Australasians also hurried off, first to Niagara Falls, and then to Boston where they defeated the British team in three straight matches at the Longwood Cricket Club.

The challenge round at Forest Hills was one of the more memorable in Davis Cup history. It was the first world-class tennis event ever played at the new home of the West Side Tennis Club. The Tudor-like clubhouse, newly sowed grass courts, and temporary wooden stands which, along with the clubhouse seats, accommodated some twelve thousand spectators, were all completed in a little over a year after the United States Davis Cup team defeated the Aussies in June 1913 at the West Side courts in Van Cortlandt Park at 238th Street. It was only after completely inspecting the grass that the Davis Cup committee officially awarded Forest Hills the privilege of holding the challenge round matches, which were to be played on Thursday, Friday and Saturday, August 13, 14, and 15. The American team was composed of McLoughlin and Bundy from California, and the two *Titanic* survivors, Williams, of Philadelphia and Karl Behr, of New York. The Australasians, led by Captain Brookes and Tony Wilding, also included A. W. Dunlop and S. Doust.

The stage was set on Thursday afternoon: the weather was perfect. More than twelve thousand people, the largest crowd ever to watch tennis, overflowed the stands. In the first match, Wilding rather easily disposed of Williams. Then the legendary Brookes and the new idol of American tennis, McLoughlin, came on the court and produced one of the finest Davis Cup matches of all time. No one who saw the match would ever forget it. It began Al Laney's love affair with the game of tennis.* It was a battle of youth and power against wizardly court craft and experience. Games followed service to nine–all in the first set; Brookes had his chance in the eighteenth game when he reached 40–love on McLoughlin's service, but Mac served three aces and then went on to win the game. The battle of the services continued; the crisis came in the thirty-first game: Brookes, serving, got to 40–15 but lost the game; Mac ran out the set with two aces in the next game. He then took the next two sets and the match, 6–3, 6–3. Many persons at the time said that the brilliance and popularity of this dramatic match became one of the clinching arguments for moving the National Championship from Newport to Forest Hills in 1915.

McLoughlin and Bundy, on the second day, lost the doubles match to the best team in the world, Brookes and Wilding. On the third day, the first match between Brookes and Williams was to decide the fate of the cup for the duration of the war. Brookes raced through the first three games and was never headed, winning the first two sets at 6–1, 6–2, Williams making many errors and double-faults. In the third set, however, Williams regained his touch and carried Brookes to 7–all, when he lost his service and, most thought, the match; but Williams pulled out the set at 10–8. "The Gallery went wild," wrote the American tennis journalist, Edward C. Potter Jr.,

and was in commotion from the time Williams launched his attack. Williams ran to the dressing room as soon as set point was scored, but

---

*Al Laney, *Covering the Courts: 50-Year Love Affair with the Game of Tennis* (1968). This delightful classic will be referred to throughout this book, especially in Chapter 11.

Brookes remained. The applause continued and intensified and Brookes was annoyed by it. He put his hands to his ears, which had the effect of redoubling the pandemonium. It was not until he took his hands away and went to the dressing room that the gallery calmed down. When play was resumed, Williams lost his touch. Brookes was grim and relentless and forced the fight, taking Williams' serve in the ninth game for the set and match, which gave the cup to Australasia.[4]

Many years later, in her book *Crowded Galleries*, Dame Mabel Brookes described the Brookes-Williams match rather more dramatically than Potter. One must recall that, in 1914, the average member of the upper-class crowd at Newport was an Anglophile, while the average American at that time was an Anglophobe. Dame Mabel, who had written rather bitterly of the pro-German and anti-"Limey" values of the crowd at the Davis Cup matches in Pittsburgh, wrote of this deciding match at Forest Hills as follows:

The final day was as stifling as New York can turn on in August. The stands, holding 14,000 people, were packed with hatless, white-shirted men and brightly dressed women, and the kaleidoscope of color rose up steeply, enclosing the tennis-courts in an airless pit. On the side nearest the clubhouse, a special stand with official boxes had been erected, and I was assigned one near the service line. The feverish tension of the crowd was almost tangible and even the tennis officials reflected the tempo. War had not touched them at that period; America was determined not to join in any European conflict, and her sympathies were not necessarily pro-British. That we were Australians had no significance in those days. We were "Limeys" to the man on the bleachers, and there was no sentimental pull. The only thing that mattered was that U.S.A. should hold the Cup. . . .

Norman, playing like a machine, won the first two sets, 6–2, 6–3. The crowd, after the first few games, settled down to watch just another tennis match with the Master giving a lesson to a younger player who knew some of the answers but not enough to pull the game his way. The applause was generous, but lacking in fire, for all the while they saw the Davis Cup being again packed up. It stood on a table behind the umpire's chair—symbolic of a nation's supremacy in the world of tennis, and in the collective opinion of the crowd, rapidly being regained by the "Limeys." Then Norman dropped a service and Williams, a keen fine player, full of tennis lore, put on the pace, kept his own service and captured another of Norman's. The crowd took a hand in proceedings. They queried the umpire's and the linesmen's decisions, they shouted encouragement to their side and loudly called "out" to all Norman's subsequent line-balls. They shouted on the impact of service, groaned at a point won, and behaved as if all baseball and football crowds had joined in a concerted rooting match. Norman hung on, but the din broke his concentration and on some occasions he was at a loss to know if the crowd or the umpire had called "fault." Williams, keen for the set, kept up the pressure and finally won it, 10–8, in an uproar that seemed not possible from only 14,000 throats. Norman—drooping, distressed, his concentration wrecked—stood on the base-line while the upsurge of sound broke over him; then, placing his racquet and ball (he had been serving) on the grass, stuffed his fingers in his ears.

From then on there was pandemonium—bottles bowled across the court, the crowd howled anew, some jumped over the barriers, followed by the police. Lindley Murray (the next U.S. champion) was sitting below me as umpire on the base-line, and I leaned down and in the din pointed to Norman, still standing fingers in ears. He understood, ran across and brought Norman back to the side-lines. In dumb show I indicated the club-house, where Dick Williams had already gone for the short third-set interval of rest, and pulled out his soggy shirt to remind him to change. Lindley Murray went with him and the crowd ceased shouting and commenced to simmer down. Cramped with sitting and excitement, they milled about the hot-dog stands, and drank soda-pop and smoked while groundsmen cleaned up the court and re-marked the base-lines. I sat alone, confused by the almost inhuman display, too young to feel anything but fright and resentment. The unbridled feeling had not scared Norman, however—he was fighting mad. I dared not think what was going to happen in the final stages of the game. Presently the galleries resettled in their places to await the end of the interval.

Dick Williams came on the court amid cheers, and a minute afterwards, Norman. As he passed by the Davis Cup he gave it a little reassuring pat and a twirl which was, I knew, quite unpremeditated. Once more he had regained his poise, and there would have to be more than shouting and pop bottles to get him rattled. There was a moment's silence as he passed the Cup and came on to the court. Then the crowds recognized that all they had done was yet not enough, and he was returning, unbeaten, for more;

and they started to applaud and the noise rose in volume until the cheering voices became a roar, and I held on to the side of the box and wondered at the dramatic change of heart in fourteen thousand people. A ball-boy handed Norman his discarded racquet and the sound from the gallery lifted almost to hysteria. It was an ovation, a recognition of pure fighting guts. It was also hard on Dick Williams. He played well and doggedly, but the end was in sight. The crowd knew it and so did Norman. The show was virtually over, and it was a tame finale, almost an anticlimax. Tony, beaten by Maurice McLoughlin three sets to one, left immediately for England to enlist. We followed in three days. . . . on the *Mauritania* in an unaccustomed blackout, leaving the Davis Cup behind in safety. We were given a luxury suite, for there were exactly nineteen passengers on board.[5]

Beneath the sociological and historical surfaces of life, as the French say, the more things change the more they remain the same. Dame Mabel's possibly biased account of Forest Hills in 1914 might well have described the goings-on at Flushing Meadow in our day. Similarly, in reading the *New York Times* for those Challenge Round days in August 1914, I could not help noticing other reminders of French wisdom: among them, an article, "More Marines in Nicaragua," which noted that we were sending fifty-seven officers and men down there in anticipation of trouble; another, "Baby in Furnace Five Days," noted that a maid at 247 West 72nd Street had hidden her unwanted baby in the furnace; or, "Wild Negro Chef Kills 6, Wounds 4: Slays One After the Other." So much for the theory of the good old days when lawn tennis spectators all behaved like ladies and gentlemen, and before the world went mad.

After beating Wilding in the last match of the challenge round, McLoughlin was universally recognized as the tennis champion of the world. But he came and went like the comet he was often called, for he lost the championship to Williams at the end of August and never again won an important match. For Wilding the match marked the end of all fun and games. On the evening of May 8, 1915, in a trench near Neuve Chapelle, Belgium, he was talking tennis with a friend, reliving that final match against the Comet. "We can't always be at our best," he concluded with a tired smile as he dropped off to sleep. The next morning, his body was pulled out of the trench in a mixture of shrapnel, earth, and sandbags, and a gold cigarette case, given him by Craig Biddle, fell out of his pocket.

It is surprising how little first-class tennis in America was affected by the First World War. After all we were in it for a very brief time. Nevertheless, the fact that so many of the players had such worthy war records was noticed by all at the time.

———

Moving the National Championship from Newport to New York was undoubtedly the most important change from the old order in lawn tennis to the new. As there had been agitation for some years to make this important move, the Newport people made every effort to make this year's tournament the best ever. And it was. President Wrenn of the USNLTA was in charge and his control of every detail was never relaxed. For years, due to the leisured habits of the Society crowd, play had been limited to mornings before lunch; many matches this year were scheduled in the afternoon. High barriers were erected behind the baselines of the championship court so that strolling ladies in brightly colored parasols would not spoil the players' vision, as in previous years. A thousand extra seats were available in new stands, making for a capacity crowd of four thousand (compared to the twelve thousand at Forest Hills). The turf was also improved and played truer than ever.

It was surely appropriate that R. Norris Williams, the last aristocratic millionaire tennis champion, won the last National Championship to be played at Newport, beating his friend McLoughlin in straight sets in the finals. Nobody expected him to beat Mac, few even expected him to take a set. After all, Mac had played brilliantly all season, taking the only matches against Australasia in the Davis Cup. The two friends, moreover, had met four times in their careers, Mac winning them all—at Bayridge and Newport in 1912, in the Newport finals in 1913, and at the recent Longwood tournament. But Dick played well all week, losing only one set in the whole tournament to Billy Johnston in his first match (such was the luck-of-the-draw that year).

And so ended, after thirty-four years, the last predominantly upper-class season in American tennis. The genteel traditions of Newport were soon to be replaced by the commercial traditions of New York. The final decision on this fateful move was to be made at the annual meetings of the USNLTA in New York City the following February.

For most of the years when the U.S. National Championship was being held at Newport, the best tennis in New York City was played at the West Side Tennis Club which was founded in 1892. The club was first located on Central Park West between 88th and 89th Streets. After six years, due to population pressure, the location became too valuable and the club moved to 117th Street, near Columbia University, where it remained for a decade before moving to 238th Street and Broadway, in what is now Van Cortlandt Park. The property was the size of two city blocks and it looked as if the club was now to have a permanent home. As the members wanted a club of national and international standing with the best facilities in the world, a substantial clubhouse, a dozen grass courts, and fifteen clay courts were eventually built. The club began as an all-male club (with no family memberships, but a limited number of women players were allowed their own membership) and remained so throughout the amateur era. Membership was based on congeniality and the ability to play good tennis. It was the only first-rate club in America devoted exclusively to tennis. As we have seen, Davis Cup matches were held at the club in 1911 and again in 1913.

But when the Van Cortlandt estate wanted their property for other uses, another move became necessary. After a thorough search, the club decided on a ten-acre plot of ground adjacent to the railroad station at Forest Hills, Long Island, which was purchased in 1913 for $75,000. Forest Hills, part of the Anglo-American garden city movement of that day, was planned by Frederick Law Olmstead for the Russell Sage Foundation Homes Company. It was to be an ordered, "homogeneous and congenial community" of neo-Tudor-style homes. In simple fact, by gentleman's agreement, it was a white Protestant community built in an age when thousands of immigrants from Southern and Eastern Europe were passing through Ellis Island to New York. The Long Island Railroad tunnel had recently been completed, and it was a fifteen-minute ride from Penn Station, the Eastern Seaboard railroad center of the nation. As we have seen, the present Tudor-style clubhouse and courts were completed in time for the Davis Cup matches against Australasia in August 1914. After the success of the matches, it was obvious to a majority of American tennis players that Forest Hills was the logical place to hold the National Championship, but it took a while for logic to win out over sentiment.

Many leading tennis players, including Maurice McLoughlin, although he was too polite to say so publicly, wanted the Nationals moved out of the stultifying Society atmosphere of Newport. The matter, however, was not brought up officially until the annual meetings of the USNLTA in 1911; nothing was done that year. S. W. Merrihew, in his February editorial in *ALT*, commented at length on the annual meeting, from which I quote the following:

> No one will attempt to deny the force of sentiment; and Newport is almost all sentiment. . . . No one who has come under the spell of Newport can ever forget it; and therefore nothing but solid reasons will avail to bring about a change.
>
> Yet when we put the arguments against Newport in the scale—as we must—we find ourselves swayed in the other direction. . . . That we must make a change seems to be certain; but when it is made it should be for the better, a change that will rebound to the good of lawn tennis the country over.[6]

Nothing was done for three years. At the annual meeting in 1915, however, all the forces for both permanence and change came to a head now that there was a concrete alternative to Newport at Forest Hills. The Forest Hills members, led by Julian Myrick, who had run the recent Davis Cup matches flawlessly and was eventually to be president of both the USLTA* and the West Side Club, had lobbied for the change to New York for some years. Everybody who came to the annual meeting at the Waldorf-Astoria in February was ready to discuss the proposed move to New York.

In advance of the annual meeting, the forces in favor of New York organized a "Tennis Players' Committee" of ten men, eight from New York plus Dwight F. Davis of St. Louis and Clarence J. Griffin from San Francisco. Two lawyers who had always been active in USNLTA affairs, Karl Behr and Lyle Mahan† of New York, led the committee which first circulated a letter

---

*The "N" or National was dropped in 1920, and the "L" for Lawn in 1975, when the stadium courts at Forest Hills were changed from grass to clay. It is the United States Tennis Association today.

†Lyle Mahan was not a top tennis player but was active in tennis circles, at Newport and New York. His famous father, Alfred Thayer Mahan, had been president of the Naval War College at Newport, among many other accomplishments. He was also an intimate friend of both Theodore Roosevelt and Henry Cabot Lodge. Lyle was a graduate of Groton and Harvard.

outlining the reasons for the change and asking the member clubs to vote directly by proxy in favor. There followed a kind of lawyer's brief outlining the advantages of New York which is summed up as follows:

1. Tennis is now national in extent.
2. New York is the playing center of the nation: of the 100 players ranked this year, 58 were from the New York area, 13 from New England, 13 from the Middle West, 6 from the Coast, and 8 from the South. Only 36 ranked men played at Newport this year; 70 or more would have played at Forest Hills.
3. New York is the Railroad Center of the Nation. Newport is two train rides and a boat ride from New York.
4. Playing conditions: Only the championship court at Newport is of top rank in terms of turf and background; but even there, between the hours of eleven and twelve when all important matches are played, the sun shines directly in to the eyes of the player in the north court. The other courts have inferior turf and no backgrounds except moving spectators, mostly society women.
5. The new West Side Club has better playing conditions—27 courts better than the average at Newport and six championship courts better than the one at Newport. Stands for twelve thousand compared to four thousand at Newport.
6. The Nationals to be held in September when the weather is fine and the regular season is completed.
7. The number of entries will be regulated, poor players eliminated, and more ranking players included.
8. Players' environment and accommodations: Forest Hills will be a tennis players' rather than a Society environment. Amusement, entertainment, and hotel accommodations will be far better in New York.
9. For the first time the mass of tennis lovers—college men and schoolboys—will be able to attend; hardly any young men and boys were ever seen at Newport.
10. The right of the majority of players from the East, South and West to compete in the National Championships and to watch them.[7]

A document was also sent out by those who opposed the move away from Newport. It was largely an appeal to tradition, and noted the fact that, of the thirteen men who had won the Championship, eight—Sears,

Slocum, Campbell, Hovey, Larned, Clothier, Wright, and Williams—favored remaining at Newport, two were neutral—Whitman and McLoughlin—and only one—Holcombe Ward—favored New York. (Wrenn, as president of the association, felt it improper to take a stand either way, while H. L. Doherty, the Englishman, was not contacted).

The annual meeting at the Waldorf-Astoria was called to order at about five o'clock. Participation was the greatest ever recorded; 171 votes were cast in 1914, on the amateur rule, while 248 votes were cast that night on the Newport-New York decision.

After routine business was completed, the meeting was adjourned for dinner. A "darkey" orchestra played in the background. At one point, a New York supporter, who had written some verses about the superiority of New York over Newport, surreptitiously passed them on to the bandleader who had his men render the verses to the tune of "Tipperary," a popular song of the day. After dinner, Henry W. Slocum, who had the honor of speaking first, gave a sentimental and charming speech, from which I quote in part:

> Now, gentlemen, they call us, I think, "sentimental old has-beens," those of us who want to keep the tournament at Newport. . . . I never in my life go to Newport and go through the gateway of the Casino into the grounds, the beautiful grounds there, and hear the band playing, and see the beautiful women standing around (laughter)—just think of Behr and Mahan objecting to beautiful women (laughter)—that ought to cost them at least twenty-five votes. . . . I am mighty glad to be enrolled on the side of the question with such sentimental fellows as Dr. Dwight and Dick Sears, and even such sentimental men as "Old Bill" Clothier and "Old Bill" Larned. . . .[8]

Slocum surely represented the solid, old-stock establishment, mostly from Boston and Philadelphia. They loved Newport and distrusted commercial New York. Thus he noted that of the twenty elected officials of the association (four officers and sixteen members of the executive committee), seventeen, "from Bob Wrenn down," were in favor of Newport.

Karl Behr, who spoke next, was far more vigorous and animated than Slocum and, according to S. W. Merrihew in *ALT*, got slightly more applause. He began as follows:

> We have on our committee, gentlemen, 130 active tennis players and leaders of the game in twenty different states of the country. . . . There is no

doubt in the minds of these tennis players that this Championship belongs to no state; it belongs to no section; it does not belong to the West Side Club; it does not belong to the Newport Casino, but it does belong to the tennis players of the country. (Applause)[9]

New York, Behr went on to show, had 107 clubs (or 41 percent of the total clubs) within commuting distance, while Newport had barely 10 (4 percent) within an equal distance. The New York area also had half of the first 100 men ranked that year. Numbers were clearly on the side of Behr and his followers.

The second man to speak in favor of Newport was a young and confident (if not arrogant) Boston Brahmin, George Peabody Gardner, Jr. A member of the famous Harvard class of 1910, which included T. S. Eliot, Walter Lippmann, and John Reed, among other eminent persons-to-be, Gardner had won the Intercollegiates as a freshman and had been a track star in his last three years at Harvard. He spoke clearly and well. One paragraph of his speech, however, might well have tipped the scales in favor of his opponents; coming in the middle of his speech, it was "the most sentimental of the evening and evoked hisses from the astonished auditors." Young Gardner, with supreme confidence, spoke as follows:

It has been argued as to the background, the wavering background of purple, white and yellow umbrellas. This almost justifies—"almost" I say, justifies the Newport side in saying "Granted the umbrellas, we prefer the background of waving umbrellas to the background of bottle-throwing baseball fans" (hisses)—of the baseball fans whose knowledge of the game is so limited, and whose conception of sportsmanship is so slight (hisses) that they have to have signs telling them when to applaud and when not to applaud, and unfortunately they sometimes get their signals mixed.[10]

Julian S. Myrick, an insurance salesman possessed of little eloquence, spoke with conviction and a barrelful of facts about the qualifications of the West Side Club. His was probably the most convincing speech for his side.

The speeches and discussions were still going strong by eleven o'clock. Though cut short to allow for a summing up and final vote, the meeting lasted till one in the morning. The final vote was 129 for New York and 119 for Newport; a change of only six votes would have given the Championship to Newport. It was this pivotal meeting in the history of American tennis that set the stage for the further democratization of tennis, the decline of pure amateurism, and steadily increasing commercialism.

===

Californians took all the honors at the first National Championship to be held at Forest Hills, in 1915. After beating Williams in a five set semi-final match, Billy Johnston beat McLoughlin in the finals. He and Clarence J. Griffin took the doubles title from McLoughlin and Bundy in a five set final match. Two Californians did not meet in the singles final again until Budge beat Gene Mako, in the 1938 championships.

Dick Williams beat Billy Johnston for the 1916 singles title. Again, the doubles final was an all-California affair, Johnston and Griffin beating McLoughlin and Ward Dawson. Never again was there an all-California final in the national doubles.

In the meantime, Woodrow Wilson had sent General John J. Pershing to pursue Pancho Villa into Mexico and bring some order along the Mexican border. And the chances of America being drawn into the war against Germany were increasing. Williams, soon after his victory, left for the gentleman's officer training camp at Plattsburgh, New York. Many other tennis players, college athletes in general, and gentleman-businessmen trained there, too, at that time. The United States declared war on Germany in April 1917, and the official Championship was replaced by a patriotic tournament which was won by a brilliant engineer from California, R. Lindley Murray, who was kept out of the services because of his value on the home front. Murray also won the official Championship when it was resumed in 1918, beating a rising star from Philadelphia, William T. Tilden, Jr., in the finals.

The officers of the USNLTA were extremely proud of tennis's contribution to the war effort. Many leading players became officers in the three services. George Church, incidentally, followed fellow Princetonian Hobey Baker, into aviation. Karl Behr took the lead in organizing those who stayed home in a series of exhibition matches in order to raise money for Red Cross ambulances. Some forty were paid for in this way; two women stars, Mary K. Browne (National Champion in 1912, 1913, and 1914) and Molla Bjurstedt (Champion in 1915, 1916, 1917, and

1918) played each other in some fifty exhibition matches to raise money for the cause.

Dick Williams, who began as a Second Lieutenant in the Field Artillery, went almost immediately to France where, due to his fluency in French, he was soon a Captain and staff officer. Among other honors, he won the Croix de Guerre for bravery in the Second Battle of the Marne. During one leave, he played with Suzanne Lenglen, on the Riviera, where many men in the AEF gathered after the war was over. In February 1919, 168 American officers were entered in a tennis tournament at Nice to decide the Championship of the AEF. Among them were such famous players as Lieut.-Colonel Dwight Davis, Captain Watson Washburn, and Lieutenant Clarence Griffin. Captain Williams won the tournament, defeating his old Harvard teammate, Captain Watson Washburn, in the finals.

That same February, as if to signify the end of the ancien régime, the USNLTA accepted the resignations of William J. Clothier and Albert L. Hoskins from its executive committee. Clothier had served continuously since 1902 and Hoskins since 1906. All the officers and members of the executive committee as of 1906 had by now either died or resigned. Furthermore, the father of American amateur lawn tennis, James Dwight, had died in 1917.

CHAPTER 7

Two Philadelphia Gentlemen: William J. Clothier, Father and Son

I don't care a straw for Greek particles or digamma. . . . If he'll turn out a brave, helpful, truthtelling Englishman and a gentleman and a Christian, that's all I want.
—*Tom Brown's School Days*

THE ANGLO-AMERICAN GENTLEMAN'S CODE CAN BE WELL PLACED WITHIN a concrete historical setting by taking a more or less detailed look at the total way of life of two generations of the Clothier family of Philadelphia. William J. Clothier and his son and namesake have been associated with the tennis establishment for just two years short of a century, from 1896 when Old Bill, at the age of 15, entered his first National Championships at Newport, to 1994 when Young Bill, at the age of 79, was serving on three USTA committees—Chairman of the International Players Committee, member of the USTA Olympics Committee, and member of the Executive Committee of the International Tennis Hall of Fame, at Newport.[1]

In Philadelphia, the three leading Department Stores throughout most of the twentieth century were Strawbridge and Clothier (Quaker), John Wanamaker's (Presbyterian-Episcopalian), and Gimbel Brothers (Jewish). Gimbels has recently been torn down.

William Jackson Clothier was the ninth and youngest child, and fourth son, of one of the Strawbridge and Clothier founding partners, Isaac Hallowell Clothier, and his wife Mary Jackson Clothier, daughter of a prosperous Quaker merchant with solid real estate holdings in Philadelphia. The Clothiers had come from a small English village near Glastonbury in Somersetshire to Burlington, New Jersey, in 1713, and finally settled in the nearby Quaker town of Mount Holly at the time of the Revolution. In Mount Holly, a member of what was now the third Clothier generation in America, young Caleb Clothier, whose father was an Elder in the Monthly Meeting, was impressed by the charismatic preaching of Elias Hicks when he visited there. At the famous Hicksite Separation in 1832, in which the Hicksites split off from orthodox Quakerism, Caleb joined the Hicksites before moving to Philadelphia where he became an active Quaker and abolitionist while following his trade of bricklaying. His first son, Isaac Hallowell, was born in the city and attended the Hicksite Friends Central School. At 17 he entered the employ of a leader of the Hicksite Friends, George Parrish, an importer of British dry goods.

At about the same time, another young Friend, Justus Strawbridge, two months younger than Isaac, entered the employ of Joshua Baily, a successful merchant and leader of the Orthodox Friends. Justus and his brothers had grown up on a farm near Mount Holly. At Joshua Baily's suggestion, he attended the Orthodox Meeting at 12th Street, the wealthiest Meeting

131

in Philadelphia. It was there that Justus met a schoolteacher, Mary Lukens, whom he married in 1863. They had five sons.

Justus Strawbridge and Isaac Clothier became partners in 1868. Isaac's father-in-law, William Jackson, tore down two buildings he owned at 8th and Market streets, and built a five-story store which he leased to the new partners. The firm prospered (attracting both Orthodox and Hicksite business) and still remains in family hands at the original location. In the second generation, Isaac's oldest son, Morris Lewis Clothier, became the senior and managing partner in 1903, the first president when the firm was incorporated in 1922, and chairman of the board in 1927, where he remained until his death in 1947. The Strawbridges have dominated the firm ever since, especially under the leadership of G. Stockton Strawbridge, who became a vice president in 1948 and president in 1955. No Clothiers are still active in the business.

While Justus Strawbridge served on the boards of the Orthodox Friends colleges of Haverford and Bryn Mawr, the Clothiers were the First Family of (Hicksite) Swarthmore college for two generations. Isaac served on the Board of Managers for many years along with his friend and summer neighbor at Jamestown, Rhode Island, Joseph Wharton, a Swarthmore founder and chairman of the board until his death in 1907, when Isaac Clothier took his place as chairman. Isaac and his oldest son Morris were constant benefactors of Swarthmore. In addition to chairs in Latin and Physics, they made many other gifts over the years. And the family, led by Morris, gave Clothier Hall in memory of their father. Its tall, gothic, churchlike tower dominates the campus to this day.

All the Clothiers in the second generation graduated from Swarthmore except the youngest, Bill, who went on to Harvard after his freshman year. The daughters were good students and active in extracurricular activities, especially Hannah Hallowell who graduated in 1891 and spent the rest of her life in Swarthmore as the wife of William I. Hull, holder of the Joseph Wharton Chair in History and a well-known William Penn scholar. Although Isaac Clothier was slight of stature and no athlete, he loved all sports, especially football, in which all his sons participated. Morris was captain and halfback on the 1888 team which beat the University of Pennsylvania 44–6. Isaac Hallowell, Jr., played on the team in 1914, when his older brother, Walter, was the manager. As an alumnus, Walter was a great booster of first-rate football at Swarthmore in those days before intellectual snobbery took over the campus. "I understand it's difficult to get into Swarthmore these days," wrote James Michener ('29) in the nineteen sixties. "I'm glad I came along when it was still Swat'more and its football team arrived by trolley car, Saturdays at noon."[2]

═══

Proper families along the Eastern Seaboard, from Boston to Charleston, have tended to divide themselves into those who prefer either the fashionable and stylish, or the more solid and simple ways of life. Back before the First World War, for example, stylish Philadelphians spent their summers at such famous resorts as Bar Harbor, on Mount Desert Island, in Maine, or at Newport, Rhode Island. Their more solid and plain peers (often kinsmen) preferred Northeast Harbor, on Mount Desert, or Jamestown, on the island of Conanicut, opposite Newport on Narragansett Bay. Joseph Wharton and Isaac H. Clothier, plain and solid Philadelphians of the highest order, were the patriarchs of Jamestown in their day. Before World War II, as one sailed across the bay from Newport, their two shingled mansions on the rocks, Clothier's "Harbor Entrance" and Wharton's "Marbella" still dominated the Jamestown shoreline. In those days in late August each year, members of the Clothier, Wharton, and other Jamestown summer clans took the ferryboat each day to Newport during Tennis Week at the Casino.

Young Bill Clothier was an avid spectator in the years before he entered his first casino tournament at the age of 15, in 1896. He was by far the best athlete in the family. Self-taught at tennis, and too young to play with his older brothers, he built his solid and patient game through endless solitary hours banging the ball up against the barn door. Born in the Hicksite Quaker suburb of Sharon Hill, he grew up at the new family estate, "Ballytore," on the Main Line and attended the Haverford School. He entered Swarthmore, in 1899, where he was president of the freshman class, joined the family fraternity, Phi Kappa Psi, and played on the varsity football, ice hockey, and baseball teams.

Because he had seen all the good tennis players who came from Harvard to Newport each summer, he transferred up to Cambridge after his freshman year, and entered Harvard in Franklin Roosevelt's class of 1904. At Harvard he joined one of a small group of exclusive final clubs called the Owl, along with several other good athletes, including Beals Wright, U.S. Champion in 1905. As one of the most respected men in his class, he was honored at graduation by being chosen one of its three marshals (Franklin Roosevelt was another). He concentrated on team sports and played on the varsity football and ice hockey teams. Ice hockey was always his favorite team sport and, thus, was another good reason for transferring from mild Philadelphia up to colder New England. In the meantime, his tennis was steadily improving. In 1902, he became Intercollegiate Champion and reached the fourth round at Newport where he was beaten by the great Englishman, R. F. Doherty. The next year, he reached the finals for the first time where he was beaten by H. L. Doherty, R. F.'s brother. He was defeated in the finals again in 1904, the year he graduated from Harvard. In 1905 he was a member of our first Davis Cup team to play in England but lost in the quarterfinals at Newport. In 1906, he finally won the United States National Lawn Tennis Championship, exactly a decade after he entered his first Newport tournament.

Clothier won the all-comers in 1909 but was beaten in the challenge round by his good friend and frequent doubles partner, William A. Larned. He reached the semifinals three more times, losing to Maurice McLoughlin in the last National Championships to be held at Newport (1914). McLoughlin subsequently lost to R. Norris Williams in the finals but even so was ranked number one in the nation that year. Clothier was ranked in the First Ten eleven times between 1901 and 1914. In the course of twenty-four years of competitive tennis, he won the Canadian, Pennsylvania State (five times), and New York State Championships, the Eastern Championships, at the Longwood Cricket Club, and all the main invitational tournaments included in the Eastern Grass Court Circuit. His favorite tournaments in the Circuit were held at the Seabright Lawn Tennis and Cricket Club (where he was a life member), in Rumson, New Jersey, and at the Meadow Club, in Southampton, Long Island. If business permitted, he usually spent what was called "tennis week" in each place, staying with Bernon Prentice at Rumson, and with George Wrenn at Southampton. Both were Harvard men and members of the tennis team as undergraduates. Bernon Prentice, tournament chairman at Seabright for many years, was well known for his donation of a beautiful trophy called the Prentice Cup which has been competed for by teams from Oxford and Cambridge versus Harvard and Yale every other year for over a half-century.* George Wrenn played doubles on the Davis Cup team in 1903 (with his brother Bob who was National Singles Champion in 1893–94 and 1896–97, and Harvard's greatest all-around athlete in his day).

Clothier won the singles and doubles titles at the Meadow Club four times and was runner-up in the singles at the age of 39, in 1920. Southampton was the favorite summer resort for at least two well-known Philadelphia sporting gentlemen and their families, Joseph Sill Clark, of the famous cricket and tennis family, and George Stuart Patterson, the city's best all-round cricketer in the 1890s and captain of the Gentlemen of Philadelphia when they played all the first-class county teams in a cricket tour of England in 1897.†

In February 1906, William J. Clothier married Anita Porter. The beautiful daughter of Judge William W. Porter, Anita belonged to one of the most distinguished families in the history of Pennsylvania.[3] Her first American ancestor, Robert Porter, came from Londonderry, Ireland, to Londonderry, New Hampshire, around 1720, soon thereafter coming down to Pennsylvania where he bought a farm four miles outside of Norristown (less than twenty miles from the present Clothier estate in Valley Forge). His son, Andrew Porter, was a school teacher, a Lieutenant Colonel in Washington's army, and Surveyor-General of Pennsylvania for many years. David Rittenhouse Porter (1788–1869) was one of Pennsylvania's better nineteenth-century Governors, and is remembered for, among other things, his deft handling of the Philadelphia Anti-Catholic riots in 1844. Both his son and grandson (Anita's grandfather) were members of the Pennsylvania bench.

Such a handsome couple belonging to two distinguished families was

---

*Prentice's son, Sheldon, was at St. Paul's School with young Bill Clothier. I spent a week or so with Sheldon at a navy "transit camp" in the South Pacific, just before he lost his life on his first assignment aboard a carrier.

†The Philadelphia Gentlemen played against W. G. Grace, famous British batsman and the most popular man in late Victorian England. George Stuart Patterson's son, A. Willing Patterson, was on the Harvard-Yale tennis team which played in the Prentice Cup Matches held in England in 1931. He was also National Squash Champion in 1940. He learned squash at St. Paul's School which had the first courts in America. He and his wife had Althea Gibson as their houseguest when she first played at the Merion Cricket Club in 1953 (see below).

expected to have a large and elaborate wedding which was planned for February 21. In the meantime the groom was thrown from his horse which had slipped on ice. He broke his pelvis and was in bed when the wedding ceremony was performed on the appointed day in front of only the immediate family at "Ballytore."

The young couple settled in Wynnewood, where they lived until moving permanently in 1926 to their large and beautiful estate, "Valley Hill Farm," which they built in 1911 near Valley Forge, in Chester County. Purchasing the original one hundred acres in 1910, Clothier added more and more land over the years. Although starting out in investment banking (with financial help from his father), he spent most of his business life as president and owner of the Boone County Coal Company in West Virginia. "In addition to my regular business," he wrote for his Harvard twenty-fifth anniversary record book (1929),

> I am interested in operating my farms outside Philadelphia, consisting of some eight hundred to one thousand acres. We raise various kinds of stock, including horses, sheep, pigs, poultry and cows—the dairy end of this business being the largest department, and contributing most largely toward the success of the undertaking. Outside of my time devoted to these businesses and such charitable work as I am identified with, my attention is pretty well occupied by different forms of athletics, *each in their season*.
>
> Apart from tennis, which I try to play consistently for exercise in the summer, my greatest form of diversion and exercise is riding to hounds. I am Master of Foxhounds of Pickering Hunt, having been interested in the hounds we now own since leaving college in 1904. Foxhunting is an old sport in the territory outside of Philadelphia. As the Kennels are situated on my place in the country, with the club house immediately adjoining, a large portion of my recreation life is devoted to this form of exercise. In a modest way we have a racing stable, from which we make entries in the hunt meetings in this general vicinity. (My italics)[4]

As a devout Quaker all his life, Clothier took his charities seriously. He was a director of the Philadelphia Charity Ball, the Graduate Hospital of the University of Pennsylvania, the Boy Scouts of America, the Freedoms Foundation at Valley Forge, and the American Friends Service Committee. He of course belonged to the best clubs in the city, in addition to the Pickering Hunt Club where he was Master of Hounds

(MFH) for forty years until his resignation in 1951.* When the International Tennis Hall of Fame was founded at Newport in 1954, he served as its first president.

As the master of "Valley Hill Farm," Clothier surely lived the ideal life of the gentleman-sportsman in the best Anglo-American, Eastern Seaboard traditions. Visiting young Bill in the 1930s at the time of the annual Christmas party held in the big house for the hired hands and their wives and families, I found the scene right out of a Trollope novel. Of course, Clothier was an extremely well-disciplined and rigidly organized man, refusing any social invitations on weeknights, especially on Fridays, because of his full hunting regime on Saturdays in season, and tennis during the summer; at least two mornings a week for many years, he was up and following the hounds by six and behind his office desk in town by nine-thirty; he never engaged in sports on Sundays and often attended the nearby Valley Meeting of the Society of Friends.

Handsome, powerfully built, and fearless (he broke almost every bone in his body, several more than once, at one time or another), he was the essence of the strong, silent man,† his wife once noting that, at the Tennis Ball at Newport one summer, he sat next to the tournament chairman's wife and never spoke to her once. He naturally looked down on his fellow Philadelphian, Bill Tilden, disapproving of his theatrical and flamboyant ways. A staunch Republican, he had no use for his charming Harvard classmate, Franklin Roosevelt.

---

*Just as the French courtier has always been most proud of his friends at court and his way with women, so the British gentleman has been most proud of his acres and his horses. While Bill Clothier was MFH at Pickering, Robert Earley Strawbridge, Justus's oldest son, avidly modeled himself on the British country gentleman at his estate in Bryn Mawr. During the hunting season he often took a house at Melton Mowbray, Leicestershire, where he was so popular that his fellow British huntsmen made him MFH of the Cottesmore pack, one of a handful of the most distinguished in the world. Bill's older brother, Isaac Hallowell, Jr., was also an avid horseman; for decades all fashionable Philadelphians as well as the thousands who attended the Devon Horse Show each spring knew him as the ubiquitous manager, in top hat and cutaway coat, of the whole spectacular show (the best in the nation); he also rode and exhibited at the National Horse Show in Madison Square Garden where he won many medals.

†Anthony Wilding, the Beau Brummel of his day at Wimbledon, referred to Clothier as "a fine loose-limbed man with the frame of a guardsman," in his tennis memoirs, *On the Court and Off* (1913).

If William J. Clothier was deadly serious, silent, and shy, his beautiful and vivacious wife, Anita, was full of fun and took the lead in everything worthwhile in the life of her city and state. Though she ran a large establishment, raised three children, and rode to the Pickering hounds on Saturdays, her volunteer work won her the Gimbel Award, in 1942, as the most distinguished Philadelphia woman of the year. A few years later, she received the Meritorious Service Medal from the Governor of Pennsylvania. The Clothiers had five children, three living to maturity: Anita, their older daughter, married a Proper St. Paul's and Princeton Philadelphian, young Bill was the middle child, and his younger sister, Carolyn, married a fine Stanford athlete and Rhodes Scholar who became a successful lawyer and banker. Bill, among Philadelphia's more eligible bachelors for many years, finally married an Austrian lady at the age of 47, in 1962, the same year his father died.*

In 1950, the big house on the hill burned to the ground, along with many sentimentally valuable memorabilia, including Clothier's tennis trophies. Five years later, Anita Clothier died. When William J. Clothier died, in 1962, he left three children, Anita, Bill, and Carolyn, seven grandchildren, and seven great-grandchildren.

William J. Clothier II was born in 1915 and, like his father, attended the Haverford School. In 1927, he went away to Camp Jennessee, at Saranac, New York, in the Adirondacks. He went back every summer for seven years, learning more about camping and sports than about tennis, until the last two years when he was put in charge of a tennis program on the newly built tennis court.

In January 1929, Bill and another young Philadelphian, Lawrence White,† went up to St. Paul's School in Concord to take the places left vacant by two young boys from New York who had run away from the school. One of them, Alastair B. Martin, became a famous court-tennis player and is now enshrined in the Hall of Fame at Newport (see below).

Bill arrived at the school at the beginning of its Augustan Age

---

*He once took Grace Kelly to Newport for the opening of the Tennis Hall of Fame and a ball at "The Breakers."

†The direct descendant of William White, the first Episcopal Bishop of Pennsylvania, Lawrence White was a first cousin of R. Norris Williams, National Tennis Champion in 1914 and 1916 (see above).

(1929–1938) under the great rector, Samuel S. Drury. From its founding days under the Reverend Henry Augustus Coit, the school had been intimately connected with upper-class traditions in Philadelphia. Coit had been trained for the ministry in the city and his wife was the gregarious and charming daughter of one of its most prominent and prolific families. Both St. Paul's and Philadelphia were the main centers of American cricket in the eighties and nineties. Like Arnold of Rugby, Coit, was no sporting enthusiast; but he rather liked cricket, according to August Heckscher, an historian of the school, "not, as has sometimes been supposed, because it was English, but because it was quiet and gentlemanly and was played without raucous cheering."[5] Richard Henry Dana III (his father wrote *Two Years Before the Mast*), captain of the cricket team and the leading boy in the class of 1870, persuaded the reluctant rector to sanction a new cricket field of fifteen acres which was largely leveled and cleared of rocks by the students; cricket was done away with in 1903 and the cricket field is now the Lower Grounds, the center of football, baseball, tennis, and track in the Drury years.*

St. Paul's has long had a close affinity with the amateur tennis establishment. The small tennis elite at the school in Bill Clothier's day, for example, played on an idyllic dirt court in the middle of the woods which was built by the Reverend Godfrey M. Brinley, who had graduated from the school in 1883, won the Intercollegiate Singles Championship in 1886, and returned to the school to teach for forty-two years (1888–1930). Besides William J. Clothier, two other members of the Tennis Hall of Fame, Julian Myrick and Francis X. Shields, sent their sons to St. Paul's. Myrick was, as Tilden once put it, the "czar" of American lawn tennis during the Golden Age of American Sport in the 1920s. It was he who led the move of the West Side Tennis Club from the Upper West Side of Central Park to Forest Hills on Long Island, a garden city so named by the Cord Meyer Development Corporation which purchased six hundred acres of farmland there in 1906. Myrick then brought the National Championships down from Newport to Forest Hills in 1915. His son, William Washborn Myrick, was in the class behind Bill Clothier.

---

*It was quite natural that the youngest of the five Clark brothers and the best cricketer among them, Percy H. Clark, sent six sons to the school in the Drury years; and they all spent their summers at Northeast Harbor, Maine, which was also the summer home of the Drurys.

Cord Meyer, Jr., entered the school in 1933; Frank Shields's son went there in 1955 and was an excellent oarsman.

In the Anglo-American gentlemanly spirit of the times, all boys (including this author) at St. Paul's in those years before World War II were expected to play team sports—football, ice hockey, and baseball or rowing in the spring, all of which was a matter of firm tradition rather than any written rules.* One of the few to specialize in tennis in the spring was Bill's classmate, Alvah W. Sulloway. Bill and I were of the minority (usually the better athletes) who played baseball in the spring rather than following in the great rowing traditions at the school.† But I remember most fondly those many spring and fall days spent on the Brinley Court in friendly, hard-fought matches with Clothier, Sulloway, and others. Especially enjoyable as a variation from school routine were the Sunday afternoons when Alvah's father, Frank J. Sulloway, a lawyer in Concord, had some of us in for a game of doubles at his court in Concord. It was only while researching this book that I realized that Mr. Sulloway, a class behind Bill's father at Harvard, was beaten by Mr. Clothier in the third round at Newport on his way to the championship in 1906. In the spring of their senior year, Al Sulloway and Malcolm Muir beat Bill Clothier and Lee Ault in the finals of the School Championships. The match was held on the Sulloway Court in Concord. At Anniversary weekend, a half-century later, in 1984, a return match on the Sulloway Court was planned, but buckets of rain intervened.

After graduation from St. Paul's, Bill played in his first Eastern Circuit tournament in August, at the Meadow Club in Southampton. In the men's singles, he lost to Dwight F. Davis, Jr., in the first round (Davis, whose father gave the Davis Cup, was 26 while Bill was only 18). Bill and his father lost in the second round of the doubles, and Mr. and Mrs. Clothier were beaten in the mixed doubles by the team which eventually

---

*August Heckscher, author of the latest history of the school and New York City's main WASP intellectual and cultural leader for many years now, was editor of the school's magazine and a guard on the *fourth* Delphian football team. (Every boy in the school was a member of either the Delphian, Old Hundred, or Isthmian Clubs. Bill Clothier was a Delphian, Hobey Baker and myself Isthmians, and all the Clark brothers Old Hundreds.)

†I, for example, was captain of the baseball team at St. Paul's and captain of the freshman tennis team at the University of Pennsylvania.

won the event. At the end of the month, Bill and his father were beaten in the semifinals of the Father and Son Championship, held for the first time at the Germantown Cricket Club rather than at Longwood, in Boston.

Bill Clothier followed his father to Harvard where he majored in anthropology under such famous teachers as Ernest Hooten, Carlton Coon, Klyde Kluckhohn, and Alfred Kidder. He went in for football which then demanded spring training. He admired his football friend, Joe Kennedy, but had little use for his younger brother, Jack, in or out of the White House. Bill joined the A.D., usually considered one of the two best final clubs (Porcellian was the other) at the top of Harvard's small fashionable world.

The summer after his freshman year, Bill again played in several circuit tournaments. He lost in the early rounds at Southampton, and at Newport he was beaten in the third round by the giant Czechoslovakian, Roderich Menzel. At the end of August, Bill and his father won the Father and Son Championship; this was the first time a National Singles Champion had ever won this tournament which had been held since 1918. The Clothiers beat the Sulloways rather easily in the third round.*

The next year, the Clothiers won the Father and Son Championship again in a hard-fought and truly historic final match against Dwight F. Davis and his son. Just thirty years after winning the Singles Championship in 1906, William J. Clothier and his doubles partner, Dwight F. Davis (three times U.S. Doubles Champion with Holcombe Ward) won the Veteran's Double Championship. The final was one of the great matches at Longwood that year; it was held on the Clubhouse Court and by the third and deciding set, hundreds of spectators were jammed around the court. That summer of 1936 was the high-water mark of the Clothier family's participation in the top levels of tournament tennis. They did play in the Father and Son several more times, but in 1937 were beaten in the finals by the Canadian team of R. N. Watt and M. Laird Watt, who had two legs on the Challenge Cup. (They lost in 1941 to Gardnar Mulloy and his father.)

Bill graduated from Harvard in 1938 and went to work for his father's Boone County Coal Company, in Clothier, West Virginia (pop. 140). As

---

*The Sulloways won the Father and Son in 1938.

social life was rather limited, he drove fifty miles in the evenings to play ice hockey on the Charlestown team.* As the war approached, Bill joined the Federal Bureau of Investigation in September 1941. When the Japanese struck at Pearl Harbor, he was on his way to the Los Angeles field office. During that time he met the then czar of California tennis, Perry Jones, and they became good friends. In 1942, the OSS (Office of Strategic Services), recently formed by Wild Bill Donovan, a New York lawyer and charismatic socialite, took over intelligence gathering in Europe, while Hoover and the FBI were assigned to Latin America. Bill was assigned tours of duty in Chile and Peru where his cover was as an archaeologist studying pre-Columbian architecture. He became fluent in Spanish. He also spent some time in Cuba. All the while, he indulged his lifelong amateur interest in anthropology (back in Philadelphia, he was president and a director for many years of the Pan-American Association). Near the war's end he was stationed in San Francisco, where the United Nations Conference was being held. He resigned from the FBI in March 1946 to join the Philadelphia investment and brokerage firm of Janney & Company.

In the meantime, Allen Dulles, who had been close to Donovan in the OSS during the war, became the director of America's first intelligence service in 1947.†

The first generation of leaders in the CIA were largely drawn from private school and Ivy League college backgrounds. With some money of their own, they wanted to serve their country in the dangerous postwar years. According to Stewart Alsop, the top levels of the CIA in the first amateur generation were riddled with old Grotonians and St. Paul's men, just as Britain's secret intelligence service was, in its heyday, riddled with old Oxbridgians. At any rate, along with others of his breed, Bill spent a decade or so in the postwar years as a collector of foreign intelli-

---

*Even today he remembers the Charlestown-Huntington rivalry which equaled anything he had ever experienced: "It was a good thing we lost the playoffs in Huntington. I would have feared for my life."

†When Hitler invaded Poland in 1939, the United States was the only world power that lacked a secret intelligence service. When Secretary of State Henry Stimson discovered that a six-man team in the State Department had broken the Japanese code, he cut off funding at once. As he put it in his patrician way, "Gentlemen do not read one another's mail."[6]

gence for the CIA office in Philadelphia. Richard Helms, director of the CIA during the late 1960s, became a good friend of Bill's. A native of Philadelphia, educated at posh schools abroad before attending Williams College, Helms spent two years after college as a United Press reporter in Berlin, where he covered the rise of nazism, and conducted an interview with Hitler. During the war, he worked in the OSS with Allen Dulles in Berlin, and then joined the CIA at its founding in 1947. An ardent tennis player, always dressed in long white pants even in humid Washington summers, Helms has played from time to time on the Clothier courts at Valley Hill Farm.

While Bill was patriotically serving his country in the CIA, he was also devoting more and more of his spare time to tennis administration, never, however giving up playing both competitive lawn tennis (in 1960 he lost to Adrian Quist in the quarterfinals of the veteran's singles) at Forest Hills and court tennis at the Racquet Club in town where he served on the board of governors for many years and as president (1971–76). At his tennis base at the Merion Cricket Club, on the Main Line, Bill built up the Pennsylvania Lawn Tennis Championships from a mainly local tournament, to the best on the Eastern Grass Court Circuit, and one of the best in the world. He served as chairman of the Tennis Committee between 1948 and 1952, when he was made tournament chairman where he remained for over two decades until the tournament's final demise in 1974.

Bill's important positions as a member of the Executive Committee of the United States Lawn Tennis Association, as well as his chairmanship of the International Play Committee and the Grass Court Circuit Committee over the years was a vital factor in his making the Merion tournament so important in the years before the rise of professional tennis. He is also one of the few Americans to belong to the All-England Club at Wimbledon. He has visited Wimbledon every year since 1957, where he arranged for foreign players to come to America, both to play at Merion and at other clubs in the Circuit. As he once told a reporter from *World Tennis*, on the occasion of his winning the coveted Marlboro Award in 1960 for his distinguished service to tennis: "There are times when I would gladly trade with any impresario for an equal number of spoiled opera singers. But the fact is that, with dozens of tournaments on the calendar clamoring for good players, somebody has to organize itineraries and such. . . . Ever since we included overseas players at Merion, interest and attendance has taken a decided upswing."[7]

In order to make the Merion tournament the best on the circuit, Bill and several hundred members of ten committees went to work on April 1 each year to prepare for the midsummer tennis week. The week before the tournament, Bill moved into a room at the club in order to be more on top of things. Perhaps the essence of the Merion tournament during Bill's leadership was the unusual hospitality and friendliness shown to the players. All out-of-town players were made to feel that they were honored guests with all membership privileges. They were housed in private homes along the Main Line, and a large number were fed free of charge at the club. As an official of both the Pan-American Association and the Council of International Visitors, Bill was used to entertaining foreign dignitaries in all fields. Bill not only invited the first black player to participate at Merion, Althea Gibson in 1953 (when many other private clubs on the East Coast still were closed to blacks), but also arranged for her to stay with the A. Willing Pattersons, in Radnor. Willing was on the Harvard tennis team in 1931, went abroad for the Prentice Cup matches in 1931, and was national squash champion in 1940. As a member of staff at the American Friends Service Committee, he was a natural volunteer for this pioneering assimilation of a black at Merion. That his wife was a Delano kin of Franklin Roosevelt was also appropriate. Some said at the time that the Pattersons were too cordial to their guest, who came back again in 1958, when she won the tournament as well as the National Championship at Forest Hills. A decade later when Arthur Ashe won the tournament, Bill arranged through the Council of International Visitors to have him stay at the home of Holland Hunter, a professor of economics at Quaker Haverford College. Hunter's wife, Helen, was a professor of economics at Bryn Mawr. Her mother, Helen Taft Manning, a famous dean at Bryn Mawr, was the daughter of President Taft.

In 1952 Bill founded the Philadelphia Tennis Patrons Association which he led for twenty-five years. It had a profound impact on Philadelphia tennis, making it possible for underprivileged children to learn to play the game. It was appropriate that Bill remained a good friend of Ashe's from the time Arthur first went to Merion in the sixties. The program of the Patrons Association was given a boost in 1983 when the

Arthur Ashe Youth Tennis Center was founded in the city's outskirts, partly due to their friendship.

In spite of Bill Clothier's gentlemanly and nonassertive style, he was the first man in Philadelphia tennis in the years between the end of the Second World War and the coming of professional tennis. Philadelphia's tennis eminence centered at the Merion Cricket Club under his leadership. In 1986, Bill was inducted into the Pennsylvania Sports Hall of Fame and was the recipient of the Jack Kelly Award. In 1992, he was elected to the Collegiate Tennis Hall of Fame by the Intercollegiate Tennis Coaches' Association in Athens, Georgia. (Arthur Ashe was one of his sponsors.)

The Clothier tennis dynasty is now in its third generation. Bill's son, Morris, was an all-American squash player while representing Franklin & Marshall College during the 1980s. He also took up Court Tennis, eventually winning the National Amateur Championships three times. He is currently the number one amateur player in the United States. During the past year (1992–93) Morris and his partner won the National Squash Racquets Championship (amateur) in doubles. He also won the National Mixed Doubles Championship. At the age of 29, he is a vice president of Lazard Frères in New York City.

CHAPTER 8

Racism and Anti-Semitism: The Gentleman's Achilles Heel

I always was uncomfortable in snooty private clubs.
—Billie Jean King

At the same time that I was turned away from a public movie theatre, I was treated royally at the most exclusive country clubs in the United States.
—Arthur Ashe

AFTER THE FIRST WORLD WAR, THE ARISTOCRATIC IDEALISM OF THEODORE Roosevelt and Woodrow Wilson was replaced by the bourgeois realism of Harding, Coolidge, and Hoover. Wilson was indeed prophetic when he said to young Franklin Roosevelt that "it is only once in a generation that a people can be lifted above material things."[1]

The authority of the values of the WASP establishment reigned supreme throughout the booming twenties, the last Anglo-Saxon decade in American history. Beneath the surface optimism of this decade of boosterism, business, and ballyhoo, however, all too many paranoid members of the Protestant establishment were obsessed with the growing mongrelization of "their" country. Between 1880 and 1920, for instance, some fifty million immigrants, largely Catholics and Jews from Southern and Eastern Europe, were added to a nation which had been predominantly Protestant and of Northern and Western European stock since its founding days in the eighteenth century. Thus a Proper Bostonian and Franklin Roosevelt's Harvard contemporary, Lothrop Stoddard, wrote *The Rising Tide of Color Against White-World Supremacy*, which almost immediately became an "international sensation" after its publication in 1920. The following year, the eminent Harvard psychologist, William McDougall, published his Lowell Lectures under the title *Is America Safe for Democracy?* in which he questioned whether democracy would survive the mongrelization of a Nordic civilization. Racial and ethnic prejudice in America took an extreme form in anti-Semitism, which thrived in the 1920s when H. L. Mencken's *Smart Set* became the bible of the educated classes; Mencken's sneering values are revealed in the following paragraph in his *Prejudices: Fourth Series* (1924):

> The Jews could be put down very plausibly as the most unpleasant race ever heard of. As commonly encountered they lack many of the qualities that mark the civilized man: courage, dignity, incorruptibility, ease, confidence. They have vanity without pride, voluptuousness without taste, learning without wisdom. Their fortitude, such as it is, is wasted upon puerile objects, and their charity is mainly a form of display.

In the same year that our first National Lawn Tennis Championship was held at Newport (1881), Czar Alexander II, often called the Abraham Lincoln of Russia after his 1861 emancipation of the serfs, was assassinated on March 3; his reactionary son, Alexander III, was made Czar and the Jewish pogrom became official policy of the new regime. The formula was simple: a third of the Jews were forced to emigrate, a third accepted baptism, and a third were starved to death. Just as Herbert Spencer was being honored at New York's Delmonico's Restaurant for scientifically proving the Anglo-American gentleman's right to rule, and as Boston Brahmins were founding The Country Club in the suburb of Brookline, a flood of Jewish refugees from Russia entered the ports of Boston, New York, Philadelphia, and Baltimore. And American Jewry changed beyond recognition in the next four decades. As of 1880, for example, a very small number of largely German Jews were living in 173 cities and towns throughout the nation. By 1920, a majority of some four million American Jews were from Eastern Europe and living in the five cities of New York, Philadelphia, Baltimore, Boston, and Chicago. While Jews made up only 3 percent of the population of New York City in 1880, by 1920 they constituted some 30 percent (while there were but 250,000 Jews in all America in 1880, there were almost 400,000 in New York's Lower East Side alone by 1920).

From the beginning these Jewish immigrants thrived on the Horatio Alger values of urban America, and their children were especially successful in rising up the educational ladder. In Theodore Roosevelt's Harvard class of 1880, for example, there were no Jews and only three Catholics—no Boston Irish, no Italians, no one whose name ended in *i* or *o*, and no blacks. By the early 1920s, over a fifth of Harvard's freshman classes were Jews, which led President Lowell in 1922 to advocate the adoption of a Jewish quota. While Lowell's ideas leaked to the press and his prejudices made headlines, most other colleges at the time were covertly following similar admission policies; Yale and Princeton never were as diverse as Harvard and were far more anti-Semitic during the interwar years. And the undergraduate clubs at all three institutions were even more rigidly exclusive of Jews than the admissions offices. When Franklin Roosevelt resigned as Secretary of the Navy in 1920, for example, he was given a testimonial dinner by his Harvard Club, the Fly. A fellow Grotonian, Francis Biddle, was the toastmaster and asked Felix Frankfurter, who had become a friend of FDR's during the war, to be a speaker. "When several of the members of the club would not go to the dinner," wrote Biddle in an autobiography, "and one refused to speak to me because I had asked Frankfurter to speak, I realized how strongly anti-Semitic feeling permeated Harvard clubs. I felt deeply humiliated."[2]

This last Anglo-Saxon decade, when hoards of middle- and upper-class WASPS were moving to the suburbs, joining clubs, deriding differences, and denouncing Jews, also produced the second great renaissance in American literature. Just as a homogenous, provincial, transcendental, and small-town New England produced our first literary renaissance in the generation of Hawthorne, Emerson, Melville, and Thoreau, just before industrialization and materialism caused the decline of their world, so the members of the lost generation of the twenties came to maturity in a period of national transition from an Anglo-Saxon, class society to an ethnically heterogenous mass society. Edmund Wilson, John Dos Passos, F. Scott Fitzgerald, Robert E. Sherwood, Thornton Wilder, Stephen Vincent Benét, William Faulkner, Ernest Hemingway, and Thomas Wolfe were all born within five years of one another at the turn of the century; all came from solidly middle-class and primarily old-stock families; and all, save Hemingway and Faulkner who never went to college, studied at Harvard, Yale, or Princeton at a time when these campuses were still small and relatively homogenous, class communities.

Of all the members of this creative generation, F. Scott Fitzgerald has left us the best portrait of the WASP establishment. In this decadent and dying decade, all of Fitzgerald's gilded Yalemen were eventually doomed to destruction: on May Day 1919, his Gordon Sterrett, once voted the best-dressed man in his class at Yale, blew his brains out after a party at the Ritz; Dick Diver, whose career at Yale closely resembled Fitzgerald's at Princeton, was finally defeated, spiritually and emotionally, by compulsively destructive, millionaire expatriates, the sick Nicole and her vicious sister. And the "hard malice" of Tom Buchanan, "the best end ever produced at New Haven," destroyed his own marriage and Gatsby as well.

In his most perfect novel, *The Great Gatsby* (1925), Fitzgerald created the classic portrait of the WASP establishment's encounter with the New Man. James Gatz, become Jay Gatsby, who once went to Oxford, and had apparently made a fortune in bootlegging under the expert tutelage of Wolfsheim, the famous fixer of the 1919 World Series, bought himself a great mansion at West Egg, where he settled down to watch the Green Light across the bay on the estate of Tom Buchanan and his wife, Daisy. Gatsby had centered all his idealistic dreams on Daisy ever since he had met and fallen in love with her during the War, at an officer's club dance in Daisy's hometown in the South. While waiting and watching the

Green Light, Gatsby gave his famous parties. Fitzgerald's brilliant descriptions of his rootless and destructive guests, who had nothing in common but their shared vulgarity and their money, will ever remain the classic portrait of what was then called Café Society, and has now become the Jet Set or Celebrity Society of the likes of John McEnroe, and which, according to the late Andy Warhol (McEnroe's portrait painter), will eventually include each of us for fifteen minutes.

If Gatsby's world symbolized the New Man's corruption of the American Success Dream, the Buchanans stood for the corruption of the same dream by the establishment: "They were a careless people, Tom and Daisy—they smashed up things and creatures and then retreated back into their money."

And Tom was impressed with his caste superiority as well as his inherited money. "Have you read 'The Rise of the Colored Empires' by this man Goddard," he asked Nick Carroway, the narrator of *Gatsby* and Fitzgerald's alter ego, in the course of a dinner table conversation. "The fellow has worked out the whole thing," Tom continued. "It's up to us, who are the dominant race, to watch out or these other races will have control of things. . . . His idea is that we're Nordics. I am, and you are, and you are . . . and we've produced all the things that go to make civilization—oh, science and art, and all that. Do you see?"

===

The country club and suburban boom came to an abrupt halt after the Stock Market Crash in November 1929. About a quarter of the private country clubs were forced to close during the depression; it was not until the golfing Eisenhower years that the number of clubs held steady at about 2,000 and gradually began to increase.*

Two months before the Crash, Big Bill Tilden won his seventh and last National Lawn Tennis Championship at Forest Hills. If Hemingway and Fitzgerald represented a great creative generation in American literature, its Golden Day reflecting the lingering sunset of WASP hegemony in America, so Big Bill Tilden was a conspicuous part of the Golden Age of

---

*Two excellent discussions of the country club are Robert H. Boyle, *Sport: Mirror of American Life* (1963), and Dick Miller, "The Saga of the American Country Club," in *Town & Country* (August 1978).

Sport which included such other giants as Bobby Jones in golf, Babe Ruth in baseball, Red Grange and the Four Horsemen of Notre Dame in football, Jack Dempsey and Gentleman Gene Tunney in boxing, and Man o' War on the turf. In the next chapter we shall turn to an analysis of Bill Tilden's life and place in tennis history. Appropriately enough, he was the last cricket-club-bred gentleman to win our National Tennis Championship.

———

We have seen how Francis Biddle was humiliated by the anti-Semitism of his Harvard clubmates in 1920. While most of them were country-club Republicans and remained so, Biddle, a Roosevelt Progressive from his youth, became a Democrat in 1932 and played a leading role in the party, as a founder of the Americans for Democratic Action and United States Attorney General under Franklin Roosevelt and as a judge at the Nuremberg Trials under Truman. One of the major differences between men like Biddle, Acheson, or Harriman and most of their Groton and Harvard-Yale peers (all too often haters of "That man Rosenfelt"), was that they were anti-anti-Semitic as against the uniform anti-Semitism of their class.

In striking contrast to the *excluding* style of the 1920s, moreover, the 1930s were marked by an *including* ethic under Franklin, and especially Eleanor Roosevelt. A majority of blacks, for example, voted for Hoover in 1932 and then replaced Lincoln's picture on their walls with one of Franklin Roosevelt after 1936; at the same time, wealthy and prosperous Jews followed their ethnic rather than economic interests and were ardent supporters of the New Deal. No wonder Franklin Roosevelt was called a "traitor to his class," largely because of his economic policies but also because he was an affirming aristocrat (like his cousin Teddy before him) who believed in assimilating all men and women of talent and worth, regardless of background, into the establishment. And his pioneering wife, Eleanor, resigned from the Daughters of the American Revolution after their refusal to allow Marian Anderson to sing in their hall in Washington. The anti-Roosevelt litany of the day included the following cynical bit of doggerel:

You kiss the negroes;
I'll kiss the Jews.

We'll stay in the White House

As long as we choose.[3]

It was no wonder that Endicott Peabody, before the Fiftieth Anniversary celebration of Groton in the spring of 1934, let it be known among alumni that they should not return to Groton for the ceremonies unless they were prepared to be polite to the President and his First Lady.

The New Deal of the 1930s brought many members of minority groups into the mainstream of American life, and started them on their way to middle-class respectability. Similarly in tennis, the traditional, Eastern grass-court establishment was invaded by the sons of California, largely from middle- and lower-middle-class backgrounds; these eager new boys and girls from the West won the prizes and the hearts of spectators at staid old Wimbledon as well as at Forest Hills.

During World War II, when all Americans regardless of ethnicity or race fought side by side against a common enemy (and their racist leader, Adolf Hitler), fostered a new sense of belonging among non-WASPs. As an Italian American infantryman who landed at Anzio put it: "When we marched on Rome and I was continually greeted as an Americano like all my buddies, I realized for the first time that I was not merely a dago or wop Italian, but a real American."[4] In choosing the air force elites, of course, 20/20 vision was far more important than ancestry.

But the more important break came after the war. First, many veterans who would never have thought of it before, took advantage of the GI Bill and went to college and even to graduate and professional schools. At the same time, the unprecedented expansion of the postwar economy brought many new men, including a large number of ambitious and smart hyphenated-Americans into important positions in business, the professions, politics, and arts and letters. And consequently there was an ever-increasing pressure to accept these men and their families in elite urban and suburban clubs as well as the elite colleges. And it was at the elite levels of this new credential society that club anti-Semitism was felt most strongly. "Never did clubs, as clubs, seem more forbidding," wrote Cleveland Amory, "than to the younger generation of the 1960s" and "the blanket anti-Semitism prevailing in so many clubs is an excellent example of this inhibition."[5]

This blanket, club anti-Semitism probably led Gladys Heldman and Joseph F. Cullman III to take the lead, in the last decade of amateur tennis, in eventually bringing about the Open (pro) era. Both were born and bred in the same New York, upper-class, German Jewish world (often referred to as "Our Crowd").

Joseph F. Cullman III, whose German Jewish grandfather had started a tobacco company back in the 1870s that was later to buy out Benson & Hedges, was born to several generations of wealth and a product of Hotchkiss and Yale. He was like a Jewish version of Frank Merriwell. Educated in the heart of the Eastern Seaboard establishment, where he experienced his share of thoughtless, and not so thoughtless, anti-Semitism, Cullman was surely aware of the Eastern Grass Court Circuit then played at such anti-Semitic clubs as the Longwood Cricket Club, the Newport Casino, the Meadow Club, the Seabright Lawn Tennis and Cricket Club, and the Merion Cricket Club. Nor was he ever invited to join any of the leading men's clubs, such as the Links, in New York City: "I am on some pretty good boards, as you can see," he once told two sociologists. "It would have been normal with the connections I've got to have been asked to join one of those clubs, but I wasn't. And, you know, I survived very well without it. But I can recall it. It didn't go unnoticed."[6] Long denied access to the amateur lawn tennis establishment, he has responded by playing an important role in Open Tennis ever since 1968, when his Philip Morris (he was chairman of the board) sponsored the first U.S. Open at Forest Hills. In 1990, in his seventy-eighth year, he was enshrined in the Tennis Hall of Fame in Newport; he was chairman of the Hall of Fame executive committee at the time.

Gladys Heldman was the daughter of George Z. Medalie, lawyer, judge, and civic leader, who was a member of the executive committee of the American Jewish Committee and also of the Harmonie Club. Gladys and Joe Cullman spent many hours on the tennis courts of the Century Country Club in Westchester County, perhaps even more exclusive and fashionable than the Harmonie within the old family, "Our Crowd," Jews of New York."*

Gladys graduated with honors from Stanford and then went on to take an M.A. in medieval history at the University of California, Berkeley, where her new husband, Julius Heldman, was an instructor in chemistry; Julius is

---

*In the first issue of *World Tennis* (June 1953), Lloyd Budge wrote an article on a tennis tournament at the Century Country Club.

an excellent tennis player, National Boys' Champion in his youth, and today a keen player as well as a student of tennis style and tactics. Gladys, who did not take up tennis until after her two children were born, worked at it six hours a day and soon became a first-class player. Meanwhile, Julius moved his family to Houston, Texas, where he worked for the Shell Oil Company. In 1951, Gladys won the famous River Oaks tournament and was ranked number one in Texas that year. In 1954, she even played at Wimbledon.

In the meantime, in 1947, just forty years after he founded his *American Lawn Tennis* in 1907, S. Wallis Merrihew died;* several years later *ALT*, the great monthly of the amateur era, came to an end. Gladys Heldman's main claim to fame was her founding of *World Tennis* in 1953.† In contrast to the evenhanded and patrician voice of Merrihew, Gladys Heldman and her allies were ideologues of the first rank: "Setting off editorials like exploding fireworks," wrote the late David Gray of those exciting founding days,

> *World Tennis* demanded freedom, open tennis, democracy, and common sense. There were dragons everywhere. "Country Club" was one of our dirtier epithets. Not because country clubs as such were objectionable but because they exemplified the exclusivity of the sport. The country clubs and, behind them Wimbledon, Forest Hills, and most of the great tournaments were middle-class, even upper-middle-class, occasions. Those who controlled the game seemed happy to see it confined to the rich. We, the readers and disciples of *World Tennis*, knew that our game was good enough to be a popular sport, an exercise for the masses, for those who didn't possess straw hats and fancy striped blazers.[7]

Young David Gray, a fine British tennis journalist, like many of his progressive peers, surely worshipped "St. Gladys, at her preaching cross," leading the way to the great tennis expansion of the 1970s which took place largely outside the gates of the traditional cricket and country clubs.

The exclusionary policies of private clubs, both the urban men's clubs and the suburban country clubs, became media issues in the 1960s. Interestingly enough, the clubs' admission policies were criticized on the basis of

---

*I have always been horrified that Merrihew has never been inducted into the Hall of Fame in Newport.

†Tilden died the same month the first issue appeared; his picture was on the cover.

their racist and sexist policies rather than their anti-Semitism. It all began at the West Side Tennis Club in 1959 when Ralph Bunche, then Assistant Secretary of the United Nations, sought memberships for himself and his son, both tennis enthusiasts: "The roof fell in on the club president, Wilfred Burglund," wrote Robert Minton, historian of the club,

> who Bunche said had told him that Negroes and Jews were not accepted for membership. The incident was front-page news, and five days later Burglund resigned as president and Bunche was invited to join the club. Today Arthur Ashe is an honorary club member, and during the Open [1975] there are black pros, umpires and spectators on the veranda [previously limited to lily-white members of the club and their guests].[8]

In that unusual year of 1962 in tennis, another issue of club racism made national headlines: Carl T. Rowan, the black Deputy Assistant Secretary of State for Public Affairs, was refused membership in the Cosmos Club, one of Washington's oldest and most distinguished social and intellectual organizations. "The disclosure of this rejection in 1962 precipitated an upheaval within that club," wrote the *New York Times* in 1968. "Admission rules were changed and important members resigned. The controversy also led to the withdrawal of the membership proposals submitted on behalf of President Kennedy."[*] The 1968 *Times* article went on to report how a women's tennis team at the exclusive Chevy Chase Club refused to play a scheduled match with a team from the Indian Spring Country Club because it included a Negro on its team, Mrs. Carl T. Rowan. When he first heard of the underground debate and gossip about the women at Chevy Chase, Carl Rowan just laughed: "We found it morbidly funny," he said, "that at the time this nation was deeply involved in a great struggle in Southeast Asia, and when the great cities were facing chaos and decay . . . , the supposedly elite people of this country could be running around holding secret meetings to figure out how to keep one Negro woman off a tennis court." Finally, one of the

---

*A year earlier, President Kennedy's friend and Chief of Protocol, Angier Biddle Duke, felt it necessary to resign from his favorite club in Washington, the Metropolitan, because of its racial policies which interfered with his duties towards diplomats from Africa. And he was joined by several other distinguished New Frontiersmen. Today Duke is Southampton's most distinguished citizen and a Meadow Club member. Rigid anti-Semitism no longer rules at the Meadow Club which is thriving as never before.

main causes of the disintegration of WASP authority in this country in the 1960s was revealed in the last lines of this *Times* article which must be quoted in full:

> The Chevy Chase Club has also been the target of complaints from the Jewish members of other country clubs including the predominantly Jewish Indian Spring.
>
> They said that although Chevy Chase in recent years had allowed Jews to play on the tennis courts, it had been made clear to them that they were not welcome to use the bathrooms and locker facilities. They had to change in their cars, they said.[9]

———

That the racial and ethnic snobberies of the upper-class club should have been an important factor in producing the decline of upper-class authority in post–World War II America was perhaps inevitable, but also a tragedy. For in our mobile society, as Tocqueville saw over a century ago, where the organic and inherited ties of family, class, and caste have been so steadily weakened, especially after World War II, exclusive clubs and other upper-class associations such as selective private schools and colleges gradually served as the main agents of social control and traditional, rather than purely formal and legal, authority. "So severe are Boston's leading clubs," Cleveland Amory wrote of familistic and conservative Boston on the eve of the Second World War, "that even the bluebloods have to watch their step to gain admission."[10]

These exclusive associations became the main rungs in the ladder of upward social mobility. Between the two world wars, the Episcopal church schools and the Big Three colleges, combined with memberships in the proper college, city, or suburban clubs were the main status-ascribing institutions in the making of the American gentleman. And exceptional athletic ability has always been an entrance ticket to this associational ladder of class assimilation, as the fabulous life and tennis career of Francis Xavier Shields showed so well.

———

Before World War I, upper-class WASPs thought all Irish Catholics belonged to the servant class or lower. Many Proper Protestants were more anti-Irish Catholic than anti-Semitic. It was in this climate of opinion that Frank Shields was born in 1910 on Manhattan's Irish Catholic Lower East Side.* He was rescued from his birthplace by Frederick Alden, headmaster of the Columbia Grammar School, a private school for upper-class Jewish boys, most of whom lived near its location at 93rd Street and Central Park West. To keep the school in the public eye, Alden sought out the best young athletes in the city and gave them scholarships. Though Shields was a fine all-around athlete, starring in baseball and basketball, Alden gave him a scholarship for his tennis ability. He was thrilled when Frankie, at the age of 14, took the Third Avenue El downtown to the Seventh Regiment Armory and reached the final of his first tournament, the National Boys' Indoor Championships. Three years later, while still at Columbia Grammar, he reached the semifinals at Forest Hills where he was beaten by the French star Henri Cochet.

That fall of 1928, Shields went off to Roxbury, a boarding school just outside New Haven which specialized in getting backward sons of the rich and athletes on scholarship into college, especially Yale. As a schoolboy, Frank made two lifelong friends: his doubles partner at Columbia Grammar, Julius Seligson, and his Roxbury friend, Sidney Wood, Davis Cup partner and many times opponent on the tennis circuit. He later was in the insurance business with Seligson for many years and in the laundry business with Wood for a short time until Don Budge took his place. Frankie did a little more studying at Roxbury than he had at Columbia Grammar (none at all), but never made it to Yale. Instead, he spent the first four years of the thirties on the tennis circuit. In 1930, he was beaten in the Forest Hills final by John Hope Doeg. The next year he reached the finals at Wimbledon but had to default to his friend Sidney Wood. He had his best tennis year in 1933, reaching the finals in all the seven tournaments he entered on the circuit and winning four including Newport. Although he lost to the great Australian, Jack Crawford, in the Forest Hills final, he was ranked number one in the United States that year. Many expected a long reign as champion but he had a poor year in 1934, his last full year on the circuit. That year, after playing in the Pacific

---

*The material on Frank Shields is from a fine biography by one of his sons: William X. Shields, *Bigger Than Life: A Biography of Francis X. Shields* (1986).

Southwest tournament in Los Angeles, he stayed on in Hollywood where he was on the payrolls of MGM and Sam Goldwyn for several years. Though far handsomer than Clark Gable, he could not act.

While Shields was no womanizer, he was constantly sought out by wealthy and fashionable women. His lifelong admirer and benefactor was Mrs. Barger-Wallach, a wealthy Newport hostess who had won the U.S. Ladies Championship in 1908, two years before Frank's birth. He always stayed with her at Newport during the biggest, partying Tennis Week of the season. At most tournaments, he stayed with friends rather than sleeping on army cots set up by the host clubs or at nearby hotels where the top stars were put up.

Unfortunately, Frank Shields's good looks and Irish charm were more than matched by his Irish thirst. Always a perfect gentleman when sober, he was an ugly and often dangerous drunk when off on one of his ever-increasing binges. His three high-born and loyal wives all eventually divorced him because of alcoholism.

After separating from his second wife in Hollywood, Shields moved back to New York where he lived alone in a one-room fourth-floor walk-up apartment. A bachelor now, Frank joined the exclusive Racquet Club which had two court tennis courts. He soon became so proficient at the game that he was asked up to Tuxedo to play an exhibition match. He stayed with Stanley Mortimer and his wife Kathy (Averell Harriman's daughter) who were the leaders of the club colony. Frank was introduced to Stanley's younger sister Katharine (Goody) who had just been divorced from Oliver Biddle, of Philadelphia. Frank saw Goody again in Southampton and immediately pursued her with all his charming ways. They finally married and settled down in Old Westbury. Frank was now at the top of blue-blooded New York society and also in one of his non-drinking periods. As a witness to his now secure establishment position, he was chosen Davis Cup captain in 1951, which involved half a year of travel with expenses paid but no salary; this great honor turned out to be a tragic disaster.

Shields gathered together a team of five young players: Dick Savitt, who had won both the Australian and Wimbledon titles earlier in the year, Victor Seixas, who had been runner-up to Frank Sedgman at Forest Hills, Tony Trabert, Herbert Flam, and Budge Patty, 1950 Wimbledon winner who lived more or less permanently in Europe. In various combinations they won three interzone matches at 5–0 against Japan, Mexico, and Canada. Shields now had to decide on a smaller squad to take to Australia where they were to first play Sweden and then challenge the Australians. He decided on Savitt, Seixas, and Trabert, and he and Goody (the children were left with their trusted English nanny) set out with the small team for California, where they were to further train at the actor Charles Farrell's (Frank's good friend) Racquet Club. When the plane landed the players found out that Shields had added another player, Ted Schroeder; the addition horrified them and produced a controversy which increased steadily until the final challenge round against the Australians. Although Schroeder had been a Davis Cup mainstay since the war, he had not played the Eastern Circuit at all in 1951 or played at Forest Hills since 1949. It was just unfair to play him this year! To further stimulate paranoia, Jack Kramer was added as coach. All agreed that he was a fine coach but he was also a close friend of Schroeder's. He was, moreover, the most strong-willed tennis champion of the modern era, and all suspected that he would influence Shields's choice of Schroeder for one of the two singles positions.

The team arrived in Australia on November 3, almost two months before the challenge round which was to be played the day after Christmas. It looked as if Savitt and Schroeder were to play the singles, but there was a lot of tennis yet to be played at the New South Wales Championships in Sydney, and the Melbourne Championships. And Seixas played like a world champion: in the Sydney final he beat Mervyn Rose of the Australian team, who had previously upset both Savitt and Schroeder. At Melbourne, he beat Schroeder and lost a close final to Sedgman. Seixas felt he needed a rest, and Savitt had lost to Sedgman in forty-five minutes, so Shields chose Trabert and Schroeder to play the singles against Sweden, which the United States won 5–0 (Bjorn Borg's great coach, Lennart Bergelin, played both singles and doubles for Sweden). Many members of the press felt that Shields was being manipulated by Kramer in playing Schroeder. Savitt was enraged. Later, when the selections for the challenge round were officially announced at the Hotel Australia in Sydney—Schroeder and Seixas in the singles and Trabert and Schroeder in the doubles—Savitt knew he had been had and stormed out of the room. He never spoke to Shields again and refused all future offers to play on our Davis Cup teams. The Australians won

3–2, Sedgman easily winning both his singles matches and the doubles with Kenneth McGregor.

It had been a depressing trip and Shields had probably made the wrong decision in not playing Savitt: Harry Hopman, the great Australian captain, thought he did. But nobody had anticipated Shields's final humiliation when one of the wire-service reporters, who spent most of his time hanging around the bar at press headquarters in the Hotel Australia, finally figured out the "real" reason for leaving out Savitt, and he wrote a story accusing Frank Shields of being an anti-Semite. (Savitt had been the first Jew to ever win Wimbledon.) The story spread like wildfire, nine thousand miles away in the United States, without Shields being able to do anything about it. This was the first totally depressing blow he had ever suffered in his charmed life. How could people believe this unfair story? After all, he had spent his youth at an all-Jewish school where most of his teammates had been Jewish boys. And his oldest friend and business partner was Julius Seligson, a Jew, as were most of their clients, many of whom took their business elsewhere after the incident. Julie stuck by him. Nobody publicly stood up for him. Needless to say, he fell off the wagon for the first time since he had become Davis Cup captain.

Although nobody will ever know for sure whether anti-Semitism influenced Shields or Kramer in their overlooking Savitt, it must be said that the mores of the upper-class world in which Shields lived took blanket anti-Semitism for granted.

CHAPTER 9

William Tatum Tilden II: A Philadelphia Gentleman as World Champion

Do not think that tennis is merely a physical exercise. It is a mental cocktail of very high "kick."
—William T. Tilden II

THE GREAT TURNING POINTS IN HISTORY HAVE USUALLY PRODUCED PIVOTAL men whose lives have both mirrored and shaped their eras: Washington, father of his country; Lincoln, the great emancipator and preserver of the Union; Franklin Roosevelt, war leader and founder of the welfare state in America; and Martin Luther King, Jr., hero of the civil rights movement. In this history of the rise and decline of amateur lawn tennis, William Tatum Tilden II, a gentleman from Philadelphia, was preeminently *the* pivotal man. He was the last cricket-club-bred National Champion and eventually became the first National Champion to turn professional. "I was practically born into the Germantown Cricket Club," Tilden wrote in *Me—The Handicap*, his first autobiography (1929). "In the days when tennis in the United States was Newport and Society, it can easily be seen that I was born to be a little tennis snob. God only knows how I escaped that fate. I suppose the U.S.L.T.A. officials would regard my escape as engineered by others than the Lord. Anyhow, somehow or someway, the Little Snob turned out to be the Tennis Bolshevic." Tilden was here referring to his running battle throughout the twenties with the officials of the USLTA over the amateur issue. But the term "Bolshevic" (nonconformer) caught the essence of his whole amateur career. As will be seen later in this chapter and in the two following chapters, Tilden was the most exciting, catalyzing, frustrating, self-aggrandizing, and ultimately revolutionary force in modern tennis.

Though a gentleman by birth and breeding, Tilden was also possessed by the will and temperament of a genius, two aspects of his personality which were often at odds. At the same time he was no tennis prodigy but a self-made genius, as it were. His fellow townsman and hero, Dick Williams, was both a tennis prodigy and an impeccable gentleman without the will or temperament of a genius. When Williams won our National Championships in 1914, Tilden, at age 21 (only two years younger than Williams), did not even qualify for entry. Two years later, at Forest Hills, Williams won his second championship, while Tilden was put out in the first round. Tilden did not win his first U.S. Championship until the age of 27, in 1920; he was ranked number one that year, a position which he held for ten years in a row (the only American, man or woman, ever to do so).

Tilden was rightly proud of his thirty-two-year reign in top tennis circles both here and abroad. "In 1913, largely because there was no one else available, and because by some strange chance I had played several good matches in a row," he wrote in his often self-deprecating style,

> I was entered in the National Mixed Doubles Championships with the marvelous little Californian, Mary Kendall Browne. Mary was a miraculous doubles player, so good that despite the handicap of having me as a partner she successfully won all our matches and I acquired the first of my seventy national titles. My last, the United States Pro Doubles, was won with Vincent Richards in 1945, thirty-two years later. Maybe I'm not a fossil after all![1]

Tilden won the first of his five U.S. Men's Doubles Championships in 1918, with young (age 15) Vincent Richards, his first and greatest protégé. He is the only man to have won our National Singles Championship six years in a row (1920, 1921, 1922, 1923, 1924, 1925). He won it one more time just before the great Stock Market Crash in November 1929. In addition to his unequaled record on grass at Forest Hills, he also won the U.S. Clay Court Championship in singles seven times, first in 1918, and then six times in a row, 1922 through 1927.

In Tilden's day, the highest honor in tennis was to be chosen to play on our Davis Cup team. Tilden played in more Davis Cup matches than any amateur in history (28), winning his first match in England in the summer of 1920, against a young member of the French Davis Cup team, and then winning fifteen challenge round matches in a row before his first defeat by young René Lacoste, at the Germantown Cricket Club in 1926. Finally, in 1920, Tilden was the first American to win the Gentlemen's Singles Championships at Wimbledon and then, just before turning professional, in 1930, he won Wimbledon for the third time at the age of 38, the oldest winner since Arthur Wentworth Gore won it for the last time in 1909, at the venerable age of 41 (Tilden was and remains the only Wimbledon Champion to win his first and last championships ten years apart).

Tilden dominated American amateur tennis during the decade of ballyhoo and celebrity worship. As "Big Bill" he became tennis's first celebrity, along with such other heroes of Sport's Golden Age as Jack Dempsey, Babe Ruth, Bobby Jones, and Red Grange. Tilden was surely the loneliest of them all, as Westbrook Pegler wrote in 1930: "He is as famous as Babe Ruth in his own country and just as famous in other countries where nobody ever heard of Babe Ruth, but the mysterious Mr. Tilden, though he glories in his celebrity . . . nevertheless is a stranger to the public and to the sports writers. . . . His temperament has withstood description in a thousand attempts and defied popular understanding, and the people know him only as a figure, a celebrity, not as a person."[2] Even the hard-boiled Pegler dared not mention in print one of the possible reasons why this urbane, proud, and haughty celebrity was incapable of real friendships with anyone, though he did write at the end of his piece that "Mr. Tilden also fancies himself as a patron of young boys who wish to play tennis."

Many years after one of Tilden's protégés, Junior Coen, had given up big-time tennis, he summed up his old patron as follows: "He manufactured friendships. He did that because everyone needs friends, and I guess I would question now whether Bill ever had a real friend. Life would revolve around the people he *made* his friends at the time. The sex thing was there, I now know, although I never once saw it. The key was friendship. He took these little kids and helped them in order to get their comradeship."[3]

The wound is often the bow, just as it is the injured oyster which produces the pearl. And young Bill Tilden was driven to become far more than just a perfect Philadelphia-Gentleman-Sportsman in the style of his aristocratic hero, Dick Williams; for surely he must have been cruelly wounded when he first became aware of his then strictly tabooed tendency towards homosexuality. And he spent much of his life trying to conceal his cruel wound. According to Frank Deford's definitive biography, *Big Bill Tilden*, he was primarily asexual throughout most of his life, never spending a night alone with an adult, man or woman.*

Big Bill Tilden came of pure English stock. His mother's parents, David and Selina Hey, came to Philadelphia from Yorkshire in the middle of the nineteenth century. David set up his own wool-importing firm which soon prospered. Their children, including their daughter Selina, grew up in unostentatious comfort.

The English Tildens were a large clan spread all over the County of Kent at the time of the Norman Conquest. The first Tilden in America landed,

---

*Throughout this chapter, I have leaned heavily on Deford's fascinating biography of Tilden.

with his wife, seven children, and seven servants, on Cape Cod in 1634, and within a year became a ruling elder in the settlement now called Scituate. The family eventually produced three branches in America.

The New England Tildens, who were Loyalists at the time of the Revolution, went north to Canada where they prospered: Tilden-Rent-A-Car is the Canadian equivalent of Hertz. The New York branch produced Samuel Tilden, Governor of the State and famous Democratic candidate for President in 1876, who was cheated out of the White House in the only certified case of presidential vote fraud in our history. The southernmost Tilden line settled in Maryland and Delaware and produced the first William Tatum Tilden who was born in Newcastle County, Delaware. After his physician father's death, he was brought by his mother to Philadelphia and sent to the great Central High School for boys. Spurred on by his ambitious mother, he did well in school and always held some sort of part-time job. When he graduated, he was already working his way up in David Hey's woolen firm. His rapid rise in the world was a real-life example of the Horatio Alger sagas. For Mr. Hey immediately took a special interest in him and eventually invited him to his home for lunch after church, on an April Sunday in 1879, where he met Selina, the boss's daughter; they fell in love and were married the following November, and soon had three healthy children, born in 1880, 1881, and 1883. The Tildens lived in a modest house on Germantown Avenue where Selina ran a cultured and happy home for her husband and three children until 1884, when a diphtheria epidemic took the lives of all three children between November 29 and December 15 of that terrible year. They were buried in a hastily purchased family plot in the nearby Ivy Hill Cemetery. The once-happy household was never to be the same again.

In 1886, nevertheless, Selina gave birth to a second son, Herbert Marmaduke* Tilden, who was his father's son from the very beginning. Tall and handsome, he was already engaged to a beautiful girl while at the University of Pennsylvania. He was an outgoing, regular fellow, tennis champion of the Germantown Cricket Club and winner of the Intercollegiate Doubles Championship in his senior year at Penn. Upon gradua-

---

*Fourteen Tildens earned Harvard degrees between 1799 and 1905, two with the given name Marmaduke.

tion in 1908, he was taken into his father's firm, by then the William T. Tilden Company, as assistant treasurer.

Selina became pregnant again six years after Herbert's birth. She hoped for a girl to replace the two daughters she had lost, but she produced another son, born February 10, 1893. She named him William Tatum Tilden, Jr., and called him Junior, a name he came to hate, especially when his teasing playmates called him June or Junie. He changed it to 2nd or II soon after both his parents and older brother had died. At Forest Hills in 1918 he was entered as William T. Tilden, Jr., in 1919 as William T. Tilden 2nd.

Junior Tilden was born at "Overleigh," a large Tudor-like mansion, on McKean Street, less than three hundred yards from the main (Mannheim Street) gate of the Germantown Cricket Club, then the center of fashionable Philadelphia cricket. The Tildens had moved there at the same time as Stanford White's firm completed the distinguished new Georgian clubhouse in 1892. Tilden Sr. had risen rapidly in the world of business and civic affairs. An elder in the Presbyterian Church* and a popular speaker, he was soon a pillar of Philadelphia leadership, eventually becoming a three-time president of the Union League Club, the citadel of Republicanism in the city. He even had hopes for public office and entertained a steady stream of Republican leaders at "Overleigh," including Teddy Roosevelt and William Howard Taft. His long leadership at the Philadelphia Board of Education resulted in a school being named after him. A self-made man and proud of his success, he lived in a more ostentatious style than most of his neighbors. Along with his expensive clothes and an inevitable carnation in his buttonhole, he was noted for flashy automobiles; the finest of chauffeur-driven limousines always stood ready for his use.

Rarely home for dinner, Mr. Tilden left the rearing of Junior strictly up to his wife.

Although named after his father, Junior Tilden, like so many great historical leaders from Alexander the Great and Napoleon down to Douglas MacArthur and Franklin Roosevelt, was definitely a *momma's boy*. From the first he was a delicate and different child. His beloved mother, still influenced by the tragic events of 1884, was obsessed with health and hy-

---

*Always class-conscious, Big Bill became an Episcopalian.

giene and kept him out of school until he was 15. While being tutored at home he also absorbed his mother's twin passions for music and the proper use of the English language. Many years later, his diction and accent—slightly British in the clipped, Eastern upper-class style of his day—immediately impressed the largely Oxford- and Cambridge-bred spectators at the Old Wimbledon, on Worple Road, where he won his first championship. To this day, I myself remember being impressed with his class accent and manner when I served as a ball boy for one of his exhibition matches in the early thirties. In *Me—The Handicap*, Tilden wrote that his accent earned him "the reputation of being high-hat" and attributed it to "the fact that Mother insisted that I speak English, not one hundred per cent American slang."

Young Tilden spent many delighting hours sitting beside his mother while she played the piano. Though in later life he studiously avoided discussing his youth, he was always ready to talk about his adored mother and her fostering his love of music. "If I had to give up tennis or music," he once admitted after becoming World Champion, "I would give up tennis." All his adult life, in fact, he held the performing artist in higher esteem than the athlete: "Why should the outstanding athlete be more universally known," he often asked, "than the creative artist?" But his love of music and other arts remained largely at the level of appreciation and secondary to his own creative gifts which he devoted to the art of lawn tennis.

Tilden's love of both the arts and tennis was first developed at the Tilden summer home in the Onteora Club, an exclusive resort in the Catskills not entirely unlike Tuxedo Park, except that it attracted a goodly share of artists and intellectuals in contrast to the mainly fashionable and wealthy gentry who populated Tuxedo. Tilden wrote:

> The Onteora Club is worthy of a few passing words, because it was here that my natural love for artistic things, inherited from my mother and never quite understood by my father, gained its first real impulse to grow, a growth which has led me into rash excursions into stage and screen work, and what some people are kind enough to term literature. . . . Here writers, actors, musicians of all kinds, people who did things, whose names meant something to the big world, spent their vacations . . . and indulged that child-like spirit of "Makebelieve play" so typical of creative temperaments

in their lighter moments. Here Maude Adams, a spirit as charming, whimsi-
cal and lovable as Sir James Barrie whose works she played so wonderfully,
had her summer home. Here Madame Louise Homer of the Metropolitan
Opera Company with her husband Sidney Homer, the composer of so
many famous songs . . . made their headquarters for some years. Mark
Twain was a frequent visitor . . . [as was] John Alexander, the portrait
painter, uncle of Fred Alexander, the tennis star.[4]

Junior Tilden took up tennis at the age of 5 at the family's Onteora
home, spending hours on the packed gravel driveway banging the ball
against the back of the house. There were no teaching professionals in
America in those days, so he modeled his game on those of his brother
Herbert and Frederick B. Alexander, Princeton captain and Intercollegiate Doubles Champion at the time, both of whom were advocates of
the big-serve-and-volley game. In the summer of 1901, at the age of 8, he
won the 15-and-under Boys Championship of the Onteora Club. His opponent in the final, Dean Mathey, was two years older (Mathey later captained the Princeton team and won the Intercollegiate Doubles in 1910
and 1911). Tilden vividly remembered that first victory many years later
when he wrote: "Mathey was decidedly favored to win. He almost did. In
fact he led by one set 6–1, and was 5–0 and 40–30 in the second set but
something went wrong and he stopped dead. I emerged to win that set at
7–5 and the last at 6–0. Frankly, I knew I was pretty good." Tilden loved
to show people his first tennis trophy, a little pewter cup marked *Onteora
Club, Boys Singles, 1901*. This first victory set a pattern of coming-from-
behind-to-win which he repeated in some of the most famous matches of
his career.

In 1908 when Junior was 15, his sheltered life at home with his mother at
"Overleigh" came to an end when she was stricken with a kidney disease
and completely paralyzed. Junior was sent to live with two maiden ladies,
his favorite aunt, Mary Hey, and his cousin, Selina Hey. They lived in a
modest house on Hansbury Street, the other side of the Germantown
Cricket Club from the Mannheim Street entrance. Tilden lived with these
two beloved relatives who spoiled him to death throughout the rest of his
life in Philadelphia. He was sent to the Germantown Academy, the oldest
and one of the best schools in Philadelphia. Three years later Junior suffered the first and greatest loss in his life when his mother died. At the same

time he graduated from "G.A.," as his school was often referred to, and went on to the University of Pennsylvania. He remained at Hansbury Street, while brother Herbert and his young bride moved into "Overleigh." Tragedy soon struck again: "In 1915, my last year in college," Tilden wrote, "my father and brother both passed away suddenly, following short illnesses, my brother leaving his wife and two young children, Miriam and Billy*. I did not complete my last year in college on that account, but went to work with the *Evening Ledger*, thus beginning my newspaper career, a career which in later years was to weigh so heavily on the minds of the officials of the United States Lawn Tennis Association."[5] Tilden was referring here to his later being accused of cashing in on his tennis fame by writing for newspapers, whereas his writing had in fact preceded his tennis fame. While writing for the *Ledger*, Tilden took on an unpaid job helping to coach the tennis team at the Germantown Academy.

His father's death in 1915 and his taking on the teaching job at his *alma mater* marked vital turning points in Tilden's tennis career. In the first place, the job at G.A. was the intellectual spark which led him to become one of the keenest students of the game of tennis who ever lived. Perhaps a genius is someone who is never satisfied with traditional answers but rather is driven to take infinite pains to get to the very roots of his art or science. As he later wrote:

> I began to study tennis from the standpoint of geometry and physics, began to work out carefully a strategic and psychological approach to the game. Thus my first real pupil, and my most successful, was myself. I believe sincerely that my subsequent skill is directly traceable to the pains I took in learning enough to teach my old school team. . . . I am glad to say I am still learning (age 55).[6]

Big Bill Tilden lived for tennis and wrote about it profusely.† His many articles and books analyzing the game were absolutely first-rate, unequaled by any tennis player before him or since. His technical articles

---

*William T. Tilden III, captain of the Princeton tennis team in 1936.

†His tennis fiction—including numerous moralistic short stories for boys and one novel about a teenager's worship of his older brother, who rose to tennis fame only to be eventually corrupted by a rich member of the thinly disguised USLTA—was self-revealing but artistically thin. He also wrote a number of unsuccessful plays.

and book, moreover, were written with style and clarity, especially his masterpiece, *Match Play and the Spin of the Ball*, which was the culmination of many years of thought originally stimulated by his teaching at the Germantown Academy. A half-century later, Frank Deford wrote about the influence of Tilden's great classic as follows:

When John Newcombe won his first Wimbledon in 1967 someone asked him where he had originally learned to play the game. "Reading Bill Tilden's book," he said with some surprise, as if "Didn't everybody?" When Arthur Ashe and Stan Smith traveled on a State Department tour through Africa in 1970, they suddenly chanced upon a beautiful young teenage player in Dar es Salaam, Tanzania. They could not believe his form, his strokes, his understanding of tennis, for there was neither anyone around to teach him nor to play against him. It turned out that his father had brought 'Tilden's book' with him from India and taught his son from it, working with him for months in front of a mirror before permitting the boy to hit a ball, and then requiring him to play exactly as it was written in the book. The boy (who subsequently earned a tennis scholarship to an American college) was literally, to his limits, a Tilden image; it was like finding an Eskimo speaking first-century Latin.[7]

While the teaching job at the Germantown Academy stimulated Tilden to become a lifelong student of the game, his father's death allowed him to begin his slow rise to the top as a player. Until then he had limited his play to local tournaments in and around Philadelphia during May and June. Many years later he told S. Wallis Merrihew that his father had not been impressed with his tennis potential and made him spend every summer with the family at Onteora rather than branching out by playing the big-time, summer circuit at Seabright, Southampton, Longwood, Newport, and so forth. This was the case even after he was first noticed by the press when he took a set from the unbeatable Dick Williams in the finals of the Pennsylvania State Championships in 1912, or when he won the National Mixed Doubles Championship, then held at the Philadelphia Cricket Club, with Mary K. Browne in 1913 and 1914. His arrival on the national tennis scene, then, only began when he entered and did quite well at Seabright in the summer of 1916 and was subsequently accepted at Forest Hills, only to be beaten in the first round. While he had been ranked for the first time in 1915 in Class 6 (61 to 70), he was elevated to the Second Ten (11 to 20) in 1916. There was no ranking in 1917 due to the war. In 1918, Tilden won two national titles: the National Clay Court, his first singles title and, as we have seen, the National Doubles, at the Longwood Cricket Club, with Vincent Richards. At Forest Hills, he was beaten in the finals by R. Lindley Murray, a brilliant engineer from California who was kept out of uniform because of his valuable contributions to the war effort at home. Tilden was ranked number two behind Murray.

Tilden spent 1917 and 1918 in the Army Medical Corps, stationed in Pittsburgh; the great improvement in his tennis was largely due to his commanding officer, a Colonel Brooks, who was an avid tennis enthusiast and encouraged Tilden to play in as many tournaments and exhibition matches as possible. "Due in great measure to Col. Brooks," Tilden later wrote, "1917 and 1918 saw my tennis make a great stride forward at a time when most players were going back." Tilden also had a good year in 1919 but again was beaten in the Forest Hills finals, this time by William M. Johnston who had spent the war years in the U.S. Navy. S. Wallis Merrihew wrote of Tilden's slow rise to runner-up status as follows:

> From 1912 or 1913 until the end of 1919 he was a promising player who nearly always failed to fulfill. His game was brilliant but dependable only on rare occasions. He began as an aggressive player, whose service and volleying stood out prominently, but who failed in the pinches and became erratic without apparent cause; and then he became an exponent of the backcourt and chop game, with medium paced drives and frequent chops as his habitual weapons. . . . He was runner-up in two championships, those of 1918 and 1919; and in both of them he came to the final round with a pretty widespread belief that he might win. In both cases he failed to win a set. Yet in 1919 he had beaten William M. Johnston decisively at Newport. . . . from the rout at the hands of Johnston there had to come one of two things—either a new Tilden, conscious of his shortcomings and working desperately to overcome them, or a Tilden willing to go along, always in the near-Champion class.[8]

Winston Churchill once said that there was all the difference in the world, in all of life's endeavors, between being Number One and being two, three, or four. In contrast with all too many gentlemen, I might add, no genius has ever been satisfied with being number two. It was thus in 1919 that Tilden proved his genius. At the age of 26, determined to be number one, he set out to strengthen his game, stroke by stroke, especially building a new backhand drive. This was before the great California and Florida booms of the 1920s, and before indoor courts were readily available in the Northeast, so Tilden went up to Providence, Rhode Island, to work for J. D. E. Jones of the Equitable Life Insurance Company, who owned one of the few indoor tennis courts in America at that time. Mr. Jones was an excellent tennis player, later winning the National Father and Son Championship with his son, Arnold, who also became National Junior Champion. Tilden wrote of his Hartford winter as follows:

> My job was to coach Arnold between insurance interviews or possibly to hold insurance interviews between coaching Arnold; Mr. Jones never told me which. The family had its own private court and here it was that every day all through the fall and winter of 1919–1920 I worked on my offensive backhand. . . . By May, the stroke had become offensive to my opponents. All through those months I forgot I had a defensive slice and went out to hit every backhand with a flat drive. Every day held hours of discouragement when I felt I would never master the gosh-darned stroke, but in the end it paid off.
>
> The spring of 1920 found me with a new and reliable stroke on the backhand; ready and waiting for the Davis Cup, Wimbledon, Forest Hills and Billy Johnston. I will always feel that to Mr. Jones and my Providence friends I owe my last step up the championship ladder.[9]

All students of the game of tennis and its history are familiar with the uniqueness of Tilden's taking that winter off in Providence in order to perfect his backhand drive. For it illustrated the very essence of his genius and rage for perfection in his art. The last British champion, Fred Perry, greatly admired Tilden's passion for perfection: "What a different attitude from that of today's generation," Perry wrote of Tilden in 1984, "not to mention a lot of players in the past, who have never troubled to learn anything new in tennis." It is why Perry (like so many others including myself) finds "the pattern of play nowadays so boringly predictable in most matches. The players are still doing exactly what they did when they first started on the professional circuit." In contrast, according to Perry, "Tilden was never the same player two days in a row."[10]

After coming down from Providence in the spring of 1920, Tilden was chosen for the Davis Cup team by captain Sam Hardy, of the famous San Francisco tennis clan. Williams and Johnston were to play the singles, Williams and his close friend from Yale, Chuck Garland, the doubles, while Tilden was chosen as a "possible replacement." Nobody but Tilden knew how much his game had improved over the winter when the team sailed for England at the end of May with two objects in mind—winning Wimbledon and the right to challenge Australia by winning two preliminary Davis Cup ties in England.

To everyone's surprise, of course, Tilden won at Wimbledon where he was a sensational success with the British crowds, who loved his habit of crying "peach" whenever his opponent made an exceptional shot. He was the first American to win this world grass court title which had eluded several generations of his countrymen ever since Joseph and Clarence Clark, of the Germantown Cricket Club, played their exhibition match at Wimbledon in the 1880s. Due to his great victory, Tilden was chosen to play both singles and doubles with Johnston; and they beat both the French and British Davis Cup teams without losing a match. Tilden returned home in a triumphant mood and ready to wrest the title at Forest Hills from his old nemesis and respected friend, William M. Johnston, thus becoming recognized as the number one tennis player in the world.

The Tilden-Johnston final at Forest Hills that September of 1920 was generally recognized at the time to have been the greatest in the history of the championship. Tilden won the first set 6–1 and Johnston the second 6–1, when the two men proceeded to play three sets of almost perfect tennis amid incredible drama: Tilden won the third set and was on his way to winning the fourth and the match when Johnston lifted his game a notch and won the set; the match stood at a dead even tie 6–1, 1–6, 7–5, 5–7 when suddenly all hell broke loose: an airplane from nearby Mitchell Field, while photographing the event, suddenly went out of control right over the stands surrounding the court and crashed to the ground just outside; the engine was found buried three feet into the ground and Tilden claimed to have felt the ground shake under his feet. The umpire feared panic and the two players agreed that the play must go on. Tilden won the fifth set 6–3 and the first of his six straight National Championships. On that day of final victory, Tilden's strokes, off both his backhand and forehand sides, were superb and constantly varied. He altered his big serve between a high-kicking American twist, a sharp slide, and a blinding flat one down the middle of the court which soon became known as his famous Cannon-Ball Serve. Altogether he served twenty clean aces, the last one winning the final point of the match.

Tilden and Johnston were now chosen to lead the Davis Cup team down under to bring back the cup which had remained there ever since August 1914, when Norman Brookes and Anthony Wilding defeated Maurice McLoughlin and Dick Williams at the West Side Tennis Club, at its new location in Forest Hills. In memory of Anthony Wilding, the challenge round was held at the Domain Cricket Club, in Auckland, New Zealand. Tilden and Johnston defeated Brookes and Patterson without losing a match and brought the cup back to America where it remained for seven years (the longest continuous stay in any one nation in the history of the cup).

The Tilden era of world tennis had now begun. At the same time, Tilden and Johnston came to be known as Big Bill and Little Bill, the series of famous matches between them being billed as David and Goliath battles. American crowds usually love the underdog and they invariably favored Little Bill, the gentlemanly David, whenever he battled with Big Bill, the volatile, irascible, and flamboyant Goliath-Villain. Many believed that Tilden was not above throwing the first two sets of a match in order to capture the popular underdog role as he battled back to dramatic victory. He did this twice in 1921, in winning the challenge round at Wimbledon and in the opening match against Japan in the Davis Cup challenge round (the only time in history when Japan reached this level of international tennis).

Tilden's Wimbledon victory in 1921 was one of the two most mysterious and controversial of his career. The USLTA sent him abroad that year to defend his Wimbledon title and consolidate his position as World Champion. He sailed in May with Arnold Jones and his father on the *Mauritania*. Having played competitive tennis constantly for a year—at home, in New Zealand, and in Europe—he was emotionally and physically exhausted by the time he reached St. Cloud, on the outskirts of Paris, where he was to play in the Clay Court Championships of the World.* He won rather easily but immediately afterwards had to be hospitalized in Paris and operated on for a bad case of boils. Upon arriving in London, he entered a nursing home where he remained for the three weeks preceding Wimbledon. Fortunately, in this last Wimbledon to be played at Worple Road, the titleholder stood out. Tilden almost literally got out of his sickbed to meet the winner of the all-comers, Brian Norton, the young South African. This colorful little underdog immediately delighted the crowd by easily taking the first two sets from the tall and broad-shouldered World Champion. Few in the crowd knew how weak Tilden still was. Just when Norton seemed to be the sure winner, however, Tilden suddenly replaced his hard-driving game with an onslaught of soft slices, chops, and deft drop shots, which he described in *My Story* with his usual clarity of style:

> With the start of the third set I changed tactics and began a series of drop shots. The great throng around the court, overwhelmingly British both in nationality and sentiment, had never seen this shot [Tilden invented it] and for some strange reason decided it "wasn't cricket." Came whistles, even boos and catcalls, which, strange to relate, annoyed and upset Norton more than they did me. He grew angry at what he felt was a discourtesy to a sick man. I went to 3–0 when Norton blew up. He threw the rest of the third set and after an effort to hold me at the beginning of the fourth when I again reached 3–0, Norton repeated the sorry mistake. Convinced I could not stand on my feet for a fifth set, he threw the fourth as well.
>
> His judgment proved almost correct. He went into a lead in the fifth set which he held to 5–3 and twice needed but one point for victory. On the first I smacked over a service ace. On the second occurred one of the most remarkable psychological breaks that I remember in tennis.
>
> After a prolonged exchange of drives I hit one which I was certain was going out to give Norton the match. I had started for the net to shake hands when the ball dropped squarely on the sideline of the court. Norton, aware of my for-

---

*These were not the French Championships which, up until 1925, were open only to Frenchmen.

ward motion, decided I was coming into the net to volley and he attempted a difficult passing shot—which missed. Had he realized it, hitting the ball back anywhere at all in my court would have been enough because I had already passed up the match [Tilden was actually carrying his racket in his left hand].

His error brought the score to deuce. Making a dying effort, I pulled out my last bit of reserve and ran out the set 7–5 with the best tennis I played that day. I remember little of the end of the match or how I got back to the clubhouse. Once there, for the first time and last time in my tournament career I fainted dead away.[11]

This last match of the so-called vicarage-garden-party era at the Old Wimbledon was certainly one of the most bitterly fought and fascinating in the history of Wimbledon down to the present day. Ted Tinling, the great guru of the open era of Wimbledon, wrote of the Tilden-Norton match in his book *Love and Faults* (1979): "Fifty-seven years have now elapsed since this unfathomed mystery, but by many accounts the match had a weird quality throughout. I know many connoisseurs who were present and all accept the fact that a deep, psychological, probably homosexual, relationship affected the results."[12] It is interesting that Tinling, in our sex-obsessed age, should have been so much more open about homosexuality than any of the many other writers I have read, both in discussing this match and other aspects of Tilden's career. "Clearly Norton had a deep infatuation for Tilden," he wrote in his detailed discussion of their Wimbledon match. On the other hand, A. Wallis Myers, dean of British tennis writers at the time, wrote that "Norton missed a great many shots because of his sympathy for Tilden's suffering from the crowd." The contrast between Tinling and the various contemporary observers of the match provides us with a nice measure of the moral climates of our age as against Tilden's. What was nobody's business in Tilden's day has become everybody's business ever since the almost total elimination of privacy in America after 1968, a condition so tragically illustrated in Arthur Ashe's being forced to discuss on television the most intimate aspects of his private life.*

---

*It is my impression that, in our "let-it-all-hang-out" age, when personal problems have become social problems and political issues, there will be fewer homosexual geniuses than ever before in history. More about this in Chapter 11.

As we have already seen, Julian S. Myrick led the successful fight, in 1915, to move the U.S. Lawn Tennis Championships from Newport to Forest Hills. From then on "Mike" Myrick gradually consolidated his power at the USLTA until he became the virtual dictator of amateur tennis, both in and out of office, throughout the Tilden era. He became president of the Association in 1920, the year Tilden became World Champion. And for the rest of Tilden's amateur days, as Tinling wrote, "Myrick and Tilden . . . were constantly at each others throats. The U.S. Authorities were scared that the original effete image of American men's tennis . . . could be revived by the world's No. 1 player projecting a homosexual aura."* On the contrary, Tilden, if anything, did more to project a new, red-blooded, and masculine image of tennis than any other player of his time. In the 1920s, moreover, even his closest protégés were unaware of his homosexuality, which is why his tragic arrest in Beverly Hills, many years after his amateur days were over, came as such a shock to so many. Here again, I think, Tinling was projecting our own age's obsession with sex back on an era which was, in official tennis circles at least, far more obsessed with the preservation of simon-pure amateurism. It was Myrick who was responsible for hanging Kipling's idea of the amateur gentleman's code over the marquee steps of the West Side Tennis Club: "If you can meet with Triumph and Disaster . . ."

Tilden was all in favor of amateurism too, but he also was in the habit of living like a king.† He had his first fight with Myrick and the USLTA over who was to pay his way abroad to defend his Wimbledon title in 1921. "Figuring that I had an income of my own," wrote Tilden,

> the Association decided not to take care of my living and traveling expenses completely on this trip. When they extended the invitation to lead an American group abroad, they informed me that I would be graciously al-

---

*The "original effete image" refers to the pre–World War I era when red-blooded Americans saw polite tennis players as "Little Lord Fauntleroy" blue bloods.

†He inherited two sizable fortunes, and made more money through his writing while still an amateur than most professional athletes earned at the time. He died in relative poverty.

lowed one thousand dollars. Out of that enormous sum I was supposed to pay my boat fare over and back, live three weeks in Paris—and the four weeks in London! Anyone who had ever made such a trip has a pretty good idea of how far that amount would go. Besides, I felt it beneath the dignity of the United States to have its champion travel in any way except first class. I so notified the Association, and told them that unless they were willing to pay my complete expenses, both traveling and living, I had no intention of going abroad. That was where matters stood in early April.[13]

In the meantime, Tilden and his Davis Cup teammates were invited by President Harding to play some exhibition matches at the White House. Since he had known Presidents Roosevelt and Taft as a boy at "Overleigh" and was now coming to consider himself a king among kings, Tilden felt perfectly comfortable in discussing his disagreement with the USLTA with President Harding. Before long the Association announced that Tilden would be sent abroad with all expenses paid. Tilden of course always took a suite at the best hotels in London, Paris, Berlin, and elsewhere. He kept a permanent suite at his favorite Algonquin, in New York, even though he rarely spent a combined total of a month there in the course of a year. He was also in the habit of regularly entertaining hosts of friends—celebrities, protégés of one sort or another, and the inevitable hangers-on—who usually partied until the early hours of the morning. While liquor flowed freely among his guests, Tilden sipped endless glasses of ice water. Tilden always and everywhere picked up the tab. "He traveled," according to Al Laney, "like a goddamn Indian Prince."

Because in 1921 a new stadium was being built at Forest Hills to take care of the enlarged crowds Tilden was attracting to tennis, our National Championships that year were held at the Germantown Cricket Club. It was the last unseeded championship, and Tilden, Johnston, and Richards, three of the best players in the nation, were all in the same quarter of the draw: Johnston, after winning a bitter battle with Richards in the third round, played Tilden in the round of sixteen. As he had been accused of winning over Johnston in 1920 only because of his big serve, Tilden vowed to beat him with ground strokes alone this time. And an overflow crowd of more than 12,000 watched him win in four sets without serving an ace; he then went on to his second straight title by beating a fellow Philadelphian and Penn man, Wallace Johnson.*

Having consolidated his position as World Champion, Tilden no longer needed to go abroad; let the challengers come to the champion. The Nationals in 1922, played at Germantown again, were seeded for the first time. Anticipating another Tilden-Johnston final, the tournament was ballyhooed as the "match of the Greek Gods." In those simon-pure days, cups were the only booty, and in all the traditional tournaments, a three-time winner was allowed to take possession of the valuable prize. By 1922, Bill Larned, Maurice McLoughlin, Lindley Murray, Dick Williams, as well as Johnston and Tilden had each won the cup twice. For the first time, if Tilden and Johnston reached the finals, one of them would take the cup home. Their records in matches between them were remarkably similar, even though Tilden had won the last two championship battles. They each had won five of their ten matches, with Tilden taking twenty sets to Johnston's nineteen. They played the final at Germantown before an overflowing and partisan crowd which felt that Little Bill had a good chance to win over the master. Little Bill came out and quickly won the first two sets with ease, his backhand equaling his famous forehand. Tilden then made his stand, and Johnston let him run out the third set 6–2. After the intermission, Little Bill won the first three games of the fourth set. The crowd roared its approval. As the two men crossed over, Tilden spied the hated Mike Myrick sitting next to the umpire's stand: "Just to annoy me," Tilden thought to himself. "Well Bill, it's been a great match," said Myrick, with a smirking smile on his face. "It's damned well gonna be," Tilden heatedly replied. He then proceeded to take six straight games to win the fourth set, and then the match 4–6, 3–6, 6–2, 6–3, 6–4. It surely was a match to please the Gods. And Tilden carried the cup across the Cricket Club lawn to Auntie Hey's house on Hansbury Street where it was placed in a prominent place in the living room. The loss broke Johnston's heart: "I just can't beat the son of a bitch," he mourned in dismay, all alone in the locker room. Many fans went home weeping for their favorite loser, Little Bill.[14]

Hardly a month after beating Johnston in this come-from-behind classic, Tilden was playing a free exhibition match before a sparse crowd in

---

*Johnson was tennis and squash coach in my days at Penn.

Bridgeton, a small and ancient Quaker town in South Jersey, when he scratched the big finger of his right hand on a rusty chicken-wire back-stop. True to form, he was trying his best to retrieve an opponent's smash in a pointless match and in a set which he easily won at 6–0. Blood-poisoning set in and his whole finger was only saved by his favorite doctor's skillful amputation of the finger just above the second joint. By all odds Tilden's tennis career should have been over. Instead, he changed his grip slightly and, some said, played better than ever, even though the finger pained him for the rest of his life.

In spite of the accident, the next two years were probably the best of Tilden's tennis career. In 1923, he played through the Nationals at Germantown with the loss of only one set and beat Johnston in a fifty-seven-minute final 6–4, 6–1, 6–4. He also won the doubles with Brian Norton and the mixed doubles with his old friend Molla Mallory.

In the meantime, a young and unknown Frenchman, René Lacoste, was beaten in the second round of the singles by Tilden's friend, Frank Hunter. He had been fascinated by Tilden ever since, as a young boy, he first saw him play at St. Cloud in 1921. During this first visit to America, the young French aristocrat took every opportunity to watch Tilden play, analyzing his strokes and especially his tennis mind, all of which he carefully recorded in his little black notebook. He was preparing himself to take the lead in winning the Davis Cup for his beloved France.

The Finest Five Years in Tennis History: The French Musketeers Finally Topple Tilden

Tilden always seems to have a thousand means of putting the ball away from his opponent's reach. He seems to exercise a strange fascination over his opponent as well as the spectators. Tilden, even when beaten, always leaves an impression on the public mind that he was superior to the victor. All spectators seem to think he can win when he likes.

—René Lacoste

THE FIVE YEARS, BEGINNING IN 1924, WHEN TILDEN'S GAME REACHED ITS peak, and ending in 1928 when Tilden and Lacoste played their last great Davis Cup match in the brand-new Roland Garros stadium on the outskirts of Paris, were surely the finest five years in the history of tennis (see Figure 6). It is symbolically most appropriate, perhaps, that they fell not too long before Tilden finally made up his mind to turn professional. In these five years, as Tilden's game was eclipsed by three brilliant Frenchmen—René Lacoste, Jean Borotra, and Henri Cochet—there were more dramatic matches, especially in the Davis Cup challenge rounds, more unexpected triumphs, and more crowd-delighting tournaments than during any five-year stretch before or since.

Tilden went through the whole year of 1924 without a defeat. He was more dominant than ever in the Davis Cup challenge round, winning both his singles matches in three quick sets. In our first National Championships to be played in the new concrete stadium at Forest Hills, he probably played the finest tennis of his life in beating Johnston in the finals in three straight sets—the first set in twelve minutes and the whole match in less than an hour. In the last three games of the match, Tilden allowed Johnston only three points. Several decades later, Al Laney wrote of this match that "Tilden was at his absolute peak, and I have not since seen the like of it."[1]

While Tilden's tennis game reached its peak of perfection that September at Forest Hills, the Wimbledon a fortnight earlier in the summer was more indicative of the shape of things to come when two Frenchmen, Jean Borotra and René Lacoste, became the first non-English-speaking players to reach the gentlemen's finals, which Borotra won in five sets. Three Frenchmen subsequently won Wimbledon six years in a row: Borotra in 1924 and 1926, Lacoste in 1925 and 1928, and Henri Cochet in 1927 and 1929. This is the only time in the history of tennis when players from one nation have won Wimbledon six years in a row (that is, since the British lost their Wimbledon monopoly with Tilden's victory in 1920).*

---

*Americans won Wimbledon *five* times in a row between Kramer's win in 1947 and Savitt's in 1951; the Australians won it five straight times between Newcombe's victories in 1967 and, after Laver's wins in 1968 and 1969, again in 1970 and 1971; Borg won it five times for Sweden, 1976 through 1980.

FIGURE 6

The Finest Five Years in Tennis History, 1924–1928

1924

Wimbledon   Borotra defeated Lacoste in finals: 6–1, 3–6, 6–1, 3–6, 6–4.
First non-English-speaking finalists and winner.

Davis Cup   (Germantown, Pa.) U.S. defeated Australia 5–0.
Tilden and Richards played all 5 matches, losing only one set (in the doubles).

Forest Hills   (First Championship played in new stadium) Tilden defeated Johnston in finals: 6–1, 9–7, 6–2. (Johnston defeated Lacoste in quarterfinals).

1925

Wimbledon   Lacoste defeated Borotra in finals: 6–3, 6–3, 4–6, 8–6.

Davis Cup   (Germantown, Pa.) U.S. defeated France 5–0.
Tilden defeated Borotra: 4–6, 6–0, 2–6, 9–7, 6–4.
Tilden defeated Lacoste: 3–6, 10–12, 8–6, 7–5, 6–2 (Heroic match).

Forest Hills   Tilden defeated Johnston in finals: 4–6, 11–9, 6–3, 4–6, 6–3.
(Lott defeated Brugnon in 2nd round; Williams defeated Borotra in 3rd; and Richards defeated Lacoste in 4th quarterfinals).

1926

Wimbledon   Borotra defeated H. Kinsey in finals: 8–6, 6–1, 6–3.

Davis Cup   (Germantown, Pa.) U.S. defeated France 4–1.
Lacoste defeated Tilden: 4–6, 6–4, 8–6, 8–6 (First Leaf of Autumn).

Forest Hills   Lacoste defeated Borotra in finals: 6–4, 6–0, 6–4.
BLACK THURSDAY: Cochet defeated Tilden in quarters leaving three Frenchmen in semifinals.

1927 The Finest Year in Tennis History

Wimbledon   Cochet defeated Hunter in quarters: 3–6, 3–6, 6–2, 6–2, 6–3.
Cochet defeated Tilden in semis: 2–6, 4–6, 7–5, 6–4, 6–3 (in the famous third set, Tilden led 5–1 and then lost 17 points in a row and the match).
Cochet defeated Borotra in finals: 4–6, 4–6, 6–3, 6–4, 7–5 (Borotra had six match pts).

Davis Cup   (Germantown, Pa.) France defeated U.S. 3–2 (team effort to tire Tilden succeeds).
Lacoste defeated Johnston: 6–3, 6–3, 6–2.
Tilden defeated Cochet: 6–4, 2–6, 6–2, 8–6.
Tilden-Hunter defeated Borotra-Brugnon: 3–6, 6–3, 6–3, 4–6, 6–0.
Lacoste defeated Tilden: 6–3, 4–6, 6–3, 6–2.
Cochet defeated Johnston: 6–4, 4–6, 6–2, 6–4.

Forest Hills   Lacoste defeated Tilden in finals: 11–9, 4–6, 6–2, 6–4.

1928

Wimbledon   Lacoste defeated Cochet: 6–1, 4–6, 6–4, 6–2.

Davis Cup   (Roland Garros, Auteuil, France) France defeated U.S. 4–1.
Tilden defeated Lacoste: 1–6, 6–4, 6–4, 2–6, 6–3. Heroic first match; France won other 4 matches easily.

Forest Hills   USLTA deprives Tilden of amateur status; Cochet defeated Hunter in finals.

The French victory at Wimbledon in 1924 was but the first successful step in its quest for world leadership in tennis which began at St. Cloud, in 1921, when 16-year-old René Lacoste saw Tilden win the World Hard Court Championships. At the time, Jean Borotra was 23 and had just given up his native Basque game of pelota in favor of tennis. Henri Cochet was just short of 20 and a year away from his first big win when he became the World Hard Court Champion. These three rising young stars, along with Jacques Brugnon, three years older than Borotra and a brilliant doubles player, soon became known as the "Four Musketeers." In the Dumas spirit of "one-for-all-and-all-for-one," these Musketeers set out to win the Davis Cup for the honor of their beloved country rather than for personal glory alone. As Tilden put it: "To play against this French team called for an advanced course in psychology almost as much as a supreme tennis game because when you played any one of these fellows, you played the whole team. They were always on hand to support and encourage a teammate, and on the court you could feel the combined psychology of the team pressing on you from the sidelines as well as from across the net."[2] Never had there been a sports group so devoted to a common cause, nor four men so strikingly different in social background, personality, and tennis styles.

Borotra, a man of many talents, was a graduate engineer who was already a highly successful businessman while playing world-class tennis; he was a clever linguist with a calculating mind, a master at masking his intentions both on and off the court.

Cochet was a street gamin from Lyons with little culture; a self-made man full of God-given talent, he loved to play the game but hated to practice; his natural talent for tennis was matched by the luck of the Devil.

Lacoste, the youngest of the Musketeers and their recognized leader, was born to a highly cultivated family of great wealth; his parents totally backed his passion for tennis. Of little natural athletic ability, he made himself into a scientific tennis machine, spending far more time practicing than in match play. Above all, Lacoste was a proud, upper-class Frenchman determined to lead his France to greatness in his chosen field. When his mission was accomplished by winning the Davis Cup in

America, in 1927, and defending it in France, in 1928, he retired the next year at the age of 25. And he made his own sporting-goods fortune under the sign of "The Crocodile."

Brugnon, the oldest of the Musketeers, was colorless and the least interesting; his contribution was in the doubles, where he was quietly supreme.

Tilden admired and respected Lacoste, with whom he also felt a transnational class affinity; he was baffled and a bit in awe of Cochet's God-given athletic ability and tennis genius; and he was possessed of a jealous hatred of Borotra. He wrote of Lacoste and Borotra as follows:

> Take René Lacoste. He had the detached, stolid, phlegmatic exterior bearing popularly associated with the Anglo-Saxon; inside, he was subtle, shrewd and analytical, with a scientific approach to tennis that made him seem ruthless and cold-blooded. His nickname, "Crocodile," perfectly describes his personality. . . . Borotra was the artist and charlatan of the French, undoubtedly, the greatest showman and faker in tennis history. Technically, his game left much to be desired. There was no shot in his entire repertoire, with the possible exception of his deadly overhead, which he hit according to the tenets of good form. Yet his unbelievable speed of foot, his swift eye, his muscular reflexes so fast that he seemed almost inhuman, allowed him to produce first-class results with a completely second-class technique. Borotra's personality was far more intriguing than his tennis. He was what passes for "typically" French. That is to say, he had all the charm, warmth, glamour and complete insincerity which is Paris.[3] No man on the tennis tour today has ever described an opponent like Borotra with such deft charm.

The Musketeers reached the challenge round of the Davis Cup for the first time in 1925. At the Germantown Cricket Club, the American team made a clean sweep of all five matches, even though Tilden was extended to five sets by both Borotra and Lacoste. On the first day, he squeezed out a five-set victory over Borotra and then, on the last day, played an heroic, come-from-behind match to defeat Lacoste 3–6, 10–12, 8–6, 7–5, 6–2. He had underestimated Lacoste and was two sets down and behind 0–4 in the third before he knew what hit him: "The monotonous regularity with which that unsmiling, drab, almost dull man returned the best I could hit often filled me with the wild desire to throw my racket at him," Tilden said later. Somehow, Tilden, after dramatically pouring a pitcher of ice water over his head, came back to take the third set at 8–6, but not before surviving four match points at 5–6. He finally won the last two sets and the match, giving up only three points in the final four games. Tilden was exhausted; Lacoste was fresh as a daisy and, as always, appeared unmoved; his dispassionate mind was busy recording his mistakes and plotting the best ways of beating Tilden in 1926.

Tilden won the U.S. Championship in 1925 for the sixth time in a row, beating his old friend Johnston in the finals, for the last time. American tennis and Tilden still reigned supreme, but it would be another story the following year.

Tilden's invincibility was challenged for the first time in 1926 when he suffered three important losses. In February he lost his first important match since first winning Wimbledon in 1920, when Borotra beat him 13–11, 6–3, in the National Indoor Championships held at the Seventh Regiment Armory in New York City. Tilden's second loss came in the Davis Cup challenge round against France at the Germantown Cricket Club. In the second match of the third day, with the tie already won, Tilden lost to young René Lacoste. It was the first loss of his long Davis Cup career. Unfortunately, in the third set, Tilden rushed to the net and stopped quickly to make a drop shot. His knee went out. He should have defaulted on the spot and rested the knee for a week or two. But team captain Dick Williams, who was out on a side court playing a friendly game of doubles, was inexcusably unavailable to make the decision. Tilden felt the only honorable thing to do was to finish the match, which he did and lost.

The press rightly played up the defeat, one of them labeling it the "First Leaf of Autumn." The members of the French team were beside themselves with joy, even though they had lost the challenge round and only managed to beat a 34-year-old lame champion in a meaningless match. But they had *beaten him for the first time* and that was the point.

Within five days, Tilden was beaten again, this time by Cochet in a five-set, quarterfinals battle at Forest Hills. At the same time Borotra beat Billy Johnston and Lacoste beat Dick Williams. Three Frenchmen survived the quarterfinals which came to be known as Black Thursday. For the first time since 1917, Tilden was not to be in the finals, which Lacoste won easily over Borotra to become the first non-English-speaking player to win the U.S. Championship.

The guard was changing and the French knew it. Borotra, Lacoste, and Cochet had all beaten Tilden in important matches. The Musketeers left New York with a psychological lien on the Davis Cup for delivery the next September.

The year 1927 was surely the most exciting in tennis history. Determined to regain his position as World Champion, Tilden went abroad in the early spring of 1927, with his good friend and doubles partner, Frank Hunter. Having built up his knee through a rigorous program of ice skating all winter, he began the trip with a series of victories in Germany, the Netherlands, and Belgium, before going to Paris where he defeated both Lacoste and Borotra in some exhibition matches before the French Championships at St. Cloud. Lindbergh landed in Paris during the first week of the Championships, and many expected him to attend the finals between Tilden and Lacoste. Though he did not, thousands of avid fans were turned away from the finals, many watching from trees. It was an unbearably hot and humid day, and the match dragged on for over three hours. Tilden could have accepted victory after the third set when Lacoste developed cramps; unable to accept victory on these terms, he allowed his much younger opponent a half-hour to be taken from the court and revived by a massage. Later on, when Lacoste lurched for the net-post, Tilden allowed him as much time as he wanted to recover his breath. In the broiling sun, even a linesman wilted and Cochet took his place on a service line. After his massage, Lacoste took the fourth set, winning the last seven games in a row. Games followed service in the fifth set until Tilden broke service and led 9–8 with his serve coming up. Twice he reached match point with only one cannon ball between him and victory. The first time he served what appeared to be an untouchable ace. Both Tilden and Lacoste apparently thought so and were coming forward to shake hands when Cochet called it out. Tilden did not question the call but worked back to match point again, only to miss an easy shot. Tilden now double-faulted on the first match point against him and Lacoste won the marathon battle 4–6, 6–4, 5–7, 6–3, 11–9. "There followed a tennis demonstration I have never seen repeated," wrote Al Laney many years later. Here was an heroic defeat which Tilden twice almost won. In accord with his rigid sportsman's code, he never, at the time or later, mentioned Cochet's close line call, even though it obviously upset him and contributed to his finally double-faulting on match point. "I doubt that there ever has been a tennis battle," wrote Al Laney, "waged with more perfect sportsmanship under trying conditions, or with greater mutual admiration between adversaries."

Several weeks later at Wimbledon, Tilden met Cochet in a semifinal match which was one of the strangest of all time, even stranger than Tilden's mysterious win over "Babe" Norton in the 1921 final at the Old Wimbledon. As Al Laney later wrote:

> This meeting of Cochet and Tilden was, of course, one of the most famous tennis matches ever played. I can still speak of it in detail because I kept the point score and notes made that day, but I could not explain it then and I cannot now. . . . Tilden, having noted what happened to Hunter* went all out from the start to win quickly. He unleashed a withering attack of unanswerable speed. Drives from both wings, either "flat" or carrying top spin, were hitting the lines, out of reach or too swift to return, and the service often brought no reply at all. [Tilden easily won the first two sets 6–2, 6–4.]
>
> And then, with the beginning of the third set, Tilden launched his most devastating attack. Never on that side of the Atlantic had he struck with such real violence. Cochet searched in vain for an effective weapon to stem the tide as Tilden went steadily on, literally hitting through his man, dominant, domineering, and arrogant. It was the Tilden of 1921–25 back on top, piling up the games. He seemed in a big hurry to get it over with. After banging his way to 5–1 with a cannonball Cochet could not reach, Tilden threw the two balls† remaining in his hand over the net behind his service and could hardly wait for Cochet to gather them in and serve what we all thought would be the last game.[4]

Now the unbelievable happened: from 15–all in that amazing seventh game of the third set, Tilden, hitting all out to win quickly, lost the next three points; they changed ends and Tilden waited impatiently for Cochet to take his place and then proceeded to lose his serve at love as his trusted cannon balls sailed out of court or into the net. From 15–all in that seventh game, in fact, Cochet won seventeen points in a row, going

---

*Hunter lost to Cochet in the quarterfinals after winning the first two sets.

†Tilden and most top players of his day usually held three balls in their hand when serving; thus, in case of a let on the first serve, play was continuous because of the two rather than one ball remaining in hand. This was even more important in club tennis without ball boys. Today almost nobody begins with three balls, indicating perhaps the present, rather than future, orientation of the younger generation. They seem, moreover, to prefer delay to continuous play these days; hence the interminable bouncing of balls before serving which began with James Scott Connors, also the inventor of the *grunt* among other crudities of body behavior.

from 1–5 to 5–all and 30–0 before Tilden won a point. Cochet ran out the set at 7–5 and the match 2–6, 4–6, 7–5, 6–4, 6–3. When they talked in the dressing rooms after the match, Tilden had to agree with Laney that he had passed his physical peak—though he hated to admit it.

Cochet then went on to beat Borotra in a hair-raising final, in which he again recovered from two sets down to win. Borotra, moreover, had six match points, the third of which became part of Wimbledon lore: leading 5–3 and 40–30 in the fifth set, Borotra served and dashed to the net; a rapid exchange of volleys followed which ended when Cochet won with a stroke which Laney and others thought was a double-hit; the players looked at the umpire, expecting him to call "not up" and announce Borotra's victory. He said nothing, play proceeded, and Borotra lost three more match points (one a net cord) as Cochet climbed to 5–all and then victory 4–6, 4–6, 6–3, 6–4, 7–5.

No wonder that Al Laney, in his fifty-four years of watching big-time tennis here and abroad (1914–1968), found the 1927 Wimbledon to be the "most dramatic and exciting" of them all.*

The week following Wimbledon, the French Davis Cup team beat Denmark in the European zone final and sailed for America soon afterwards. The entire French nation seemed to be involved in this Sixth Crusade when their heroes, Les Mousquetaires, set forth to fight for the honor of France which all patriots hoped, and many expected, would lead to final victory. As the boat-train pulled out of the Gare St. Lazare, the cocky and handsome Cochet leaned out of a window and called: "First the Davis Cup and then the American Championships. We bring back both this time, yes?"

After playing in the annual Southampton invitation tournament and in the national doubles at the Longwood Cricket Club, where they also beat Japan in the Interzone Finals, the Musketeers arrived at Germantown in high spirits. Lacoste was especially pleased with his victory over Japan's Harada, whose game was so similar to Billy Johnston's.

The French strategy involved beating Tilden as a team; thus, according to the plotting Lacoste, the draw was all-important. He hoped to play Johnston first, leaving Cochet to wear down or beat the great Tilden in the second match. Brugnon and Borotra were to wear out Tilden in the doubles, leaving Lacoste and Cochet fresh and rested for the third day. Things went accord-

---

*No Wimbledon Champion during the first quarter-century of the pro era (1968–93) ever came from two sets down in the finals to win.

ing to plan. Lacoste easily beat Johnston in the first match, while Tilden needed four hard-fought sets to beat Cochet. On the second day, Tilden played brilliantly as he and Hunter won the doubles in five long sets, loaded with lobs and other tactics calculated to tire Tilden (during the intermission after the third set, Lacoste urged his teammates to prolong the match to five sets). The picadors had done their job well in the first two days.

On the third day, a hot and sultry Saturday, before an overflow crowd of some 15,000 in temporary wooden stands, a tired and aging (34) Tilden faced a refreshed and much younger (23) Lacoste and lost in four sets. Even at Germantown, Tilden had always been the unloved heavy. "But now," wrote Frank Deford,

> he strode from the court, alone, head bowed in defeat, his long legs reaching out over the land he had crossed all his life, the people began to rise and cheer him. It was not for his match so much; he had not played that well. The cheers were for him. And many began to cry for him too. Tilden, totally unfamiliar with this expression, was for once completely at a loss as an actor. At last he thought to raise his hands above his head, like a boxing champ, and the crowd hurled down another tumultuous roar for him.[5]

With the score now tied at 2–all, a French victory depended on Cochet. Tilden and Lacoste watched the match sitting side by side in the front row of the stands. In spite of the hot afternoon sun, the always phlegmatic and cool Crocodile was so emotionally spent that he needed two sweaters and an overcoat to calm his nervous chills. After Cochet easily won over the slow and heavy-breathing Johnston, Tilden and Lacoste stood up, bowed formally, and departed for the dressing rooms.*

---

*Nobody at the time realized that their hero, Billy Johnston, was suffering from the early stages of tuberculosis. Many years later, in 1938, when Don Budge was making up his mind whether or not to turn professional, he contacted his admired older friend, Billy Johnston, for advice. "To my surprise," Budge wrote in his autobiography, "Johnston turned out to be more vehemently in favor of my signing than anyone else I had talked to. He said: 'I was offered thirty-to-forty thousand to sign a few years ago, and I thought I would,' 'Then a lot of people started telling me not to. They gave me that line about having to go to the back doors. They told me the country needed me to play tennis for the Davis Cup. . . . Well, you know what happened. A year or so later, I came down with TB. I needed money then, but I couldn't get my hands on it. All those friends who had urged me to stay amateur for the sake of Uncle Sam turned their backs on me as soon as I needed them. Take the money Don. The pats on the back don't last very long at all.'"[6]

At last the Davis Cup belonged to France. And soon afterwards Lacoste won his second U.S. Championship at Forest Hills, beating Tilden in three brilliant sets 11–9, 6–3, 11–9. Tilden felt the match was perhaps the greatest in his career; Al Laney agreed that "it was one of the finest exhibitions of tennis techniques and skills ever seen."* Yet Tilden could not win, even though he had opportunities for turning the tide in each of the three sets. Age defeated him, yet he once again won the admiration of the wildly cheering crowd, in defeat as he never had in victory.

Lacoste, who had defeated Tilden all three times they met during this brilliant tennis year, was now the undisputed Champion of the World as well as leader of the conquering Musketeers. Champagne flowed every evening on shipboard as the heroes carried the cup home to France. The Crocodile went to bed early each night, always of course paying his share of the tab.

The Musketeers had no sooner landed in France than the tennis authorities there began to build the most charming tennis facilities in the world, on a tree-laden spot on the edge of the Bois de Boulogne and not far from the racecourse at Auteuil. It was named the Stade Roland Garros, after a French aviator who was killed in the First World War. Here the French were to host the first challenge round in the history of the Davis Cup not to be played on grass; the red clay courts, typical of those used all over the Continent, were calculated to slow the ball down and favor the steady baseline defensive player over the big serve and net-rushing attacking game. At any rate, Roland Garros was and still is famous for matching the charm of Paris in the spring. It was an ideal setting for the first meeting on French soil between the defending Musketeers and the American challengers, led by Big Bill Tilden. All of Paris was waiting for the promised battle with "Beeg Beel" in the summer of 1928 (which almost never took place).

When Tilden moved on to Paris, it was not only as star of the American Davis Cup team but also as team captain, by official appointment of the USLTA. In the meantime, back in America, the vindictive USLTA officials, Mike Myrick in the lead, decided to go for the jugular, and

---

*In 1974, when *Tennis* magazine asked Danzig to rate the greatest matches he had ever seen, he listed this Lacoste-Tilden match at the top.

banned Captain Tilden from further play for violating the "Amateur Writer Rule." During Wimbledon, he had written a number of articles for a British syndicate, which appeared in over a hundred newspapers including the *World*, in New York. Everyone was shocked, even the newly appointed team captain, Joseph Wear; the USLTA was shocked in turn that most Americans took Tilden's side. French officialdom was most shocked of all: they had built Roland Garros and were selling tickets like hot cakes, all in anticipation of a great showdown between the Musketeers and Beeg Beel. The affair reached the highest levels of state, when finally Myron Herrick, our Ambassador to France, was ordered from above to straighten things out so that Tilden could play.

Tilden's suspension was lifted just two days before the challenge round began. He and Lacoste were to play the first match. The court had been heavily watered the night before, in order to slow it down in Lacoste's favor. The Crocodile, having just won Wimbledon (beating Tilden in the semifinals for the fourth time in a row) was a 2–1 favorite. Tilden was upset by the amateur controversy and seemed to be unable to concentrate during the first set which he lost 6–1. "About all I had," he wrote, "was my years of match experience, what few brains God gave me, and an overwhelming determination to win that contest at all costs. I couldn't hit Lacoste off the court so I chose to try to outfox, outmaneuver, out-spin and out-steady the great Frenchman from the baseline. On the face of it, this seemed the most ridiculous tactic one could choose against Lacoste, but it was my only chance."* Tilden stuck to his plan to outsteady Lacoste with chops, slices, and drop-shots from the baseline, except when (at the urging of his colleagues during the intermission) he tried to blast Lacoste off the court in the fourth set, which he lost. Tilden continued:

> I reached 4–3 in the fifth set after several desperate and probably lucky recoveries, when on Lacoste's service once more came a break which sounds like Fiction. At 15–all in the eighth game we had a long exchange and finally Lacoste hit deep to my backhand corner, voluntarily rushing to the net behind his shot. I hit a long, slow, rather high backhand chop down the line to his high forehand. I knew Lacoste's pet angle volley shot which he played about eighty per cent of the time from that position. Tired and drawn, but

---

*In winning the 1975 Wimbledon singles, Arthur Ashe beat Jimmy Connors by using much the same tactics as Tilden did in beating Lacoste.

hopeful, I started running across to my forehand court, hoping that Lacoste was unaware of my intent and would play his favorite stroke. Evidently he was watching the ball so intently that he had no idea of my maneuver. Sure enough, he hit the sharp-angled forehand volley I expected. I was almost at the umpire's chair and far beyond the sideline as I reached the ball just before it bounced the second time. Desperately, blindly, I connected with it *below the level of the net post* and between it and the umpire's chair, then crashed into the concrete rim of the court, over which I catapulted into the bosom of a large and deeply pained dowager. From her lap I looked back to find Lacoste still at the net. My shot had fallen good behind him in his backhand court. (My italics)[*7]

Lacoste was completely unnerved and Tilden quickly ran out the set and the match. The fading giant had won with one last gasp. Though he by no means played his best tennis, the match was one of the finest examples of his genius.

The match marked, above all, a fitting climax to the finest five years in the history of tennis. For, after France's successful defense of the Davis Cup, Tilden was again suspended from the amateur ranks and missed playing at Forest Hills in 1928 for the first time since he had lost in the first round in 1916. Lacoste, after leading France to their first Davis Cup victory in 1927 and a successful defense at the new Stade Roland Garros the following year, retired at the age of 25.

After his reinstatement as an amateur, Tilden went abroad with the Davis Cup team in 1929 to challenge the French. The Americans lost once again 3–2, Tilden losing the opening match to Cochet and then beating Borotra on the last day. At Wimbledon, he lost to Cochet in the semifinals. Back in in America, he won the U.S. Championships for the last time.

The year 1930 was Tilden's last as an amateur. He won Wimbledon and then went to France where he won the only match in a 4–1 loss to the French Davis Cup team. He spent a lonely summer on the Circuit

---

[*]Ever since July of 1928, that point has been embedded in my memory; we boys discussed it endlessly; later in the summer, in the Junior Championships of our club, I played in the finals with an older boy (he was 17 and I 13) who modeled his game entirely on Lacoste's, down to the inevitable white hat. I of course was Tilden, and fortunately, like my idol, won.

and lost in the semifinals at Forest Hills to John Hope Doeg of California. He signed a professional contract on the last day of the year

．

=====

Professional tennis began in 1926 when an American promoter, C. C. ("Cash and Carry") Pyle, stole Suzanne Lenglen from the amateur ranks for the then-princely sum of some $75,000. As a supporting cast to the Great Suzanne he signed up the most popular American women, Mary K. Browne, and three American men, Vincent Richards, Howard Kinsey, and Harvey Snodgrass. The first year's tour was a financial success. Eventually Pyle retired as interest in the new pro-game declined. Richards took over leadership and searched all over Continental Europe for new talent (playing pros hardly existed in England or America at the time), finally signing up a Czech pro, Karl Kozeluh, who was reputed to be the best tennis player in Europe even though he had never played in a major tournament. But Richards still needed a great name to draw the crowds. His talented and dramatic friend, Big Bill Tilden, was just the ticket. Richards signed him on for a tour with Kozeluh which opened at Madison Square Garden, on February 18, 1931 (see Figures 7 and 8). A crowd of 13,500 paid a gate of $36,000 to see Tilden mop up the Czech at will. Then the Tilden Tennis Tour, Inc. hit the road, zig-zagging across the country from Boston to Chicago to Los Angeles. Tilden drove the promoters crazy by winning all the time and inspiring an epidemic of "Big Bill Cancels Czech" headlines in city after city.

As professional tennis players were barred from all clubs by the British and American tennis associations, the pro tours were reduced to winter matches indoors in a variety of inadequate facilities. Arenas had to be booked well in advance so as not to conflict with basketball and hockey games. The more easily available gymnasiums at colleges and schools were often too small. Above all the tours were utterly exhausting. There was no air travel and railroad schedules were too rigid, so most of the travel was by night in automobiles, with a truck carrying the huge and heavy canvas court and other equipment.

The pro tour had a lean year in 1932 as Tilden played Richards and lesser lights. The next year Richards brought the German Champion Hans Nusslein to America to tour with Tilden. But gates steadily declined until 1934, when Ellsworth Vines, United States and Wimbledon

FIGURE 7

World's Tennis Championship

MADISON SQUARE GARDEN

NEW YORK CITY

Wednesday evening, February 18, 1931

William T. Tilden, 2nd

First Professional Appearance

VS.

Karel Kozeluh

World's Champion Professional

3 Out of 5 Set Match

for the

World's Indoor Professional Championship

Presented by

Jack Curley and Burt Cortelyou

in association with

TILDEN TENNIS TOUR, INC.

PRICES

$1.00 $2.00 $3.00

and a few Courtside Seats at

$5.00

TICKETS NOW ON SALE

A. G. SPALDING & BROS.

518 FIFTH AVENUE. Tel. Murray Hill 2-1291

105 NASSAU STREET. Tel. Cortlandt 7-2900

AMERICAN LAWN TENNIS, INC.

461 EIGHTH AVENUE

Tel. Medallion 3-3190

JACK CURLEY

1476 BROADWAY

Tel. Bryant 9-1600

AND AT THE BOX OFFICES

MADISON SQUARE GARDEN

8th Ave., between 49th and 50th Sts.

TEL. COLUMBUS 5-6800

Source: American Lawn Tennis, January 20, 1931.

FIGURE 8

Tilden Tennis Tour, Inc.

226 West 47th Street, New York, N. Y.

Presents

"Big Bill" Tilden { 7 Times U. S. Champion
10 Times Ranked 1 in U. S.
11 Years on U. S. Davis Cup Team

"K" Kozeluh { 5 Years World's Pro Champion

And other World-Famous Stars to be Announced

In a

NATION-WIDE TENNIS TOUR

Playing in

NEW YORK, MADISON SQUARE GARDEN	February 18
BALTIMORE	February 19
BOSTON	February 20
CINCINNATI, 149TH ARMORY	February 22
YOUNGSTOWN	February 23
CHICAGO	February 25
DETROIT	February 28
OMAHA	March 2

Indoor or Outdoor

Book Now   *Book Now*   *Book Now*

Write BURT CORTELYOU, General Manager, Tilden Tennis Tour, Inc., 226 West 47th Street, New York, N. Y., for terms, details and dates.

All indoor matches played on specially constructed courts of cork carpet supplied by the Armstrong Cork Company.

In writing give approximate seating accommodations, and for indoor matches give actual size of open floor space.

Entire tennis equipment, including net, backstops and balls, supplied by A. G. Spalding & Bros.

The new Spalding-Tilden Diamond Top Flite racket used by Tilden on sale at all matches, or obtainable by order from TILDEN TENNIS TOUR, Inc., 226 West 47th Street, New York, N. Y., or through any SPALDING dealer.

On Sale at the Matches

TILDEN'S TENNIS BOOKS

"Glory's Net"—A thrilling novel of love, tennis and amateurism	$1.00	"The Phantom Drive"—Short tennis fiction stories	1.00
"Match Play and the Spin of the Ball"	3.00	"The Pinch Quitter"—Short stories for boys	1.00
"Match Play and the Spin of the Ball"—abridged edition	2.00	"Tennis for the Junior Player, the Club Player and the Expert"—A textbook of instruction	.50
		"Shooting Stars of 1930"	.50

also

"AMERICAN LAWN TENNIS"—the leading magazine on the game.
"*Tennis*"—Official organ of the U. S. L. T. A.

All these can be ordered by mail from TILDEN TENNIS TOUR, Inc., 226 West 47th Street, New York, N. Y. BURT CORTELYOU, *General Manager*.

Source: American Lawn Tennis, January 20, 1931.

Champion, made his pro debut at Madison Square Garden before a turn-away crowd of 16,000, a goodly proportion in black ties. Tilden clobbered him in a little over an hour. Allison Danzig wrote in the *New York Times* that Vines's game was "far superior to his showing as an amateur." But playing one-night stands in 93 cities and towns across the country was pretty hard on the old man and Vines ended up winning 58–35. The Tilden-Vines tour set a pattern for the pro tours. Year after year most of the best amateurs turned pro and challenged the then Pro Champion. "By the time I signed," wrote Don Budge, "Tilden, Vines and Perry had also all turned professional, but pro tennis then, as right up to 1968, had to struggle with talent and showmanship, but without tradition and honor."[8] In many ways Tilden was the virtual founder of professional tennis and took the lead right up until America's entrance into World War II. The postwar era of pro tennis will be discussed in later chapters.

Here it should be said that Big Bill was still playing top-flight tennis in his late forties when he toured with Don Budge. "He just loved tennis," Budge once said of Tilden. "The last time we toured, in 1941, he was almost fifty, and I beat him something like 55–6, but let me tell you: he loved it and tried like hell every game. One time I asked him: 'Bill, what will you do when you can't play tennis anymore?' He just looked at me and said: 'Hmmmph. Kill myself.'"[9]

CHAPTER 11

Big Bill Tilden:
A Gentleman Possessed by Genius

Talk not of genius baffled. Genius is master of man.
Genius does what it must, and talent does what it can.
—Edward Robert Bulwer-Lytton

THE GENTLEMAN AND THE GENIUS WERE ALWAYS AT WAR WITH ONE another in the fascinating mind of Big Bill Tilden. As Frank Deford put it,

> On the one hand he was the most scrupulous sportsman, obsessed with fair play, but on the other, designing and irritating—from the moment he showed up with the armful of rackets, the polo coat (sometimes complete with silk muffler), and underneath it the white V-neck with red and blue piping, that became known generically simply enough as the Tilden sweater. As he approached the court, he would, with graceful disdain, throw one racket far out before him, a pearl before swine, soliciting a "rough" or "smooth" from the other player. For warm-up, after carefully selecting a racket, plunking the strings like violins, he would proceed with his repertoire, showing off for the crowd at the expense of his poor opponent. The other player often appeared to intrude on the relationship between the crowd and Tilden. When it was about time to start, he would call out gaily, "I'm ready whenever you're exhausted, partner."[1]

Great classics are often written at the end of heroic ages. It is highly appropriate that at the end of the amateur age, in 1968, Al Laney published his great history of amateur tennis, *Covering the Court: A 50-Year Love Affair with the Game of Tennis*, a book in which Tilden was often the protagonist. Laney's love affair began just before the Tilden era in 1914 when, as a teenager from Florida, he went out to Forest Hills (instead of up to the Polo Grounds to watch his beloved Giants as he had intended) and watched Norman Brookes and Anthony Wilding take the Davis Cup from the defending Americans, R. Norris Williams and the "California Comet," Maurice McLoughlin. For over half a century he made a life and living out of his love for tennis. His great book is a magnificently romantic tribute to the amateur game.

Al Laney had watched Tilden rather casually during his rise to become the Tennis Champion of the World during the early twenties. On the whole, he disliked him and underestimated his ability, predicting, for instance, an easy victory for Johnston in the 1924 final. Like many others, Laney at first despised Tilden's blatant showmanship, occasional outrageous tantrums, unreasonable arrogance, and quarrelsome and intimidating behavior towards linesmen and tennis officialdom in general. In spite of his bias, Laney thought a great deal about the 1924 final in the days and weeks which followed and finally had to admit to himself that he had been wrong about Tilden: "At any rate," he wrote, "here was where I made a sad farewell, so to speak, to Little Bill, whom I loved, and swung over completely to Big Bill, whom I did not yet esteem as I was to later, but whom I now recognize beyond possible doubt as the greatest, king of them all."

On a trip abroad not long after that famous Tilden-Johnston final at Forest Hills, Laney took along a bag full of clippings, largely consisting of interviews with and articles about Tilden. Among the clippings was an article on Tilden's temperament and genius by an obscure sportswriter named Wilson, which became central to Laney's thinking during his next ten days at sea. He later wrote about his thoughts on that voyage as follows:

> Most people who wrote or spoke about Tilden, the most controversial figure the game has known, said that he reached the heights by conquering his temperament. I also accepted this view until Wilson suggested that the only trouble with this explanation of Tilden's greatness was that it was not true. Tilden did no such thing, it was suggested. He did not conquer his temperament. On the contrary he used it and made it serve him in achieving his triumphs.

> This view, though it upset conventional belief, was immensely interesting, but I had put it aside for future consideration. Now in the leisurely days at sea I took it up again, pursuing it to a point where it could reveal something previously obscured. I had been repelled though fascinated by Tilden's personality, but having had this now obvious fact revealed, he had become an object for closer observation and study. In the light of what I had seen and was to see later, I believe the observation to have been correct, and I note that Tilden remained to the end of his long career just as mercurial, irascible, and easily upset and sent into rage as he had been in the years of his rise to world supremacy.

> He seemed to have learned early that when he tried to curb his temperament, to rein it in, he lost matches; that when he gave it unleashed play, he won. The time required to learn and apply this lesson may account for the fact that Tilden did not reach the top until after his twenty-seventh birthday. Wilson said that "one must play around with the word genius to estimate justly this wizard of the courts," and there is justification for the feeling that for Tilden, temperamental release and free flow did amount to a special genius.

"The grand, almost regal manner with which Tilden is wont to destroy his opponents," Wilson wrote, "the insouciance with which in September he reverses a July setback; the overwhelming drama and color his personality and methods infuse into his game, make him quite the most magnificent champion of tennis history."

The many times Tilden pulled out a match after being within a point or so of defeat were cited to support this rather extravagant appraisal, and it was contended that "this unconscionable relish of his for the prolonged battle and deferred rush to victory, is not volitional but belongs to the temperament and the peculiar genius of the man."

Tilden could never accept defeat. If on occasion he lacked the natural spark to ignite his game, he crowded on the temperament. He could tap a vein of something like divine frenzy by pulling out all the stops in that often deplorable but priceless temperament. Tilden could play superlative tennis while boiling with anger against an opponent. . . .

Tilden, in short, became the greatest of champions because he could turn creative artistry into unparalleled performance.[2]

It would be hard to find a more enlightening analysis of the relationship between genius and temperament than in Laney's thoughts on Tilden's tennis game.

Genius is a rare quality of mind, while talent, in sport at least, is a far more prevalent gift of God. Both Dick Williams and Little Bill Johnston were highly talented (gifted) tennis players but by no means geniuses. Tilden's great genius lay in his supreme confidence in his ability to dominate (mastermind) his opponent psychologically. In his first book, *The Art of Tennis*, written in his hotel room while he was playing in his famous first Wimbledon, Tilden wrote that "the primary object in match tennis is to break up the other man's game." And he applied this psychological maxim with great style in beating the World Champion, Gerald Patterson, in the challenge round. Patterson took the first set easily at 6–2 and everyone expected him to run out the match with ease. Quite suddenly it seemed, Tilden gained psychological mastery of the match: "A subtle change came over Patterson's game," wrote a British reporter in great surprise. "Things that looked easy went out, volleys that ought to have been crisply negotiated ended up in the net." In winning the next three sets with ease, the reporter concluded that "the Philadelphian made rather an exhibition of his opponent."[3]

The very essence of Tilden's genius was his psychological will to power over his opponents: "When two players start a match," he wrote in his masterpiece, *Match Play and the Spin of the Ball*, "it is always a battle to see who will dominate and who will be pushed around. One player or the other will ultimately impress his tennis personality upon the other. The one who does will win, because by so doing he forces the recognition of impending defeat upon his opponent." His psychology of gamesmanship included being the first one to toss his racquet, thus forcing his opponent to choose between rough and smooth and the first one to ask his opponent if he is ready to play, as if to say: "I'm ready whenever you're exhausted, partner."

Tilden's psychology of dominance derived from his deep-seated sense of himself as a fine artist whose instrument was his racquet. The words of his longtime friend and famous opera singer, Mary Garden, summed up his own tennis creed when she said: "Now you listen to me, Bill, and then don't listen to anyone again. You're a tennis artist and artists always know better than anyone else when they're right. If you believe in a certain way to play, you play that way no matter what anyone tells you. Once you lose faith in your own artistic judgment, you're lost. Win or lose, right or wrong, be true to your art."[4]

René Lacoste soon saw that Tilden was an artist who always played tennis for his own satisfaction: "He does not seek approval of the public," Lacoste wrote in a brief but perceptive book, *Lacoste on Tennis*, "but only the satisfaction of his own mind. . . . He seems to exercise a strange fascination over his opponents as well as his spectators. Tilden, even when beaten, always leaves an impression on the public mind that he was superior to the victor."*[5]

---

*Tilden, Mary Garden, and René Lacoste, of course, lived in a world which equated the amateur athlete and the fine artist, who were supposed to be above mere money values, and sharply differentiated them both from the professional athlete and the commercial artist who were essentially businessmen. The Pennsylvania Academy of the Fine Arts in Philadelphia, the oldest and most distinguished art school in the nation, for example, was still educating its students to become fine artists in Tilden's day. "Any talk about making money was thought to be prostituting the arts," said a professor of the old school who is now forced to teach his students how to market themselves in the highly competitive (and cynical) world of modern "pop" art. In his popular lectures in an overcrowded classroom, he begins with the jarring and unromantic fact of modern life: "The art world today is an industry." The tennis world is, too.

Fred Perry, England's last World Champion, had a great respect for Tilden's tennis brain and consummate knowledge of gamesmanship. I wondered if he had read any of Tilden's writings when I read his second autobiography, especially when he wrote as follows:

When Tilden walked on the court he was the king; he dominated the scene. When I played I had one or two simple ruses to get the spectators looking at me instead of my opponent. When we got halfway on to the court I would throw the racket in front of me and call, "rough or smooth?" Then after we had warmed up for a couple of minutes, I would say loudly, "Any time you're ready." As far as the public was concerned, one player—me— had made two decisions already, so I was the one people were watching. Tilden noticed this, as he noticed everything else, and in our professional matches he eventually asked me if I would allow him to make the first moves instead of jumping the gun. Another ruse of mine, when I went to the net, was to hit the ball and then move my body behind it, making it a little more difficult for my opponent to pick up the white ball against the white background of my shirt, and maybe upsetting his timing slightly. The *only player* who ever noticed this maneuver was Bill Tilden. Tilden never missed a trick. (My italics)[6]

Gamesmanship seems to be the very opposite of the gentlemanly ethic. But reality is never either/or but both/and or more-or-less. One should always think of continuums rather than categories. Thus at the gentlemanly end of the continuum stands Dick Williams, without a drop of gamesmanship in his nature. Somewhere in the middle was Tilden, the grandly ambivalent, gentleman-genius, at one moment an obsessive moralist and follower of the cricket creed and another a master psychologist and often irritating gamesman. At the far opposite end from Williams stood Fred Perry, a single-minded follower of the winning-is-everything ethic. Born on the other side of the tracks as the son of a Labor M.P. in class-conscious England, Perry was proud of the fact that he never aspired to the upper-class cricket ethic. He wrote in his 1984 autobiography:

I hear a lot about Englishmen being good losers. Hogwash! There's nothing good about losing. . . . It should be the end of the world if you lost a tennis match at top level. . . . I was a loner, though I traveled most of the time as part of a team and had a lot of friends, I always made it my business to know more about my opponents than they knew about me. I was pretty crafty. If I ever said, 'Good shot'—which I very seldom did—they were never sure if I meant it or not. Nor did I ever believe in the gesture of throwing a point away in order to acquire the reputation of being "a good sport." I didn't aspire to being a good sport: "champion" was good enough for me.

It would be hard to find a more honest and clearly stated description of the *success ethic*; or, as they say, nice guys finish last.

Tilden was obsessed with honor and sportsmanship, having been reared, as we have seen, at the heart of the upper-class, cricket ethic in Philadelphia. Refusing to accept points which he thought he didn't deserve, he was forever throwing points, games, and whole sets when he was convinced that the linesman or umpire had made a bad decision. He once threw a whole set in a challenge round match because of a bad call in his favor on set point. Often his flamboyant moralism was as irritating as his temper tantrums. A moral despot, he was convinced that he was always right: "Would you like to correct your error?" he was in the habit of asking livid linesmen. Though he had the same will to win as Perry and all great champions, he nevertheless insisted on playing the game for fun: "Play tennis without fear of defeat and because it's fun or don't play it at all," he wrote. "Champions are born in the labor of defeat." Frank Deford quoted Sam Hardy, Davis Cup captain and closer to Tilden than most men, who said that Tilden "never makes a serious business of winning tournaments. To him, the fascination of playing is paramount, the victory a minor consideration. He is as excited and happy over a match that he has lost as over one he won. This accounts for many of his defeats. It is the penalty he pays for his mercurial temperament, but then, without this temperament, he could never be, as he is, the most brilliant and daring player in the world."[7]

A few comments on Sam Hardy's perceptive insights into Tilden's genius are in order here. In the first place, Hardy clearly saw that winning was not everything to Tilden, even though being the best and most exciting tennis player in the world surely was. Above all, Tilden loved the process more than the prize, which was what made him the essential amateur with little in common with so many of today's most successful pros. To jump ahead in our story for a moment, it would seem to me that

Tilden may well have had more in common with John McEnroe, a pro, than with Fred Perry as an amateur. Both Big Bill and Mac were driven by a rage for perfection, not in order to make money but to satisfy deep elemental urges. They were both possessed by genius, one in a gentlemanly age and the other in an age of incivility and bad manners. In other words, it is not either/or as between amateurs and professionals. It is rather that more amateurs seemed to love and enjoy the process as Tilden did whereas all too many of today's pros too often seem to be enduring the process in order to make money, or so it more and more seems to me. Perhaps we should admit that the amateur sportsman is far more fun to watch than the money-motivated pro; that the funless tennis of the modern pro tour is becoming more and more boring.

In Tilden's day, a whole generation of American boys were reared on the values of Frank Merriwell of Yale. I once knew a man whose immigrant, blue-collar father sent him to Yale in the 1930s because of his admiration for the honorable values he found in the Frank Merriwell stories. While Tilden was very probably an avid fan of true-blue Frank, he was definitely a regular reader of the *St. Nicholas* magazine whose didactic stories and articles carried Merriwell's sporting moral code on down to 1943 when it stopped publication. Tilden not only read *St. Nicholas* in his youth; he wrote for it later on. In fact, by far his best discussion of the unwritten tennis code of his day is to be found in an article on "Sportsmanship in Tennis," which he published in the June 1921 issue of the magazine, and from which I quote the following lines:

> The American amateur athlete is above all else a clean sportsman. It is one of his characteristics and the underlying principle of our scholastic and intercollegiate athletic system. Good sportsmanship is also inherent in American manhood.
>
> Now this whole question of good and bad sportsmanship is essential. A nation whose men have been trained to the practices of honesty, generosity, and fair play is bound to have a policy of broad-minded liberality in all its international dealings. The opposite is likewise true. It has been found that following the doctrine of "Might is Right" in sports results in giving an entire people the same point of view.
>
> There is just this difference between amateur and professional sport: the former insists upon honesty, generosity, and fair play among its followers;

but although there is a desire to maintain an equally high standard in pro-fessional athletics, it has been found that, when money is a consideration, fair play is apt to make a hasty exit from the scene. For this reason, the games of golf and tennis grip their followers in such a manner that all are loyal to the sport itself and to all the high standards sportsmanship signifies. (Can we say the same of organized baseball?)

Indeed, it is the inherent honesty of these two games that above all else grips their players and holds them with a steadfastness that the higher-salaried stars of the diamond rarely, if ever, feel.

I am a tennis player. . . . What a strange contrast tennis offers to most other sports! Take the matter of officials. There is no paid umpire to render deci-sions. In fact the men who act as umpires and linesmen in the biggest tourna-ments are there only to relieve the contestants themselves from the strain of watching the ball. Their purpose is not to enforce law and order. And the un-written code of the game is that, in case of doubt on any decision, you must give your opponent the benefit of that doubt by yielding him the point. . . .

It is the law of the game of tennis that the word of a linesman or umpire is final; it cannot be questioned. Their decisions end the matter. Conse-quently, there has grown up a fine clean spirit of sportsmanship, an unwrit-ten law, to the effect that no matter how flagrant the error may be on the part of one of these officials, if it is against you, no thought of questioning it may arise. It's also the law of the game never to take anything that is not due you. This unwritten code transcends the written one to such an extent that when one profits by a mistake on the part of an official he takes the law into his own hands and gives justice to his opponent. Naturally, this de-mands a rare courage, for you are seemingly discourteous to the umpire or linesman, as the case may be, yet only by so doing can you hold your self-re-spect. It is the recognized method of returning to your opponent that which is justly his due.

Let me explain by citing several historical incidents. Some years ago, in a famous Davis Cup match in which England was pitted against Australasia, those two great sportsmen and wonderful exponents of tennis, J. C. Parke, of England, and Norman E. Brookes, of Australia, were fighting out a match that would prove the turning-point of the tie. Parke was at his best, an occasion when he played superbly. It seemed apparent to all that he had Brookes beaten. He was leading two sets to one and match point in the fourth. Then it was that he drove Brookes far out of court with a deep

Teddy Tinling (left) and Big Bill Tilden, photographed on the Riviera, in 1930; Teddy, at 6 feet, 7 inches, was the taller. Tinling, who died in 1990, just short of his eightieth birthday, was a keen student of the game for 7 decades. He knew everybody from the great Susanne Lenglen to Steffi Graf. Master of Ceremonies at Wimbledon for many years, he was inducted into the Tennis Hall of Fame at Newport in 1986. *(American Lawn Tennis)*

"Little Bill" Johnston, showing his famous Western forehand. Having learned the game on the public courts of San Francisco, he came East and won the U.S. Singles Championship in 1915, and repeated it in 1919. For the rest of his career, he played in the shadow of Tilden, who defeated him in the finals in 1920, 1922, 1923, 1924, and 1925. As the underdog with perfect manners he was, nevertheless, far more beloved than Tilden. *(American Lawn Tennis)*

The Four Musketeers of France with Pierre Gillou, Davis Cup team captain: left to right, Brugnon, Cochet, Gillou, Lacoste, and Borotra. The team finally toppled Tilden and won the Davis Cup at Germantown Cricket Club in 1927. (*American Lawn Tennis*)

René Lacoste beginning his typical backhand stroke. Born of wealthy parents with no great athletic ability, he was a self-made tennis machine who became the best player in the world in 1926 and 1927, and who was the real leader of the French Musketeers. He first came to Forest Hills in 1923, losing in the second round; in 1924, he lost to Johnston in the quarter-finals; in 1925, he also lost in the quarters to Richards; but he finally won the U.S. Championship in 1926. (*American Lawn Tennis*)

Tilden takes a line (acts as line judge) at the Lacoste-Cochet semi-final match at Forest Hills in 1926. In our status-obsessed age, no world champion would stoop to such a low-level job. (*American Lawn Tennis*)

Henri Cochet was a natural genius who took the ball on the rise yet never seemed to be hurried. In 1927 he won the first of his two Wimbledon singles titles "in a manner not equalled before or since": in the quarter-finals, he beat Frank Hunter after losing the first two sets; in the semis, Tilden won the first two sets and led 5–1 in the third, only to lose 17 points in a row and the set 5–7, and the match in five sets. Cochet then beat Borotra in a five-set final, Borotra winning the first two sets and having six match points. Typical of that ancient age of honor, Borotra lost one of those match points when he informed the referee that Cochet's ball, which landed out, had touched him first. (*American Lawn Tennis*)

Jean Borotra was known as the "Bounding Basque," as this photograph explains. He captivated the Wimbledon crowds as no one had done before, or has since. He won the singles title twice, the doubles three times, and the mixed once. He competed at Wimbledon first in 1922 and last in 1964—a span of 42 years. He then went on competing in the veteran's until 1977, becoming the only person to have competed in all the anniversary celebrations, fiftieth , seventy-fifth, and one-hundredth (1977). (*American Lawn Tennis*)

Sidney Wood (top left) and Frank Shields (bottom right), two American boys who had once played on the Roxbury (Connecticut) School tennis team together, reached the finals at Wimbledon in 1931. Both were fine sportsmen at the top of their games. Unfortunately, Shields injured his knee in a previous match and was ordered to default by the Davis Cup captain. He probably would have won (he was seeded third to Wood's seventh). Wood's win by default (called a "walk-over" at Wimbledon) is still unique in the history of that tournament. *(American Lawn Tennis)*

Frederick J. Perry (left) defeated "Gentleman Jack" Crawford of Australia in the 1933 final at Forest Hills. As Crawford had already won the Australian, French, and British championships that year, this defeat deprived him of becoming the first man to win what later was called the Grand Slam. *(American Lawn Tennis)*

J. Donald Budge (left), from Oakland, California, beat Baron Gottfried von Cramm of Germany in the finest and most dramatic tennis match ever; it was the final match in the 1937 Inter-Zone Final Davis Cup tie played at Wimbledon; Budge won in five sets and the U.S. won 3–2. *(American Lawn Tennis)*

The Merion Cricket Club, on Philadelphia's Main Line; here, exactly 25 years after Brookes and Wilding had taken the Davis Cup Down Under (in 1914), the Australians beat the Americans in 1939, just as Hitler's armies were marching. (*American Lawn Tennis*)

After the most important match of the Davis Cup tie at Merion in 1939, Captains Walter Pate of the U.S. and Harry Hopman of Australia are congratulating the winner, Adrian Quist, while the loser, Robert Riggs (left) looks dejected. Clinton Mellor (right) was a Merion member and official referee of the tie. (*American Lawn Tennis*)

American Tennis Greats sitting on the porch of the Merion Cricket Club during the Intercollegiates, 1934. From left to right: Dwight Davis, donor of the Davis Cup; Joseph S. Clark, first Intercollegiate Champion; Julian Myrick, Tennis Czar during the Tilden era; Henry Slocum, U.S. Singles Champion in 1888–1889; and Bill Clothier, U.S. Singles Champion in 1906. Behind Clothier sits Hope Montgomery Scott, the model for Tracy Lord, heroine of her friend Philip Barry's most successful play, *The Philadelphia Story*. (William J. Clothier II)

William J. Clothier and his son (left) defeated Dwight Davis and his son for the U.S. Father and Son Championship on August 29, 1936, exactly thirty years after Bill Clothier, Sr., won the U.S. Singles at Newport on August 29, 1906. (William J. Clothier II)

Two Americans, Elwood Cooke and Bobby Riggs (right), both impeccably dressed, enter the Centre Court at Wimbledon for the 1939 Singles Final. Riggs won the singles, doubles, and mixed that year, thereby parlaying a hundred-pound bet with a London bookie into $108,000. Afraid to bring this small fortune home, he left it in a London bank vault for the duration of the war. (*American Lawn Tennis*)

Bobby Riggs (left) congratulates Jack Kramer on his winning the Professional Lawn Tennis Association's Singles title in 1948. (*American Lawn Tennis*)

drive, and immediately followed in to the net. Brookes lobbed, but he lobbed short. It meant the match for England if Parke won the point; quite possibly, it meant the Davis Cup as well. Parke swung hard into the ball and drove it through Brookes's court for a kill. But his racket, following through in a long downward flight, touched the net so very slightly that none of the officials saw it.

"Game, set, match, Parke!" called the umpire.

Brookes came forward, smiling, hand extended in congratulations. Parke remained where he had hit the ball, his face turned to the umpire.

"Mr. Umpire," he said. "I hit the net."

"You are sure, Mr. Parke?" came the reply.

"Quite," he answered.

Brookes stood silent, still ready with congratulations.

"The point is Mr. Brookes's. Deuce!" called the umpire.

Play recommenced. Parke lost that game. Brookes, quick to seize his last chance, could not be stopped. The match, and ultimately the Davis Cup, went to Australia.

Was it wrong for Parke to speak? That question was rather freely discussed at the time. Tennis men all know it was not, that Parke lived up to the traditions of the sport, just as all of us hope and trust we shall do when such occasions arise.

Tilden goes on to describe several more instances of sportsmanship at critical points in important matches, incidentally noting that "hardly a great match goes by without some incident that shows the true sportsmanship of tennis players." And he concludes his article in his typically romantic style: "It is my sincere belief that tennis is a great power for good among the boys of this country, for it is not only a game demanding perfect physical condition, but a mental keenness, fine nerve-control, and, by no means least, the highest spirit of sportsmanship. For it is always to be remembered that tennis and good sportsmanship have been, are, and will be synonymous."

═══

For one reason or another, Tilden's effeminate mannerisms became more and more obvious as he grew older. His beloved Aunt Hey remarked on the change as did others around the Cricket Club, sometimes less kindly. At any rate, in 1939, at the age of 46, he left Philadelphia and the social rigidities of Eastern Seaboard Society forever and settled in permissive Los Angeles where the sun shines every day and he was able to play tennis and give lessons all year round.

Ironically enough, Tilden finally disgraced himself before the world in permissive Southern California. Those were the days when the Los Angeles Tennis Club, under the leadership of Perry Jones, was still the breeding ground of future American champions. Jack Kramer, at the age of 15, often played hooky from school, took two buses and a trolley car (one and a half hours each way) to the club just to play with the great Tilden: "He was a strange guy, but he couldn't have been nicer to me," Kramer told Frank Deford. "That was almost a decade before he got arrested for going after little boys, but he certainly never acted improperly with me—and I'd never heard of that at the time either. Whatever was wrong with Bill, he had it in check then."[8] That was in 1936 during one of Tilden's periodic visits to Hollywood.

About a decade later, after Tilden had moved out to Hollywood for good, he and Bobby, a spoiled young boy he had met at the Los Angeles Tennis Club, were apprehended by two Beverly Hills police officers, just before ten o'clock in the evening on November 23, 1946. They were driving along Sunset Boulevard in Tilden's classy Packard clipper. Bobby was at the wheel (illegally) while Tilden, according to the cops, had his left arm around him, "holding him very tightly, and, it appeared, with his right hand on the boy's lap." The cops ordered Bobby to get out of the car and then noticed that his fly was open, four buttons undone.

To protect the boy, Tilden stubbornly insisted on pleading guilty, contrary to the professional advice of his lawyer who was horrified that the old champion was still "hung up on this sportsman thing," as he put it. Had Tilden followed his lawyer's professional advice and pleaded not guilty he would have gotten off and avoided disgrace, for Bobby was a handsome and dissolute 14-year-old whose divorced parents had no desire to punish Tilden. The boy was, in sexual ways, probably more sophisticated than Tilden. On the afternoon of the arrest, he had had sex with a young girl, so he told Tilden, who then asked him where he had learned so much about sex: "In the private school I just left," Bobby replied casually. In short, after a careful study of the facts, the probation officer on the case felt that Bobby was not hurt by Tilden as much as by his pam-

pered environment and divorced parents. Tilden nevertheless was convicted and sent to Castaic Honor Farm, a minimum-security facility of
some five hundred inmates, located in an isolated area some forty miles
north of Los Angeles. He served seven and a half months of his year's
sentence and was released in August 1947.

Free again, Tilden soon found out that most of his Hollywood benefac-
tors, many of whom had paid him well for tennis lessons, now dropped him.
Only David Selznick, Joseph Cotton, and Charlie Chaplin remained loyal.
Perry Jones, a prim and prissy bachelor, often rumored to be a homosexual
himself, had never liked Tilden much and now barred him from the L.A.
Tennis Club entirely. Giving fewer and fewer lessons (now mostly on Chap-
lin's court), Tilden was forced to move into cheaper and cheaper rooms.
Somehow he managed to write a second autobiography, publishing it as *My
Story* in 1948. It was little more than pages of name-dropping, an ultimately
embarrassing book. He also wrote his first play in years; the *Los Angeles
Times* found it well written but positively "malodorous," considering the
plot included a mentally ill mother, a kidnapped son, and sibling incest.

Unfortunately the aging and lonely champion became more and more
lax in his dress, his personal hygiene, and his morals, finally stooping to
cruising around high schools and YMCAs until he was arrested again for
molesting a young hitchhiker. This second offense could have been prosecuted as a felony, but the same judge who had heard Tilden's first case only
charged him with a probation violation, sending him back to the Castaic
Honor Farm for a year; he was released early, just before Christmas 1949, a
few days before an Associated Press poll of sportswriters rated him the best
athlete of the half-century. Tilden got more than twice the votes of any of his
rivals, including Ruth, Dempsey, Bobby Jones, and Red Grange.

This second arrest was a blow to Tilden and reinforced his reputation as a
degenerate back East in Philadelphia. At the Germantown Cricket Club,
where he had been made an honorary life member, his picture was taken
down from its honorable place on the wall, right opposite the main entrance
to the clubhouse, and all efforts were made to expunge his name from official memory (today the picture hangs once again in its old place of honor).
Except for Vinnie Richards, almost no one, including once-doting protégés
like Sarah Palfrey Danzig and Carl Fisher, stood up for him. "They didn't,
they didn't, myself included," Carl Fisher, by then a prominent Philadelphia
osteopath, ashamedly confessed to Frank Deford, many years later.[9]

Tilden was still a member of the Professional Tennis Players Association, which he had helped to found after World War II. True to form, when he was found dead at the age of 60 in 1953, in a shabby room in a run-down apartment house on a side street just off Hollywood and Vine in Los Angeles, he was fully dressed, with bags packed, and ready to depart for Cleveland, where he was entered in the United States Professional Tennis Championships.

A memorial service was held the following week at a local mortuary, attended by a few friends, including Ellsworth Vines, Pancho Segura, and Johnny Doeg, as well as Gussie Moran and Noel Brown, two of his last protégés. No one came, nor were messages or flowers sent, from the USLTA or from Philadelphia. "Tilden was in a nice brown suede jacket and a new clean white sweater with red deer figures running across the chest, which Joseph Cotton had bought for him to lie in," wrote Frank Deford. "Then Big Bill was cremated, because it was cheaper to get him across state lines that way, and shipped back to Philadelphia. For $115, a small stone was bought, and it reads WILLIAM T. TILDEN 2ND 1893–1953. That is the only monument of any kind, anywhere in the world—at Forest Hills, at Wimbledon, in Germantown, anywhere—that pays tribute to the greatest tennis player who ever lived. And the trophies are in a Los Angeles warehouse. There is nothing else at all."

He was buried in the family plot, at the foot of his beloved mother and beside his older brother, Herbert, in the Ivy Hill Cemetery, not far from the Germantown Cricket Club.

———

At this point it is important to stress the fact that Tilden's Merriwell moral code in tennis was but a reflection of the unwritten ideals of his whole class and generation. A fascinating recent book by Walter Isaacson and Evan Thomas, *The Wise Men: Six Friends and the World They Made* (1986), is a detailed study of how six amateur public servants—Averell Harriman, Dean Acheson, Robert Lovett, John McCloy, Charles Bohlen, and George Kennan—were the unofficial leaders of the last WASP establishment to dominate the values of Americans as a whole during the three decades between the coming to power of Franklin D. Roosevelt in 1933, and the assassination of John F. Kennedy in 1963.

Merriwell values still pervaded the whole establishment during those three decades which witnessed America's rise to become the unquestioned leader of the Free World. Sportsmen, as we have already seen in the case of Frank Shields, had a definite advantage in their rise into the ranks of the upper class as well as the establishment. The last leader of the establishment, John Jay McCloy, for instance, was born north of Market Street (across the tracks) in Philadelphia two years after Tilden's birth in then fashionable Germantown. His determined, widowed mother paved his way to success by "doing hair" for a wide circle of fashionable friends of Senator George Wharton Pepper's wife. She not only made her living among Philadelphia's gentry, she also absorbed their values which she passed on to her beloved son. No natural athlete, McCloy was taught to "run with the swift," had the winner's instinct, and made himself into a first-rate club tennis player. While working his way up in a Wall Street law firm, he rented a room in Forest Hills where he became a member of the West Side Tennis Club as well as the exclusive Heights Casino in Brooklyn. S. Wallis Merrihew once wrote a column in *American Lawn Tennis* (February 15, 1925) on young McCloy's spirited match with Tilden at the Heights Casino. Though McCloy lost to the master, he carried him to 7–5 in the second set. Eventually, he was known on Wall Street as the man who once beat Tilden. During World War II, McCloy worked closely with the ancient Wise Men's mentor, Henry Stimson, at the War Department, before becoming President of the World Bank and High Commissioner of occupied Germany. Following Harriman and Acheson, blue-blooded Grotonian-Yalemen both, McCloy was the last unofficial chairman of the American establishment. Always guarding his private and independent, amateur status, he probably turned down more offers of Cabinet posts than any other man in our history.

Perhaps Big Bill Tilden is best placed generationally by noting that he was born in 1893, the same year as Dean Acheson, one of the Wise Men, and John P. Marquand, the classic novelist of their class.* Acheson, the son

---

*It is interesting that during the decade when Tilden was at the height of his reign as King of Tennis, T. S. Eliot of Harvard published *The Waste Land* (1922), Sinclair Lewis of Yale published *Main Street* (1920), *Babbitt* (1922), and *Arrowsmith* (1922), and F. Scott Fitzgerald of Princeton published *This Side of Paradise* (1920) and *The Great Gatsby* (1925). At the same time, there were two Nobel Prize winners who did not go to college—Ernest Hemingway, who published *The Torrents of Spring* and *The Sun also Rises* in 1926, and William Faulkner, who published *Soldier's Pay* (1926) and *The Sound and the Fury* (1929).

of an Episcopal Bishop, graduated from Groton and Yale and took a law degree from Harvard. Instead of going on to Wall Street, he went to Washington where he clerked for Justice Felix Frankfurter of the Supreme Court and then built up a fine law practice. Never entirely sympathetic with Roosevelt, he became President Truman's close confidant and Secretary of State. He was probably more responsible for the Truman Doctrine than Truman and more responsible for the Marshall Plan than General Marshall. Finally he was a friend and occasional advisor of President Kennedy. By the way, it is interesting that, just as Arthur Ashe, a cultivated black man, was the last best example of the gentlemanly values of amateur tennis, so John F. Kennedy, a cultivated Irish Catholic, was the last Protestant establishment President of the United States. Marquand, whose many successful novels established him as the leading anthropologist of upper-class mores in America, was convinced that Kennedy was admirably equipped to carry on these class mores: "Five days before Marquand died, the week of the Democratic Convention," wrote a *New Yorker* editor in 1960, "he surprised us (for we had understood that he was a Republican) by announcing that it was his intention to vote for Senator Kennedy and by contributing, as his share of the talk, a charming and touching personal anecdote about the nominee's grandfather, whom he called Honey Fitz."

In his classic book *The Late George Apley* (1936), Marquand's Boston Brahmin hero, not long before his death in 1933, wrote to his son about his (Apley's) newly-born grandson. "I hope, when he grows up, that . . . he will see what so many of you have forgotten, that there must be certain standards, that there must be certain formulae in art and thought and manners. There must be a class which sets a tone, not for its own pleasure, but because of the responsibility which it owes to others. In a sense it may be what the demagogues call a privileged class, but it must know how to pay for its privileges."

Marquand knew that it was only with the traditional establishment of upper-class authority and the hegemony of its mores throughout society that a civilization would ever be able to defend itself against total domination by money-power, on the one hand, or some form of democratic despotism, on the other.

The Grass Court Circuit Becomes a Melting Pot, and Perry Jones Leads a Second California Invasion of the Eastern Establishment

All close balls are good. If you remember that, you'll never cheat an opponent. In tournament tennis, you don't question a call by the umpire or a linesman. You continue to play. And don't *think* too much when you play a big match. Just try to hit the ball well. Oh, yes, keep your sneakers clean.
—Perry Jones

THE LAST AND GREATEST PERIOD OF UPPER-CLASS POLITICAL DOMINANCE in America spanned the years between March 1933, when Franklin Roosevelt entered the White House, and January 1949, when Harry Truman's first term ended. In those turbulent yet hopeful years, the American people went through the Great Depression, took the lead in waging the wars against Hitler and Japan, in creating the United Nations, in San Francisco, and in putting through the Marshall Plan which revitalized our Western European allies for the long cold war against Russian communism. In that last year of the first half of the twentieth century, the United States stood at the head of the Free World, proudly looking forward to the rest of the great "American Century," as that Calvinist Yaleman, Henry Luce, had so confidently predicted in an essay in *Life* magazine.

During these very same years, America produced—in Ellsworth Vines, Donald Budge, Robert Riggs, Jack Kramer, Richard Gonzales, and others almost as great—the greatest generation of talented and world-class tennis players in the whole history of the game. This great generation, whose stars were all bred in California, was also the most democratic one to play for glory on the clean-cut lawns of the staid and snobbish cricket and tennis clubs along the Eastern Seaboard.

Just as the leadership of the Roosevelt democratic revolution in politics included such patricians as Henry Stimson, John G. Winant, Dean Acheson, Averell Harriman, Francis Biddle, and many other members of their class, so the new era of democratized tennis was still run by gentlemen of the same patrician class who still dominated the clubs along the Eastern Tennis Circuit as well as the USLTA Davis Cup selection committees.

But unfortunately, democratization and bureaucratization are two sides of the same coin. As Alexis de Tocqueville saw so many years ago, one cannot have one without the other. Tocqueville saw too that democratization leads to the worship of money. Thus this Golden Age of democracy sowed the seeds for the eventual plutocratization of American society as well as the game of tennis, both of which processes began in the egalitarian and class-destroying late 1960s and were consummated and vulgarized during the Reagan-Bush era of naked greed. Finally, as we shall see, the production of great tennis players in America steadily declined after 1950, as did the quality of American political leadership.

221

In the history of American tennis, the year 1930 witnessed a change in generations and the class origins of the most prominent players. In the first half of the year, Tilden, the last representative of the cricket club aristocracy, strode across Europe, collecting thirteen singles trophies, thirteen doubles, and nine mixed, including the Championships of Germany, Austria, Italy, and the Netherlands before being beaten in the French finals by Henri Cochet. Finally, on July 9, at the age of 37, Tilden won his last amateur Championship at Wimbledon.

In the meantime, a new generation of American tennis players was coming to the fore, symbolized in September, at Forest Hills, when John Hope Doeg, a native of California and a Stanford graduate, won our National Championship, defeating young Frank Shields in an extremely exciting final round.* In the previous year at Forest Hills, Tilden had beaten both finalists, Shields in the third round and Doeg in a bitterly fought, come-from-behind, five-set semifinal. As a nice measure of generational change, of the eight quarterfinalists in 1930, only Tilden and Hunter were of the older generation; all the other six were under 24, five of them, including Shields, under 20. Doeg beat Hunter in the quarters and Tilden in a bitterly fought semifinal battle. This was Tilden's first loss to an American in our Championships (or any other important tournament) since 1919, when Billy Johnston easily defeated him in a three-set final. As another gauge of change, Jean Borotra was put out in the first round by Berkeley Bell, an unseeded Texan. Tilden might have met two future champions who were in his part of the draw, but both lost to lesser players, the new sensation from California, Ellsworth Vines, in the third round, and Fred Perry, then a little-known Englishman, in the fourth.

The Doeg-Shields final, though not a great match, generated tremen-

---

*In the second round, Doeg had a real battle in beating W. Barry Wood, Jr., all-American football player from Harvard, 6–2, 6–2, 5–7, 4–6, 6–2. Wood was the ideal gentleman scholar so admired by Endicott Peabody of Groton, and his public school peers in England. Wood learned his tennis at the Longwood Cricket Club and graduated from the nearby Milton Academy before going on to college where he became the finest scholar-athlete in Harvard history. For three successive years, he won varsity letters in football, ice hockey, and baseball. In his senior year, he was awarded a tennis letter, was captain of the football team, president of the student council, and a member of *Phi Beta Kappa*. After graduating *summa cum laude*, he went on to a distinguished career in medicine, being a vice president of the Johns Hopkins University, in charge of medical education, when he died in 1971. No multidimensional man like Barry Wood can be found at Flushing Meadow today.

dous excitement and tension as these two handsome young giants went at each other like two pit bulls, as Allison Danzig wrote:

> It was a match that will linger long in memory as a superb exhibition of both tennis and the acme of good sportsmanship. Here were two strapping youths who both carried dynamite in their services and volleys, who scorned to temporize, who asked no mercy and never gave any, but who could give away points, regardless of the juncture, to rectify a possible mistake in their favor and give them not as charity but in the spirit of noblesse oblige and without quibbling or fuss.[1]

The year 1930 marked the fiftieth anniversary of the first U.S. Men's Championships at Newport as well as the beginning of a new democratic era. This new democracy, however, meant a change in personnel rather than a change in the traditional social structure of the game or its manners and mores. New wine, as it were, was poured into old bottles. The Grass Court Circuit, played at the older cricket and tennis clubs along the Eastern Seaboard between Boston and Philadelphia, still constituted the heart of the American game (see Figure 9). The players were largely college boys as they had been since the days of Dick Sears and Joe Clark, of Harvard. But since the 1920s, they were coming increasingly from California, the Deep South, and Texas rather than the older Ivy League colleges (see Figure 10). And the Eastern "Big Three"—Harvard, Yale, and Princeton—were replaced at the top after World War I by the California "Big Three"—USC, UCLA, and Stanford.

In 1930, the Intercollegiate Championships were held at the Merion Cricket Club soon after the close of the academic year. They had been held there since 1900; after 1934 they would move to clay courts and be held all over the country. Clifford Sutter, of Tulane, defeated Julius Seligson, of Lehigh in the 1930 finals. Sutter then went on to win the famous Longwood Bowl, at the Longwood Cricket Club. As we have seen, Longwood was organized in 1877 on the old Sears Estate; the Bowl was first competed for in 1891, nine years before the first Davis Cup matches were played there in 1900. The young sensation from California, Ellsworth Vines, was beaten in the second round at Longwood but went on to win the Metropolitan Grass Court Championship at the distinguished Crescent Athletic Club in Brooklyn, defeating Frank Hunter in a classic come-from-two-sets-down five-setter.

In addition to ancient Longwood, the three most important, and so-

FIGURE 9
Grass Court Circuit: Men's Singles, 1930

May 29   Orange Lawn Tennis Club, South Orange, New Jersey
Final Round   Frank Shields d. John Van Ryn

June 23   Merion Cricket Club, Haverford, Pennsylvania
National Intercollegiate Championships
Final Round   Clifford Sutter (Tulane) d. Julius Seligson (Lehigh)

July 3   Nassau Country Club, Glen Cove, Long Island (Men's Invitation)
Final Round   Frank Hunter d. Edward Jacobs

July 14   Longwood Cricket Club, Chestnut Hill, Massachusetts
Longwood Bowl (Men's Invitation)
Final Round   Clifford Sutter d. Sidney B. Wood, Jr.
(Ellsworth Vines defeated in second round)

July 19   Crescent Athletic Club, Bay Ridge, Brooklyn, N.Y.
Metropolitan Grass Court Championships
Final Round   Ellsworth Vines d. Frank Hunter 1–6, 4–6, 6–4, 6–4, 6–1
Semifinals   Vines d. Frank Shields 2–6, 6–3, 6–4, 5–7, 12–10

July 28   Seabright Lawn Tennis and Cricket Club, Rumson, N.J. Invitation
Final Round   Sidney Wood d. Ellsworth Vines 6–2, 6–2, 6–0

Aug. 4   Meadow Club, Southampton, Long Island Men's Invitational
Final Round   Sidney Wood d. Wilmer Allison 4–6, 6–3, 2–6, 6–2, 6–4

Aug. 9   Westchester Country Club, Rye, N.Y. Eastern Grass Ct. Champs.
Final Round   Clifford Sutter d. Gregory Mangin 4–6, 8–6, 7–5, 4–6, 6–1

Aug. 18   Newport Casino, Newport, R.I. Newport Men's Invitational
Final Round   William T. Tilden d. Wilmer Allison 6–1, 0–6, 5–7, 6–2, 6–4

Aug. 25   Longwood Cricket Club, Chestnut Hill, Mass. National Doubles Champs.
Final Round   George Lott and John Doeg d. Wilmer Allison and John
Van Ryn 8–6, 6–3, 4–6, 13–15, 6–4

Sept. 6   West Side Tennis Club, Forest Hills, N.Y. National Championships
Final Round   John Doeg d. Frank Shields 10–8, 1–6, 6–4, 16–14
Semifinal   Doeg d. Tilden 10–8, 6–3, 3–6, 12–10
Quarterfinals   Doeg d. Hunter 11–13, 6–4, 3–6, 6–2, 6–4
Round of 16   Van Ryn d. Fred Perry 4–6, 6–3, 6–4, 6–1
3rd Round   G. Lyttleton Rogers (Irish Champ) d. Vines 4–6, 4–6, 6–4,
6–1, 6–4

2nd Round   Doeg d. Barry Wood (Harvard Football Captain) 5 sets
1st Round   Berkeley Bell d. Borotra 3–6, 6–2, 12–10, 7–5

Sept. 19   Los Angeles Tennis Club, Pacific Southwest Championships
Final Round   Ellsworth Vines d. Gregory Mangin 14–11, 6–3, 6–4

First Ten 1930:   1. Doeg (Stanford) 2. Shields (Roxbury School)
3. Allison (U. Texas) 4. Wood (Roxbury School)
5. Sutter (Tulane) 6. Mangin (Georgetown)
7. Lott (U. of Chicago) 8. Vines (USC)
9. Van Ryn (Princeton) 10. Bitsy Grant (North Carolina)

cially prominent, men's invitation tournaments were held each year at Seabright, at the Meadow Club, and at the famous Newport Casino. The Seabright Lawn Tennis and Cricket Club, in Rumson, New Jersey, where solid, old-family New Yorkers spent their summers-by-the-sea for many years, held its forty-fourth invitation tournament in 1930; Sidney Wood, in a brilliantly conceived and executed match, softened up Vines's powerful game and beat him in an easy three-set final.

The Meadow Club in Southampton, the most stylish summer resort on Long Island, celebrated the fortieth anniversary of its tournament in 1930; Sidney Wood, a member of the club then and now, defeated Wilmer Allison, Wimbledon runner-up from the University of Texas, in a thrilling five-set final.

If tennis weeks marked the height of the local social season each summer at Seabright and Southampton, Tennis Week and the tennis ball at Newport were the scenes of a national gathering of socialites largely drawn from the Eastern Seaboard gentry. Newport cottages, great and small, were filled with houseguests from Charleston, South Carolina, north to Philadelphia, New York, and Boston. In spite of the depression, opulent Newport remained in full swing throughout the thirties. Barbara Hutton's famous coming-out party during Tennis Week in 1931 was attended by young Fred Perry, who was staying with an heir to the Lea & Perrin sauce fortune at "Bonnycrest," a medieval-like castle he had brought stone by numbered stone from Scotland to Newport, where it sat overlooking the beautiful harbor, out of which the America's Cup competitors sailed. Perry wrote:

> There were servants all over the place. Goodness knows what our socialists back in England would have thought. When I woke up on my first morning a butler in striped waistcoat was standing over me with my morning tea. Then he brought me a dressing gown and fetched a bowl of water so that I could test the temperature to see if it was to my liking for my bath. I had to giggle when he had gone, thinking about this common fellow from Ealing sitting up in bed, putting his finger in a bowl of water and saying to the flunky, "A little warmer, if you please."[2]

For the first sixty-seven years of the twentieth century in America countless college tennis players spent several summers on the Eastern Grass Court Circuit which served as an informal socializing ritual, expos-

FIGURE 10

Intercollegiate Singles Champions: 1883–1987

1883–1920

Year	Name	School
1883	Howard A. Taylor (fall)	Harvard
1883	Joseph Clark (spring)	Harvard
1884	W. P. Knapp	Yale
1885	W. P. Knapp	Yale
1886	G. M. Brinley	Trinity (Conn.)
1887	P. S. Sears	Harvard
1888	P. S. Sears	Harvard
1889	R. P. Huntington, Jr.	Yale
1890	Fred Hovey	Harvard
1891	Fred Hovey	Harvard
1892	William Larned	Cornell
1893	Malcolm G. Chase	Brown
1894	Malcolm G. Chase	Yale
1895	Malcolm G. Chase	Yale
1896	Malcolm Whitman	Harvard
1897	S. G. Thompson	Princeton
1898	Leo Ware	Harvard
1899	Dwight Davis	Harvard
1900	Raymond Little	Princeton
1901	Fred B. Alexander	Princeton
1902	William J. Clothier	U. of Penn.
1903	E. B. Dewhurst	Columbia
1904	Robert LeRoy	U. of Penn.
1905	E. B. Dewhurst	Columbia
1906	Robert LeRoy	Harvard
1907	G. Peabody Gardner, Jr.	Harvard
1908	Nat Niles	U. of Penn.
1909	Wallace Johnson	Yale
1910	R. A. Holden, Jr.	Harvard
1911	E. H. Whitney	Harvard
1912	George Church	Princeton
1913	Richard Williams, 2nd	Harvard
1914	George Church	Princeton
1915	Richard Williams, 2nd	Harvard
1916	G. Colket Caner	Harvard
1919	Charles Garland	Yale
1920	Lascelles Banks	Yale

1921–1967

Year	Name	School
1921	Philip Neer	Stanford
1922	Lucien E. Williams	Yale
1923	Carl H. Fischer	Phila. Osteopathic
1924	Wallace Scott	U. of Wash.
1925	Edward Chandler	California
1926	Edward Chandler	California
1927	Wilmer Allison	Texas
1928	Julius Seligson	Lehigh
1929	Berkeley Bell	Texas
1930	Clifford Sutter	Tulane
1931	Keith Gledhill	Stanford
1932	Clifford Sutter	Tulane
1933	Jack Tidball	UCLA
1934	C. Gene Mako	USC
1935	Wilbur Hess	Rice
1936	Ernest Sutter	Tulane
1937	Ernest Sutter	Tulane
1938	Frank D. Guernsey	Rice
1939	Frank D. Guernsey	Rice
1940	Donald McNeill	Kenyon College
1941	Joseph R. Hunt	U.S. Naval Acad.
1942	Frederick R. Schroeder, Jr.	Stanford
1943	Francisco Segura	U. of Miami
1944	Francisco Segura	U. of Miami
1945	Francisco Segura	U. of Miami
1946	Robert Falkenburg	USC
1947	Gardnar Larned	Wm. & Mary
1948	Harry E. Likas	U. San Francisco
1949	Jack Tuero	Tulane
1950	Herbert Flam	UCLA
1951	Tony Trabert	Univ. of Cincinnati
1952	Hugh Stewart	USC
1953	Hamilton Richardson	Tulane
1954	Hamilton Richardson	Tulane
1955	Jose Aguero	Tulane
1956	Alejandro Olmedo	USC
1957	Barry MacKay	U. of Mich.
1958	Alejandro Olmedo	USC
1959	Whitney Reed	San Jose State College
1960	Larry Nagler	UCLA
1961	Allen Fox	UCLA
1962	Rafael Osuna	USC
1963	Dennis Ralston	USC
1954	Dennis Ralston	USC
1955	Arthur Ashe, Jr.	UCLA
1956	Charles Pasarell	UCLA
1957	Bob Lutz	USC

1968–1987

Year	Name	School
1968	Stan Smith	USC
1969	Joaquin Loyo-Mayo	USC
1970	Jeff Borowiak	UCLA
1971	Jimmy Connors	UCLA
1972	Dick Stockton	Trinity (Tex.) Univ.
1973	Alex Mayer, Jr.	Stanford
1974	John Whitlinger	Stanford
1975	Billy Martin	UCLA
1976	Bill Scanlon	Trinity (Texas)
1977	Matt Mitchell	Stanford
1978	John McEnroe	Stanford
1979	Kevin Curren	Texas
1980	Robert Van't Hof	USC
1981	Tim Mayott	Stanford
1982	Mike Leach	Michigan
1983	Greg Holmes	Utah
1984	Mikael Pernfors	Georgia
1985	Mikael Pernfors	Georgia
1986	Dan Goldie	Stanford
1987	Andrew Burrow	Miami

FIGURE 10 (continued)

Summary

1883–1920 IVY ERA

Harvard	16	
Yale	8	
Princeton	5	
H-Y-P	29	80%
Penn	3	
Columbia	2	
Brown	1	
Cornell	1	
Trinity	1	
Other Ivy	8	20%
Total	37	100%

1920–1967 CALIFORNIA-South

USC	9	
UCLA	6	
Stanford	3	
Oth. Cal.	4	
California	22	47%
Tulane	8	
Miami	3	
Rice	3	
Texas	2	
South	16	34%
East	5	11%
Mid West	3	6%
Other	1	2%
Total	47	100%

1968–1987 CALIFORNIA

USC	3	
UCLA	3	
Stanford	6	
California	12	60%
South	6	30%
Mid West	1	5%
East	0	–
Other	1	5%
Total	20	100%

FIGURE 11

I Was a "Tennis Bum" and Am Glad of It

By AN OLD TIMER

THESE days when so many of the boys are panning the games which made them, I think it only fair to present the other side of the picture, for in viewing the question from a retrospective and admittedly mature viewpoint I am free to confess that tournament tennis owes me nothing and would quite likely take the same course if I had it to do over again.

Although never a top notcher I was good enough to win a few minor tournaments and to receive invitations to Newport, Southampton, etc., and to take part in exhibition matches, receive tennis rates or gratuitous board at numerous resorts and country clubs during the playing season. In order to take advantage of this I deliberately chose a business which was seasonal and permitted comparative freedom during the summer and part of the winter months. Undoubtedly I curtailed my earning power and neglected to amass the wealth which numerous of my classmates acquired through keeping the nose to the grindstone but to my mind there were compensations.

Except for spectacular achievements in science, politics, and so forth the world largely measures success by position made possible by wealth. Money is the recognized key to luxury, comfort, independence, culture and general affluence. In these days of keen competition and specialization those who achieve this goal must concentrate to the exclusion of all else. Self-discipline, self-denial and a single purpose is the prescribed method of attaining the pinnacle in any endeavor, but in looking around among the many friends who have arrived I question whether it was worth the price.

moderation is the ideal course to pursue. Today the danger lies in overemphasis of sports and it is true that the young Davis cup player is called upon to extremes in his devotion to the game. This will undoubtedly be met by holding the event biennially instead of yearly as the large number of competing nations at present make it almost a continuous affair but in general I can heartily commend the youngster who is fortunate enough to show adaptability in the game to make the most of it.

It has been said that any fool can *exist* but it takes a clever man to *live*. Most of the players of my day who were skillful enough to play tournament tennis successfully were clever enough to keep a sense of proportions and balance. They learned how to live then and so far as I know have never had occasion to feel handicapped by their tennis careers when taking their various stations in life.

Tournament tennis enabled me to enjoy my young manhood (between twenty and forty) to the fullest extent. I associated with nice people, travelled under the pleasantest conditions, saw the high spots of the country and the Southern British colonies (unfortunately I never played the European circuit) and put up at the best quarters under the most congenial circumstances. In other words I enjoyed the privileges that wealth and security are supposed to offer but with this exception—I had them during my youth and I like to believe I was at the same time storing a reserve of health and a worldly broadening for later years.

Possibly it all reverts to the old saying of "Abuse and Not the Use" which causes the harm, or the admonition that

Source: American Lawn Tennis, November 20, 1930.

ing boys from a variety of backgrounds, especially after 1930, to the manners and sportsmanship values of a secure upper-class subculture. Sometime after World War I, those who played regularly for a number of years began to be called "Tennis Bums," a species nicely defined by "An Old Timer" in 1930 (see Figure 11).

One of the more socially perceptive of this species, William F. Talbert, is today the grand old man of American tennis, who has served as chairman of the Hall of Fame at Newport (he was inducted in 1967) and chief referee at the National Open at Flushing Meadow. All the while he has always been an elegant, man-about-town New Yorker, the kind that always gets the right table at "21." He first came East in 1938 to play in the Intercollegiates at the Merion Cricket Club. He lost in an early round but got to the semifinals in 1939, his senior year in college, and then went on to First Ten ranking thirteen times between 1941 and 1954, winning the Newport, Southampton, Seabright, Rye, and Orange singles titles each once, the national doubles four times with Gardnar Mulloy, and the mixed-doubles four times with Margaret Osborne before she married their mutual friend, Willie DuPont.

Talbert was diagnosed as a diabetic at the age of ten. An avid sports fan, he finally got permission from the family doctor to take up tennis. His father lost his job in the depression, and young Billy went to work at 14, eventually working his way through the University of Cincinnati. In 1984, when asked by Stan Hart why he took tennis so seriously in his youth, he replied: "For two reasons. One was that I was poor, and tennis was leading me to places I had never known about. I was being invited into a new world. And two, I wanted to prove that being a diabetic, I could do the same things anyone else could do."[3] No one has written about the socializing role of the circuit with more insight than Talbert, in his autobiography, *Playing for Life*. He begins his chapter on "The Circuit" with his impressions of the Merion Cricket Club on his first visit in 1938:

> There was quite a bit to learn at Merion, and not all of it on the court or in the locker room. . . . There was something rich and heady in the atmosphere. Merion was a repository of Philadelphia's Main Line traditions. The clubhouse, the lawns, the people themselves had that patina of security—the tone that comes with social position established and reinforced over a period of

generations. . . . There was a wonderful sense of leisure being used with good taste and decency. Most of us tennis players came from homes nothing like the great Main Line houses, and from public courts that had little in common with Merion's tailored grass, but they took us in like blood brothers.[4]

Talbert goes on to talk of the role of the clubs along the circuit in the general democratization of tennis in his time:

Tennis can hardly be called "a gentleman's game" anymore—not in the stuffy sense of the term. Long before I took up the game, it had stopped being the exclusive property of the rich. It is played far more commonly on concrete and asphalt playgrounds than on private lawns. Kids who have to peddle newspapers to buy their first rackets have become stars in the sport. . . .

It's true that clubs . . . insist on certain standards of behavior that aren't required in, say, a football game between the Detroit Lions and the Chicago Bears. But that, I think, is because to these people tennis is more than just a sport—it's a function of society. And a tennis tournament is more than a series of games played on a lined court—it's a social event in which the obligations of host and guest, they feel, ought to be maintained. . . . "Tennis week"—the week of the tournament at any of the old Eastern clubs—is usually the high point of the summer social season. It's at the time of the Casino Invitational, for example, that some of Newport's most festive débuts are held.* An invitation to a house party at Southampton is all the more prized if the date falls during the Meadow Club tournament. As the players move along the tournament route, like strolling minstrels visiting courts, the doors of the summer houses swing open, the guest rooms start to fill, the orchestras strike up that peculiarly thin music reminiscent of expensive hotels, and the terraces light up to full lantern power.

The players themselves are the lions of this society. The game is their cachet, admitting them to places they might never reach with their other credentials. The circuit is a fantastic kind of melting pot. It's where a young man whose parents speak broken English and who has never worn a tie at the dinner table could find himself seated, at dinner, with the daughter of an Ambassador or a Supreme Court Justice—and possibly near His Excellency or Mr. Justice himself. Or where a fellow working his way through

---

*While Fred Perry danced at Barbara Hutton's debut, Billy Talbot knew Brenda Frazier and Gloria Vanderbilt in their glamorous debutante days at Newport.

school by baling wastepaper on a janitor's gang, whose folks might or might not be able to pay the next month's rent, could find himself accepted without prejudice in this sort of company. All you had to do was recognize that there were some obligations on the guest's side too.[5]

Unlike all too many of the players who talked tennis morning, noon, and night with their buddies, young Talbert made every effort to cultivate friendships with club members, especially successful businessmen, observing their sartorial style and eventually becoming a Brooks Brothers gent *par excellence* (see Figure 12). He was proud of the fact that he exchanged Christmas cards with Henry Ford for many years after they had

FIGURE 12

Source: American Lawn Tennis, September 5, 1930.

first met at Tennis Week in Southampton. And he never missed writing the proper thank-you notes to the important amateur officials as well as the fashionable hostesses with whom he had stayed during the week. Talbert's old doubles partner, Gardnar Mulloy, had told Stan Hart in *Once a Champion* that he was often paid off under the table, so Stan asked Talbert if he had. "No," Talbert replied, "I was put up in homes. . . . I wrote my thank-you notes and was invited back." Then he continued: "Gardner says a lot of things for effect . . . things that will open people's eyes to make them pay attention whether they are true or not true."

Writing thank-you notes was also vital to success on the European amateur circuit. Richard Evans, a British tennis journalist, quoted Boro Jovanovic, Yugoslavian champion in 1961 and runner-up in the doubles at Wimbledon the following year, as follows: "I had to remember all the names of all the tournament directors' wives and write to thank them for everything they had done for me last year and please could I play again next year. Only then did I start negotiating for expenses and maybe air tickets. Agents? Hah, what were agents? We did everything ourselves."

"With his dark good looks and five languages, all spoken in a deep cultured voice," continued Evans, "Jovanovic found all this a great deal easier than a lot of players, but most of them, out of necessity, got by." The days of letter-writing ended with the amateur era. "Heaven knows," Evans, an expert on the pro tour, asked himself, "how some of today's pros would manage if they suddenly had to write a letter!"[6]

The upper-class, Tennis Circuit melting pot so nicely described by Bill Talbert continued down to the end of the amateur era. We have already seen how William J. Clothier II, who made Tennis Week at Merion one of the finest on the Circuit during the fifties and sixties, arranged for Althea Gibson and later, Arthur Ashe, to be put up by fine Main Line families. Althea's hostess was a kinswoman of President Franklin D. Roosevelt, and Ashe's, a granddaughter of President William Howard Taft. In a diary kept during the year 1973, Arthur Ashe wrote with nostalgic affection of his amateur days on the circuit:

> Just look at me, at the same time that I got turned away from a public movie theatre, I was treated royally at the most exclusive country clubs in the United States. We all learned to expect to be catered to. We were put up at a magnificent estate, somebody's teen-age daughter or friend drove

us around at our beck and call, we ate at the house or signed checks at the club, played golf there and got invited to all the tennis week parties. . . . We were called tennis bums, and I suppose, yes, that is an accurate description, as far as it goes.[7]

It was during the depression that a second generation of talented California boys and girls came East to play for fame and glory. While the first generation of Californians to invade the East before the First World War were predominantly from the San Francisco Bay Area, the second generation came predominantly from Southern California; they learned to play on public courts and eventually found their way to the Los Angeles Tennis Club, where Perry T. Jones ran the junior program of the Southern California Tennis Association (SCTA) with an iron hand.[8]

As we have seen in Chapter 5, the Los Angeles Tennis Club had been founded in 1920. The founders, among them several members of the Sutton clan, had elected Thomas C. Bundy, May Sutton's husband, the first president of the club. In 1924, Perry T. Jones was put in charge of the junior development program of the SCTA. Two years later, at the suggestion of Miss Elizabeth Ryan, the Tennis Patrons Association of Southern California was formed by a distinguished group of L.A. Tennis Club members (including Bill Tilden). Elizabeth Ryan, born to an aristocratic family in Los Angeles where she learned to play tennis, had gone abroad in 1912 and played for the rest of her active tennis career in all the capitals of Europe, including the last Women's Championship of Imperial Russia, which she won in 1914. She envisaged Los Angeles as becoming one of the capitals of world tennis, and with her support, the famous Pacific Southwest tennis tournament was born the next year under the direction of Perry T. Jones. Bill Tilden was the first winner and the list of subsequent winners is almost as distinguished as that of Wimbledon. The Pacific Southwest was soon recognized as a brilliant climax of the Eastern Circuit season (see Figure 9 above).

"Declared by players and fans alike to be one of the most interesting and successful tournaments in the world," according to an article in *American Lawn Tennis* in October 1931, "the fifth annual Pacific-Southwest championship, Southern California's tournament of champions, was held on the seventeen beautifully surfaced cement courts of the Los Angeles Tennis

Club. . . . The tournament is sponsored yearly by the Tennis Patrons Association of Southern California, the Southern California Tennis Association, and the Los Angeles Tennis Club. Perry T. Jones, secretary of the S.C.T.A., did a most efficient job of managing the whole affair." Ellsworth Vines defeated Fred Perry, the handsome and impeccably tailored Englishman, in a come-from-behind, five-set final; he also won the doubles with Keith Gledhill, making it a clean sweep for the home team.

Perry T. Jones was the Ward McAllister of Los Angeles Society in the 1930s: Just as Ward McAllister, the ultimate snob, organized and civilized the "400" of Gilded Age Newport and Fifth Avenue, so Jones, also a snobbish, organizing genius, set out to make his beloved Pacific Southwest a major fixture of fashionable Los Angeles Society. His patrons were "allowed" to purchase boxes at "The Tennis," host tables at "The Tennis Ball," and house, feed, and entertain visiting tennis celebrities. According to *American Lawn Tennis*, the 1931 Pacific Southwest turned out to be one of the finest Society events of the year. The first Sunday of the tournament was set aside to honor the two visiting British stars, Fred Perry and Pat Hughes, with a series of exhibition matches; it was entirely fitting that Wimbledon winners that year—Sidney Wood, Singles Champion; George Lott and Mrs. Lawrence A. Harper, Mixed Doubles Champions; and John Van Ryn and George Lott, Doubles Champions—all won their exhibitions. On Monday, Harold Lloyd gave an elaborate luncheon for the visiting stars at his Santa Monica beach house. On Monday evening the Tennis Patrons Association gave a dinner-dance at the famous Ambassador Coconut-Grove restaurant. A prominent socialite dowager gave another dinner-dance there to meet the tennis stars on Tuesday. On Wednesday, Charles Farrell, romantic movie star of that day, and his actress wife, entertained at their Beverly Hills mansion. On Thursday, the players were taken on a tour of motion picture studios and entertained at luncheon by Douglas Fairbanks on the United Artists set. Miss Constance Bennett, a pretty young screen star at the time, gave the final event of the tournament, a dinner-dance at her home on Saturday night. On Sunday Perry T. Jones was delighted when a crowd of over four thousand watched the final matches on the center court; it was the largest crowd ever to witness a tennis match on the Pacific Coast. It is surely little wonder that when a poll was taken in the 1950s, asking leading tennis players which tournaments they enjoyed most, Wimbledon and the Pacific Southwest were listed either first or second in every player's response.

The late Ted Tinling immediately recognized Jones's genius when he visited Southern California with his lifelong friend, Elizabeth Ryan, in September 1933:

> Jones had a tremendous caste sense. The movie stars, Loretta Young, Marlene Dietrich, Bette Davis, Myrna Loy, Norma Shearer, Kay Francis, Claudette Colbert, and a host of equally famous men, came regularly to the tennis matches. . . . The movie colony was not well thought of by the older Los Angeles residents. Jones wanted the money and the status the socialites represented, but he also wanted the famous faces arrayed around his stadium court, so he arranged for both cliques to have their own groups of court-side boxes, clearly separated on opposite sides of the arena. Jones allowed me the privilege of being one of his socialites, but once I was seated in direct line across the court from Norma Shearer and Adonis-like Robert Taylor, another time from Janet Gaynor and Charles Farrell, and I readily confess to wishing I was sitting among the stars on the opposite side.[9]

It was surely Perry T. Jones's organizing genius which made the Pacific Southwest a major prestige event in Los Angeles High Society and on the international tennis scene. Both Jones and the Patrons Association, however, saw the tournament as a means to the primary end of making Southern California and the Los Angeles Tennis Club the major producer of tennis talent in America (and the world) for the two decades after 1930. In the first place, the great success of the tournament made it possible for young boys and girls in Southern California to see, and model their games after, the very best men and women tennis players in the world. Secondly, the success of the Pacific Southwest attracted more and more wealthy persons to the Patrons Association, thus providing Jones, the czar of the SCTA junior development program, the financial means to discover, groom, train, and provide financial assistance for his boys to compete in tournaments up and down the State of California. He had enough resources to send his boys East to compete in the USLTA-sponsored Junior Championships held each summer on the grounds of the Culver Military Academy, in Indiana; and later, to the Eastern Grass Court Circuit. Finally, for the best, he could provide trips to Europe and Wimbledon.

Perry T. Jones loved tennis with a single-minded passion which overshadowed any need he might have had for women or money. His mother had been a Southern Belle and he was a Victorian bachelor and a bit of a snob. Although he had won the Singles Championship of Los Angeles back in 1918, his tennis form was awkward, his backhand positively bizarre; he had no gift for teaching tennis. His talent lay in his ability to discover and foster budding tennis talent; most of the players he brought to the Los Angeles Tennis Club had already learned to play on public park courts; Jones gave them a chance to improve themselves through tournament competition which he sponsored as head of the junior program of the SCTA and also by playing at the Los Angeles Tennis Club, with the best of their age group, with older members, and with visiting tennis greats such as Bill Tilden.

Jack Kramer was probably the best player produced by the Jones system. Jack was born in Las Vegas, Nevada, where his father was a workman on the Union Pacific Railroad. He was 13 when his father was transferred to San Bernardino, on the outskirts of Los Angeles. The next year, he entered his first tennis tournament, the Dudley Cup, in Santa Monica. He arrived on the scene with one old Tilden Topflight racket, wearing an old brown sweater. "It was like another world," Kramer wrote in his autobiography, *The Game*. "The other kids all had on perfect tennis whites, Tilden V-neck sweaters, and they all carried two or three shiny new rackets. It was quite a gathering. Little Bobby Riggs was there, little Joe Hunt, little Ted Schroeder. Throw in little Jack Kramer, and there were present at this one junior tournament four boys who would win six U.S. National titles within the next dozen years."[10]

"Before I left Santa Monica, stunned and beaten," Kramer continued, "someone suggested that I see a man named Perry Jones at the Los Angeles Tennis Club." Jones liked young Kramer from the beginning, and vice versa: "He was Mister Jones if you wanted to go anywhere. Mister Jones wasn't a snob the way a lot of people pegged him, but he was very prim and proper. I was a conscientious kid and Mister Jones especially liked the way my father handled me, so he kept his eye on me from the first."

One incident in particular may help explain why Jones liked Jack's father. As Kramer wrote in *The Game*:

The moment I started to show any kind of big head Dad would call me "Cocky" and stick me right back in my place. One time when I was just starting to win, I began to think I was a big shot, and I carried on a running argument with an umpire. When he called me for a footfault, I blew my stack altogether and threw my racket over the fence. I looked up then and saw my father approaching the umpire's chair. I felt like a million dollars: my old man was going to show this guy that his boy couldn't be pushed around. Yes, sir!

After a few seconds of conferring with Dad, the referee suddenly stood up, waved his arms, and announced that the match was over, the win going to my opponent by default. My father had called it off. Our discussion was very brief. "Cocky", he said, "if you ever do that again, you'll never go back on a tennis court as long as you live in my house."

Kramer never lost his temper on the court that badly again. And he made it a point not to dispute line calls or umpire decisions, noting that today "players, the press and the fans make too much fuss over the quality of officiating."

In 1937, Jack Kramer won his first national title. That year, Mister Jones, so Kramer wrote,

> paid my entrance fee of $25 and enrolled me as a junior member in the Los Angeles Tennis Club. He also put me on the Spalding Free List, which meant that I didn't have to buy my rackets, and he gave me $50 and sent me off to Culver, Indiana, to play in the National Boys' fifteen-and-under [it's now sixteen-and-under]. My father scraped up $100 in cash, and gave me a blank check, signed, in case I needed it. I came back with $7 and the check, uncashed, plus the national singles and doubles championships. In one year I had come completely out of the blue to become the best boy player in America.

The junior membership in the Los Angeles Tennis Club meant everything to young Jack Kramer over the next few years. He wrote:

> I could get matches against Vines, Tilden, Riggs, Gene Mako, Joe Hunt, Ted Schroeder, Jack Tidball, Frank Shields, and—often as not—the players on the UCLA and Southern Cal teams. Sidney Wood would come in for long periods from the East, and Kovacs from Northern California. My parents arranged it with Montebello High School to adjust my schedule so that I could have all my classes in the morning and thus be able to commute to

the club in the afternoons. It wasn't easy, and it was an hour and a half each way. But once I got there I played till dark. It was paradise.

This paradise created by Mister Jones at the L.A. Tennis Club produced more first-rate young tennis players than any club in the history of tennis (see Figure 13). Nine of Jones's boys—Ellsworth Vines, Robert Riggs, Jack Kramer, Richard Gonzales, Gene Mako, Ted Schroeder, Edward "Budge" Patty, Joseph Hunt, and Robert Falkenberg (a definite member of the group who was unaccountably left out of Figure 13)—are now enshrined in the Hall of Fame, in Newport. Of the nine, Vines, Riggs, Kramer, and Gonzales were all-time World Champions, while Mako, Schroeder, Patty, Hunt, and Falkenberg were Champions in their day. Also included among Mister Jones's boys were seven Intercollegiate Champions: Keith Gledhill (1931), Jack Tidball (1933), Gene Mako (1934), Joe Hunt (1941), Ted Schroeder (1942), Bob Falkenberg (1946), and Herb Flam (1950); Gledhill and Schroeder won for Stanford, Tidball and Flam for UCLA, and Mako and Falkenberg for USC. Joe Hunt won the doubles for USC in 1938, and the singles in 1941 while playing for the U.S. Naval Academy.

For over a decade and a half, the boys from the L.A. Tennis Club virtually owned the USLTA National Boys (18 and under) Championships at Culver, winning the singles fourteen times in the eighteen years between Keith Gledhill's win in 1929 and Herbert Flam's second win in 1946 (Frank Parker won it in 1932, and Don Budge in 1933). The L.A. Tennis Club winners were as follows: Gledhill (1929), Mako (1934), Riggs (1935), Julius Heldman (1936), Joe Hunt (1937), David Freeman (1938), Schroeder (1939), Robert Carruthers (1940), Budge Patty (1941–42), Falkenberg (1943–44), and Herbert Flam (1945–46).

The Junior Champion from the L.A. Tennis Club in 1936 was Julius Heldman who went on to become an instructor in Chemistry at Stanford, where he met his future wife, Gladys, who graduated in 1942. He played top club tennis while working his way to the top in the oil business. At the same time, he was a keen analyst of the differing tennis styles of the great players, which he wrote about with clarity and insight. Gladys and *World Tennis*, which she founded in 1953, were primary forces behind the coming of open tennis; she also was the virtual founder of the women's professional tour which grew out of her supporting Billie Jean

FIGURE 13

Perry T. Jones and the Southern California Junior Champions

Photographs by Thelner Hoover

Tennis racket rendering after a frame made by
George Toley, 1949.

Bob Peacock, Dorothy Bundy, Les Stoefen, Gracyn Wheeler
Ted Olewine, Herb Flam, Doug Woodbury, Ruby Bishop, Jack Tidball
Maureen Connolly, Welby Van Horn, Bob Carruthers, Gene Mako,
Budge Patty, Dave Freeman, Julius Heldman, Barbara Winslow, Richard Gonzales
Nancy Chaffee, Helen Pastall, Beverly Baker, Louise Brough,
Ellsworth Vines, Bobby Riggs, Ted Schroeder, Joe Hunt, Jack Kramer.

Source: Patricia Henry Yeomans, *Southern California Tennis Champions Centennial, 1887–1987*

King in her bitter battles with the male chauvinist, Jack Kramer, who took over the Pacific Southwest after Jones retired in 1970. The last straw in the King-Kramer battles came in 1970 when Kramer set aside $12,500 for the Men's Champion and only $1,500 for the Women's Prize.*

Jack Kramer carried on the Jones tradition down into the Open era. Billie Jean resented those traditions and values from her first meeting with Perry T. Jones at the tender age of 11 when she played in her first tournament at the L.A. Tennis Club. She had grown up in Long Beach, California, the daughter of a fireman, and arrived at the tournament dressed in a blouse and shorts, both handmade by her mother. Mister Jones refused to allow her to be in the photograph taken of the players because she did not have on the proper white dress; boys wore pants and girls wore dresses. She also resented the fact that, as director of the junior development program of the SCTA, Jones awarded travel money to promising boys and not to her. In other words Billie Jean Moffitt (King) found Jones to be a "snooty sexist" from the very beginning, and of course resented both Jones and Kramer and their sexist values all her ideological life. Due to her resentment of Kramer, she insisted that the battle of the sexes, where she trimmed another male chauvinist pig, Bobby Riggs, at the Houston Astrodome in September 1973, be held on the Friday night of Tennis Week at the Los Angeles Tennis Club, where Kramer was directing the Pacific Southwest Open.

Billie Jean and Bobby were not too different when they were young kids in Southern California. Both were raised in very religious and close-knit families; both were bright, short in stature and tall on talking, and both were independent nonconformers. Mister Jones felt about the same way towards Bobby when he was one of the boys around the Tennis Club in the 1930s as he later did about Billie Jean in the 1950s. And, unlike his great friend Kramer, Riggs found Jones to be a dictatorial snob: "I was short—five feet, seven and a half when I stopped growing—my tennis gear sometimes needed laundering, and I always spoke up to Jones, letting him know how I felt about discrimination against kids like myself, who didn't happen to come from Pasadena or Beverly Hills or the other upper-class areas of Los Angeles," he wrote in 1973 in an utterly charm-

---

*Kramer, in my view, was one of the last *real men* in American tennis administrative circles.

ing autobiography, which fittingly ended as follows: "I have put in my will that I want to be cremated. I want to have half of my ashes spread over the stadium court at Forest Hills and half over the center court at the Los Angeles Tennis Club, where I grew up and played so many matches. I figure that should be in the year 2018, roughly 6,750,000 [vitamin] pills from now."[11] Bobby Riggs was a delightful and delighting free spirit who had no time for holding grudges, especially against the greatest tennis club in America and its guiding genius during the days of his youth.

Perry T. Jones wanted all his players to look and dress like future champions. He took almost every one of them to LaBelle Tailors where he personally supervised their being fitted for their first white flannel trousers. At the age of 13 Jack Kramer first saw Ellsworth Vines at the L. A. Tennis Club. At 6 foot 2½ inches tall, imperially slim and immaculately dressed in white flannels, Vines reminded young Kramer of his idol, Fred Astaire. That Mr. Jones preferred Vines and Kramer (well-dressed and polite) to Bobby Riggs and Billie Jean King (less concerned with dress and manners) had nothing to do with the class snobbery which Riggs and King both so despised. But who, I should like to ask, is to say that class snobbery is any worse than classless slobbery? For snobs are often the product of leveling upward and confident ages, while reverse snobbery or slipshod slobbery (in dress, manners, grammar, professional pride, and craftsmanship in general) are insidious social diseases of leveling downward and despairing ages such as our own. Perry Jones, it must be said, was no simple snob. Nobody has written about this complicated man with more subtlety and wit than the hard-boiled and prize-winning columnist for the *Los Angeles Times*, Jim Murray: see his column on the occasion of Jones's death in 1970 (see Figure 14).

———

While the five great, world-class Californians—Vines, Budge, Riggs, Kramer, and Gonzales—dominated American tennis between 1930 and 1949, there was also a solid core of lesser champions always ready to defeat them at any time. In addition to the Perry Jones men already mentioned—Ted Schroeder, Budge Patty, Joe Hunt, Bob Falkenberg, all Wimbledon or U.S. Singles Champions (see Figure 13), and Lester Stoefen, Herbie Flam, Welby Van Horn, Keith Gledhill, and Gene Mako—there were many fine players from Texas, the South, the Middle West,

FIGURE 14

JIM MURRAY

Last of the Victorians

Someone once said of the late Perry T. Jones that he was a "combination of Marie Antoinette and Stanley Ketchel."

He was the last of the Victorians. He came from a prosaic-enough background. He was never what you might call rich, but whenever you were around him you could almost hear the sterling silver tea service rattling.

Perry drank out of china cups, and he had the exaggerated respect for "manners" one finds in the overprivileged. He was bridge-party American. Pasadena Gothic. But, inside, he was like a fighter who never stops moving in. He had some of the instincts of a guy who hops freights.

It took awhile to know Perry—like, a decade if he liked you, a quarter of a century if he could tolerate you, and never if he considered you common.

He had standards but they were not rigid. Hardly anyone ever called him "Perry." He met with kings and prime ministers, movie czars and real czars, dukes and earls. He knew every dowager on Orange Grove Ave. as well as Doheny Drive. But his world was bounded on the south by Clinton Ave., on the north by Hollywood—and on the east by Wimbledon and the west, Australia. The Los Angeles Tennis Club was his castle, but all tennis was his domain.

A Kingmaker

He could never play the game very well. He couldn't teach it at all. He just loved it—the way a widowed mother loves her only child. He never had time for anything else once he found tennis — neither a wife nor a fortune. Not politics, diplomacy, government or philosophy. His idea of a foreign policy was "Win Wimbledon!"

He could look out his office window any afternoon and see the crowned heads of tennis. It must have made him feel like Talleyrand—because he crowned them.

He made Southern California the tennis incubator of the world—by providing the best competition, facilities, cooperation and instruction. A tennis player might grow up in Cincinnati or Montebello, Richmond, Va., or Arequipa, Peru, or the Philadelphia Main Line. He was nothing till he had tested and honed his game against the California superstars who came out of Perry Jones' assembly line. Everywhere he looked on his desk was an autographed picture of tennis greats of the half-century who owed this man a great deal. The Davis Cup itself was on it for awhile.

Bow Ties, Tinted Glasses

Fussy, arbitrary, demanding, he wore bow ties and tinted glasses and no day was too hot for him to appear with his collar unbuttoned or sleeves rolled up. He could spot a tennis player 20 blocks away—but he was not like some mentors who didn't care if their proteges pulled wings off birds or dealt blackjack in the dorm as long as they could score an ace or bring the Davis Cup back to America. Perry once barred Pancho Gonzalez because he was a school dropout, an antic which almost got him picketed and prosecuted. But Perry stood his ground and held his serve and, years later, someone asked Pancho if he forgave him and Pancho growled "For what? For making me go back to school?"

I thought Perry was the most exasperating old man I ever met for the first 10 years of our acquaintanceship. The last 10, I always looked forward to our meetings. He never gave up trying to reform me. I found his devotion to a game that America seems to have passed by, at first, quaint, and then, admirable. In a world of reeds, he was a tree. He didn't run his empire by poll. He took a sampling of one man—a Mr. Jones.

They jimmied up the game in recent years. They tried to get it on the Eye and over by midnight. It must have been traumatic for Perry but he would have put in points-after-touchdown to advance tennis. "Some people think the game is shot through with gold," he once told me. "But I can tell you, since 1923, tennis has been a struggle. We have never made as much as $10,000 from our (Pacific Southwest) tournament. I would have to beg, borrow, and, if not steal, at least juggle to keep the other 70 tournaments going and send our great players to Wimbledon and Forest Hills."

Perry Jones was tennis' door-to-door salesman. It was not a job he liked, but it was for a game he loved.

There was an empty chair at the recent Pacific Southwest tournament and no answer on a phone which would always be busy this time of the year. Perry Jones had carried the match with Death to deuce as long as he could. I hope tennis survives him. And, though I loathe the stuff, I hope, too, that the "tea committee" survives. I'd even serve on it for Perry's sake.

and the Eastern Seaboard. First and foremost among them was Frank Parker who was ranked in the First Ten for all seventeen years between 1933 and 1949. His greatest achievements were winning our National Championship at Forest Hills twice (1944–45) and being the first American to win the French Championship twice (1948–49).

Gardnar Mulloy, the Iron Man of American Tennis, in the style of the Britisher, Arthur Gore, was an all-around athlete from Miami, Florida. He ranked in the First Ten for fourteen years between 1939 and 1954. His most characteristic achievement was winning the Wimbledon Doubles Championship with Budge Patty, in 1957, at the age of 43. Mulloy and his father won the National Father and Son Championship in 1939, 1941, and 1942.*

While William F. Talbert has been discussed above, it should be said here that he held a First Ten ranking thirteen times between 1941 and 1954. His greatest singles victory was his defeat of Pancho Gonzales in the 1949 Southampton finals where, at the age of 31, he came from two sets to one down to win 6–4, 5–7, 3–6, 7–5, 6–2. He also won the doubles that year with Gardnar Mulloy. Talbert and Mulloy were one of the greatest doubles teams of all time.

Sidney Wood, a gifted player from Southampton, Long Island, held a First Ten ranking ten times between 1930 and 1945. His greatest achievement was winning Wimbledon in 1931, when his old school friend, Frank Shields, had to default in the finals because of an injury. Wood had first played at Wimbledon at the age of 15 where he created quite a stir when he appeared on the court dressed in white knickers and plaid stockings to play his first round match with the great Lacoste, from whom he took all of four games. One of the great stylists of his or any other time, Wood possessed a tennis mind almost equal to Tilden's. He never reached the very top level because of his slight build and continuing poor health. "Of all the tennis players I have watched pass in review," wrote Allison Danzig,

---

*For seventy years between 1918 and 1987 the Father and Son Championships have been held on grass. Other First Ten men to have won this family prize over the years are as follows: William J. Clothier and Son (1935–36), Sidney Wood and Son (1956), Richard Savitt and Son (1981); Hamilton Richardson and Father (1953–54), Frank Froehling and Father (1962–63 and 65–70), Peter Fleming and Father (1974), Richard Leach and Father (1985). One wonders whether this patriarchal relationship at the First Ten level will continue much longer in this atomized age of professional tennis.

"Wood, more than any other, symbolized the spirit that plays the game for the sheer love of playing. None could attach smaller consequences to victory or accept defeat more light-heartedly."*[12] In this sense, Sidney Wood was one of America's last aristocrats in the style of R. Norris Williams.

Sidney Wood's school friend and fellow habitué of Southampton over the years, Frank Shields, has already been thoroughly discussed above; here it should be said that he ranked in the First Ten seven times between 1928 and 1935, while being number one in that famous tennis year of 1933.

Finally, Bryan M. (Bitsy) Grant, lawn tennis's "Georgia Peach" from Atlanta, was a 5-foot 4-inch, 120-pound giant-killer who ranked in the First Ten eleven times between 1930 and 1941. According to Allison Danzig, he was, pound for pound, the greatest tennis competitor the world had ever seen (or seen since, I should say). "On second thought," Danzig wrote, "you can strike out the 'tennis.' For sheer fight and bull-dog tenacity in hanging on against overwhelming force, I never saw his superior in any game."[13] Grant won the Southern Championships eleven times between his first win at the age of 16 and his last, exactly a quarter-century later. He won the National Clay Court singles crown in 1930, 1934, and 1935 and the doubles with George Lott in 1932. His great matches and frequent upsets at Forest Hills were legendary. First and foremost, in 1933, he beat the defending champion, Ellsworth Vines, in three straight sets, in the fourth round. The next year, he lost a five-set battle with Budge, in the third round, and then, in 1935, beat Budge in the quarterfinals. In 1936, he lost in the quarters to Perry who was playing his final and finest year as an amateur. In 1937, he carried Baron von Cramm to five sets before losing in the semis. He also played in the Davis Cup team that year, beating both John Bromwich and Jack Crawford in the American Zone Finals. No one ever counted on beating Bitsy without a battle. He surely was, along with Ty Cobb and Bobby Jones, one of the three wonders of the Atlanta sports world in his day.

Three great doubles players should be added to this supporting cast of players on the Circuit during the 1930s: Wilmer Allison of the University of Texas, John Van Ryn of Princeton, and George Lott of the University of Chicago. Allison, the greatest native Texan ever to play the game, won the U.S. Singles

---

*Fred Perry looked upon Wood's sportsmanship as simply a lack of the champion's "killer instinct," a character trait Perry admired above all else and possessed in abundance.

Championship in 1935, while he and Van Ryn won the U.S. doubles in 1931 and 1935 and the Wimbledon doubles in 1929 and 1930. In 1931, Van Ryn won both the Wimbledon and French doubles titles with George Lott. Van Ryn, by the way, was the last Big Three (Harvard-Yale-Princeton) man to rank in the First Ten until two Yalemen, Donald Dell* and Eugene Scott, were so ranked in the lean tennis years of the 1960s (1962; Dell-7th and Scott-8th).

George Lott was ranked in the First Ten seven times between 1924 and 1933, after which he turned pro. At the same time, he was certainly one of the five best American doubles players of all time: he won the U.S. doubles title five times with three different partners, Wimbledon twice with different partners, and the French once. His favorite partner was his last, Lester Stoefen, one of Perry Jones's boys, with whom he won the U.S. doubles in 1934 and Wimbledon in 1933–34. Born the only child of well-to-do parents, Lott was raised in Chicago where he went to college and still resides. Though born to privilege, he behaved in the big-shoulder and macho, Chicago manner, the very opposite from Tilden whom he thoroughly admired as a tennis player, even when teasing him at times for his *flitty* (as it then was called) ways. Lott closely resembled Tilden in one important sense: they both wrote about tennis. While Tilden was far better known as an author, George Lott is a keen analyst of the game, about which he has written many clear, and sometimes stylish, articles over the years.

At this point, it should be said that the two interwar decades marked a Golden Age in American doubles play. Not since the turn of the century, when the Doherty brothers† dominated Wimbledon and Holcombe Ward, Dwight Davis, and Beals C. Wright held sway in America, have

---

*Donald Dell, founder and chairman of Pro Serve, and Gene Scott, publisher of *Tennis Week*, are among the more powerful members of the present American tennis establishment.

†In 1897, Reginald F. Doherty and his younger brother, H. Lawrence, won the first of their eight Wimbledon doubles titles. They became the first foreign players to win the U.S. doubles title, in 1902; they won it again in 1903. At the same time, Holcombe Ward and Dwight F. Davis won the American crown for three years before the Dohertys (1899–1901), while Ward won it three years after them with his new partner, Beals C. Wright (1904–1906). As we have seen, Laurie Doherty was the first foreigner to win the U.S. singles title (1903); he also won the Wimbledon singles five times in a row (1902–1906), a record unmatched till Borg equaled it between 1976 and 1980.

such a talented group of doubles players been produced in this country, to say nothing of the great French Musketeers. The best American doubles teams playing in the interwar years, according to George Lott, were Vincent Richards and R. Norris Williams, Tilden and Richards, Keith Gledhill and Ellsworth Vines, Wilmer Allison and John Van Ryn, Francis T. Hunter and Tilden, Charles Garland and Williams, Howard and Robert Kinsey, Don Budge and Gene Mako, and, too modestly, Lott and Lester Stoefen, in that order. "Richards and Williams," wrote Lott, "were never beaten in major competition. They won the U.S. Doubles and the Challenge Round Doubles in 1925 and 1926. They formed the best doubles combination I ever saw or played against. Williams, in his day, was the finest doubles player of all time. Richards was not far behind and they blended perfectly."[14]

One would imagine that Tilden was too egotistical to be a good doubles player; he was, in addition, a backcourt, rather than a forecourt, singles player. But Tilden was a genius and had a fine doubles record. In fact, as we have seen, he won his first national title in mixed doubles, with Mary K. Browne (1913–14); he also won the men's doubles with 15-year-old Vincent Richards, in 1918, two years before his first national singles title. Tilden and Richards won the American title two more times (1921–22) when they broke up due to personality problems; they might have gone on to produce one of the best ever records in doubles. At any rate, Tilden won the U.S. doubles with Brian Norton in 1923, and with his good friend Frank Hunter in 1927; he and Hunter also won the Wimbledon doubles that year as well as the famous doubles match in the Davis Cup challenge round against France at the Germantown Cricket Club. It was a terrible mistake to have played Tilden that day, softening him up for the loss to Lacoste and the cup on the last day. Richards won the doubles at Wimbledon, in 1924, with Frank Hunter, in addition to his two wins with Williams at Forest Hills, before turning pro.

The brilliant Indian summer of the Golden Age of Doubles, including the war years and up to 1949, produced two of the finest doubles teams to ever play the game: Mulloy and Talbert and Kramer and Schroeder. In every one of the U.S. Doubles Championships between 1940 and 1948, either Billy Talbert or Gardnar Mulloy were in the finals and they won it as a team four times. Never were two players so consistent over so long a period of time.* During this same period, Jack Kramer won the U.S. doubles in 1940 and 1941 with Ted Schroeder, in 1943 with Frank Parker, and in 1947 again with Schroeder. The team of Talbert and Mulloy never won Wimbledon, though Mulloy did win there at the age of 43, with Budge Patty, as we have seen. Kramer won the doubles at Wimbledon twice, in 1946, with Tom Brown, a strictly amateur tennis player and lawyer from San Francisco, and in 1947, with Bob Falkenberg, one of Perry Jones's boys who went on to make a business fortune in Latin America.

One time, many years later, George Lott told Stan Hart that Kramer was the best doubles player he had ever seen. I would venture to say that the best American doubles players of all time were Holcombe Ward, Dick Williams, Vincent Richards, George Lott, Jack Kramer, Gardnar Mulloy, Billy Talbert, and John McEnroe. Most of them would surely rank in anybody's First Ten in American doubles.

---

*Between 1949 and 1954, Talbert won the U.S. indoor doubles title five times, three times with Don McNeill, and once each with Budge Patty and Tony Trabert.

CHAPTER 13

Gentleman Jack Crawford of Australia and Fred Perry, the Last Great Englishman

Crawford and I were great friends. Though we were keen rivals we respected each other's game . . . there was never an argument.

—Frederick J. Perry

The English have always liked good losers rather than winners. . . . One can imagine the impact Perry had on Britain of the 30's, for he was the first Englishman to see tennis as a battle rather than a game.

—Ted Tinling

IF THE TILDEN-FRENCH MUSKETEERS ERA OF THE 1920S PRODUCED THE most dramatic five years in the history of amateur tennis, the eight years between 1932 and 1939 certainly produced more all-time, world-class tennis players. Tilden, Lacoste, and Cochet were outnumbered by the four self-made democrats, Vines, Perry, Budge, and Riggs, as well as two aristocratic stylists, Gentleman Jack Crawford of Australia, and Baron von Cramm of Germany (see Figure 15). While the central drama of the 1920s focused on the gallant campaign of the Musketeers to defeat Tilden, the great tennis of the thirties lacked the same, sustained dramatic intensity because all four of the democrats, Vines, Perry, Budge, and Riggs, turned professional after two or three years as amateur champions. (See Jack Kramer's discussion of this problem below.)

Ellsworth Vines won both Wimbledon and Forest Hills and was ranked number one in the world (see Figure 15) in 1932. But he did not win his two singles matches in the Davis Cup challenge round against the French, at Roland Garros, which turned out to be one of the worst examples of Gaelic gamesmanship in the history of the cup. Before the matches began, everything pointed to an American victory: Vines was the best player in the world and the captain of the French team, Lacoste, unable to play because of ill health, had to persuade a reluctant Borotra to take his place at the last moment. In the first match of the tie, Vines played Borotra, thirteen years his senior, who felt like an ancient lamb being led to slaughter. But before a patriotic and partisan crowd, including the President of France, Borotra rose to the occasion and defeated a listless Vines in four sets. Cochet also defeated Allison in four. On the second day American spirits were lifted when Allison and Van Ryn won the doubles in five long and extremely exhausting sets. But then, in the first match of the third day, Allison lost to Borotra in a bitter and unfair battle which decided the tie in favor of France.

Gamesmanship was an issue right from the start. The court had been so soaked down before the Allison-Borotra match, obviously to slow it down for Vines's cannonball serves, that the match was delayed while it dried out enough to be playable. The tennis balls were stored courtside in a refrigerator-like container in order to slow them down as well. At any rate, Allison got off to a running start, winning the first two sets easily; then Borotra came back strongly to win the next two. After a long rally in the fourth game of the fifth set, Allison seemed near collapse; he was

FIGURE 15

World First Ten, 1924–1928 and 1932–1939

1924

1. W. T. Tilden (USA)
2. Vincent Richards (USA)
3. J. O. Anderson (Australia)
4. W. M. Johnston (USA)
5. R. Lacoste (France)
6. J. Borotra (France)
7. H. Kinsey (USA)
8. G. L. Patterson (Australia)
9. H. Cochet (France)
10. M. Alonso (Spain)

1925

1. W. T. Tilden (USA)
2. W. M. Johnston (USA)
3. Vincent Richards (USA)
4. R. Lacoste (France)
5. R. N. Williams (USA)
6. J. Borotra (France)
7. G. L. Patterson (Australia)
8. M. Alonso (Spain)
9. B. I. C. Norton (S. Africa)
10. T. Harada (Japan)

1926

1. R. Lacoste (France)
2. J. Borotra (France)
3. H. Cochet (France)
4. W. M. Johnston (USA)
5. W. T. Tilden (USA)
6. Vincent Richards (USA)
7. T. Harada (Japan)
8. M. Alonso (Spain)
9. H. Kinsey (USA)
10. J. Brugnon (France)

1927

1. R. Lacoste (France)
2. W. T. Tilden (USA)
3. H. Cochet (France)
4. J. Borotra (France)
5. M. Alonso (Spain)
6. F. T. Hunter (USA)
7. G. M. Lott (USA)
8. J. F. Hennessey (USA)
9. J. Brugnon (France)
10. J. Koseluh (Czechoslovakia)

1928

1. H. Cochet (France)
2. R. Lacoste (France)
3. W. T. Tilden (USA)
4. F. T. Hunter (USA)
5. J. Borotra (France)
6. G. M. Lott (USA)
7. H. W. Austin (England)
8. J. F. Hennessey (USA)
9. H. L. de Morpurgo (Italy)
10. J. B. Hawkes (Australia)

FIGURE 15 (continued)

1932
1. H. E. Vines (USA)
2. H. Cochet (France)
3. J. Borotra (France)
4. W. L. Allison (USA)
5. C. Sutter (USA)
6. D. Prenn (Germany)
7. F. J. Perry (England)
8. G. von Cramm (Germany)
9. H. W. Austin (England)
10. J. H. Crawford (Australia)

1933
1. J. H. Crawford (Australia)
2. F. J. Perry (England)
3. J. Satoh (Japan)
4. H. W. Austin (England)
5. H. E. Vines (USA)
6. H. Cochet (France)
7. F. X. Shields (USA)
8. S. B. Wood (USA)
9. G. von Cramm (Germany)
10. L. R. Stoefen (USA)

1934
1. F. J. Perry (England)
2. J. H. Crawford (Australia)
3. G. von Cramm (Germany)
4. H. W. Austin (England)
5. W. L. Allison (USA)
6. S. B. Wood (USA)
7. R. Menzel (Czechoslovakia)
8. F. X. Shields (USA)
9. G. de Stefani (Italy)
10. C. Boussus (France)

1935
1. F. J. Perry (England)
2. J. H. Crawford (Australia)
3. G. von Cramm (Germany)
4. W. L. Allison (USA)
5. H. W. Austin (England)
6. J. D. Budge (USA)
7. F. X. Shields (USA)
8. V. B. McGrath (Australia)
9. C. Boussus (France)
10. S. B. Wood (USA)

1936
1. F. J. Perry (England)
2. G. von Cramm (Germany)
3. J. D. Budge (USA)
4. A. K. Quist (Australia)
5. H. W. Austin (England)
6. J. H. Crawford (Australia)
7. W. L. Allison (USA)
8. B. M. Grant (USA)
9. H. Henkel (Germany)
10. V. B. McGrath (Australia)

1937
1. J. D. Budge (USA)
2. G. von Cramm (Germany)
3. H. Henkel (Germany)
4. H. W. Austin (England)
5. R. L. Riggs (USA)
6. B. M. Grant (USA)
7. J. H. Crawford (Australia)
8. R. Menzel (Czechoslovakia)
9. F. A. Parker (USA)
10. C. E. Hare (England)

1938
1. J. D. Budge (USA)
2. H. W. Austin (England)
3. J. Bromwich (Australia)
4. R. L. Riggs (USA)
5. S. B. Wood (USA)
6. A. K. Quist (Australia)
7. R. Menzel (Czechoslovakia)
8. J. Yamagishi (Japan)
9. G. G. Mako (USA)
10. F. Puncec (Yugoslavia)

1939
1. R. L. Riggs (USA)
2. J. Bromwich (Australia)
3. A. K. Quist (Australia)
4. F. Puncec (Yugoslavia)
5. Frank A. Parker (USA)
6. H. Henkel (Germany)
7. W. D. McNeill (USA)
8. Elwood T. Cooke (USA)
9. Welby Van Horn (USA)
10. Joseph R. Hunt (USA)

Source: Official Encyclopedia of Tennis, edited by the Staff of the United States Lawn Tennis Association (1972).

playing for the third day in a row. But he held on and led 5–3, and 40–love on his own service, only to lose two match points and the game. In the next game, Borotra noticed that his big toe was sticking out of his rope-soled, canvas shoes; he had already changed his shoes twice but obtained permission to change again; he now sat on the back of a ball boy, in the middle of the court, while two other ball boys changed his shoes once again. Allison and the rest of the American team saw the move as nothing but blatant gamesmanship. Still the Americans almost won the match and the tie. In the next rally, Borotra faced his fourth match point on his own serve; his first ball went into the net; his soft second serve slowly floated several inches out; Allison banged the ball high in the stands as he walked to the net to shake hands with Borotra; but there was no call of out. "Allison looked quickly and disbelievingly at the linesman," wrote Alan Trengove, in his excellent story of the match. "The man would not change his mind. 'Thieves! Thieves!' cried an American fan. Even many of the French fans booed the decision, for despite their delight in any French victory over America they were proud of the Musketeers' reputation for sportsmanship and did not want to retain the cup unfairly."[1] Allison won only one more point and lost the match. Vines now played a brilliant final match, handing Cochet his first Davis Cup defeat since France took the cup from Tilden and his teammates at Germantown, in 1927. After France won the Davis Cup in 1932, it never won it again for fifty-nine years, when Captain Yannick Noah led the French team to victory over the Americans, at the Palais de Sports Ger land in Lyon, France, in 1991.

The French officials were by no means the only gamesmen in Continental Europe, as the British-German Davis Cup tie held in Berlin earlier in 1932 clearly showed. The German team that year, led by Dr. Daniel Prenn and Gottfried von Cramm, reached the the Interzone Final for the first time. They lost a close tie to the American team. In the previous round, Germany defeated Great Britain in a memorable tie, especially for Fred Perry who suffered the most bitter defeat of his career in the final match which decided the tie in favor of Germany: "One point—just one little point—ruined the 1932 season for me," he wrote many years later. "And it happened in Berlin, right in front of Adolf Hitler."[2]

The tie was held at the Rot-Weiss Club in Berlin, where the court was sixty feet below ground level in order to avoid the wind; the court was heavily watered to slow down the game. The British team came to Berlin soon after Wimbledon, where Austin had reached the final and had a good chance to win it for the first time for England since Gore had done so in 1909, the year of Perry's birth; but Vines was on and trounced him in fifty minutes, in one of the most lopsided finals ever. Emotionally drained after his Wimbledon loss, Austin was beaten by Dr. Prenn in the opening match; Perry defeated Cramm in the second match and, the next day, won the doubles with Pat Hughes. Still not up to par, Austin lost to Cramm on the third day, leaving Perry to play the deciding match against Prenn.

The court had been thoroughly soaked before the match which exactly suited Dr. Prenn's slow-moving baseline style. He won the first two sets easily. The court began to dry by the third set which Perry won and was then led up many steps to the clubhouse for the ten-minute break. Perry wrote of the German gamesmanship which followed the break as follows:

> When the time came to go back to the court, the officials told me they would take me down by the back way to avoid the crowds. How kind these Germans are, I thought. When we got down there the back gate was locked, so I had to climb all the way up the steps to the clubhouse again, where I found Herr Prenn still easing his limbs on the massage table. Then down to the court—the right way this time.
>
> I was good and mad by now. I won the fourth set 6–0 and went 5–2 up in the fifth, with Prenn serving to save the match. All through the match he had been serving solidly and slowly, and had not been foot-faulted once. . . . Eventually I had him at match point. Although our captain, Roper Barrett, was not there on this occasion, he had always drummed into us the need for extra caution at match point in Davis Cup ties away from home. We were never to hit the ball anywhere near a line. . . .
>
> Prenn served and went the wrong way as I hit a forehand down the line past him. As I moved up to the net to shake hands and to prepare to celebrate Britain's 3–2 victory, I noticed a hell of a row going on at the baseline. The baseline judge had called a foot-fault on Prenn, his first of the match, so he had one more serve to come. He saved the replayed match point with a volley and I didn't win another game. Prenn took that fifth set 7–5 and Germany was in the European Zone final.[3]

The behavior of the German and French officials, in Perry's defeat in Berlin and Allison's in Paris, never would have been tolerated at Wimbledon or Forest Hills. The amateur spirit of sportsmanship was a uniquely valuable, Anglo-American upper-class virtue in those days of their confident world hegemony, both material and moral.*

The Prenn loss haunted Perry for the rest of the 1932 season, especially as he lost two more five setters in a late August visit to America: first he suffered a humiliating loss in the fifth set in the Newport quarterfinals to David N. Jones, a 6-foot 3-inch basketball player at Columbia University, who only ranked eighteenth nationally at the time; he next lost to Sidney Wood at Forest Hills in the fourth round, after winning the first two sets.

Fred Perry, a highly disciplined man, went back to England, after winning his favorite Pacific Southwest, determined to be the fittest player in the world in the fifth set. He trained all winter with one of England's famous football clubs, and had the first of his four great seasons as an amateur in 1933.

Frederick J. Perry was born in Stockport, a Midland textile town not far from Liverpool. His father, Sam Perry, went to work as a spinner at the age of 10 and steadily rose to become a union president at 21 and a JP (Justice of the Peace, the most honorable unpaid position in English county government) before he was 30. He was also a Wesleyan preacher and devoted temperance worker; on his twenty-first birthday, Fred received a promised hundred-pound reward for abstaining from alcohol. (He was later known as "Monsieur Limonade" in Paris.)

After the First World War, Sam Perry moved his family to the London suburb of Ealing, where Fred attended the County School, winning his colors in both cricket and football. He also became a first-class table-tennis player, eventually winning the World Championship at Budapest, the

---

*Within this moral context, it is worth noting that, in less than a year from Prenn's defeat of Perry, he was kicked off the German Davis Cup team as part of Hitler's first Jewish purge. Of Russian-Jewish origins, Prenn was raised in Germany where he was a widely respected player and a tenacious competitor of high moral character; after the affair he fled to England. The German LTA caved in to the Nazis without a fight, all Jewish members of the association resigning. Frau Nelly Neppach, German Ladies Champion in 1925, committed suicide. There were *no official protests* made by the tennis associations of *any other nation*. Austin and Perry did write a protesting letter to the *Times*.

first non-Hungarian to do so. Fred saw his first, top-level lawn tennis at the age of 15, while the family was on holiday at Eastborne; one day he wandered off alone and came upon the famous Devonshire Park tennis grounds, where he climbed over a wall to watch a tournament. The young boy, impressed with the stylish and expensive automobiles presumably owned by the tennis players, then and there vowed to become a lawn tennis champion.

Perry was not a teenage wonder in lawn tennis. He worked hard, however, and, by the age of 20, qualified for the 1929 Wimbledon where he reached the third round. Though pleased with his modest success at his first Wimbledon, Perry now set to work even harder at improving his game, which he modeled on Henri Cochet's, especially on his consummate skill at taking the ball on the rise: "I spent five and a half months in the autumn and winter of 1929–30," he wrote, "working at perfecting the early ball and I confess that sometimes I thought I would never manage to master it. . . . For hours and days and weeks I worked at it."⁴ Then on a magical Sunday morning, he hit the ball perfectly and immediately stopped playing for a week in order to preserve the feeling of the finally jelled cross-court shot taken on the rise; he returned next Sunday and knew that he had it for the rest of his playing days.

All the while Fred was working at a sports shop in Cheapside. At the same time, his father became part of Ramsay MacDonald's second Labour Government, as an M.P. representing the town of Kettering in Northamptonshire. Now a successful but not wealthy man, Sam Perry, M.P., saw his son's tennis potential and urged him to give up his job, agreeing to support him financially for a year while he devoted himself full-time to improving his game even further. In April 1930, Fred had his first chance to test his new "early-ball" skills at the British Hard Court Championships at Bournemouth. He reached the final round where he was beaten by Britain's number one player, Henry Wilford "Bunny" Austin, already a Wimbledon semifinalist and Davis Cup player.

Three years older than Perry, Austin was a public school (Repton) and Cambridge man with a classically stylish tennis game. Twice runner-up at Wimbledon, against Vines in 1932 and Budge in 1938, Austin was always at his very best in Davis Cup play. While Perry won all his eight matches in the four years when the English held the cup, Austin only lost twice. His fine game, aristocratic style, and first-rate record have been obscured by the fame of his more flamboyant Davis Cup partner. Austin was the last English gentleman to play world-class lawn tennis and the last Englishman to reach the final round at Wimbledon (1938).*

Fred Perry's first big break in lawn tennis came in the 1930 Wimbledon Championships when he beat an Italian Baron and First World War ace, Umberto de Morpurgo, in the third round. The baron, ranked in the World First Ten, was a fierce competitor. He immediately went ahead 5–1 in the first set before young Perry got started by first saving a set point and then going on to win the set 10–8; by that time, the Wimbledon "bush telegraph" was spreading the word until hardly an inch of space was left on Court Three. Even more important was the fact that a committee of the LTA was meeting in a room overlooking the court to decide on who was to fill the last vacant spot on a British team which, in the late summer, was to be sent on a six months' tour of the United States and South America. Perry created a sensation by winning the match in four sets and was chosen to travel to America, all expenses paid by the LTA,† thereby letting generous Sam Perry off the financial hook for the rest of 1930.

When the team boarded the *Mauritania* at Southampton, Perry was so proud of his white team blazer with the Union Jack crest and crossed rackets that he almost wore it to bed. After the first lunch on board, the team captain told Perry to unpack and then join him in his cabin for tea, where he clearly laid down the rules with a calm sense of class authority: "We don't expect you to win even one round in most tournaments. . . . If you get knocked out in the first round, I want to see you watching our

---

*Austin was the first player to wear shorts at Wimbledon. They were immaculately pressed and of Bermuda length. It is relevant to the thesis of this book to note that Austin was a prominent member of the Oxford Group, or Moral Rearmament, a sectarian movement during the 1930s, at a time when many members of the Anglo-American upper classes were doubting themselves and the secular values of their class. While most sectarian movements, according to sociologists, have arisen among the down-and-out masses, the Moral Rearmament movement attracted "up-and-outers," who became born-again Christians at conversion sessions held in fashionable drawing rooms. In 1938, the year he lost to Budge in the Wimbledon final, Austin published a widely read book on Moral Rearmament.

†Just as *Who's Who* is assumed to be British, with its American counterpart *Who's Who in America*, so the LTA is naturally British as compared to the American USLTA. A bit of British smugness this.

matches and practicing every day. As captain of the team, I represent the LTA and while you are on the tour you will respect and adhere to the regulations laid down about dress and deportment on and off the court. If you want to go your own way you will be on the next boat back to England and you will never play for your country again."[5]

In those days, team members carried their belongings in large steamer trunks. Class customs required that a gentleman's wardrobe include a minimum of a black tie and dinner jacket, white tie and tails, a blue blazer and tweed jacket in addition to the white team blazer, a gray flannel suit, a polo coat and a chesterfield, or dark blue coat, for the evening, and several pairs of flannel trousers, gray and white. Young Perry, a brash loner much like Jimmy Connors before he set out, was swiftly acculturated into the mores of the Anglo-American upper classes on that first trip to America. He did not win many matches and was put out in the fourth round at Forest Hills. But he did win his first National Championship in Argentina.

In 1931, Perry was ranked for the first time in the World First Ten, number four, behind Cochet, Austin, and Vines and ahead of Shields and Wood. He just missed the big wins that year, losing to Sidney Wood, the eventual winner, in the semifinals of Wimbledon, to Vines, the eventual winner, in the semis at Forest Hills, and again to Vines in the finals of the Pacific Southwest. The highlight of his year was that first visit to California. As he wrote in his autobiography: "My first trip to California in 1931 marked the start of a new era and changed my life forever. I became an annual visitor to the Pacific Southwest tournament and very much a man-about-Hollywood, where the life style suited me down to the ground. I played the Pacific Southwest tournament for five years, losing the 1931 final, winning it the next three times and again getting to the final the following year. As a three-time winner I was awarded the trophy permanently, but I gave it back to the tournament for perpetual competition." As a reward for his first visit to Los Angeles, a date was arranged for him with Jean Harlow, "stunning in a black dress and with platinum-blonde hair," as Perry remembered it. They had a splendid dinner followed by visits to several night spots, all tabs signed by Miss Harlow for the Metro-Goldwyn-Mayer publicity department. Such was life for poor boys in those ancient amateur days of luxury and fun without affluence.

If 1927 had been the finest year in tennis history, the year 1933 was a very close second. For one thing, both years marked crucial turning points in Davis Cup history: in 1927, France became the first non-English-speaking nation to win the cup; in 1933, the British won the cup for the first time since 1912 (see Figures 16 and 17).

In 1933, the Davis Cup team to beat was the American one. Vines was the best player in the world and had handed Cochet his first Davis Cup defeat since 1927 in the challenge round the previous year, when many people felt that Allison had been cheated out of a victory over Borotra in the critical match of the tie. But Vines hit his amateur peak in 1932 and then slipped badly in 1933, losing to both Austin and Perry when Britain won the Interzone Final (4–1) and the right to challenge France.

In the 1933 challenge round at Roland Garros, Fred Perry's gamesmanship may not have been too wise. Conventional tennis wisdom at the time expected the British to beat the French rather easily, especially as Borotra had announced his retirement from Davis Cup singles play, forcing team captain Lacoste to pair the aging Cochet with an inexperienced, 19-year-old, André Merlin. But for Perry, at least, this challenge round proved to be an exhaustingly dramatic ordeal.

In the opening match, Austin easily defeated Merlin. Perry followed by winning the most important match of the tie, beating Cochet in five long sets, after which he passed out on the dressing room floor. Perry's discussion of this match provides great insight into his own and the French minds. He begins with an outline of two of his gamesmanship ploys. "One of my methods of injecting a little gamesmanship into a big match was to vault the net if I won and congratulate my opponent, thereby giving the crowd the impression that this Perry fellow was fit enough to play another five sets. . . . I had another trick up my sleeve if I was involved in matches with a ten-minute break at the end of the third set. I'd start by wearing off-white gabardine trousers and an off white shirt. Then, after the rest period, I would re-emerge in dazzling white duck trousers and a fresh white cotton shirt, my hair neatly parted. The crowd always thought I looked twice as fresh as the other man, but of course it was just window dressing."[6]

At the end of the Cochet match, of course, Perry vaulted the net in his immaculate white gear to shake his victim's hand. Perry went on to describe the psychological problem of the match with Cochet as follows:

FIGURE 16

The Davis Cup: Champion and Runner-Up Nations, 1900–1990

Year	Champion Nation	Runner-up	Venue	Number of Competing Nations	Year	Champion Nation	Runner-up	Venue	Number of Competing Nations
1900	USA	British Isles	Boston	2	1950	Australia	USA	New York	25
1901	no challenge				1951	Australia	USA	Sydney	27
1902	USA	British Isles	New York	2	1952	Australia	USA	Adelaide	29
1903	British Isles	USA	Boston	2	1953	Australia	USA	Melbourne	30
1904	British Isles	USA	London	3	1954	USA	Australia	Sydney	31
1905	British Isles	USA	London	5	1955	Australia	USA	New York	34
1906	British Isles	USA	London	3	1956	Australia	USA	Adelaide	33
1907	Australasia	British Isles	London	3	1957	Australia	USA	Melbourne	36
1908	Australasia	USA	Melbourne	3	1958	USA	Australia	Brisbane	37
1909	Australasia	USA	Sydney	3	1959	Australia	USA	New York	39
1910	no challenge				1960	Australia	Italy	Sydney	40
1911	Australasia	USA	Christchurch	3	1961	Australia	Italy	Melbourne	42
1912	British Isles	Australasia	Melbourne	3	1962	Australia	Mexico	Brisbane	42
1913	USA	British Isles	London	8	1963	USA	Australia	Adelaide	49
1914	Australasia	USA	New York	7	1964	Australia	USA	Cleveland	46
1915–18	no competition				1965	Australia	Spain	Sydney	43
1919	Australasia	British Isles	Sydney	5	1966	Australia	India	Melbourne	46
1920	USA	Australasia	Auckland	6	1967	Australia	Spain	Brisbane	48
1921	USA	Japan	New York	11	1968	USA	Australia	Adelaide	49
1922	USA	Australia	New York	11	1969	USA	Romania	Cleveland	51
1923	USA	Australia	New York	17	1970	USA	F.R. Germany	Cleveland	50
1924	USA	Australia	Philadelphia	22	1971	USA	Romania	Charlotte	51
1925	USA	France	Philadelphia	23	1972	USA	Romania	Bucharest	52
1926	USA	France	Philadelphia	24	1973	Australia	USA	Cleveland	53
1927	France	USA	Philadelphia	26	1974	South Africa	India	(default)	55
1928	France	USA	Paris	33	1975	Sweden	Czechoslovakia	Stockholm	53
1929	France	USA	Paris	29	1976	Italy	Chile	Santiago	53
1930	France	USA	Paris	28	1977	Australia	Italy	Sydney	55
1931	France	Great Britain	Paris	30	1978	USA	Great Britain	Palm Springs	50
1933	Great Britain	France	Paris	31	1979	USA	Italy	San Francisco	49
1934	Great Britain	USA	London	27	1980	Czechoslovakia	Italy	Prague	51
1935	Great Britain	USA	London	28	1981	USA	Argentina	Cincinnati	51
1936	Great Britain	Australia	London	23	1982	USA	France	Grenoble	57
1937	USA	Great Britain	London	25	1983	Australia	Sweden	Melbourne	58
1938	USA	Australia	Philadelphia	24	1984	Sweden	USA	Gothenburg	61
1939	Australia	USA	Philadelphia	25	1985	Sweden	F.R. Germany	Munich	62
1940–45	no competition				1986	Australia	Sweden	Melbourne	69
1946	USA	Australia	Melbourne	19	1987	Sweden	India	Gothenburg	70
1947	USA	Australia	New York	22	1988	F.R. Germany	Sweden	Gothenburg	74
1948	USA	Australia	New York	29	1989	F.R. Germany	Sweden	Stuttgart	79
1949	USA	Australia	New York	26	1990	USA	Australia	St Petersburg	84

FIGURE 17
Wimbledon and Davis Cup Winning Nations, 1877–1987

Wimbledon Winners			*Davis Cup Winners*		
Before World War I					
1877–1914			1900–1914*		
England	28	(74)	England	5	(42)
Ireland	4	(10)	Australasia	4	(33)
Australasia	4	(10)	USA	3	(25)
	38	(100)		12	(100)
				*Not held 1901, 1910		
Between the Wars					
1919–1939			1919–1939		
USA	9	(43)	USA	9	(43)
France	6	(29)	France	6	(29)
England	3	(14)	England	4	(19)
Australia	3	(14)	Australia	2	(9)
	21	(100)		21	(100)
After World War II					
1946–1967			1946–1967		
Australia	10	(45)	Australia	16	(73)‡
USA	8	(36)	USA	6	(27)
France	1	(5)		22	(100)
Peru	1	(5)†			
Spain	1	(5)			
Czechoslovakia	1	(5)			
	22	(100)			
Open Era					
1968–1987			1968–1987		
USA	7	(35)	USA	9	(45)
Sweden	5	(25)	Australia	4	(20)
Australia	5	(25)	Sweden	4	(20)
Czechoslovakia	1	(5)	South Africa	1	(5)*
Germany	2	(10)	Czechoslovakia	1	(5)
	20	(100)	Italy		(5)
				20	(100)

*India defaulted in the final round,
protesting apartheid.

†Alejandro Olmedo, Wimbledon winner in 1959, learned his tennis in his native Peru and was recruited to play for USC before becoming a U.S. citizen.
‡In the years between 1950 and 1968, when Harry Hopman captained the team, Australia lost only four times, including 1968, when all his top men had deserted the amateur ranks. Back in 1958 when the United States beat the Australians, Olmedo, not yet an official citizen, won both his singles matches and the doubles with Richardson, in the challenge round.

Vaulting the net after such a grueling match definitely was the boxer's shuffle on my part.* In the privacy of the dressing room I passed out completely, then came round to find myself on the massage table with Roper Barrett and Maskell fanning me. My condition, due as much to mental strain as physical exertion, was hushed up for tactical reasons, and as a precaution I was rested from the doubles. . . .

It's hard for anyone who wasn't there at the time to understand the particular strain of playing the Challenge Round of the Davis Cup in Paris. We were trying to take the Cup away from the French on their own territory and Paris was a seething cauldron. You never knew what was going to happen and everything you did was like another step along a tightrope. The court was purpose-built to suit the Frenchmen and spike the Americans' game, so the French had every advantage to start with, and the 15,000 people who were jammed into Roland Garros Stadium that day were all frenzied Frenchmen, whistling and jeering. If there was a bad call, it took four or five minutes to silence the eruption. It's a very nerve-racking thing to play tennis in that kind of charged atmosphere. And to try to beat Cochet, who, let's face it, was my idol, on his own territory, in the Davis Cup Challenge Round and in such a decisive match, was a staggering responsibility. I think, when I beat him, the bottom dropped out of my act. I think it was the sheer joy and relief of thinking, "My God, we made it!"[7]

On the second day, Borotra and Brugnon easily won the doubles. In the opening match of the third day, 15,000 Frenchmen, including the President of the Republic, cheered themselves hoarse as Cochet, playing his last match for France, came from behind to win in five sets. It was now up to Perry to beat Merlin, which he did in four close sets. The British had won the cup for the first time since 1912. Captain Roper Barrett, who had been involved with British Davis Cup leadership, as player and/or captain, ever since 1900, when he and his partner lost the doubles to Dwight Davis and Holcombe Ward in the first Davis Cup tie ever played, lovingly hugged the cup as if it were a new-

---

*Two points should be noted here: first, tennis is far more like boxing than any other nonteam sport; two loners attempt to break down their opponents, mentally as well as physically. Secondly, Perry mentions his snow white "ducks," which reminds me to stress the fact that the amateur age of white flannels, so often referred to derisively today, is not quite accurate; flannels were rarely worn after the First World War; Dick Williams was the first star to wear cotton ducks in the twenties and by Perry's time everyone wore them, a few dudes, like Perry, wearing the more expensive gabardine which needed to be dry-cleaned just like flannels.

born baby.* After the national anthems of both countries were played, Perry retreated to the dressing rooms where he passed out for the second time.

That evening, Cochet temporarily purloined the cup and persuaded Perry to accompany him through the night spots of Paris; the two famous friends and a growing crowd of hangers-on sang the "Marseillaise" and "God Save the King" and emptied the champagne-filled cup at every rendezvous (while others drank, Perry "sipped," as he put it). The escapade lasted all night, ending when the sacred cup was returned to its proper place at 7 A.M. the next morning.

Perry now went on to win Forest Hills and the Pacific Southwest, thereby setting the tone for his next three years (1934–36) as reigning Champion of the World.

———

In 1933, John Herbert Crawford, of Australia, ranked number one in the world, even though Fred Perry reigned supreme in September (see Figures 15 and 18). Crawford began the year by winning his third straight Australian singles title. At the time, a first-rate American team of Vines, Allison, Van Ryn, and Keith Gledhill was touring Australia, playing in the major State tournaments. In the Australian Championships at the end of the tour, Crawford beat Gledhill in the singles final after putting out Allison in the semis. Vines, who was expected to win the Championship, was put out in the quarters by a 16-year-old boy from Sydney, Vivian McGrath.† Vines and Gledhill won the doubles, beating the top Australian team of Crawford and Gar Moon, in the finals.

John Herbert Crawford, widely acclaimed as the father of modern Australian lawn tennis was, in many ways the Tilden of Australia.[8] Born

---

*Roper Barrett was a Wimbledon singles finalist in 1909, the year of Perry's birth.

†Young McGrath was the first world-class player to hold a tennis racket with two hands. At the age of 20, in 1937, he won the Australian singles title, beating another two-handed player, John Bromwich, who was three years younger. McGrath was a right-hander and used two hands for his backhand, on his left side; Bromwich was a left-hander with a two-handed backhand on his right side. McGrath burned out at an early age but Bromwich became one of the finest doubles players in history. The third two-handed player was also an Australian, Geoff Brown, who got to the singles, doubles and mixed doubles finals at Wimbledon in 1946, without losing a set; he lost all three finals. The last two-hander, in the twenty years after 1930, was Pancho Segura, who won the intercollegiates three years in a row (1943–45) and turned professional in 1947. After Segura there were no world-class two-handers until Jimmy Connors, who became the first two-hander to win Wimbledon (1974).

FIGURE 18

Australian, French, British, and American Men's Singles Champions,
1930–1949

	Australian	French	British	American
1930	Moon	Cochet	Tilden	Doeg
1931	Crawford	Borotra	Wood	Vines
1932	Crawford	Cochet	Vines	Vines
1933	**Crawford**	**Crawford***	**Crawford**	**Perry**
1934	Perry	Cramm	Perry	Perry
1935	Crawford	Perry	Perry	Allison
1936	Quist	Cramm	Perry	Perry
1937	McGrath	Henkel	Budge	Budge
1938	**Budge**	**Budge**	**Budge**	**Budge**
1939	Bromwich	McNeill	Riggs	Riggs
1940	Quist	not held	not held	McNeill
1941	not held	"	"	Riggs
1942	"	"	"	Schroeder
1943	"	"	"	Joe Hunt
1944	"	"	"	Parker
1945	"	"	"	Parker
1946	Bromwich	Bernard**	Petra***	Kramer
1947	Pails	Asboth	Kramer	Kramer
1948	Quist	Parker	Falkenberg	Gonzales
1949	**Sedgman**	**Parker****	**Schroeder**	**Gonzales**

* First non-Frenchman to win title.
** First Frenchman to win since Cochet.
*** Y.F.M. Petra first Frenchman to win since Cochet; no Frenchman has won Wimbledon since.
**** Parker is the only American to have won the French Championships twice, let alone twice in a row.

Of the twenty American Championships, Perry won three, and Vines, Budge, Riggs, Parker, Kramer, and Gonzales won twice (all six American two-time winners turned pro, as did Perry). The five one-time winners, Doeg, Allison, McNeill, Schroeder, and Hunt, remained in the amateur ranks and all graduated from college. None of the six Americans who turned pro—or Perry—were college graduates.

in 1908, on a large and prosperous farm near the town of Albury, right on the border between New South Wales and Victoria, he was the next-to-youngest of six children. His mother was a good tennis player and his father average, and they both played constantly with Jack's two much older brothers on the family tennis court; too young to play, Jack was usually the ball boy; but he also spent hours hitting a tennis ball against the side of the barn. He first took up the game seriously at the age of 12, at Manly, a beautiful beach resort on the north bank of the entrance to Sydney Harbor, one of the most spectacular in the world. His only teacher was his 22-year-old brother. At first young Jack got only a few games; after about a year, he got a set, then two sets, and eventually took all three sets. He was soon playing on grass as a junior member of the Manly Lawn Tennis Club. At the age of 17, in 1925, he won the Junior (under 21) Singles Championship of Australia, as well as the doubles, with Harry Hopman who was two years older. Hopman was slight and swift-moving, while Crawford was a more leisurely, 180-pound six-footer in his youth and a hefty 210-pounder by the time he won Wimbledon in 1933.

Before turning 21, Crawford had won the Queensland, New South Wales, and Victorian Singles Championships as well as the doubles with Harry Hopman. He and Hopman were as closely linked as Hoad and Rosewall were later on, and they now dominated the men's game while still juniors. The tennis public loved it and the Lawn Tennis Association of Australia immediately set about inviting top players from England, France, Japan, and America to come "down under" and cross swords with Crawford who was rapidly becoming a national hero. Within a few years, tennis in Australia changed from a minor to a major sport, largely due to the popularity of Gentleman Jack Crawford. His doubles partner, Harry Hopman, was in the long run perhaps equally important in Australian tennis history: he was the first Aussie to wear shorts and, after 1950, led Australia to world leadership in amateur lawn tennis.

Gentleman Jack's stylish tennis form and courtly manners were classic examples of old-school majesty and grace; he reminded one of a young man who had come for an afternoon of tennis at the Vicar's. He was always dressed immaculately, in polished white shoes,* sharply-creased,

---

*During World War II, when my ship spent ten days in Sydney for rest and rehabilitation, an Australian Army Colonel took me for a game of tennis at the White City Club, scene of many Australian Championships and Davis Cup matches; I was impressed with the perfectly polished tennis shoes lined up at the foot of each member's locker. While Australia had a much more socialized economy and egalitarian distribution of wealth than ours, at least in the 1940s, their social system was far more Victorian, as far as class authority and deference were concerned. No locker-room attendants at the Germantown or Merion cricket clubs at that time or since were ever required to keep club members' shoes polished.

old-fashioned flannels, and what we would now call a white dress shirt, with sleeves buttoned at his wrists; he might unbutton and roll up his right sleeve as a match progressed. His majestic style had never been seen, or imagined, before in Australia. When he first played at Wimbledon, however, Englishmen of the older generation immediately saw the similarity of his game to the famous classical style of the Doherty brothers. Crawford's influence on the Australian game lasted through several generations and was called "The Crawford Style" for years. Crawford was, like Tilden in America, the last of the classic baseliners. He attacked from the baseline, using the court as a chessboard, maneuvering and parrying with intelligence and subtlety. Instead of power, he relied on accuracy, control, and disguise. Tilden was also a master at "chess tennis."

Throughout his tennis career, Crawford suffered from asthma and insomnia, which caused several sad losses. At the same time, he had one of the finest records in Australian history, winning eleven Australian titles as well as countless State Championships; he won three titles at Wimbledon and three at Roland Garros; he won the Australian mixed doubles title three times with his beloved wife; and finally, he played on nine Davis Cup teams. His most famous victory was his win over Vines in the "greatest ever" Wimbledon final, in 1933; his most famous loss was administered by Perry in the Forest Hills final that same year.

In 1933, the Australian Davis Cup team chose to challenge in the European Zone where, in spite of Crawford's two singles victories, the team lost to the British in the Zone Finals. In the meantime, Crawford beat Cochet to become the first non-Frenchman to win the championship of France. He then went to London where he beat the reigning champion and odds-on favorite, Ellsworth Vines.

After more than two hours of play, in this classic Wimbledon final, the score stood at two sets all and twenty games each. In the fifth set, Crawford served first and, after unbroken services, reached 5–4 when, lifting his game to his limit on Vines's serve, he took the final game at love, raising the chalk as four winners hit the line. An Englishman, S. A. E. Hickson, who was witnessing his fifty-third final since umpiring at the first Wimbledon, declared that "for sustained quality of play, mutual attack in the service, and the tense excitement of the last phase, the two-hour contest which Crawford and Vines waged was Wimbledon's greatest match."[9] The very essence of Crawford's character was caught by an Australian writer who concluded his discussion of the match as follows: "With Crawford, however, results can to some extent be placed on one side; there is little doubt that the classic displays of stroke-making he gave and the personality that gained him such respect and affection made an even greater and more lasting impact on the game of lawn tennis."*

Jack Crawford was lawn tennis's finest example of the gentlemanly ideal at a time when the Anglo-American empire was still at its peak of power and moral authority. In this sense, he was the very antithesis of his friend Perry.

═══

The United States Men's Singles Championship at Forest Hills in 1933 turned out to be disastrous for Vines and tragic for Crawford. Vines, who had won at Forest Hills in 1931 and 1932, was humiliated by Bitsy Grant in the fourth round, as we have already seen. It was his last match on grass as an amateur and he cut the gut out of his racket afterwards, saying wearily, "I'm through!"

Crawford, who had already won the Singles Championships of Australia, France, and England, was beaten by Fred Perry, in a come-from-behind, five-set final, thereby losing his chance to become the *first* to win what later was called the "Grand Slam." The finals were played on a hot and humid day. Crawford was tense, over-tennised, and suffering from insomnia and asthma; he had hardly slept a wink for his whole two weeks in New York: "I used to play tennis all afternoon at Forest Hills," Crawford later told Stan Hart, "go back to that hot little hotel room and play tennis all night, going over and over in my mind matches I had played years before."[10] The first three sets of the final were brilliant, Crawford leading two sets to one at the ten-minute rest period. "I went off to the changing room, to put on my fresh white clothes," wrote Perry, "but Crawford just sat in a courtside box with his wife, smoking a cigarette. He didn't even change out of his sweaty

---

*Paul Metzler, *Tennis: Styles and Stylists* (1969). Metzler, a multidimensional gentleman, was not only a keen student of tennis but also a diplomat attached to the Australian Embassy, in Washington, at the time this book was published. Wimbledon official, Brame Hillyard, held Metzler's view of Crawford when he "insulted" Perry by telling Crawford that the "best man" did not win the 1934 Wimbledon right after Perry had beaten Crawford in a quick three-set final, (see later in this chapter).

clothes."[11] Most of the press and the spectators thought Crawford had the match won, hands down. But Perry came out all dressed up in white and, in a startling reversal of form, proceeded to win the last two sets with the loss of only one game.* Crawford had passed his peak, never winning another National Championship except the Australian, which he won once more, in 1935. For Perry, the remarkable victory began his three years of world dominance.†

The two good friends now took a four-day train trip out to Los Angeles together. Both were sick of tennis and only wanted to be off for Australia, Crawford to get home and Perry with high hopes of winning the Australian Championship. While the two Forest Hills finalists were merely going through the motions in an exhibition match before the opening of the Pacific Southwest at the Los Angeles Tennis Club, the glamorous movie star, Marlene Dietrich, the official hostess, suddenly said, in her beautiful, accented voice, according to Perry: "Well, gentlemen, I think you could at least *try*." For the second year in a row, Perry won the Pacific Southwest. When Perry Jones presented the trophy, he told Perry that, according to time-honored prophetic custom, he was also awarding him the U.S. Championship for the following year (which Perry duly won).

In spite of his very poor record in 1933, Vines was still regarded as the finest player in the world when he was on his game. At any rate, at the close of the 1933 season, he became the first American Champion to follow Tilden into the professional ranks (see Chapter 10 above). Vines's desertion of the amateur ranks may have been seen as a threat to the amateur game. For soon afterwards the USLTA made its first (and last) move to introduce open tennis when it voted, in its 1933 spring meeting, to hold an open tournament at the Germantown Cricket Club the following fall. They then petitioned the International Lawn Tennis Federation (ILTF) to approve the tournament at its June meeting in Paris.

---

*Theories of course abounded about why Crawford lost this vital match which would have made him the first Grand Slam winner. Most versions had him sipping brandy or bourbon to control his asthma. He later told Stan Hart that he had never taken a drink in any tennis match, including that one. At any rate, it has remained a legendary landmark in the history of amateur lawn tennis.

†Incidentally, Perry was the first foreigner to win the U.S. Championship since the great Englishman, H. L. Doherty, won it in 1903.

Unfortunately the USLTA sent no official to plead their case which was routinely presented to the ILTF by a Second Secretary of the U.S. Embassy, only to be turned down. Had the USLTA persisted and won out, both professional and amateur players (as in golf) might today be playing in tournaments together in some of the finest clubs in the nation, instead of in such morally vacuous places as the Cow Palace in San Francisco, the Spectrum in Philadelphia, and Flushing Meadow. The Germantown Cricket Club might be the American counterpart of Wimbledon and surely the leaders at the West Side Tennis Club might have come up with a new location with a more civilizing atmosphere than Flushing Meadow (see the end of Chapter 16 for further discussion).

Fred Perry's greatest year was 1934 when he won the Australian, British, and American singles titles, and just missed becoming the first Grand Slam winner when he injured an ankle in the second round at Roland Garros and lost to an Italian star, Georgio de Stefani.

Perry had gone to Australia at the end of 1933 as part of a British team sent out by the Lawn Tennis Association as a goodwill effort to offset the disgraceful behavior of a British cricket team earlier in the year, in the infamous "body-line" controversy which almost lost an Empire (see the discussion of this incident by C. L. R. James in Chapter 1). Fred immediately liked the easygoing and democratic ways of the Australians; throughout the visit, he played with gusto and style, easily beating Crawford in the finals of the National Championships. He played that final, incidentally, with an improvised racket which had been painted totally white just the day before; the crowd noticed the dazzling prototype immediately; after the match, a big, box kite was floated over the stadium carrying the message, "The white racket is a Slazenger." And that Perry white racket, along with Spalding's Tilden Top-Flight and Wilson's Jack Kramer, was one of the three most famous rackets of the modern amateur era.

Surely the biggest thrill in Perry's tennis career was his becoming the first Englishman to win Wimbledon since Arthur Gore's victory in 1909, which had occurred just three months after Perry's birth, in May. In the 1934 finals, he virtually blew Crawford off the court, winning three straight sets in one hour and ten minutes. Although the British had admired Perry's taking the lead in winning the Davis Cup the previous summer at Wimbledon, they cheered for Gentleman Jack rather than their "upstart" compatriot.

If the Wimbledon spectators favored Crawford over Perry during the match, official Wimbledon was downright rude to him after his historic victory. Over half a century later, Perry wrote of this rudeness as follows:

In those days there was no formal presentation of the championship trophy on court. You simply shook hands with your opponent, picked up your gear and walked back to the dressing room. . . . I went for a long soak in the bath to ease my muscles and let the significance of it all sink in with the bath water. I was the proudest bloke in a bathtub anywhere in England.

Suddenly, out in the dressing room, I overheard the distinctive voice, Brame Hillyard, Club committee man, talking to Crawford. "Congratulations," said Hillyard. "This was one day when the best man didn't win." I couldn't believe my ears. What about the two previous times I'd beaten him, in the finals of the U.S. and Australian Championships?

Hillyard had brought a bottle of champagne into the dressing room and given it to Jack, whom I so clearly remember having beaten in straight sets not half an hour before. I leapt from the tub, rushed out and, sure enough, found Crawford holding the bottle. True, I hadn't been quite forgotten: there, draped over the back of my seat, was the official acknowledgement of my championship, an honorary All England Club member's tie.

Nobody said, "Here's your tie, Fred. Welcome to the Club." Nobody even said, "Congratulations." The tie was just dropped there for me to find when I came out of the bath. Instead of Fred J. Perry the champ, I felt like Fred J. Muggs the chimp. . . .

I don't think I've ever been so angry in my life. That stuck-up attitude hurt, it really did. All my paranoia about the old-school-tie brigade surfaced with a vengeance.[12]

Perry was not one to take an insult lying down and immediately demanded, and eventually got, an apology from both Hillyard and official Wimbledon.*

---

*There was certainly no excuse for the rude treatment Perry received at the hands of Hillyard or official Wimbledon. Perry was clearly the best tennis player that day at Wimbledon and the best player in the world in 1934. On the other hand, when Hillyard called Crawford the "best *man*," he had something else in mind. One must remember that, in those far-off and far-different days, winning was not everything, nor the only thing. To many British gentlemen of that day, Perry was quite similar to the brash, arrogant, cocky, and often rudely belligerent Jimmy Connors of our day. He saw tennis as a battle rather than a game and had no respect for sporting losers.

Fred Perry had one of the finest tennis records of all time. He was world number one for three straight years, 1934–36. While Tilden had held the top world ranking for six years in 1920–25, and Cochet for four in 1928–31, Perry's three straight record held for half a century until Ivan Lendl held the world title from 1985 through 1987 (see Figures 19 and 20). His three straight Wimbledon wins in 1934–36 were not equaled until Borg won five titles in a row in 1976–80. When Perry won the French Singles Championship in 1935, he became the first man to win all four Grand Slam titles (though not in the same year). His record of eight straight wins in challenge round Davis Cup competition was one of the best ever.

Perry was, above all, a winner with the killer instinct of great champions in all sports. "Fred never missed a trick when it came to the psychology of winning," according to Ted Tinling who knew him well as a rival in business and a friend over many years. "He was a master of one-upmanship. In the locker rooms he had a sharp tongue and took every opportunity to make cutting comments, sometimes to the point of being extremely personal, with the aim of gaining a psychological advantage over an opponent. On the court, he was never averse to using a caustic one-liner to distract an opponent."[13]

In 1936, after leading the British Davis Cup team to its last ever challenge round victory (defeating Australia 3–2) and winning both Wimbledon and Forest Hills, Perry turned pro in November. In January 7, 1937, he met Ellsworth Vines, the reigning Professional Champion, in Madison Square Garden. A capacity crowd of over 18,000 turned out for this British-American battle, establishing a record for indoor tennis which remained unbroken until the vulgar, "male-chauvinist-pig" Riggs-King extravaganza at the Houston Astrodome thirty-six years later. Perry defeated Vines on that opening night at the Garden as well as in their next two matches, at Cleveland and at Chicago, when Vines was suddenly hospitalized for nervous exhaustion. Tilden filled in for a few matches. When Vines returned, Perry's momentum had been broken and Vines finally won their first American tour by the narrow margin of thirty-one matches to twenty-nine.

Mounting mistrust is one of the most important signs of social disorder and moral decline. In his 1984 autobiography, Perry nicely suggested the contrasting moral climates in America as between the prewar years

FIGURE 19
World Number One Men's Singles, 1920–1987

1920–29: Tilden 1920–25, Lacoste 1926–27, Cochet 1928–29

1930	Cochet (FR)	1950	Patty (USA)	1968	Laver (Aus)
	Cochet		Sedgman (Aus)		Laver
	Vines (USA)		Sedgman		Newcombe (Aus)
	Crawford (Aus)		Trabert (USA)		Newcombe
	Perry (ENG)		Drobny (Egypt)*		Smith (USA)
	Perry	1955	Trabert (USA)		Nastase (Romania)
1936	Perry		Hoad (Aus)		Connors (USA)
	Budge (USA)		Cooper (Aus)	1975	Ashe (USA)
	Budge (USA)		Cooper		Connors (USA)
	Riggs (USA)		Fraser (Aus)		Borg (Sweden)
1940–1945	WAR	1960	Fraser (Aus)		Connors (USA)
1946	Kramer (USA)		Laver (Aus)		Borg (Sweden)
	Kramer		Laver	1980	Borg
	Parker		Osuna (Mexico)		McEnroe (USA)
1949	Gonzales (USA)		Emerson (Aus)		Connors (USA)
		1965	Emerson		McEnroe (USA)
			Santana (Spain)		McEnroe
		1967	Newcombe (Aus)	1985	Lendl (Czech)
					Lendl
				1987	Lendl

SUMMARY: Years Number One in Four Eras

TILDEN ERA
1920–1929 Ten years, 3 men ranked No. 1
      6 years   Tilden
      2 years   Lacoste, Cochet

PERRY JONES ERA
1930–1949 Fourteen years, 9 men ranked No. 1 (WAR 1940–45)
      3 years   Perry
      2 years   Cochet, Budge, and Kramer
      1 year   Vines, Crawford, Riggs, Parker, Gonzales

HARRY HOPMAN ERA
1950–1967 Eighteen years, 12 men ranked No. 1
      2 years   Sedgman, Trabert, Cooper, Frazer, Laver, Emerson
      1 year   Patty, Drobny, Hoad, Osuna, Santana, Newcombe

PROFESSIONAL ERA
1968–1987 Twenty years, 9 men ranked No. 1
      4 years   Connors
      3 years   Borg, McEnroe, Lendl
      2 years   Laver, Newcombe
      1 year   Smith, Nastase, Ashe

Years World No. 1, 1920–1987: Tilden 6, Cochet 4, Connors 4, Perry 3, Borg 3,
McEnroe 3, Lendl 3.

*Drobny, a Czechoslovakian refugee who eventually made his home in England, was registered as an Egyptian for political purposes that year.

FIGURE 20

U.S. Number One Men's Singles, 1920–1987

1920–29 W. T. Tilden II

1930	J. H. Doeg	1950	Art Larson	1968	A. Ashe
	E. Vines		V. Seixas		S. Smith
	E. Vines		G. Mulloy		C. Richey
	F. X. Shields		T. Trabert		S. Smith
	W. Allison		V. Seixas		S. Smith
	W. Allison		T. Trabert	1973	J. Connors
1936	D. Budge		H. Richardson		J. Connors
	D. Budge		V. Seixas		A. Ashe
	D. Budge		H. Richardson		J. Connors
1939	R. Riggs		A. Olmado		J. Connors
1940	D. McNeill	1960	B. MacKay		J. Connors
	R. Riggs		W. Reed	1979	J. McEnroe
	F. R. Schroeder		C. McKinley		J. McEnroe
	J. R. Hunt		C. McKinley		J. McEnroe
	F. Parker		D. Ralston		J. Connors
	F. Parker		D. Ralston		J. McEnroe
1946	J. Kramer		D. Ralston		J. McEnroe
	J. Kramer	1967	C. Pasarell		J. McEnroe
	R. Gonzales				J. Connors
	R. Gonzales			1987	J. Connors

SUMMARY: Years Number One in Four Eras

TILDEN ERA
1920–1929

        10 years   Tilden

PERRY JONES ERA
1930–1949 Twenty Years, 12 men ranked No. 1

        3 years   Budge
        2 years   Vines, Riggs, Kramer, Gonzales, Parker, Allison
        1 year   Doeg, Shields, McNeill, Schroeder, Hunt

HARRY HOPMAN ERA
1950–1967 Eighteen Years, 11 men ranked No. 1

        3 years   Seixas and Ralston*
        2 years   Trabert, Richardson, McKinley
        1 year   Larson, Mulloy, Olmedo, MacKay, Reed, Pasarell

PROFESSIONAL ERA
1968–1987 Twenty Years, 5 men ranked No. 1

        8 years   Connors
        6 years   McEnroe
        3 years   Smith
        2 years   Ashe
        1 year   Richey**

*Seixas won Wimbledon and Forest Hills each once, while Ralston never won either title.
**Richey never won a Grand Slam title.

and our own times when he wrote as follows about his lifetime friendship with Vines which began on their first pro tour:

> For Vines and myself that was the start of a great partnership. We were in business together for the next twenty years, touring various parts of the world. We bought the Beverly Hills Tennis Club, operated it together and sold it together. Yet in all that time the extraordinary thing was that we never had a contract.
>
> By the second year of our pro tour we were sharing the operating end of it, too, and we had complete trust in each other. On the mainland USA, Vines was in charge of finances. Anywhere else, it was my job. I would say, "Well, Ellie, we took so much money, our expenses were so much, you've already had so much, and you've got so much to come," and he'd say, "Fine."[14]

It surely was in accord with the spirit of their time that the two hand-somest men ever to play world-class tennis, Frank Shields and Fred Perry, should end up in Hollywood. How different they were in other ways: Shields was a charming and idealistic alcoholic, Perry, a charming and calculating teetotaler. Shields never really cared about moneymaking even though he played with the rich and famous from Hollywood to Long Island and Tuxedo. Perry married a beautiful movie star, moved to Hollywood, became an American citizen in 1938, and served in our air force during World War II; after the war he made his pile as a shrewd sportswear merchandiser.

After turning pro, Perry's honorary membership in the All-England Club was rescinded and he was no longer allowed to wear the club neck-tie: "I was quite prepared to abide by their decision," Perry wrote of his orders to return the club tie, "because that was the rule in those days, when the word 'professional' sent a shiver through their portals."

Rebels in one generation have a way of becoming heroes in later ones. After World War II, in 1949, Perry's membership in the All-England Club was happily restored and, in 1984, on the fiftieth anniversary of his first winning Wimbledon, the Somerset Road entrance to Wimbledon was renamed the Fred Perry Gate, inside of which now stands his statue. Today, the Doherty and Perry gates memorialize the two most famous names in the history of British tennis.*

---

*Two main entrances to the Wimbledon compound.

Budge and the Baron:
The Greatest Match of Them All and the First Grand Slam

It is unfortunate in many ways that tennis is still much the domain of the rich. It is more regrettable, though, that the sport is still saddled with an image of snobbery that is not altogether fair. Even in the early thirties, when I was breaking in, tennis was becoming more than a rich man's diversion.

—J. Donald Budge

Budge made a magnificent court appearance. Dressed in immaculate long flannels, carefully whited shoes, imported woolen shirts, traditional cable-stitch tennis sweaters, and a white Davis Cup blazer, he looked every inch a champion. . . . He never questioned a call during his entire amateur career and was always a perfect gentleman, even during those rare occasions when the going got rough.

—Julius D. Heldman

WHEN FRED PERRY RULED THE LAWN TENNIS WORLD IN 1936, BARON Gottfried von Cramm ranked second and Donald Budge third. At the beginning of the 1937 season, after Perry had turned pro, Cramm and Budge became the top two amateur players in the world. The Baron, who had won the French title in 1934 and 1936 while Budge had yet to win a Grand Slam title, had a slight edge. On the other hand, Cramm, an exact contemporary of Perry, was 28 and slightly past his prime, while Budge, at 22, was just arriving at his. At any rate, within the year, in which they were the star attractions, Budge proved himself to be the unquestioned World Champion, while his good friend, Cramm, sadly, and on hindsight, tragically, became the greatest tennis player in history never to have won Wimbledon, having lost in the finals to Perry in 1935 and 1936, and to Budge in 1937.

Gottfried von Cramm, son of a German Baron, and J. Donald Budge, redheaded son of a laundry-truck driver, in Oakland, California, two of the finest gentlemen-sportsmen ever to play the game of tennis, were born at virtually opposite ends of the earth and opposite ends of the social structure; and, much like the Philadelphia aristocrat, Dick Williams, and the California redhead, Maurice McLoughlin, of an earlier day, they became fast friends for many years after their first meeting at Wimbledon in 1935.

Gottfried von Cramm was an extremely handsome, blond, and blue-eyed German aristocrat of impeccable manners. He was a supreme sportsman with a classic game very much in the style of Dick Williams; both men took the ball on the rise and played for fun and glory if not always for victory. Cramm, one of the seven sons of an Oxford-educated member of the Junker nobility, was born on the family estate, "Oelber," near Hanover, in 1909. The great estate next to his family's was owned by their good friend Baron von Dobeneck, and had one of the first *en tout cas* tennis courts in Germany; young Gottfried was soon playing there with some of the best players in Germany such as the professional, Roman Najuch, and the many-times champion, Otto Froitzheim. Since tennis players on the Continent were not encouraged to develop at such early ages as Americans, young Gottfried entered his first junior tournament in 1927, at the age of 18, losing in an early round. The next year, he moved to Berlin to study law and to improve his tennis game at the famous and exclusive Rot-Weiss Club. In 1931, he won his first national title, the Greek Singles Championship, at the same time impressing the German Davis Cup officials by reaching the fourth round at Wimbledon.

In 1932, Cramm won the first of his six German National Singles Championships* and led the German Davis Cup team to its first Interzone Final Round when they were beaten by the American team led by Ellsworth Vines. The Baron also married his childhood friend and neighbor, the Baroness Lisa von Dobeneck, and became a celebrity, both as a tennis star and as a charming member of the International Set. Between 1932 and 1937, he played seventy-four Davis Cup matches in almost every capital in Europe, losing only thirteen matches, five of them the first year. Unfortunately, his busy tennis schedule and the shallow social life led by members of the International Set were hardly conducive to marital stability, and he divorced his wife in 1937, accusing her of infidelity. He later hinted that his homosexuality may have been related to his wife's humiliating infidelities during their early married years.

In the year of his divorce, he met the famous American heiress Barbara Hutton, who had become infatuated with him while watching him play at Wimbledon. Eighteen years later, in 1955, he married her in Paris (receiving a dowry of two million dollars). This second marriage, according to Barbara's close friend who was pressed into the role of go-between, almost immediately showed signs of erosion due to his homosexuality. "The truth of the matter," she said at the time, "is that they never consummated their marriage."[1] Cramm's first marriage lasted five years, his second less than four.

Tragically for the graceful German Baron, 1937 turned out to be his last full year of world-class tennis. In August of that year, he was sent with a German tennis group on a goodwill tour of the United States, Japan, and Australia. One day after his return to Germany, in March 1938, he was arrested at his home by the Gestapo on vague charges of moral degeneracy. He was later tried and sentenced to a year in prison, the judge emphasizing his supposed homosexual relationship with a Jew named Manasse Herbst, whom he had helped financially to escape from Nazi Germany in 1936. Though he had helped his friend to escape, their sexual relationship was never proved. While Cramm definitely was a ho-

---

*He won four German titles, in 1932, 1933, 1934, and 1935, and then won again after the war, in 1948 and 1949 (the last at age 40).

mosexual, his arrest and imprisonment were undoubtedly due to his out-spoken opposition to Hitler and all he stood for.* Thus the two leading members of the first German Davis Cup team to ever reach the Inter-zone Final (1932), Dr. Daniel Prenn and Baron von Cramm, were both treated disgracefully by the Nazis.

While Perry T. Jones's boys dominated American tennis, from 1931 when Ellsworth Vines won the U.S. Championship, through 1949 when Richard "Pancho" Gonzales won it for the second year in a row, the greatest player during those years was J. Donald Budge, who was born and raised in Oakland, in the San Francisco Bay Area. Yet even he was influenced by Mister Jones, when he played in a junior tournament at the L.A. Tennis Club:

> I won my first match rather impressively and as I came off the court there was Perry Jones waiting for me," wrote Budge in his memoirs. "He beck-oned me to him and I hustled over to pick up a compliment. Instead, with a distinct frown, he looked me up and down. "Budge," Mr. Jones finally snarled, "those are the dirtiest tennis shoes I ever saw in my life. Don't you ever—don't you *ever*—show up again on any court anywhere at any time wearing shoes like that." I nodded and slunk off, properly chastised. Perry hasn't changed his demands much over the years, either. I read just recently [1969] that he told some of his juniors to get their hair cut or not bother to come back for their next match. I know he made an impression on me, for I've never gone on court since that day with even scuffy shoes."[2]

J. Donald Budge's father was a professional football star in Scotland before migrating to California in search of a better climate for his severe respiratory problem. His mother, the dominant moral influence on his life, was of Scotch descent born in San Francisco. Don was born in Oak-

---

*In a recently published diary of a Russian noblewoman who resided in Berlin during the Second World War and was close to several German aristocrats who were part of the plot to assassinate Hitler, the author suggests that her friend, Gottfried von Cramm, may have been a member of this aristocratic, anti-Nazi circle. He definitely was a sympathizer and friend of several of the plot's leaders. See *The Berlin Diaries 1940–1945* of Marie "Missie" Vassiltchikov (London, 1985).

land in 1915, his brother Lloyd in 1909, the same year as Perry and Cramm. Like their father, both the Budge boys were natural athletes and loved all sports. While Lloyd's first love was tennis, Don preferred baseball and thought very little of tennis until, at the age of 13, he was persuaded to try the game by his brother Lloyd who was then number one on the tennis team at the University of California, Berkeley. From the very first, Don's money-stroke was his backhand which grew directly out of his almost-perfect, left-handed batting swing. He began his tennis career just before his fifteenth birthday, where he was entered in the California State Fifteen-and-Under Championships by brother Lloyd. When he beat the number one seed in the first round and then went on to win the tournament, young Don was severely bitten by the tennis bug and, almost immediately, dreamed of winning the National Junior Championship. His dream came true in 1933, when, at the age of 18, he went East to Culver, Indiana, where, although unseeded, he beat the top-seeded tennis prodigy from Southern California, Gene Mako, at 8–6 in the fifth set, after losing the first two.

Don Budge had a gift for making friends with first-rate persons and learning from them. While he was a shy and awkward late-bloomer who shot up six inches during the year he went to Culver, Gene Mako had matured early and was exceedingly bright and aggressively self-confident. He was born in a cultivated, upper-middle-class family, his father being a world-renowned and highly successful artist. These two boys, both lovers of jazz, big bands, dancing, and tennis, began a lifelong friendship at Culver and, at Mako's original suggestion, played doubles together for the rest of Budge's amateur career. In 1936, they beat Allison and Van Ryn (1935 U.S. Champions) fourteen straight times before taking them in the Forest Hills final in three quick sets; they won the doubles at Wimbledon in 1937 and both the Wimbledon and U.S. doubles in 1938.

Budge was a freshman at Cal* when he withdrew (never to return) in the spring of 1934 in order to play the Eastern Grass Court Circuit, as part of an auxiliary Davis Cup squad. He did fairly well, reaching the fourth round at Forest Hills and ending up with a ranking of ninth in the U.S. top ten. The highlight of the year, and a turning point in his game, came in the Pacific Coast Championships, at Berkeley, where he lost to

---

*The University of California, at Berkeley, was called "Cal" in those days.

Perry in the finals at 5–7 in the fifth set. Although he now had a chance to play a winter schedule in South America and on the Riviera, he chose to stay home and change what Perry called his "Wild Western" forehand to an Eastern grip. He admired Perry's all-court and aggressive game and was pleased when Perry took time to help him change. But he worked throughout that winter with his old friend and coach, Tom Stowe, the pro at the Claremont Country Club in Oakland. He worked hard at perfecting the Eastern grip as well as his volley and the ability to force the action at the net. All the while, he worked at building up his strength and stamina. By the spring, he was a far better and stronger player.

Young players today are too busy making money to take time off to improve their games as Budge did that winter in Oakland. Furthermore, while Tom Stowe worked with Budge for nothing because of his faith in his ability, Nick Bollettieri, the most famous coach in America today, is primarily a moneymaker whose star students, Andre Agassi and Jim Courier, play in the extreme Western, top-spin style which Budge weaned himself away from. Only Pete Sampras, due to the free coaching of a family friend and brilliant pediatrician, took time to change his game back to the classic Budge style.

Budge played his first year of world-class tennis in 1935. At his first Wimbledon, he won an impressive upset victory over Bunny Austin in the quarterfinals. After the match, Gottfried von Cramm introduced himself to Budge and suggested that they get to know each other before playing their semifinal match two days later. In the course of a long chat on a porch bench away from the crowds, Cramm told Budge that he showed bad sportsmanship when he threw a point after a linesman had made a bad call against Austin. Budge was shocked by this criticism because he valued good sportsmanship above all else. Cramm pointed out, however, that to throw points was to embarrass the linesman before a large crowd; it is better sportsmanship to play each point as called. Before their chat was over Budge was convinced that Cramm's sporting values were better (more considerate) than Tilden's grandstanding ones (which he had been following). In his autobiography, Budge took this first talk in a long friendship very seriously and wrote about it in some detail. And he never questioned a linesman's call publicly again. Thus began a great and lasting friendship between two noble men, one born and the other bred. As Budge put it in his memoirs:

Cramm was from the old German nobility. Whereas I had grown up learning tennis on the courts at Bushrod Park in Oakland, California, Gottfried had learned with such people as King Gustav of Sweden. But his real nobility was in his human qualities, rather than his lineage; he was one of the finest sportsmen in the world and perhaps most popular of all players. He also loved tennis. . . .

From that first day I met him on the porch at Wimbledon he became one of the greatest influences upon my life. Gottfried Cramm's ideals bordered on being beautiful. I mean that.[3]

In those days of privacy and personal trust, Cramm sometimes talked to Budge about his homosexuality. In an interview with Budge in which he recalled these talks, I was struck by two things: first, I was impressed with Budge's nonjudgmental empathy with his friend's problems of homosexuality and sexual ambivalence; second, I sadly realized that such a frank friendship would be impossible on the tennis tour in our classless age where respect for privacy has declined to the point where gay-bashing is a constant threat.* Most of the tennis players who knew Cramm at all well were aware of his sexual tendencies and considered it none of their business. Johnny Van Ryn, for instance, became quite friendly with Cramm, both on the courts and at formal dinners (von and van were often seated next to one another).† He liked him, respected his game and sportsmanship, and was aware of his homosexuality. Many years later, he told Stan Hart of his being taken to dinner by Tilden and Cramm at a private, homosexual club in Berlin. It was in those days of fashionable decadence immortalized in the *Berlin Stories* by Christopher Isherwood and in the movie *Cabaret*. "There were all these tables, each with a telephone so you could call someone at the next table," Van Ryn

---

*It seems that most cultures have made more of male than female homosexuality. Thus the greatest woman tennis player of the pro era, Martina Navratilova, is an out-of-the-closet lesbian while there are no out-of-the-closet gays on the men's tour. Does this mean that there are no gays at the top level of men's tennis in our totally tolerant age? I suspect there are, if not closet gays, at least latent homosexuals among the top male stars.

†Budge was correct in calling his friend Cramm, even though most of his peers called him von Cramm. Actually it is Gottfried von Cramm, just as Tocqueville was Alexis de Tocqueville. All too many Americans (incorrectly) refer to "de Tocqueville" just as they once referred to "von Cramm."

said. "Allison and I had never seen anything like it. All those woos and such. You would see these fellows with lipstick on, dialing each other and going woo-woo: we were shocked."[4] While both Van Ryn and the Nazis knew that Cramm was a homosexual, Van Ryn and other players such as Budge also knew that the Nazis threw him in jail, as Van Ryn told Hart, "because throughout the whole tour he was telling everyone about this group, the Nazis, and how terrible they were, and he was just speaking out of school."

"I think the reason he irritated the Nazis so particularly," wrote Budge of his friend Cramm, "was not so much that he refused to go along with them, but that he looked and acted like the Nazis' propaganda said all Germans should. He was six feet tall, with blond hair, of course, cold blue eyes, and a face that was handsome to a fault. And more, Gottfried emitted a personal magnetism that dominated any scene he was a part of."[5]

The Baron's magnetism even impressed the Hollywood crowd at the Pacific Southwest when he played there in September 1937. Most of the box seat holders agreed to demonstrate their anti-Nazi feelings by walking out when he came on the court for the first time. There was great enthusiasm behind the idea, but, when Cramm came out for his first match, they just looked at him and at one another. Nobody moved. Groucho Marx summed up the mood when he later told Budge: "When I saw that man, I just felt instant shame at what I was supposed to do." They were pleased not to have protested, moreover, when, within a year, the world was told that the Nazis had thrown the charismatic Baron in jail. They later sent him to the Russian front as an ordinary private, where he won the Iron Cross, Germany's highest honor.

In their first meeting on the court, in the 1935 Wimbledon semifinal, the Baron beat Budge rather easily. While still only 19, Budge had been brought to London as a spare on the Davis Cup team behind Wilmer Allison and Sidney Wood. After upsetting Austin at Wimbledon and continually beating both Allison and Wood in practice sessions, Budge was chosen at the last minute to play second singles in place of Wood, in the Interzone Finals against Germany, also to be played at Wimbledon. He got his chance to play partly due to Wood's unselfish sportsmanship in suggesting the change to team captain Joseph Wear, just before the deadline for naming the teams. Budge admiringly described Wood's move as follows:

> "Oh, look, Cap," Wood said. "I've been thinking and thinking, and finally I just had to come over and say this. Look, I know it and you know it. Don has been playing well. He's been better than either Wilmer or me. I hate to say it, but I think you ought to replace me in the singles with Budge."
>
> Wear sighed. "Sidney," he finally said. "Thank you. Just, thank you very much. You have made this a whole lot easier for me. I agree with you and I have known it, but I have just been agonizing with myself whether I should make that decision. You've made it possible for me to."[6]

Unfortunately, Wood's sportsmanlike move marked the end of his career in major international competition. For, as we shall see, Budge won both his matches against the Germans, and when Wood asked Wear to put him back on the team in the challenge round against Britain, Wear agreed to think it over but finally felt he had to stick with young Budge.

In the 1935 Interzone Final, Budge beat Henkel and Cramm beat Allison, on the first day. The crucial match proved to be the doubles, on the second day. Allison and Van Ryn finally squeezed by Cramm and Kay Lund at 8–6 in the fifth set, after the Germans had lost five match points. On one of them, Lund volleyed for a winner and the umpire announced, "Game, set and match to Germany." But Cramm lifted his hand in protest, saying that the ball had tipped his racket as he and Lund both lunged for the winning volley.

In the locker room afterwards, Cramm was reprimanded for letting down his teammates and the Fatherland. "Let me make something straight right now," Cramm replied in a rage.

> When I chose tennis as a young man, I chose it because it was a gentleman's game and that's the way I've played it ever since I picked up my first racquet. Do you think that I would sleep tonight knowing that the ball had touched my racquet without my saying so? Never, because I would be violating every principle that I think this game stands for. On the contrary, I don't think I'm letting the German people down. As a matter of fact, I think I'm doing them credit, and until I'm asked to resign, this is the way I'll continue to play.[7]

Allison took America into the challenge round with an easy three-set victory over Henkel, and Budge made it 4–1 by beating Cramm in the final, and purely formal, match 0–6, 9–7, 8–6, 6–3. Cramm ran through the first set quickly just to show what he could do, and then eased up in the final three sets. Budge, showing the instincts of a true champion, noted that Cramm made a strategic mistake in letting Budge have this first victory over him; for Budge now knew that he could beat him, which he proceeded to do in all their future matches.

In the challenge round, Britain beat the USA 5–0, Perry and Austin both beating Allison and Budge rather easily. Allison and Van Ryn lost the doubles in five sets. At the end of the season, at Forest Hills, Budge lost to Bitsy Grant in the quarterfinals, and Perry lost in the semifinals to Allison, who went on to beat Sidney Wood in a three-set final. At the close of the year 1935, Perry, Crawford, and Cramm were ranked number one, two, and three in the world, while Budge was ranked sixth, behind Allison and Austin (see Figure 15).

As we have already seen, Perry totally dominated the tennis world in 1936, his last year as an amateur. He won both Wimbledon and Forest Hills and led the British Davis Cup team to victory in the challenge round, for the last time in history.

———

If Fred Perry dominated tennis in 1936, Don Budge was even more dominant in 1937, by far the best year of his amateur career. The great year began in January when, as a publicity gimmick, he was invited East to umpire a match on the Vines-Perry professional tour, in the Chicago area. That night, Budge made a discovery which he described as follows in his memoirs.

> I had come expecting to see Vines's hard shots sending Perry scurrying all over the court. Instead, Perry was forcing Vines every bit as much. It made no sense to me. . . . Then I saw it. Perry was taking the ball on the rise, hardly six or eight inches after it had bounced. . . . Vines, on the other hand, was waiting in a leisurely fashion and letting the ball take a nice, comfortable high bounce. . . . Vines was hitting the ball harder than Perry, but he took longer to do so. . . . I could see the split-seconds: Perry scooping up the ball, Vines rocking back for it. Before the match was even over a new

concept began to form in my mind: Suppose a man could hit the ball as hard as Vines and take it as early as Perry? Who would beat that man?[8]

Budge went back to California determined to turn that idea into reality. In the meantime, he and Tom Stowe had been working on the psychology of dominance, which Budge described as follows:

> I was to think of myself as number one at all times. If I concentrated on that belief, we felt that I would be more likely to *play* like number one. . . . hitting the ball harder and earlier aligned with this thinking perfectly, and so in the months after the Vines-Perry match I worked almost exclusively towards these two goals.
>
> My game was not pretty at first, but then I did not concern myself too much with accuracy. This is in direct contradiction to my first rule of keeping the ball in play, but I was performing a major adjustment on my game, and Stowe and I felt that the priority in this exceptional case must be with perfecting the stroke. Control and nuance came later, but by the end of the training period I was able to achieve accuracy.[9]

Perry and Budge looked upon the game of tennis as a fine art; Budge's description of his winter of 1937 almost exactly parallels Perry's description of his winter of 1929–30 in which he perfected his taking the ball on the rise, in the style of his idol, Cochet.

Partly due to that creative winter of 1937, Budge played almost to perfection during the spring and summer. He never lost a match on grass, nor any match at all until September when he lost to Henner Henkel in a small tournament outside Chicago. He was the first man ever to win the hat trick at Wimbledon (singles, doubles, and mixed doubles, with Gene Mako and Alice Marble). In the men's final, he beat Cramm in three straight sets. He beat Cramm again to win the Davis Cup Interzone Finals, and then took the lead in winning the cup for the first time since the Four Musketeers had defeated Tilden and the American team at Germantown in 1927. He finally beat Cramm again at Forest Hills and in the Pacific Southwest. He was voted the Athlete of the Year by the American Sportswriters and also became the first and only tennis player ever to win the Sullivan Award, annually presented to the outstanding amateur athlete. Like Tilden before him and unlike any American tennis player since, Budge was a national hero in that great year. Above all else, however, he played and won the greatest tennis match of all time against his friend, Baron Gottfried von Cramm, in the Interzone Finals of the Davis Cup on July 30, 1937, on the Center Court at Wimbledon. Although full reports of tennis matches are usually dull echoes of the experiences of the original observers, this match deserves to be reported in all its dramatic details. The setting of the match is best described by Budge in the following words:

> However hesitant I am to try to select the various "greatest" moments in my career—the best this, the most thrilling that, and so on—I certainly have no difficulty in naming the greatest match in which I ever played. It seemed to possess every element that could be called classic. There was high drama in every way. It was, first of all, crucial, a deciding Davis Cup match. It was competitive, long, and close. It was fought hard but cleanly by two close friends. It was cast with the ultimate in rivals, the number-one-ranked amateur player in the world against the number two. It was placed in a perfect setting, at Wimbledon, on the Centre Court, a piece of land revered in the game. There was a filled stadium. Queen Mary was on hand. Hitler listened intently to the play-by-play, and so did so many Americans that the stock-market sales sagged during the action. . . . I never played better and never played anyone as good as Cramm. Walter Pate, the United States team captain, said later, "No man, living or dead, could have beaten either man that day."
>
> I realize too that a great many sports events get better and eventually find greatness with time and the retelling, but there was instant recognition of the quality of this match. It was, in fact, Bill Tilden himself who I first heard declare that it was "the greatest tennis match ever played." He told me that, emotionally, clasping my hands, in the locker room only a few minutes after it was completed. The London *Times* correspondent wrote the next morning, "Certainly I have never seen a match that came nearer the heroic in its courage, as in its strokes, as this."
>
> I think that I realized early in the match that the crowd was slightly in favor of Cramm, but I could not be either surprised or disturbed at that reaction. The British fans had always been more than fair with me. Now, though, I was the only logical villain, for everyone loves the underdog and Gottfried was that even if he was number two in the world. I had beaten him in straight sets on this same Centre Court in the finals of the Wimble-

don tournament only a couple of weeks earlier. Besides, and more to the point, the British team was supposed to have a slightly better chance against Germany than against the United States. Rooting for Cramm was sensible as well as sentimental.

Still, as the match wore on, I got the feeling that there was no one present who was really *against* either of us. It seemed that the longer we played, the more exciting and better the tennis became, the less the crowd really cared who won. The art of the match, and the competition, seemed to become much more important than the outcome. Here we were, the best two amateurs in the game, playing for both the individual and the national championships of the world, and playing on the most important court in the world, and yet somehow the magnificence of the game of tennis prevailed over all.*

It was already late in the afternoon, nearing four o'clock, when Gottfried and I at last moved out onto the court, to bow to Queen Mary and to play. Henner Henkel had just beaten Bitsy Grant in four sets to tie the score at 2–2 in the match between the United States and Germany. Gottfried and I, the two ranking amateurs in the world, were to play for it all.

The winner of the Interzone Final still would have to meet England, the defender, in the Challenge Round, but in just about everyone's view the winner of the 1937 Davis Cup would certainly be the survivor of the United States-Germany meeting. Fred Perry, who had led the English to victory in the competition for the previous four years, had turned pro, weakening the British team to a point where it would be a definite underdog against either of the challengers.

Thus it was, that if I won this one match the United States would almost certainly get the Cup back across the Atlantic after a full decade in Europe. On the other hand, if Cramm beat me, the Germans looked just about as certain to win their first Davis Cup ever, a point not lost on Hitler himself, as it turned out. Perhaps he was still fretting about Jesse Owens.

Henkel defeated Bitsy easily, and before I really had time to console him Teddy Tinling, the tennis-clothes designer, who was acting as sort of a sergeant-at-arms, was there in the American locker room, calling me. The main part of Teddy's job this day was to move things along at a brisk pace.

---

*In all the tennis literature I have read, no paragraph has come close to this one in describing the gentlemanly ideal of tennis as a fine art.

The Royal Box was filled with The Royal Family, and it was not to be kept waiting. In hardly any time at all, Tinling had me by one arm and Cramm by the other and was marching us off to play. Gottfried and I were bustled along so that we hardly had time to acknowledge each other, and Tinling had just about swept us out into the stadium when a phone rang. None of us paid any attention, but a locker-room man picked it up and called to Gottfried. "Mr. Von Cramm," he said. "Long distance for you, sir."

"Come on, you can't keep Queen Mary waiting," Tinling said, tugging at Cramm, and myself, as well.

"But it might be an emergency," Cramm replied. I had to sympathize with Gottfried. As much as I would hate to get a long-distance call just before a match, I think it would be even worse to get a call but not take it and spend the whole match wondering who it was and what in the world it was all about. Tinling frowned but let Cramm pull free and go over and pick up the receiver. "Yes, hello," he said. "This is Gottfried Cramm." He spoke impeccable English, just as he did a half-dozen other languages. Teddy and I relaxed and did not pay much more attention until Gottfried finished speaking to the operator and suddenly switched to German. "Ja, mein Führer," was the first thing he said.

He said, in fact, little else but "Ja, mein Führer" for the rest of the conversation. He was firm throughout, though he spoke with respect. He showed no emotion. Teddy and I (and Hitler, for that matter) knew that Gottfried was less than enchanted with the Nazis. Finally, after a couple of minutes or so, Cramm hung up, turned sharply and walked over to Tinling. Teddy handed him his rackets back. "Excuse me, gentlemen," Gottfried said matter-of-factly. "It was Hitler. He wanted to wish me luck."

Not even Shakespeare could have invented a more historically dramatic setting for this greatest classic in the history of tennis. Budge now goes on to describe the match itself:

Cramm had won the toss and elected to serve first, which as it worked out, was to be the case in each set. He held that first serve at love, I came back to win mine at thirty, and we moved on that way, sharing service through the first eight games. In the ninth, I broke through. I didn't know it then, of course, but this was to be the longest game in the match—until the very last one. But then, at that time, ahead 5–4, I just felt pretty good. Hold my serve, take the set 6–4, and I'm winging.

There was no reason, either, why I shouldn't hold serve. It was moving well, I was getting it in deep, and Cramm had not been able to take more than two points off it in any game so far. Besides, I had fresh new balls. And the fact is that my reasoning was absolutely correct. I "did" serve well in the whole game. I held up the new balls and showed them to Cramm across the net. Right away, I smashed a beauty at him. It clicked right in. I never touched his return. I moved over and hit another beautiful first serve. I never touched his return. I hit another beautiful first serve. I never touched his return. I hit my fourth straight beautiful first serve. As a matter of fact, the only thing I hit in the game was beautiful first serves. And that was all he hit back. I never touched the fourth return either. Cramm had broken me back at love with four fantastic placements. I did not win the set at 6–4. He broke me again four games later, and *he* won the set 8–6.

The second set was much like the first, only now, increasingly, it was his serve that was dominant. I was holding my own and matching him, but with more difficulty. Tactically, we were both playing well, but he was having more success at getting to the net and staying there. He attacked incessantly, and kept me on the run and tried to exploit a bad patch of my forehand that showed up here.

For my part, as the set wore on, I found it more difficult to get to the net at all behind my serve. Eventually, I had to give up trying to do that altogether. Cramm was, as always, in such excellent condition that it was foolish of any opponent of his to introduce any wasted motion into the game. By trying to rush the net after I served I was using many extra steps and a lot of extra energy every time I faulted and had to go back again for my second serve. And besides, the serves I hit that did go in—well, he was passing me with a lot of those anyway. It was becoming a little discouraging. I was sure that I was playing tennis as well as I ever had before, but here I was one set down and struggling to stay even in the second. The fewer mistakes I made, the fewer still he made, and he held serve to 6–5.

Then in the twelfth game I roared right out to forty-love, but I let him off the hook and he took the next three points to catch me. We battled through two more advantages, and then for the first time, Gottfried got the advantage—and set point. He played to win it. He followed my serve in to the net and then took my return with a go-for-broke volley that swept past me and chipped the chalk off the back line. I was down two sets to none.

At this point I remember becoming more mad than analytical. Two things, in particular, kept going through my head. The first was that I was rapidly blowing what had been a very good chance to establish myself as the acknowledged number one in the world, the champion. Secondly, I knew I was doing what so many other Americans had done in past years: come over to Europe, fare well at Wimbledon, and then play poorly in the Davis Cup. That was the one thing I had promised myself not to do, but I certainly was doing it. I called myself a lot of names.

At any rate, whatever I was thinking must have been right for me, for I promptly went out and broke his serve in the first game of the third set. For the second time in the match I was ahead, and I held on to 2–1. At this point I was serving, I had new balls, and I immediately fired off a beautiful batch of first serves. If all of this sounds slightly reminiscent of something else, it was. Exactly as in the first set, the last time I had been ahead, he blasted back four straight passing shots, broke me at love, and tied up the set. I was the unwitting pioneer of the instant replay, and to say it shook me up would be every bit of the truth. Happily, it was all so astounding, I think that it also shook up Cramm. I came right back in the next game and broke "him" at love. Touché. I finished out the set at 6–4, and hurried off to the locker room for a welcome rest.

It was a warm, humid day, with just a touch of wind, the way warm days in England always are, and I was glad for the chance to take a quick shower and change into fresh clothes. Beyond that, there was little I could do. I don't remember talking to Captain Pate about much at all. How, after all, could I improve? Most matches, you know, are considered to be excellent technical performances if the number of winning placements equal the number of errors. In this match, *both Gottfried and myself were to make twice as many placements as errors* (my italics).

As a matter of fact, the only time in the whole match that one of us played poorly was when Cramm slacked off right after this rest period. I not only broke him at love in the first game, but I held my own serve and then broke him again to go ahead 3–0. Behind that much, Cramm then decided to junk the set and to try to save all he had for the final one. We went through the motions of playing it out to 6–2, and then he picked up the balls and began to serve in the fifth set, fifth match. The sun was still up and we would finish that night.

It was the first time I had ever played Cramm in a fifth set. I had a pretty good record in five-set matches, but his was unbelievable. He trained so hard and maintained such superb shape at all times that he often said that he figured that he had about a three-to-one advantage anytime a match entered a fifth set. If I had to be reminded of this fact, I knew that only a few days before he had won the key match against Czechoslovakia in the finals of the European Zone by the score of 3–6, 4–6, 6–4, 6–3, 6–2. Perhaps even more impressive than that, Cramm had won the French championships the previous year by lasting to five sets in almost all of his matches, and then finishing it off by beating Fred Perry 6–0 in the fifth set of the final. This particular victory had, by itself, resulted in giving Cramm an almost mystical edge in long matches. Of course, he was a man of such tremendous bearing and presence that the other players seemed almost eager to present him with capabilities that possibly he did not truly possess. If you were the opponent, however, coming into a fifth set it was not easy to ignore the mystique.

So now, as we entered our fifth set, I knew quite well that he would give no indication if he was tired. It didn't take them long to find out that that wasn't even worth speculating about. He took charge from the first, picked up momentum, broke my serve in the fourth game, and held his to move ahead 4–1. He had only to hold serve to run out the set easily.

In the stands there was a new, excited buzz, one of obvious anticipation. I did not notice it myself at the time, but in one section of the stadium, over where the other players were seated, there was an even livelier response. I was to hear about it in the greatest detail later.

It revolved about Tilden, who was the German coach. He had long been something of a private tutor to Cramm, and close enough to him so that he often stayed in the Cramm family apartment when he was visiting Berlin. It was Tilden who had taught Gottfried to adjust his backhand grip in 1933, and the change had played a significant role in Cramm's rise to top world-class rank. Now Tilden was coach of the whole German team. It is, of course, not at all unusual for a pro in one country to coach another nation's Davis Cup team. But it is uncommon for a coach to maintain the post when it means working against his *own* nation. That is extraordinary, and a lot of people considered it, if not downright unpatriotic, at the least a little tactless of Bill.

But if his loyalties were divided, Tilden made it plain enough that his tennis allegiance was strictly with his employer. He was seated a few rows in front of our team's show-business friends—Benny, Sullivan, and Lukas. They in turn were a few rows in front of Henner Henkel, who had come back to watch our match after beating Grant. Now, with Cramm ahead 4–1 in this last set, Tilden could not contain himself any longer.

He stood up in his seat and turned full around, looking up past Benny and Sullivan and Lukas to where Henkel was sitting. Tilden drew Henkel's attention, and then, without a word, but with only a large smug grin on his face, Tilden held up his hand, forming a circle with his thumb and forefinger—the traditional "it's in the bag" sign. Sullivan and the others saw it right away and were furious. Immediately, Sullivan leapt to his feet and began to try to tear his coat off. "Why, you dirty sonuvabitch," he hissed at Tilden. Lukas and Benny jumped up themselves and managed to pull Sullivan down and hold him. Tilden just smiled back and then sat down again, contented.

At this moment, out on the court, I was changing sides with Gottfried. I kept thinking: Is he really this invincible in the fifth set, am I going to go down just like all the others? Walter Pate threw me a towel, and I rubbed myself with it. "Don't count us out yet, Cap," I told him, perhaps with more courage than logic. "Look, I'm not tired and I feel great." And that was the truth. I won my serve at love and came back to 4–2.

I was at the net when I took the last point in the game, and in the walk back to receive serve I decided that it was time for me to try something new. The thought just struck me quickly that way; I really had no idea *what* I should try. But, after all, I could no longer take any solace in the hope that playing better than Cramm would reward me with the win. We were both playing too well, and I was the one who was two games from extinction. I had to get lucky and I had to make my own luck. Okay, without thinking too much about the odds, I planned to play it half-safe and gamble on his second serve. I decided that if he missed the first one I would creep up several steps and attack his second serve, and then come to the net quickly behind it.

Looking back, I can't really consider this good strategy, because Cramm had such a controlled first serve that it was seldom that he did not get it in. Even when he missed, it was invariably off by only a hair. But if he missed, ah, *if*—well then I was in good shape because his second serve was pretty well typed for me. His second serve tended to be a high kicker. Against most players it was terribly effective, but in my case it just so happened that I had the type of backhand that made it possible for me to pick up the serve on the rise before the ball could take off on that big bounce. Also, moving up a couple of steps in advance of my usual position gave me that much better opportunity to hit the ball before it took the big hop. This also put me in better shape to rush the net afterwards. When I had been playing my normal, deeper receiving position, I couldn't force him enough to permit me to come rushing up and try to gain the net.

I have often wondered what happened to Gottfried at this point. Maybe I just got lucky with the law of averages. But I remember how anxious he was to get the balls to serve, and I think perhaps that he became just a little too impatient. The victory was so close now that perhaps for once in his life he lost the composure that he always guarded so well. But anyway, his first service, which had been so consistent throughout the match, failed him every time but one in this game, and that one serve was to be the only point he won. The other four times he served, he missed getting the ball in by just about the same slim margin each time. Each hit in almost the identical spot, at no more than two inches back.

And each time, of course, that gave me the chance to employ my new strategy. I moved up for that second serve. And located there, as I figured, I was able to catch his second serve before it could bounce up and away. I hit each one back, hard and deep, putting Cramm on the defensive and myself at the net. Each of the four points that I won were made exactly the same way with a well-placed net volley on my second shot. I had the break I had to have, and I was back to 3–4.

He almost came right back and broke me in the next game, but twice in a row, as the score stood at his advantage, he punched backhands that went out, in the same spot, by inches. How many times in this match did these crazy things repeat themselves? After this sort of double jeopardy, I managed to hold and to tie the score at 4–4. As the tension grew to almost unbearable proportions, we matched each other's serve to 6–all. Then, remarkably and suddenly, and without, really, any shots of distinction, I broke Cramm in the lucky thirteenth game and stood ahead for the first time in hours, 7–6.

Now, at last, I had only to hold my serve to win the match and the opportunity for the United States to play England in the Challenge Round. Clearly, after hours of play, I was now immune to pressure. This is why my first serve in the game went right smack into the *bottom* of the net. That either steadied me or embarrassed me, for I did manage to get the second serve in and even to win the point. He tied at 15–all, and then we repeated the sequence: 30–15, 30–all, and 40–30, the first match point of the long afternoon.

So, I guess, I played it too safe again. I was too tentative with both my serve and second shot. Cramm took the net easily, volleyed past me, and we were deuce. I came right back with a placement of my own for a second match point, but he took the net away from me again and once more tied the game. Moreover, when he was able to repeat the ploy on the next point, he moved ahead. Later, he also had one more game point, so that by the time I gained my fifth match point it was the eighteenth point of the game, and all of five minutes had passed since we had first played a match point way back there at 40–30. Five minutes under circumstances like these are like a month of 3–2 counts in baseball.

So once more I served. It was the 175th time that day I had made a first serve. What there had been of my cannonball had gone, but I managed to get enough on this one to clear the net and send it sufficiently deep so that Gottfried could not begin to move up and gain the net from me. But he made a beautiful long return that kept me far back in the court too. All I could do was trade long ground strokes with him. I hit a good backhand.

Cramm moved over to his right-hand corner, so that we were now both on the same side of the court, facing each other down my left-hand side. He caught my shot with a forehand and hit it crosscourt. It was a beautiful shot, firmly hit, and it gave him the opening to move toward the net. He came up, crossing the court catty-cornered, following essentially the direction of his shot.

The ball was landing just inside my right sideline, a bit deep of mid-court. I had hit my last shot far back on the other side of the court, and I had begun to move back toward the center as soon as I hit it. Now, however, when I saw Cramm place the ball so far over, I had to break into a dead run if I wanted to catch up to it. I could not worry about position at all any longer. In fact, as I neared the ball, just as it bounced in, I realized that my speed had brought my body too far forward. There was no way I could brace to hit the ball. As a matter of fact, there was suddenly no way I could keep from falling.

Instead, resigned to this indignity, I did the only thing I could. I kept going at full speed and just took a swipe at the ball. What did I have to lose? I was going to fall anyway. Then, immediately after I swung, I dived for the ground, preparing to break my fall. I could tell, though, as soon as I hit the ball that I had smacked it solidly, but only as I crashed onto the grass did I turn to look. The ball whipped down the line, just past Cramm's outstretched racket. He had come up fast and could cover all but about the last two feet on the right side of the net (his left). At my angle I could not have returned the shot cross-court. I had been forced to try for a shot right down the line. Now I saw the ball slip past his reach.

By this point I was flat out on the ground, but so far outside the alley line that I could see around the net into much of the other side of the court. I could see the ball hit. I watched it kick up. But I had no perspective and no idea where the ball had landed. I waited for the call and then, suddenly, even before the linesman could begin to flatten out his hands in the "safe" sign, I could hear the cheers begin to swell. They were different cheers. The ball had landed, miraculously but perfectly, in the corner. I had hit the one possible winning shot. I was told later that the ball landed at a point less than six inches from being out *two* ways—to the side and long.

But now the roars were greater and more excited, and here I was, still lying flat out on the ground. Gottfried, the noble loser, had to stand at the net, waiting patiently for me, the winner, to get up off the ground. I rose, finally, bewildered, and rushed toward him. I tried to hug him, but before I could he stopped me and took my hand. "Don," he said, evenly and with remarkable composure, "This was absolutely the finest match I have ever played in my life. I'm very happy that I could have played it against you, whom I like so much." And then he pumped my hand. "Congratulations." Only then was it, at once, that we threw our arms about each other. I think we both wanted to cry.

I suppose it was an hour or so after the match before I was at last able to dress and leave the locker room. I think it was almost nine o'clock by this time, but the midsummer sun wasn't down yet. I walked out and glanced up into the stands, and I was shocked because there were still thousands of people there, clustered together all over the stadium. It did not seem to me that they were talking much to each other or moving around. They did not seem to be ready to leave. It was as if they just wanted to stay there where they had watched the match. I've never seen anything like that, before or since, just all those people standing there and remembering, long after I had dressed and gone.

We had to begin to prepare for playing the Challenge Round almost immediately. We managed well enough, I guess, because we beat the British 4–1, which was expected. But I don't think we were actually as well prepared as we might have been if it had not been for the excitement of the Cramm match. I know that I, anyway, could not put that match out of my mind for a long time. Even after we had played and beaten the English, there were still nights when I would wake up in a sweaty nightmare. It was always the same one. It was me behind 4–1 in the fifth set, and Gottfried was looking at me from across the net.

And even after the bad dreams ended, it was still worth speculating about what would have happened had I not pulled the match out. For one very obvious thing it is likely that if we had not won the Cup but would have had to challenge for it again the next year, 1938, I certainly would not have had the opportunity try to win the Grand Slam of tennis. I probably would have been too busy working with the team for various preliminary zone matches to concentrate on individual play. Of greater importance, it is even possible to assume that the Germans would have had the Davis Cup when the war broke out and that it would have been in Nazi hands for many years. And if winning the greatest match ever meant the chance for the Grand Slam for me, losing it may have been the first step to jail for Gottfried. Would Hitler have dared to imprison him had Cramm brought the tennis supremacy of the world to the Third Reich?[10]

After Budge won at Forest Hills in 1937, he became an authentic national hero. Everyone expected him to follow in the footsteps of Perry and turn pro. The world was at his feet and he could dictate his terms to the professional promoters who now wooed him with lucrative offers. But his friends knew how deeply indebted he felt towards the game he loved and the nation which had given him the great opportunity to become a world-renowned sportsman and tennis champion. He had won the great Davis Cup match against Cramm and brought the cup back to America for the first time since Tilden had been beaten at Germantown in 1927. And he felt obliged to be on the team for the first challenge round to be played at Germantown since 1927. Instead of turning pro, he and his best friend, Gene Mako, went to Australia. Only Mako and Allison Danzig knew that he had planned to win the four National Championships which eventually became known as the "Grand Slam," a term coined by Danzig who borrowed it from the game of bridge, the passionate pastime of many first-rate tennis players in those pretelevision days.

Budge and Mako set sail for Australia from San Francisco in the winter and twenty-one days later arrived in the summer, at Sydney, Australia. They had worked very hard at doing nothing. Budge had agreed to play in only the Victorian and National Championships as well as a limited number of exhibitions and test matches (with Mako) run along the Davis Cup format.

Unlike Vines, who was worn out by too many exhibitions which he took too seriously, Budge vowed to treat them as practice sessions, thus sharpening his game while losing most of them. He was consequently keen for both the Victorian and National Championships which he won easily, boarding ship almost immediately after the Nationals for the twenty-three-day trip home. In May, Budge won the French singles title, beating the Czechoslovakian giant, Roderich Menzel, the second-best clay-court player after Cramm in Europe, in three sets in less than an hour. He next won Wimbledon without losing a set, beating Bunny Austin in the finals, 6–1, 6–0, 6–3, in fifty-nine minutes. Of far greater importance, he repeated the hat trick for the second year in a row, again with Gene Mako and Alice Marble. This record (two Wimbledon hat tricks in a row) will never be equaled or broken as long as tennis remains a pay-for-play game. While Bobby Riggs did the same trick in 1939, as did Frank Sedgman in 1952, no man has done so since. During the first twenty years of the pro era, no Wimbledon men's singles winner ever won the mixed doubles, and only John Newcombe and John McEnroe won the Singles and Doubles Championships in the same year, Newcombe in 1970 and McEnroe (with Peter Fleming) in 1981, 1983, and 1984.

Returning to the United States, Budge first won his third Newport title in a row, beating Sidney Wood in an easy three-set final, and thus taking permanent possession of the coveted Newport Casino Challenge Cup. He then went down to Philadelphia where he led the Davis Cup team to victory over Australia, at the Germantown Cricket Club. On September 24, after seven days of rain delay, he defeated Mako in the finals at Forest Hills; he also won the doubles with Mako and the mixed doubles with Alice Marble.* He now became the first tennis player to win the four major singles titles in the same calendar year, a feat almost

---

*Mako was the first nonseeded player ever to reach the finals in our National Championships. It is also interesting to note that Mako beat Gilbert A. Hunt, Jr., in the quarterfinals. Hunt had beaten Bobby Riggs, the second seeded player, in the previous round in a spectacular and curious five-set battle 6–2, 0–6, 9–7, 0–6, 6–4. Hunt was a bit of a genius who played tennis for fun. An MIT graduate, he was a Princeton professor of mathematics all his academic life. Hunt produced another spectacular upset at Forest Hills in 1939; this time he easily beat the second seed, Frank Parker, in the fourth round 6–1, 6–1, 6–1. Like Barry Wood of Harvard, Gil Hunt was a *multidimensional man*, whose kind will never again be found at Flushing Meadow, or even Wimbledon.

accomplished, as we have seen, by Jack Crawford in 1933 (Figure 15). While 1938 was a glorious year for Budge because this "Grand Slam" eventually became his best-known accomplishment, the year as a whole produced a far lower level of big-time tennis than 1937. Thus Budge lost only one set (to Mako) in all four of his Grand Slam finals. In no important match, moreover, was Budge carried to five sets, in either tournament or Davis Cup competition. Finally, as he so sadly knew all too well, while 1938 was a great year for him, it was a hellish nightmare for his great friend and rival, Baron Gottfried von Cramm, who spent the tennis season languishing in a Nazi jail.

With good wishes from almost everybody connected with the amateur game, including USLTA officialdom and such leading sportswriters as Allison Danzig of the *Times* and Al Laney of the *Tribune*, Budge turned pro in the fall of 1938. Davis Cup captain Walter Pate, a respected member of the legal establishment, served as his legal counsel, drawing up the professional contract and advising him on a variety of legal matters. When he made his professional debut against Ellsworth Vines at Madison Square Garden on January 3, 1939, tennis officialdom turned out en masse, along with some 16,000 others. Budge beat Vines easily 6–3, 6–4, 6–2.

The pro tour followed a new pattern that year. In the first place, instead of playing in endless cow towns as well as the big cities, there were to be two tours, both limited to major cities: in the first tour Budge faced Vines whom he edged out by a match score of 22–17; in the second tour, Perry was Budge's opponent; in their opening match at the Garden in March, Budge won 6–1, 6–3, 6–0, in forty-nine minutes and then went on to beat Perry by a match score of 28–8. He was surely the recognized if unofficial Champion of the World at the end of that first pro year.

Indian Summer of a Golden Age: Riggs, Kramer, Gonzales, and the Pro Tour

Of all the tournaments, the one I remember most is Wimble-don. . . . They would send a chauffeured limousine to your hotel to take you to the matches. The linesmen walked regally on the court. I'm sure every campaigner would agree that there's no better tournament than Wimbledon; it's the premiere, number one, world's greatest event. . . .

I was invited to have tea with Queen Mary in the Royal Box. It was certainly a thrill for a hard-working, middle-class youngster like myself. She wore one of her famous hats and was very cordial and friendly. I told the Queen that I liked English history and recalled reading about the successions to the throne, King John and King Richard the Lionhearted.

—Bobby Riggs

ROBERT L. RIGGS, A YOUNG AND TENACIOUS COMPETITOR WHO LOVED TO bet on anything, became the Amateur Tennis Champion of the World for the year 1939, which turned out to be the last full tennis season for the six years after war broke out in September. That fateful year, Riggs was a wonder boy at his first and only Wimbledon and a disappointment in the Davis Cup challenge round tie with Australia which was held over the Labor Day weekend, at the Merion Cricket Club, out on the Philadelphia Main Line. On the day of the draw, Hitler launched his *Blitzkrieg* against Poland. The shadow of war hung over the Australian team; Captain Harry Hopman and Adrian Quist had enlisted in the 6th Battalion Machine Gun Corps of Melbourne.

On the first day, Riggs beat John Bromwich, Australia's number one man, and Frank Parker defeated Quist in a long five-setter. On the second day, Sunday, Great Britain and the British Commonwealth declared war on Germany. Hearing the solemn news, the Australian doubles team of Quist and Bromwich got off to a shaky start against the youthful American pair, Jack Kramer and Joseph Hunt, two of Perry Jones's boys from Los Angeles. After losing the first set, the great Australian team won the next three sets and the match. The big American disappointment came on the third day when Riggs lost to Quist and Parker was blown off the court by Bromwich in one of his finest ever Davis Cup matches. This was the first team to capture the cup for Australia as a separate nation (not Australasia). It was also the first time in the cup's history that a challenge round winner had overcome the loss of both singles matches on the opening day.

Riggs's loss to Quist was an especially bitter pill because he had defeated him the year before in the challenge round matches at the Germantown Cricket Club. The American loss was historically memorable because it was a haunting replay of another challenge round, played exactly a quarter-century earlier, when the Australasian team of Norman Brookes and Anthony Wilding defeated the Americans in a 3–2 tie at the new Forest Hills, which proved to be the last challenge round to be held until after the First World War. After that tie Brookes and Wilding were ordered home for war duty. In 1939, during the presentation ceremonies on the courts at Merion, a cablegram was placed in the hands of the newly knighted Sir Norman, instructing team captain Harry Hopman to bring his team home on the first ship available. Hopman was on his way to becoming a legendary hero in Australia and throughout the tennis world, as he led his countrymen into every challenge round for the last two decades of amateur lawn tennis (see Figures 16 and 17).

During the Davis Cup weekend, Sir Norman and Lady Mabel Brookes were guests of honor at a formal dinner for the older generation of tennis greats, given by Mr. and Mrs. William J. Clothier at "Valley Hill Farm," their beautiful estate in Valley Forge, at the western end of the Main Line. Young Bill Clothier, who was in charge of hosting the Australian team at Merion, brought his friend Frank Shields to the dinner, after a rush job of sobering him up beforehand; Shields had immediately fallen off the wagon after a chance meeting with a former wife who had also come down from New York for the tennis at Merion.

Bobby Riggs first came East to play in the Grass Court Circuit in 1936, at the age of 18. He got into the finals of three tournaments and won the Nassau Bowl. Even though he was beaten at Forest Hills in the second round by Van Ryn he was ranked fourth, which pleased him because Perry Jones had told him he had no chance of making the First Ten. From the first, USLTA officialdom (Riggs always referred to them as "120 Broadway") followed in the footsteps of Jones in finding Riggs's fox-like style often incomprehensible and always impossible to deal with. As Bobby wrote in his book *Court Hustler*:

> Once I got into the ranks of the top ten, I never had a problem supporting myself—and for two years a wife and child—as a so-called amateur player. Tournament chairmen bid against each other for my services. . . . For years I was on the personal payroll of Edmund C. Lynch, of Merrill, Lynch, Pierce, Fenner & Beane—also known in Wall Street as "We the People." . . . He liked me to play tennis with him and his friends on his estates in Southampton on Long Island, Indian Creek in Miami, and Nassau. He traveled everywhere in his private yacht. Whenever I played at Newport, I stayed aboard the boat in Narragansett Bay. I received a check for $200 every week for two years from Mr. Lynch, until his untimely death aboard a steamship on his way to Europe. . . . While I was collecting my $200 each week and making as much as $500 in expenses from tournaments, I drove a snazzy Cord convertible, one of the first cars with a front-wheel drive, stayed at the best hotels and rarely saw a bill for room and board.[1]

Of course the "120 Broadway" kind of people were shocked by Riggs in 1936, when he first arrived on the Circuit in a Cadillac, driven by his "promoter-bookmaker," a wealthy L.A. Tennis Club habitué and Riggs hero-worshiper, who spent his summer days on the Circuit betting on his hero and his friends.

In 1937, Riggs had a much-improved season on the Eastern Circuit, losing to Baron von Cramm in a five-set semifinal at Forest Hills and ending the season with a number two U.S. ranking, just behind Budge. Though he was convinced that he should have been, he was not chosen by "120 Broadway" as a member of the Davis Cup team which went to Wimbledon and beat the Germans and then the British to bring back the cup to America. In 1938, "120 Broadway" finally had to put him on the team for the challenge round against Australia; he beat Adrian Quist, which provided the needed third singles victory in addition to Budge's inevitable victories over Quist and Bromwich.

As we have seen, 1939 was Riggs's greatest year. His most famous triumph that year was winning the hat trick at Wimbledon. While few tennis buffs today recall that Budge won two hat tricks in a row in 1937–38, or that Frank Sedgman did the trick again in 1952, most of them know that Riggs cleaned up at Wimbledon in 1939, largely because he came away with more than a hundred thousand dollars (more than equal to a million today) by betting on himself with the British bookies. Right after losing to Cramm 6–0, 6–1 in the finals at Queens, his British friend and top tennis player, John Oliff, agreed to take him to his favorite bookmaker. As Oliff looked on in disbelief, Bobby bargained with the bookie as to the odds on his winning all three titles: and he left "the shop with a parlay of 3 to 1 on myself in the singles, 6 to 1 on the doubles and 12 to 1 on the mixed doubles riding on my original hundred pounds." (In those days a pound was worth about five dollars.)

After winning all three titles, Riggs was at the bookmaker's shop first thing Monday morning; he collected £21,600, the equivalent of $108,000, "the biggest bet I ever won on myself in tennis, before or since."

"As an amateur in good, if shaky, standing with my association," Riggs later recalled, "I was afraid to open a bank account with the money. I stashed it away in a London bank vault* intending to get it out the fol-

---

*When Riggs lost so quickly at Queens and then cleaned up at Wimbledon, many Riggs-watchers thought he had deliberately thrown the match to Cramm in order to improve his odds with the London bookies. Some have thought that he stashed away some thousands of green dollars in some Houston bank vault, after his humiliating loss to Billie Jean in the Astrodome. Did he bet on her? It must be said here that Riggs had nothing in common with the likes of Pete Rose of tragic baseball fame. Riggs's wagers were mostly jocular—"ten to one I can beat you while carrying a rocking-chair in my left hand"—all part of his charming persona as the imp with the luck of the devil. And, of course, there was no Houston bank vault!

lowing year. But war broke out. . . . I sweated out the Battle of Britain from a distance and nobody rooted harder than I did for the RAF to halt the German invasion of England."

Riggs came back to America and won the singles title at Forest Hills. "I was twenty-one years of age, the number one amateur player in the world, and looking for other worlds to conquer."

Riggs, however, did not quite have everything his own way. Although he was seeded first at Forest Hills in 1940, he lost in the finals to Donald McNeill, a recent *cum laude* graduate of Kenyon College. McNeill, incidentally, had won the French title in 1939, beating Riggs in the final. He was a college player of the old school who played top-flight tennis for only a few seasons before settling down to a serious business career, rising to a vice presidency of J. Walter Thompson, a high-prestige advertising agency in his day. His mother once said that she would "rather the sports writers would say Don was a true gentleman than to have him win the greatest title on earth."[2]

After being humiliated by McNeill at Forest Hills, Riggs resigned himself to one more year as an amateur, with the single-minded aim of winning the singles at Forest Hills in 1941, which he did, beating the "Clown Prince" of tennis, Frank Kovacs, in the finals.* They both joined the pro tour which opened that year at Madison Square Garden on December 26—nineteen days after the Japanese bombed Pearl Harbor. Thousands of tickets had to be given away to bellhops, taxi drivers, and so forth to help fill the stands. That night Perry injured his elbow which eventually ended his pro career; the whole tour was finally called off after seventy of ninety scheduled dates. Riggs, Budge, and other pros spent the war years, in and out of uniform, playing exhibition matches to promote wartime causes.

While 1939 was the last year of tennis at Wimbledon and Roland Garros until after the war, our National Championships continued right through the war. In 1942, Frederick R. (Ted) Schroeder, Jr., won the Intercollegiate singles, graduated from Stanford, and beat Frank Parker in the finals at Forest Hills. Soon afterwards, Schroeder joined the navy and Parker the army. The next year, Lt. (JG) Joseph R. Hunt defeated Sea-

---

*Kovacs was a beautiful tennis player who often clowned around while finding 35 ways to lose a match he should have won.

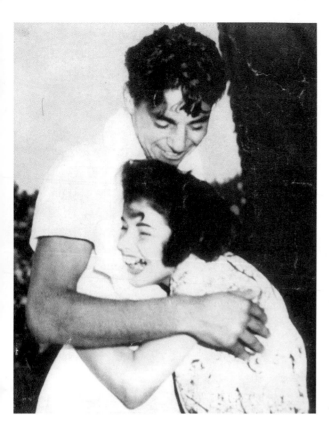

Richard "Pancho" Gonzales, a Mexican-American from Los Angeles, is congratulated by his wife, Henry, after winning the U.S. Singles title at Forest Hills in 1949. His five-set victory over Ted Schroeder, after a heart-breaking loss of the first set (16–18) in over an hour's play, has become a recognized classic final. His win brought him a fine professional contract. *(American Lawn Tennis)*

Arthur "Tappy" Larson, from San Francisco, won the U.S. Singles at Forest Hills in 1950. A psychologically damaged veteran of the First Wave to Land on Omaha Beach, he took up tennis seriously on the advice of a psychiatrist. *(American Lawn Tennis)*

Four leading pro players in 1949: left to right, Pancho Segura, an Ecuadorian-American; Pancho Gonzales; Frank Parker, born in a poor Polish-American community in Milwaukee; and the great promoter, Jack Kramer, who learned his tennis in the Perry Jones era at the Los Angeles Tennis Club. *(American Lawn Tennis)*

Budge Patty (right) and Gardner Mulloy winning the doubles title at Wimbledon in 1957. Mulloy, the Iron Man of American tennis, was 43 that year. He is still in top shape and winning senior events. (Archive Photos—Popperfoto)

Tony Trabert was the best American tennis player to come to the fore during the Hopman era of Australian dominance. In singles he won Wimbledon in 1955, U.S. at Forest Hills in 1953 and 1955, and the French in 1954–1955. No American player had the patience to win the French title again until Michael Chang won it in 1989, 34 years later. *(American Lawn Tennis)*

The Australian Davis Cup team at Merion, in 1939: (left to right) John Bromwich, Adrian Quist, Harry Hopman, and Jack Crawford. Hopman was the playing captain. He again took over the captaincy in 1950 and beat the Americans, who had won the cup all four of the postwar years (1946–1949). In the next 18 years, 1951–1968, he led the Australian teams to victory over the U.S. in the Challenge Round in every year but three. *(American Lawn Tennis)*

Roy Emerson was one of Hopman's greatest players and also an outstanding sportsman. He won the French, British, and American singles titles twice each and the Australian title in 1961, 1963, 1964, 1965, 1966, and 1967. And he won even more grand-slam doubles titles. *(Sportsworld Magazine)*

The Australian Kenneth Rosewall, along with Pancho Gonzales and Baron von Cramm, ranks with the greatest tennis players of all time even though he never won Wimbledon. He won the French and American singles titles twice and the Australian four times. In 1972, at the age of 38, he beat his compatriot Rod Laver to win the World Championship Tennis Finals in a 3-hour, 34-minute, 5-set masterpiece in Dallas, Texas. (Gerry Cranham)

Rodney Laver of Australia is the greatest tennis player ever produced by Harry Hopman and the best in the world since World War II. He is the only player, man or woman, to have won two grand slams, once as an amateur (1962) and once as a professional (1969). (E. D. Lacey)

Big John Newcombe was the last of Harry Hopman's great Australians. He won the Wimbledon singles title as an amateur (1967) and as a professional (1970–1971). He won six Wimbledon doubles titles. He had the "big game," and he was a great sportsman and crowd-pleaser. (Archive Photos—Popperfoto)

Arthur Ashe, born in Richmond, was a Virginia gentleman of the highest order, in the moral and mannerly sense. He won the first United States Open Singles in 1968 as an amateur, receiving exactly $280 in expense money. At the time of his tragic death in 1993 he was the last American of gentlemanly refinement and culture to play the game. *(Colorsport)*

Along with his friend Arthur Ashe, Stan Smith was a sporting gentleman and the last native Californian to reach the top ranks of tennis. Having learned their game as amateurs, Ashe and Smith were both college graduates, the last of their kind in the top ranks today. *(Sportsworld Magazine)*

James Scott Connors, from Belleville, Illinois, was a left-hander who used a two handed backhand to win the singles title at Wimbledon (1974); he won again in 1982. He won the first U.S. Singles title to be played at Flushing Meadow, thus ushering in the roughneck age of American tennis. Connors won the U.S. Singles title five times altogether. (Tod Friedman, *Tennis Magazine*)

In the 1980s John Patrick McEnroe dominated world tennis in much the same way that Big Bill Tilden did in the 1920s. He was, in my opinion, the best singles player of the decade and unquestionably the best doubles player. His court behavior was appalling. (Tennis Hall of Fame Library)

Ivan Lendl, a United States citizen of Czechoslovakian birth, was ranked among the top ten men in the world between 1980 and 1992. He won the French and U.S. Open Singles titles three times each and the Australian Open twice. He was never able to win Wimbledon. He was a perfect gentleman on the court. (*Tennis Magazine*)

Bjorn Borg, the first Swedish tennis champion of the Open Era, was the first winner of five Gentleman's Singles titles (1976–1980) at Wimbledon since H.L. Doherty did it in 1902–1906. He also won six French singles titles. He could never win at Flushing Meadow. (John Kelly, *Tennis Magazine*)

Photo of champions, with Duke and Duchess of Kent front and center, at the Wimbledon Centenary Championships in 1977. Gentleman Champions: Back Row—Arthur Ashe, Stan Smith, Manuel Santana (Spain), Neale Fraser (Australia), Lew Hoad (Australia), Jaroslav Drobny (Bohemia), Vic Seixas, Frank Sedgman (Australia), Dick Savitt, Tony Trabert, Rod Laver (Australia), John Newcombe (Australia), Jan Kodes (Czechoslovakia). Middle Row—Budge Patty, Jack Kramer, Yvon Petra (France), Don Budge, Ellsworth Vines, Henri Cochet and Jean Borotra (France), Fred Perry (England), René Lacoste (France), Sidney Wood, and Bob Falkenburg. (Le-Roye Productions, Kent, England)

man Jack Kramer in the Forest Hills final. Hunt had won the Intercollegiates for the Naval Academy in 1941. Don McNeill, Ted Schroeder, and Joe Hunt were all strictly amateur, part-time players; Hunt was killed not long after winning at Forest Hills and both Schroeder and McNeill followed business careers. Schroeder, who always played sporadically, had his finest year in 1949 when he won Wimbledon and lost to Gonzales in the Forest Hills finals.

While Don McNeill, Ted Schroeder, and Joe Hunt were all first-rate tennis players, they played the game as an avocation, graduated from college, and sought careers outside sport. They each won our national singles title only once; Schroeder also won Wimbledon, and McNeill won the French title. They were all middle-class boys who started life with few material advantages.

Bobby Riggs, Frank Parker, Jack Kramer, and Richard Gonzales, on the other hand, saw the game as a way up in the world and spent their whole lives in the sport; each won our national title twice and each eventually joined the professional tour. While all four men were classic examples of the Horatio Alger dream, Riggs and Kramer were of Northern European and Protestant stock, while Parker and Gonzales were of Catholic and newer immigrant origins: Parker came from a poor, Polish Catholic family in Milwaukee, while Gonzales grew up in a poor Mexican barrio in Los Angeles.

Frankie Parker, a handsome, preppy-looking young man, always neatly dressed in white shorts, was soft-spoken and a perfect gentleman on and off the tennis courts. He was ranked in the First Ten for seventeen years, from 1933 when Franklin Roosevelt entered the White House, to 1949 when Harry Truman was inaugurated and appointed Dean Acheson as his Secretary of State.* Thus Parker's tennis career exactly paralleled the greatest period of upper-class leadership in America. His career, above all, was a classic example of that class's power to assimilate and socialize talented men and women of lower-class origins into its ranks. Frankie's class socialization took place at Lawrenceville, an exclusive boy's prep school situated a dozen or so miles down the road from Princeton, New Jersey.

---

*Parker's record of seventeen years in the First Ten was second only to that of William A. Larned who ranked in the First Ten for twenty years between 1892 and 1911. Parker's record was not equaled until 1987 which marked Jimmy Connors's seventeenth year in the First Ten. Connors broke Larned's record in 1991, which marked his second decade in the First Ten (1971–91).

Although young Parker was a great success at Lawrenceville, his social class origins were far different from his preppy peers at the school. He was born Franciszek Andrezej Piakowski in Milwaukee, Wisconsin. His father left home when he was 1 year old and he and his three older sisters and brother lived, as he told Stan Hart, in "the low, low class. My mother took in washing. I worked as a ball boy at the Town Club in Milwaukee and made a dollar a week at five cents a set. Mercer Beasley, who was the pro at the club, allowed me to hit with some of his pupils and he saw something in me that made him think I might become a champion and things went on from there."[3]

Beasley and his wife Audrey took young Frankie to New Orleans where Beasley coached the Tulane tennis team. They wanted to officially adopt the boy but Mrs. Piakowski would not allow it, only letting him go because of economic necessity. Later Beasley took a coaching job at Lawrenceville where Frankie captained the tennis team and became a generally respected student leader as measured by his election as head boy at Cleve House, a high-prestige dormitory at the center of the campus. While at Lawrenceville, he won the national boys title at 15 and the national juniors at 16. At 17, in 1933, he was ranked eighth in the First Ten, having won his first of five National Clay Court Championships (a record second only to Tilden's six wins), and the first of his ten singles titles at the Spring Lake Bath and Tennis Club men's invitational, the only tournament in the Eastern Grass Court Circuit to be played on clay (the finest clay courts I have ever seen). At 18, he was passionately in love with Audrey Beasley, then in her late thirties. It was clearly a case of sociological, if not legal, incest. The boy had moved in on his mentor, benefactor, coach, and "father." And Audrey had carried on with the boy in her husband's home. When Frank became 22, he and Audrey became husband and wife.* Long after Audrey's death, Frank told Stan Hart that she was the great and only "love of his life." Certainly theirs was the most astonishing love affair in the history of American lawn tennis. After their marriage, Audrey became Frank's coach and manager.

Parker was not a natural athlete nor a great tennis player. He first

---

*After their interview, Frank wrote Stan Hart as follows: "I had nothing to do with the Beasley's divorce. It had been brewing long before I entered the picture. They had agreed to disagree, to paraphrase a phrase."

learned the game from perhaps the best coach in America (Beasley had coached Ellsworth Vines and Bitsy Grant, among others). He always worked hard at improving his game and kept himself in perfect physical shape. His placid, Polish persistence on the court was in striking contrast to the impatient, hurry-up American temperament. He never beat himself, always patiently waiting for his opponent to make the errors. Thus his two consecutive wins at Roland Garros have only been equaled by one other American, Tony Trabert (1954–55). While he won at Forest Hills twice in a row (1944–45), beating Billy Talbert in the finals, the victories came during the war years when many top players, including the best of them all, Seaman Jack Kramer, did not play. Nevertheless Frank told Stan Hart that the finest singles victory of his career was

> winning at Forest Hills against Billy Talbert. I had strived for that victory for seventeen years. I had reached the finals four times. I lost to Ted Schroeder, won it twice against Billy, and lost to Jack Kramer when I had taken the first two sets. You see, in 1944, when I first beat Billy Talbert, I had been out on Guam all year in the Army. I don't think I'd played a match all year. So when I got leave to go to Forest Hills and won it, that was my biggest moment in tennis.[4]

As we have seen, Parker played on the Davis Cup team which won the cup back from the British in 1937, and again in 1939, when the cup was lost to Australia. Although he and Audrey went to Australia with the Davis Cup team in 1946, he did not play. Schroeder was chosen to replace him in the singles, partly due to pressure put on Captain Walter Pate by Perry Jones.

Parker never won the singles at Wimbledon. He and Richard Gonzales were both sent abroad in 1949. They got along well together, in spite or because of their opposite temperaments and won the doubles titles at both Wimbledon and Roland Garros. Parker ranked fourth in 1949, while Gonzales had his greatest year and was ranked number one in the world and in the United States (see Figures 19 and 20).

The four postwar years, 1946–49, were really a continuation of the Golden Age of amateur tennis in the twenties and thirties. Jack Kramer, who dominated the first two postwar years, winning Forest Hills in 1946 and both Wimbledon and Forest Hills the following year, had learned the game in the thirties and played doubles in the famous prewar Davis Cup tie at the Merion Cricket Club in 1939. Due to bad luck and the war, he did not win our Championship until the age of 25. In 1942, after not losing a match all year, he had to withdraw from Forest Hills because of an attack of appendicitis; in 1943, he had a bad attack of food poisoning just before his semifinal match which he barely won only to be beaten badly in the finals by Joe Hunt, a naval aviator. In 1944, he became an officer in the Coast Guard, got married, and shipped out on an LST (landing ship) to join the Seventh Fleet in the South Pacific; he took part in seven engagements including the landing on Leyte. Discharged in March 1946, he entered Wimbledon in June, losing to Drobny in the fourth round, and then won the U.S. Championship in September.

After winning at Forest Hills, Kramer flew down to Australia where he and his best friend, Ted Schroeder, playing both the singles and the doubles, trimmed the Australian Davis Cup team in all five matches.* The next year, after winning Wimbledon and Forest Hills, Kramer led our Davis Cup team to a 4–1 victory over the Australian challengers at Forest Hills. He then joined the professional tour. While he was the World Champion in 1946 and 1947, Kramer did not develop his famous big-serve-and-volley percentage game until he had to battle Bobby Riggs on the pro tour.

Kramer made his professional debut against Riggs at Madison Square Garden, in New York City, on December 26, 1947, in the midst of the greatest blizzard ever to hit the city; by mid-afternoon, the snow level had exceeded that of the famous Blizzard of '88. In his autobiography Kramer described that incredible evening as follows:

> There was no surface transportation so Bobby and I, and Dinny Pails and Segura, who played the opening match on the tour, had to hike over from the Hotel Lexington. Riggs always carried the most racquets of any player—seven or eight at a time, each slightly heavier in the head where he had added adhesive tape. He had so damned many rackets that he had to number them in ink so he could tell them apart. And here he is, lugging them crosstown in a blizzard. It was like an expedition to the South Pole.
>
> We could not postpone the match so we beat our way through the rising snow on Eighth Avenue positive that we would be playing before a handful

---

*It took four days to fly down under in those pre-jet days of prop-driven planes. It surely was an improvement over the twenty-one days by boat.

of ticket-holders. But when we walked into the Garden, we could hardly believe our eyes: there were thousands of people already there and more pouring in. A total of 16,052 tickets had been sold, and incredibly, 15,114 people showed up. The *Daily News* called it "the greatest tribute to an indoor athletic event in the history of sport." Nowadays they don't get 93 percent of the ticket holders to show up for an NFL game in bright sunshine in the middle of October. The gate came to $55,730, and while 20 percent of that was the wartime entertainment tax, the gross was about equal to the Vines-Perry debut a decade before which was the only other tennis match ever to break $50,000.[5]

Riggs beat Kramer in four sets on that opening night at the Garden. Bobby also won their second match, in Pittsburgh, and stayed ahead until Kramer finally pulled ahead after nine matches to lead 5–4. The lead seesawed back and forth until their two hometown matches at the Pan Pacific Auditorium in L.A. where they each won one match, making it sixteen wins for Kramer against fifteen for Riggs. After leaving L.A., Kramer won fifty-three of the next fifty-eight matches, finishing the tour with a score of 69–20.

Kramer, always a keen student of the game, learned two important things from his first pro tour. As he himself put it:

> The trouble with the extended tour, probably in any sport, is that it will not truly reflect the rivalry. If one player is 10 percent better than the other, I guarantee you he will not just win 10 percent more matches. Rather he is more likely to win 50 percent more. Once a player establishes himself over the other, the opponent has to change his game in some way or he is conceding. But any time you change your game, you are giving up a sure strength to gamble on something new, and the chances are you were better off. In my case, when I changed it made me better, but that is rare.[6]

This first tour for Kramer was an almost perfect example of his theory. He saw early on that he was not going to beat Riggs regularly unless he changed to the big-serve-and-volley game, which later became so influential. By the time of the L.A. matches he had become comfortable with his new style and from then on, he ran away with Riggs, taking well over 90 percent of the rest of their matches and ending up with close to an 80 percent margin overall.

As he was being beaten night after night by Kramer, Riggs also saw that tour results were no real measure of ability. Still convinced that he could beat Kramer in any one tournament match with money-on-the-line, he arranged and promoted the one, first-rate U.S. Professional Championship to be held during the amateur era (see Figure 21). It was played at Forest Hills during the summer of 1948. Kramer beat Riggs in the finals and conclusively proved that he was the best tennis player in the world at that time.

———

Most of the young stars who came out of Southern California in the Jones era were from middle and lower-middle class, Protestant families of Northern European origins.* A great exception was Richard Alonzo (Pancho) Gonzales, who grew up in one of the poor Mexican American barrios of Los Angeles. During the depression, his parents and their seven children lived in two rooms. His father was a day laborer and his mother worked as a seamstress in a garment factory. Both parents originally came from the same town in Mexico; while his father was of peasant origins, his mother's family were wealthy land barons who lost everything in the Revolution; she was always immaculate and carried herself in ladylike dignity; it was she who encouraged Richard's tennis career; it was "a gentleman's game, civilized, an art," as she put it; neither his mother, nor Perry Jones ever called him "Pancho."

Pancho Gonzales was probably the greatest naturally gifted athlete ever to play the game of tennis; as a youth he excelled in marbles, paddle tennis, dice, chess, pool, basketball free throws, coin pitching, horse-shoe pitching, and table tennis; when he took up golf later in life, he shot a 75 after two months of practice. He also excelled in school in the early grades; that is until he was 13 when he fell "madly in love," as he later wrote, in his touching autobiography:

---

*The following non-WASPS reached the top levels of amateur tennis in America: Maurice Mc-Loughlin, born 1890, Nevada, Scotch-Irish; Vincent Richards, Born 1903, Yonkers, Irish; Frank Shields, born 1909, New York City, Irish Catholic; Frank Parker (Franciszek Andrezej Piakowski), born 1916, Milwaukee, Polish Catholic; Francisco Segura, born 1921, Equador, Latino Catholic; Richard Gonzales, born 1928, Los Angeles, Latino Catholic; Richard Savitt, born 1927, Bayonne, N.J., Jewish; Alejandro Olmedo, born 1936, Peru, part-Inca; Arthur Ashe, born 1943, black.

FIGURE 21

Professional Lawn Tennis Association Championships, Forest Hills, 1948

Singles

Second Round
Riggs beat Van den Bosch 6–0 6–1 6–3
Cooke beat Pelizza 12–10 4–6 6–1 10–8
Kovacs beat Harman 6–3 6–2 6–0
Segura beat Earn 6–4 6–0 6–3
Kramer beat Stubbs 6–1 6–0 6–2
Van Horn beat Nogrady 6–1 3–6 6–1 6–1
Budge beat Adler 6–0 6–0 6–1
Pails beat Sabin 3–6 6–3 6–3 6–4

Quarter-Final Round
Riggs beat Cooke 6–4 4–6 6–3 6–0
Kovacs beat Segura 3–6 3–6 6–4 6–3 6–3
Kramer beat Van Horn 3–6 16–14 4–6 8–6 6–4
Budge beat Pails 4–6 6–2 6–3 6–3

Semi-final Round
Riggs beat Kovacs 6–3 6–2 7–5
Kramer beat Budge 6–4 8–10 3–6 6–4 6–0

Final Round
Jack Kramer beat Bobby Riggs 14–12 6–2 3–6
6–3

Doubles

First Round
Budge-Riggs beat Doyle-Blauer 6–1 6–0 6–0
Stubbs-Gornto beat Seewagen-Adler 6–3 6–4 5–7 7–5
Sabin-Cooke beat Fishback-Kuhn (default)
Pails-Pelizza beat Kern Koslan 6–0 6–2 6–0
Kramer-Segura beat McKee-Kenney (default)
Earn-Harman beat Buxby-March 6–1 6–2 1–6 13–11
Kovacs-Van Horn beat Goeltz-Doeg (default)
Nogrady-Richey beat Richards-Woods 6–3 6–4 6–2

Second Round
Budge-Riggs beat Stubbs-Gornto 6–3 11–9 6–3
Pails-Pelizza beat Sabin-Cooke 6–0 6–2 6–1
Kramer-Segura beat Earn-Harman 6–2 6–2 6–3
Kovacs-Van Horn beat Nogrady-Richey 6–4 6–4 6–3

Semi-final Round
Budge-Riggs beat Pails-Pelizza 8–6 6–4
Kramer-Segura beat Kovacs-Van Horn 6–4 6–1 6–4

Final Round
Jack Kramer-Francisco Segura beat Donald Budge-
Bobby Riggs 4–6 5–7 6–2 7–5 8–6

Pro Payoff At A Glance

Gross Gate Receipts		$25,855.40
Less: Federal Taxes		4,959.48
		20,895.92
Less: Rental		3,000.00
		17,895.92
Add:—Ticket Order Service Charge	$858.71	
Entry Fees—Singles	160.00	
Doubles	80.00	1,098.71
		18,994.63
Less:—5% to U.S.P.L.T.A.	949.73	
5% to Foreign Players		
Mr. Pails	$474.86	
Mr. Segura	474.87	949.73	1,899.46
Net Gross Receipts		$17,095.17

PLAYERS

60% of 17,095..17		$10,257.10
Less: 20 Losers 1st. Round (16 Singles 4 Doubles)	$1,000.00	
4 Losers, Round of 16	400.00	
4 Winners of play-off in Round of 16	800.00	2,200.00
Prize money divisible between Singles & Doubles		$8,057.10

SINGLES			DOUBLES		
KRAMER	18%	$1,450.20	KRAMER	9%	$725.14
RIGGS	12%	966.85	SEGURA	9%	725.14
KOVACS	8%	644.57	BUDGE	6%	483.44
BUDGE	6%	483.43	RIGGS	6%	483.44
COOKE	4%	322.28	PAILS	2½%	201.42
SEGURA	4%	322.28	PELLIZZA	2½%	201.42
VAN HORN	4%	322.28	KOVACS	2½%	201.42
PAILS	4%	322.28	VAN HORN	2½%	201.42
		$4,834.26			$3,222.84

Source: *American Lawn Tennis,* August 1, 1948.

It was a blinding, choking, loyal love filled with devotion and dedication. Obvious to all, it was understood by only a few. The object of adolescent affection was my tennis racket.

My love spread from the first racket to the game itself and its many facets. The love was, and is, undying and possessive. With all due apologies to my wife, I'm wedded to it until old faltering legs doth us part. . . .

That first racket of mine, to me, was the eighth wonder of the world. Loosely strung, producing none of the banjo-like music when you twang a tightly-pulled racket of split lamb's gut . . . I never let it out of my sight. I took it to bed with me to protect the strings and a warping frame from the temperature changes of the room. I coddled it like a helpless human. . . . I shook hands with it all day, more often than a politician pumps the hands of prospective voters. Sometimes I even talked to it.

I'd say, "Good morning, Señor Tennis Racket."

And, in my own falsetto, the racket would reply, "Good morning, Señor Gonzales."[7]

From the age of 13 on, the young tennis-lover, once a very good student, spent his days dodging truant officers, all the while hanging around various tennis centers, studying the strokes of the best players and learning the complicated tennis scoring system. Eventually, this almost entirely self-taught, natural genius entered tournaments himself and within two years (1943) became the number one boy player in Southern California. In the meantime, Perry T. Jones, czar of the SCTA, found out about his truancy record and disqualified him from further play in the junior ranks. Even then, Pancho stubbornly refused to go back to school. After a two-year hitch in the navy in 1947, he turned 19, making him no longer eligible as a junior player; soon after his birthday, in May, he won the Southern California Men's Singles Championship, held at the L.A. Tennis Club. Perry T. Jones congratulated him, put him on the free list for tennis clothing and rackets, and helped him go East where he made his first visit to Forest Hills. He lost in the second round to fourth-seeded Gardnar Mulloy, in a bitter five-set battle 6–3, 6–2, 2–6, 9–11, 6–4. Two weeks later he played in the Pacific Southwest, losing to Ted Schroeder in the final round. He was ranked number seventeen nationally after this first year of men's competition. Sixteen months later, at Forest Hills, he won the U.S. National Singles Championship, which he repeated the next year.

Two of the finest natural athletes in the Tennis Hall of Fame in New-port are Frank Shields, who rose from the Irish Catholic Lower East Side of Manhattan into the posh world of Southampton, Long Island, and Tuxedo Park, New York, and Richard Gonzales, who rose to world tennis fame from a Mexican American Catholic barrio of Los Angeles. Shields, already wise to the Eastern Seaboard country club world, made it a point to befriend the young man from the West, took him to Brooks Brothers and bought him a blue blazer and rep tie, and generally smoothed his way at various clubs, especially at Forest Hills.

Both Shields and Gonzales grew up and played their amateur tennis in a class world where manners mattered as much as, or more than, money. It would be hard to conceive of the classless millionaires playing on the tennis tour today caring about blazers from Brooks Brothers or aspiring to the "polish and social graces" which young Richard Gonzales so ad-mired in Frank Shields. But of course, manners are deeply rooted in fam-ily and class authority. Gonzales's current wife, the former Rita Agassi (Andre's older sister), has written about her husband's traditional and authoritarian childhood with great sympathy and insight (see *World Tennis* 1987). She clearly showed how patriarchal and parental authority were absolutely central to his upbringing: "By today's standards," she wrote, "his father's form of discipline would be considered child abuse." No wonder young Richard perfectly understood being barred from ten-nis for skipping school by Perry T. Jones. "Contrary to general belief," he wrote in *Man with a Racket*, "I bore no animosity toward Mr. Jones. I had tried to play tennis and play tag with the truant officer at the same time. Mr. Jones had rules, and they were inflexible. It was either attend school or be suspended from tournament play. I refused to go to school. Mr. Jones simply did his duty." While writing about his confrontation with Mr. Jones concerning his school truancy at the Los Angeles Tennis Club, Gonzales included the following revealing paragraphs:

Let me digress a moment. During the last decade it has become a popular pastime to take pot shots at the brass hats of the United States Lawn Ten-nis Association, either in print or by the spoken word. Frequently you hear those totally unfamiliar with the setup comment: "The boys are okay—it's the brass hats that cause the trouble." Nothing could be more untrue. I ought to know. I caused the trouble.

To some of the disgruntled, a brass hat is a cuspidor up-side down. To me it was a badge of authority placed on an intelligent head, a symbol of leadership and organizational ability. Somebody had to wear those mythical hats.[8]

When Gonzales wrote the above lines in his autobiography (1959) he reflected both his strong patriarchal family background and the age of class authority which came to an end in America (as well as in England) in the course of the late 1960s and on into the 1970s and 1980s. Although Gonzales had an irascible and explosive temperament not unlike John McEnroe's, he sincerely believed in authority (which few of McEnroe's generation do). In many ways he was a paranoid and testy loner, trusting only a very few close friends; his married life mirrored his tennis career and included several marriages and divorces (he married a Miss Rheingold twice and divorced her twice). His bosom buddy, Pancho Segura, once said: "You know, the nicest thing Gorgo [his nickname among intimates] ever says to his wives is 'shut up.'"

Francisco "Pancho" Segura was even more of a legendary Alger hero than Gonzales. Born the same year as Jack Kramer (1921) in Guayaquil, Ecuador, he was one of nine children in a poverty-stricken family. At the age of 11 he had rickets and malaria, was weak and spindly, and was teased by the other children who called him "parrot foot." When his father got a job as caretaker of the most exclusive tennis club in Guayaquil, young Pancho learned to play the game when members were not using the courts. Too weak to hold his racket in one hand when he started to play, he developed his now-famous two-handed forehand. He made much rapid progress that the club members asked him to play on the club team in a match with the leading tennis club in the rival city of Quito. He won his match and went on to become quite a national hero (in 1940, the Guayaquil Tennis Club was renamed the Pancho Segura Tennis Club in his honor). In 1941, Pancho came up to play in our Nationals at Forest Hills where he lost in the second round to Bitsy Grant in five sets. Gardnar Mulloy, who watched the match carefully, since he was to meet the winner in the next round (Grant also beat Mulloy), was so impressed by Pancho that he got him a scholarship at the University of Miami, in Coral Gables, Florida. Pancho made the university famous when he became the only man, before or since, to win the U.S. Intercollegiate Championships three times in a row (1942, 1943, and 1944). He became a U.S. citizen while in college. Every year between 1942 and

1945 Pancho reached the semifinals at Forest Hills; after the war he lost in the quarterfinals to Gardnar Mulloy in 1946, and to Frank Parker in 1947, after which he turned pro. Both Segura and Gonzales reached the peak of their games as professionals rather than amateurs.

In 1949, Richard Gonzales was ranked number one in the world after a very uneven season. He was sent abroad with both Parker and Schroeder at the beginning of the season. Parker won the French singles title and Schroeder won the singles at Wimbledon. Gonzales lost in the singles at both Roland Garros and Wimbledon but won both Doubles Championships with Frank Parker. Back in America, he lost in the semifinals to Billy Talbert at Spring Lake. Talbert, playing the finest match of his long career, beat him again in the finals at Southampton. In between, Gonzales won the Pennsylvania State singles title at the Merion Cricket Club and the National Clay Court Championship at River Forest, outside Chicago. In a brilliantly fought final, he beat Gardnar Mulloy to win the Maude Barger-Wallach Challenge Bowl at Newport. Just before the Nationals at Forest Hills, he and Ted Schroeder won both their singles matches against Australia in the Davis Cup challenge round.

In the National Championships, Schroeder, who had won the singles titles at both Queens and Wimbledon, was seeded number one and Pancho number two. "I didn't complain," wrote Pancho in his autobiography, *Man with a Racket*. "Nor was I bitter over the way the tennis brass had rallied to Schroeder's side for the showdown. Almost to a man, the officials were pulling for Ted. He was their kind of guy—personable, poised and a good talker. To underscore how they felt about him, the USLTA awarded him the William M. Johnston Trophy during the tournament, an award that stresses 'character, sportsmanship, manners, cooperation, and contributions to the growth and development of tennis.'" (see Figure 24 in Chapter 16). In this WASP world, Pancho was inadvertently cast as the lonely villain; and he brought his wife, Henry, to Forest Hills to ease his loneliness. He touchingly wrote:

Frank Shields who had given me much encouragement during my visit to Forest Hills in 1948, again was in my corner in 1949. Frank had been the nation's top ranked player in 1933, is a sound tactician. He's also a big handsome guy who knows how to wear clothes and is poised and at ease in any kind of company. His polish and mastery of the social graces interests me as much as his tennis tips. I watched him carefully and tried to acquire some of his self assurance. I learned a lot from Frank, but to this day, I still don't know how to shake a lady's hand properly.[9]

The lonely underdog was about to play the finest tennis match of his career. He had previously lost seven of his eight meetings with Schroeder, one of the greatest "clutch" players in the game. This time the money was on the line: almost everybody knew that a lucrative pro contract awaited the winner.

The first set was all serve and volley. Schroeder won it 18–16, after one hour and thirteen minutes of furious play; Gonzales served sixteen aces to Schroeder's six and made thirty-eight placements to twenty-eight for Schroeder, and made only a few more errors. Gonzales lost the second set quickly 6–2. In the previous sixty-eight U.S. Championships, only four men—McLoughlin in 1912, Tilden in 1922, Don McNeill in 1940, and Kramer in 1947—had ever come from two sets down in the finals to win the Championship. Pancho Gonzales became the fifth (and last) player to turn this trick when he ran out the last three sets at 6–1, 6–2, 6–4. According to the *American Lawn Tennis* report of the match,

> Ted was stunned. He couldn't seem to realize he had lost. He gave the impression that he was going to throw his racket at the linesman. Was the man who had received the William M. Johnston Cup going to throw his racket at the linesman? No, it was just the result of nearly three hours of taut tennis. . . . Schroeder played tremendous tennis, but Pancho played even better. His ability to come from a two set deficit against a favored toe in this final round of the championships; his 27 service aces; and perhaps, above all, the awesome power of a game that kept improving as the match went on, will always be remembered.

Almost immediately after his great Forest Hills victory, Pancho signed a professional contract with Riggs and Kramer. His first pro tour opened at Madison Square Garden in October against Kramer who won easily in four sets. It turned out to be a disaster for Gonzales: Pancho won only four of the first twenty-six matches and only eight of the first fifty. He was not only overmatched but also immature, with no idea how to handle himself as a professional. His diet consisted mostly of hamburgers and hot dogs; he was a steady smoker and drank endless cokes on and off the court. Kramer was not above taking advantage of Pancho's immaturity and lack of discipline: "He had terrible sleeping habits made worse by the reality of a tour," Kramer later wrote.

> He couldn't get to sleep after a match under the best of conditions—and try to sleep every night when you're losing. So he'd take an afternoon nap, grab a hamburger and come out on the court dull and logy. If I won the toss, I always let him serve first because he was still half-asleep, and I could break him right off the bat. Then he'd start filling up on cokes. He'd lose again and have trouble sleeping again, and the whole cycle would repeat itself. . . . One of the great ironies of that tour was that he was a kid in perfect health and I beat him on stamina.[10]

In hindsight, Kramer saw that Pancho's win at Forest Hills in 1949 was a disaster. He should have played several more years of competitive, amateur tennis before turning pro. Budge urged him to at least win Wimbledon first before doing so.

The next nineteen years, from Gonzales's victory at Forest Hills in 1949 to Ashe's victory, still as an amateur, in 1968, were dark days indeed for American tennis, as we shall see in the next chapter.

Lean Years in American Tennis and the Reign of Harry Hopman's Australians

Hopman set high standards off the court for his teams. They wore ties and jackets when they ate in their hotel dining room, in London or on the Continent. Hopman insisted on good manners. "We were representing Australia, that was the point," he told me, "and I wanted us to behave like gentlemen in all ways."

—Herbert Warren Wind

In 1967, the USLTA was a nonprofit organization run by volunteers. Except for a small office staff in New York, there was no one who made a living from the USLTA, and it had absolutely no commercial interest in the game whatsoever. Because of it, tennis just stagnated for decades, and it took a revolution ... to move tennis away from shamateurism and the country clubs and into the legitimate professional arenas.

—Billie Jean King

THE GOLDEN AGE OF AMATEUR LAWN TENNIS IN AMERICA, WHICH BEGAN in 1920 when Big Bill Tilden became the first American to win the gentlemen's singles at Wimbledon, came to an end in 1949 when Pancho Gonzales won his famous come-from-behind victory over Ted Schroeder at Forest Hills. In the nineteen years between Gonzales's victory in 1949 and Ashe's victory in 1968, only three Americans—Arthur Larsen (1950), Tony Trabert (1953 and 1955), and Victor Seixas (1954)—were able to win the U.S. National Men's Singles Championship; only four Americans—Budge Patty (1950), Richard Savitt (1951), Victor Seixas (1953), and Tony Trabert (1955)—won the Wimbledon singles; and finally, in all those nineteen years only two Americans, Patty (1950) and Trabert (1953 and 1955) were ranked Number One in the World (see Figures 19 and 22).

Of the five Americans to win a Grand Slam event in the last nineteen years of amateur tennis, only Trabert, who won the American title in 1953, the French in 1954, and the French, British, and U.S. titles in 1955, was considered by Jack Kramer to be worthy of a pro contract. In the meantime, Gonzales had dropped out of sight after his disastrous pro tour with Kramer in 1950; his wife, however, finally convinced Kramer that he was the best man to face Trabert, in 1955. She proved to be right, and a much-improved Gonzales thoroughly outclassed Trabert, winning seventy-five matches as against Trabert's twenty-seven in their 1955–56 tour. Gonzales was now the best pro in the world and remained so for the rest of the decade. In 1960, at a time when there was little interest in pro tennis, Trabert took over Kramer's job as chief promoter. Later, Trabert had a fine career as a tennis analyst for CBS Sports during the open era, about which he has written perceptively in a book published in 1988.[1]

Something should be said here about the four Americans—Larsen, Patty, Savitt, and Seixas—who did not turn professional. In many ways the two most interesting were Larsen and Patty, both of whose tennis careers were influenced by their war experiences. Both were raised in California, Patty among the Perry Jones crowd at the L.A. Tennis Club, and Larsen in the San Francisco Bay Area. Although Art "Tappy" Larsen first played tennis at the age of 11, he only took up the game seriously after World War II on orders from his doctors: "I was so nervous and shell-shocked," he once said, "that the exercise in the open air, through tennis,

FIGURE 22

Hopman Era: Grand Slam Champions, Men's Singles, 1950–1967

	Australian	French	British	American
1950	Sedgman[1]	Patty	Patty	Larsen
1951	Savitt	Drobny[2]	Savitt	Sedgman[3]
1952	McGregor	Drobny	Sedgman	Sedgman
1953	Rosewall	Rosewall	Seixas	Trabert
1954	Rose	Trabert	Drobny	Seixas
1955	Rosewall	Trabert	Trabert	Trabert
1956	Hoad	Hoad	Hoad	Rosewall
1957	Cooper	Davidson[4]	Hoad	Anderson
1958	Cooper	Rose	Cooper	Cooper
1959	Olmedo	Pietrangeli[5]	Olmado	Fraser
1960	Laver	Pietrangeli	Fraser	Fraser
1961	Emerson	Santana[6]	Laver	Emerson
1962	**Laver**	**Laver**	**Laver**	**Laver**
1963	Emerson	Emerson	McKinley	Osuna[7]
1964	Emerson	Santana	Emerson	Emerson
1965	Emerson	Stolle	Emerson	Santana
1966	Emerson	Roche	Santana	Stolle
1967	Emerson	Emerson	Newcombe	Newcombe

1. All the Australian champions, except Savitt and Olmedo, were Australians.
2. Jaroslav Drobny was the first Czechoslovakian to win a Grand Slam tournament.
3. Frank Sedgman was the first Australian to win the U.S. title. He and his countrymen, Kenny Rosewall, Mal Anderson, Ashley Cooper, Neale Fraser, Roy Emerson, Rodney Laver, Fred Stolle, and John Newcombe, won it every year thereafter, except when Tony Trabert won it twice and Seixas, Osuna, and Santana each won it once. All in all, these nine Australians plus their countrymen, Ken McGregor, Mervyn Rose, Lew Hoad, and Tony Roche, won 47, or just over 65 percent, of the 72 titles played for during the 18 years of the Hopman era.
4. Sven Davidson was the first Swede to win a Grand Slam tournament.
5. Pietrangeli was the first Italian Grand Slam tournament winner.
6. Manuel Santana was the first Spanish Grand Slam tournament winner.
7. Rafael Osuna was the first Mexican Grand Slam tournament winner.

was the only thing that cured me." During his three years in the army, Larsen saw some of the roughest action in the European Theatre after landing on Omaha Beach on D-Day plus 30 with the 17th Cavalry Squadron of the 9th Army. Most of his buddies were killed at the landing, after which Larson fought his way to Brest as a tommy-gunner. "Suddenly, out of nowhere, a fleet of bombers began strafing and bombing us," he told Jeane Hoffman. "Our own air force had mistaken us for Nazis. Before the holocaust was over, half the troops were killed, ambulances were lined up for miles. I came through unscratched. Then and there I developed the complexes I am still trying to shake."[2] By the time he got back to California, he had developed a whole string of superstitions and jinxes. On the tennis courts, he soon transferred his fear of getting killed to the fear of getting beaten, from which he protected himself with a steady stream of superstitions: "You name 'em, I had 'em. . . . I wouldn't step on any kind of chalk line. I always had to have the winning ball to put back in play." No wonder Bill Talbert wrote the following affectionate lines about Arthur Larsen, U.S. Tennis Champion in 1950:

> The quick 140-pound champ from San Francisco . . . was an unusual character on and off the court. He could be shocking to the staid gatherings at Newport or Forest Hills, abusive to meek ballboys, and delightful to anyone around him—all within a few hours. He was superstitious beyond belief, smiling benignly as "lucky birds" flew over him or insisted on serving a "lucky ball." His blithe after-dinner speeches were hysterical—and the players, to a man, were his friends. His career ended the way he always moved—at full speed. He was seriously injured in a 1957 accident on an Italian motor scooter he had won in a tournament. Tennis lost its most colorful character.[3]

J. Edward (Budge) Patty, a Perry Jones favorite, won the Southern California junior singles title, as well as the national junior singles at Culver, Indiana, two years in a row (1941–42). He then joined the army and was sent to the European Theatre. He first caught the attention of the tennis world after the war when, as a private first class, he played along the Riviera (in the footsteps of dashing Dick Williams in 1918) and won the Allied Forces Tournament at Marseilles in 1945. As a GI who stayed behind in Europe, this handsome American expatriate soon became friends with many fashionable leaders of Continental and British society. A bit of a playboy, young Patty never took his tennis too seriously, playing for fun rather than just winning. He nevertheless made a stir in 1946 when he played in his first of fifteen straight Wimbledons, reaching the round of sixteen. In 1950, he won the Wimbledon singles title, having cut out smoking and taken training slightly more seriously. He had previously won the French title, beating his good friend and traveling companion on the European circuit, Jaroslav Drobny, in a five-set final. After these two fine victories, he came back to the United States where he was seeded number one at Forest Hills; but he sprained his ankle and defaulted in the first round. He had two more eventful years at Wimbledon: in 1953, he lost to Drobny in the third round, but only after having six match points in the longest match in the history of amateur tennis at Wimbledon (ninety-three games in all, Drobny winning 8–6, 16–18, 3–6, 8–6, 12–10). Then, in 1957 he had his last hurrah at the age of 33 when he won the Wimbledon doubles title with Gardnar Mulloy, age 43, beating the Australians, Neale Fraser and Lew Hoad, both then in their primes. Budge Patty's perfect manners and exquisite tennis style made him a Wimbledon idol for fifteen years. He eventually married and settled down as a Swiss businessman.

Richard Savitt was born in Bayonne, New Jersey, and still lives nearby, in South Orange, only a few miles from Forest Hills. A graduate of Cornell University, he had one big year at the top, winning the Australian and British Championships in 1951, while losing in the quarters to Drobny in the French and in the semis to Victor Seixas in the U.S. Championship. He was bitterly disappointed when not chosen, as we have already seen, to represent the United States in the Davis Cup challenge round in Australia. In 1952, he went on another world tennis tour but failed to win any of the four Grand Slam events. He became a success in the oil business while playing tennis largely for pleasure.

Both Patty and Savitt were outsiders in American tennis, having their greatest triumphs overseas.

E. Victor Seixas, by contrast, was a success at home. The fourth Philadelphia gentleman to win our National Singles Championship, he was born and raised in the city. An only child, his tennis-loving father often took him to his neighborhood tennis club where he taught him tennis from the age of 5. Vic was an all-around athlete at the William Penn Charter School, a few miles down the road from Bill Tilden's old school, the Germantown Academy. His first love was baseball (his grandfather had played with the Phillies) but he was better at tennis. Penn Charter, moreover, had a fine tennis coach and a first-rate program. In 1940 Vic won the Interscholastic Singles Championship, and the doubles with his Penn Charter teammate, Bill Vogt. This was the major tournament for juniors on the East Coast. At Forest Hills that year he played one of his most memorable matches, losing to third-seeded Frank Kovaks, after winning the first two sets. He was only 17 at the time. The next year, he lost a long and close match to Budge Patty in the quarterfinals of the National Juniors at Culver, Indiana, after which he entered the University of North Carolina at Chapel Hill. He played college tennis and on the circuit, breaking into the First Ten at number nine in 1942, before joining the U.S. Air Force. A slow developer like his fellow Philadelphian, Bill Tilden, Seixas did not reach his peak until 1953 when he won Wimbledon and only lost in the finals at Forest Hills, thus ranking number two behind Trabert. The next year, while he lost to Budge Patty in the Wimbledon quarterfinals, he won at Forest Hills and ranked number one in the United States for the second time.* Although losing in the quarterfinals at both Wimbledon and Forest Hills, Vic was ranked number one in the United States for the last time in 1957. Both he and Savitt were last ranked in the First Ten in 1959, exactly ten years after they both attained their rankings for the first time in 1950 (1950: Savitt 6, Seixas 8—1959: Savitt 5, Seixas 9).

Vic Seixas was always a perfect gentleman on and off the tennis court, and followed Jack Kramer as the second William M. Johnston Award winner in 1948 (see Figure 24). He was also the last Eastern Seaboard cricket club member to win our National Championship in singles. In the amateur sporting tradition, he was also a fine doubles player, winning the Wimbledon mixed-doubles title four times, the U.S. men's doubles twice, and the mixed three times. Vic played in the annual tournament at the Merion Cricket Club twenty-one times, winning it seven times. He was the last in a long tradition of Philadelphia gentleman winners at Merion, beginning with William J. Clothier 1900–1903 and 1906, Wallace Johnson 1909–10, 1920–24, R. Norris Williams 1912, 1914, 1927, and Big Bill Tilden 1918–19 and 1925.

═══

The Harry Hopman era in amateur lawn tennis began at Forest Hills in 1950, when the Australian Davis Cup team, under Hopman's captaincy, squeezed out a 3–2 victory over the United States in the challenge

---

*Back in 1951, he was first ranked number one, partly because he was chosen over Savitt in the Davis Cup challenge round in Australia, as we have sadly seen. He also beat Savitt in the semis at Forest Hills before losing in the finals to Sedgman, who became the first Australian to win the singles at Forest Hills.

round. For the rest of the amateur era, the Australians won the cup fifteen times, the United States winning only three times, in 1954, 1958 and 1963, each time losing it back to the Australians the following year. While the United States and the Australians met in every challenge round during the 1950s, the United States only reached the challenge round twice during the 1960s, winning in 1963 and losing in 1964 (see Figure 16).

For the first six decades of Davis Cup competition (1900–1959) only the British, American, French, and Australian (Australasian before 1922) teams reached the challenge round; during the 1960s, for the first time, Italy (1960 and 1961), Mexico (1962), Spain (1965 and 1967), and India (1966) all reached the challenge round and were defeated by the Australians.

Harry Hopman was a first-rate tennis player back in the Jack Crawford era. He was especially good at doubles, winning the Australian Championship with Crawford in 1929 and 1930; he was twice runner-up in the French doubles; he won the Australian Mixed Doubles Championship with his wife, Nell, in 1936 and 1937. The childless Hopmans were devoted to each other and to tennis. Hopman was a disciplinarian with rigid standards of fitness, gentlemanliness, and the big, attacking game; he was quick to punish as well as to forgive. For the last two decades of amateur tennis he was the czar of the junior development and Davis Cup programs. Hopman had been captain of the winning Davis Cup team in 1939 but then devoted himself to sportswriting in the immediate postwar years when Kramer, Schroeder, and Gonzales won and kept the cup in the United States. He became captain again in 1950 and held the position to the end of the amateur era. He never made any money out of coaching and hated the professionalization of the game, but he developed a continually renewing series of great international stars (see Figure 22). Among his top players were Frank Sedgman and Ken McGregor (1950–52), Lew Hoad and Kenny Rosewall (1953–56), Mal Anderson and Ashley Cooper (1957–58), Neale Fraser and Rodney Laver (1959–60), and during the rest of the sixties, Rodney Laver, Roy Emerson, John Newcombe, and Fred Stolle. Laver and Emerson were surely the two greatest of the Hopman era, John Newcombe, a close third. Laver, perhaps a genius second only to Tilden, is the only man in history to have won the Grand Slam as an amateur (1962) and as a professional (1969), as well as two Wimbledons in a row, as an amateur in 1961–62 and as a professional in 1968–69. Emerson, the greatest sportsman of his age, won twelve Grand Slam singles titles, six Australian and two French, two British and two American. Another fine sportsman, and the last of the great Australians under Hopman, was John Newcombe who won Wimbledon and Forest Hills as an amateur but had his greatest triumphs as a pro.

It would be wrong to end our discussion of the great tennis stars produced by Harry Hopman without a special tribute to Kenny Rosewall, one of the most beautiful tennis stylists of all time; he was the Baron von Cramm of his era; he and Cramm were surely the two greatest, world-class tennis stars never to have won Wimbledon.*

Two more important points should be made about the Hopman era. In the first place, tennis in his Australia was an extremely egalitarian game and recognized as a major sport. No other nation in the world had as many tennis courts per one thousand population as Australia and play at tennis clubs and public parks was relatively inexpensive. Hopman's genius was to take a wide variety of boys and mold them into a cohesive team of gentlemen: Sedgman's father was a plasterer, McGregor's a famous footballer, Hoad's an electrician, Rosewall's a grocer, and so forth; only Emerson and Newcombe were bred to middle-class families, Emerson the son of a prosperous rancher and Newcombe a dentist's son. Much like Perry Jones, Harry Hopman was a great organizer, disciplinarian, and believer in the virtues of the gentleman. Both men were childless, without other hobbies, and totally devoted to tennis; neither made money out of the game they loved.†

Finally, Hopman's boys dominated world tennis during a period when American tennis (as well as American sport as a whole) was moving away from its amateur traditions and turning towards professionalism. When Pancho Gonzales won Forest Hills for a second time in 1949 and immediately turned professional, he was just 21, Kramer 27, and Riggs 31. Surely Riggs,

---

*More will be said about Rosewall, Newcombe, and Laver in our discussion of the open era, in the next chapter.

†Neither Jones nor Hopman had anything at all in common with Nick Bollettieri, Millionaire.

Kramer, Gonzales, and Schroeder would have kept the Davis Cup in America for several more years had they remained amateurs.

In his incomparable autobiography, *The Game*, Jack Kramer included a stimulating chapter on pro-amateur relations during these dying days of amateur tennis which he sums up in Figure 23, where he compares the actual World Champion winners at Wimbledon and Forest Hills with his own hypothetical winners had the tournaments been "Open" to all rather than to amateurs alone. His "Open" winners are based on a careful study of the evidence—when one man was clearly the best in the world, in Kramer's estimate, he shows him as winning both Wimbledon and Forest Hills: that is, Vines in 1934–35, Kramer in 1948–50, and Pancho Gonzales in 1959. Otherwise he arbitrarily awarded each tournament to each of two top men. Though Kramer's main thesis is revealing and sound, I myself would venture to say that in 1936, 1937, and 1938, first Perry then Budge were both the amateur and hypothetical "Open" World Champions.

Two more important points: first, as both Kramer and Riggs have clearly argued above, the head-to-head pro tours were far less satisfactory than tournament play, either as a test of ability or especially as a developer of ability. There were of course Professional Championships throughout the amateur era. But, with the exception of 1948, they were of little consequence and only sparsely attended. Bill Tilden was packing for a trip to Cleveland for the Professional Championships there when he died in 1953. The professional tournament of most prestige and tradition was the U.S. Professional Championship, at Forest Hills. It dated back to 1927 when it was won by Vincent Richards. Though by now forgotten by most fans and players, the tournament in 1948 was the most memorable of them all; the report of the tournament in *American Lawn Tennis* in August of that year is a period piece in tennis history (see Figure 21). Of greatest historical interest was the Budge-Kramer semifinal. The two men were good friends and only five years apart in age; they had never played a meaningful match, however; Budge was past his prime and Kramer was at the peak of his. It was a hot muggy day. At the break, Don led two sets to one. Everything depended on the fourth set which Kramer won at 6–4 after being down 3–4. Budge won one point in the fifth set. "I have no idea why the National Anthem would have been played after our match," wrote Kramer, "but for whatever reasons, I have

FIGURE 23

Jack Kramer Rewrites History

	AMATEUR CHAMPIONS		KRAMER "OPEN" CHAMPIONS	
	Wimbledon	Forest Hills	Wimbledon	Forest Hills
1931	Wood	Vines	Tilden	Vines
1932	Vines	Vines	Vines	Vines
1933	Crawford	Perry	Crawford	Perry
1934	Perry	Perry	Vines	Vines
1935	Perry	Allison	Vines	Vines
1936	Perry	Perry	Perry	Vines
1937	Budge	Budge	Vines	Budge
1938	Budge	Budge	Budge	Vines
1939	Riggs	Riggs	Vines	Budge
1940	NOT HELD	McNeill	NOT HELD	Budge
1941	NOT HELD	Riggs	NOT HELD	Budge
1942	NOT HELD	Schroeder	NOT HELD	Budge
1943	NOT HELD	Hunt	NOT HELD	Budge
1944	NOT HELD	Parker	NOT HELD	Budge
1945	NOT HELD	Parker	NOT HELD	Riggs
1946	Petra	Kramer	Budge	Riggs
1947	Kramer	Kramer	Riggs	Kramer
1948	Falkenberg	Gonzales	Kramer	Kramer
1949	Schroeder	Gonzales	Kramer	Kramer
1950	Patty	Larsen	Kramer	Kramer
1951	Savitt	Sedgman	Kramer	Gonzales
1952	Sedgman	Sedgman	Gonzales	Kramer
1953	Seixas	Trabert	Kramer	Gonzales
1954	Drobny	Seixas	Sedgman	Gonzales
1955	Trabert	Trabert	Sedgman	Gonzales
1956	Hoad	Rosewall	Gonzales	Sedgman
1957	Hoad	Anderson	Hoad	Gonzales
1958	Cooper	Cooper	Gonzales	Hoad
1959	Olmedo	Fraser	Gonzales	Gonzales
1960	Fraser	Fraser	Rosewall	Gonzales
1961	Laver	Emerson	Gonzales	Rosewall
1962	Laver	Laver	Rosewall	Gonzales
1963	McKinley	Osuna	Gonzales	Laver
1964	Emerson	Emerson	Laver	Rosewall
1965	Emerson	Santana	Rosewall	Laver
1966	Santana	Stolle	Rosewall	Laver
1967	Newcombe	Newcombe	Laver	Rosewall

Source: Jack Kramer, with Frank Deford, *The Game: My Forty Years in Tennis.*

the distinct recollection of Don standing next to me, glassy-eyed and weaving, as 'The Star-Spangled Banner' ran on. But he was finished."[4]

———

Finally I myself would like to rewrite a manners and morals history of tennis after 1933, taking into account what might have happened had the USLTA made a more concerted effort at the annual meeting in Paris of the International Tennis Federation, and won permission to hold an "open" tournament at the Germantown Cricket Club in Philadelphia the next year. Like golf, tennis today might have still been a class game, held in classy surroundings like the Merion or Germantown cricket clubs rather than in such tasteless surroundings as the Philadelphia Spectrum, the Cow Palace in San Francisco, or vulgar Flushing Meadow. The class atmosphere of Wimbledon might have been characteristic of the modern game in America. Here, I definitely do not mean that the game should be limited to players from privileged backgrounds. As we have just seen, the class game of the thirties, forties, fifties, and early sixties was perhaps even more democratic in player personnel than today. The class code of honor was meticulously upheld by such young men of unprivileged origins as Frank Shields and Vinnie Richards through Frankie Parker on down to Arthur Ashe. And I prefer, moreover, the simple boys who found their own ways to the Los Angeles Tennis Club in the thirties to the parent-pushed boys now attending, at great parental expense, tennis academies run by such men as Nick Bollettieri, Millionaire (the greatest five-minute coach in the world, according to Jim Courier).

Most important of all, the class of gentlemen who ran tennis in 1933 still valued manners above money. This same class of gentlemen, for instance, still ran American tennis in 1951, when Earl Cochell, a First Ten player at the time, was suspended indefinitely from all USLTA-sponsored tournaments as a punishment for his rudeness at the U.S. Nationals at Forest Hills.* He was playing a fourth round match on a stadium court against Gardnar Mulloy when he lost his temper. Not only was his language on the court beyond the pale (for those days) but during the rest period after the third set, he was rude to Dr. S. Ellsworth Davenport, II,

———

*Cochell submitted a formal apology the next year and was reinstated, but only to play in tournaments west of the Mississippi.

the official referee of the tournament, who had stopped by to discuss the incident. Davenport was a very distinguished gentleman who had been referee of the Nationals since 1934 and a past president of the West Side Tennis Club where he had been a member since 1913.

Gentlemen were not afraid to exercise authority when principles were breached on those days before total tolerance and the "bottom line" took over America.

Gardnar Mulloy was one of the major "stackblowers and line-call pro-testors of his generation," according to John Sharnik. "But he doesn't hesitate to condemn the manners of the present players as inexcusable. He ascribes it to a lack of standards, not just in tennis but in society." Mulloy then went on to explain the difference between "today's brats" and "yesterday's gentlemen" as follows:

> I didn't raise my voice, I didn't use profanity and I didn't prolong it. Oh, we used to belabor the the linesmen, saying, "You're blind! or "Wanna bor-row my glasses?" Things like that. But we never gave the finger to the crowd or we would have been suspended. And that's what they need nowa-days. They need to be penalized. Why aren't they? Because the officials are afraid of them. Because commercialism has taken over. . . . .[5]

In 1960, Jack Kramer turned over the direction of the pro tours to Tony Trabert. At the same time the unofficial World Number One title gradually passed from Gonzales to Kenny Rosewall and Rodney Laver. But unfortu-nately the pros were now performing in increasing obscurity. There were no first-rate American pros and the Australian pros had little charismatic ap-peal to American audiences, who had all the money. The first year of open tennis, frankly, and despite the terrible loss that this book argues it signaled, was a godsend to American tennis when it finally arrived in 1968.

＝＝＝＝

Before leaving this discussion of amateur tennis, I should like to make the following observation: after more than a decade of reading the tennis literature for both the amateur and professional eras, an informal content analysis glaringly reveals a steady decline in the use, in a positive way, of the terms "gentleman" and "sportsman," both of which symbolized the very core ideals of the amateur game as well as the Anglo-American cul-ture as a whole up until the countercultural revolutions of 1968 and after.

John A. Kramer was not only a great champion in his amateur days but also the biggest man, after Tilden, in the professional game, from his barnstorming days in the 1940s until well into the 1970s. He was also a fine sportsman. Thus we must take into account the following criticism of the amateur game taken from his always interesting and thoughtful autobiography;

> So things are not pure in tennis today. But at least the players do have a voice and a piece of the action. In the shamateur days, we were only athletic gigolos—which is what Tilden called us—and the system was immoral and evil. I mean to be harsh. Tennis has changed so much in the last decade that it will not be long before the shamateur days are forgotten or looked upon fondly, all quaint nostalgia. I don't want the truth forgotten. Oh sure, we were kids: we had fun playing cards and chasing dames, it was nice hanging around country clubs and money, and a few of us like myself even moved up—but the overall system was rotten.[6]

While I can understand why Kramer was critical of the amateur system, I am convinced he was far too harsh when not downright wrong. The amateur system was simply not "immoral and evil" nor "rotten." But of course I lay myself open to being accused of suffering from the disease of "quaint nostalgia" as Kramer predicted. But let us look at the record by analyzing the contents of Figure 24 in some detail. All social systems, whether capitalist or communist, aristocratic or democratic, as well as amateur or pro tennis must, in the long run, be judged by the kinds of persons they produce. I should imagine that the important question to be asked here is: which tennis system has produced the highest proportion of men of "character, sportsmanship, manners, spirit of cooperation and contribution to the growth of the game?" A glance at Figure 24 reveals the following differences:

In the twenty years between Jack Kramer's win of the first Johnston Award in 1947 and Dennis Ralston's win in 1966, the committee saw fit to make the award in all but two years. On the other hand, in the first twenty pro years (1968–87), the committee made the award only half the time; the first two winners, Stan Smith and Charles Pasarell, moreover, were products of the amateur era.

Further inspection of Figure 24 reveals that, in the fifteen years after 1973 (when civility took a dive in American tennis) the Johnston Award

FIGURE 24

William M. Johnston Award Winners

Awarded to that male player who by character, sportsmanship, manners, spirit of cooperation, and contribution to the growth of the game ranks first in the opinion of the Selection Committee.

1947	John A. Kramer	1968	Stanley R. Smith
1948	E. Victor Seixas	1969	Charles Pasarell
1949	Frederick R. Schroeder, Jr.	1970	Tom Gorman
1950	J. Gilbert Hall	1971	James McManus
1951	W. Donald McNeill	1972	Roscoe Tanner
1952	Francis X. Shields	1973	No Award
1953	William F. Talbert	1974	"
1954	L. Straight Clark	1975	"
1955	Chauncey Depew Steele, Jr.	1976	"
1956	Hamilton Richardson	1977	"
1957	No Award	1978	"
1958	Thomas P. Brown, Jr.	1979	"
1959	Bernard J. Bartzen	1980	Brian Gottfried
1960	No Award	1981	No Award
1961	Eugene Scott	1982	Gene Mayer
1962	Jon A. Douglas	1983	No Award
1963	Martin Riessen	1984	No Award
1964	Arthur Ashe, Jr.	1985	Mats Wilander*
1965	Charles R. McKinley	1986	Ken Rosewall
1966	R. Dennis Ralston	1987	Tim Mayotte
1967	No Award		

*It was apparently hard to find a gentleman-sportsman among American tennis players
during the professional era, hence making the award only ten out of the twenty pro
years, two of them going to Mats Wilander, a Swede living in Monaco, and the stylish
Ken Rosewall, of Australia.

was *not* made for ten years or 70 percent of the time; in this same fifteen-
year period, only three Americans were deemed worthy of the award and
two foriegn tennis players of impeccable manners were included for the
first time.

But someone will surely say that this comparison of the amateur and
pro games is hardly relevant. While the very essence of the amateur ethic
is gentlemanly sportsmanship, the object of the pro game is tennis excellence in order to make money out of winning. It may shed some light on
this criticism to turn back to Figure 19 which lists the World Tennis
Champions for each year between 1920 and 1987. During the Perry
Jones era (1930–1949) nine men were ranked number one in fourteen

years (excluding the war years 1940–45 when there was no ranking). In the professional era, nine men were ranked number one during the first twenty years (1968–87). The men in each era as well as the number of times each held this honored ranking are listed below:

Perry Jones Era (1930–49)		*Professional Era* (1968–87)	
		4 years	Jimmy Connors
3 years	Fred Perry	3 years	Borg, McEnroe, Lendl
2 years	Cochet, Budge, and Kramer	2 years	Laver, Newcombe
1 year	Vines, Crawford Riggs, Parker, and Gonzales	1 year	Smith, Nastase, Ashe

In the first place, the nine men of the Jones era were clearly superior tennis players to the nine professionals. Hardly anyone would rate Jimmy Connors above Fred Perry. The two greatest players of the whole lot were Budge and Laver who have usually been rated at the top of any all-time World Champions list, Budge having a slight edge. But both Budge and Laver, the only Grand Slam winners, were products of the "rotten" amateur system. Laver was well past his prime when pro tennis began in 1968 and won his second Grand Slam in 1969 at the age of 31. But let us take a look at only the American players. Here we find that Budge, Kramer, Vines, Riggs, Parker, and Gonzales, as well as Smith and Ashe who both grew up in the amateur game, are not only an overwhelmingly superior group of men compared to Connors and McEnroe when it comes to "character, sportsmanship and manners," but also clearly superior as tennis players. At the moment it is too soon to judge Connors and McEnroe but, over the long run, I am confident that only McEnroe has a chance of ranking among American tennis immortals, along with Budge, Kramer, Vines, Riggs, and Gonzales. I am reasonably sure that Jack Kramer would agree with me on this. I think he would also agree that while the number of first-rate second-raters has greatly expanded in the pro era, there has been a decline in first-raters of real class. Kramer might also agree that Tilden's "athletic gigolos" of the amateur era were no worse than McEnroe's "money whores" of the present pro generation. Finally, it is my impression that Kramer might possibly have a different comparative view of pro and amateur tennis today (1994) than he did in his autobiography (1979).

The Great Revolution, 1968–1992: The Rise of Open (Pro) Tennis and the Decline of Civility

Ten years ago at the last U.S. Open played at Forest Hills, many of us believed that tennis was on the verge of liberation. It would escape from that pack of patrician gangsters who wore their khaki trousers a bit too short. It would burst out of its button-down shirt, flee the country club milieu, and moon-walk into a new era. Instead, the game seems more regimented today than ever before, and it appears that "fun" has become tennis' three-letter four-letter word.

—Peter Bodo (senior writer), *Tennis* magazine, 1987

COURT TENNIS HAD BEEN A ROYAL SPORT IN FRANCE EVER SINCE THE fourteenth century. In the years leading up to the French Revolution, Louis XIII, Louis XIV, and Louis XV were all enthusiastic about the game. On June 20, 1789, a Saturday, a tennis court achieved immortal fame when the members of the Third Estate, locked out of the normal meeting-place of the States-General at Versailles by Louis XVI, met instead in a nearby tennis court and, in the now-famous Tennis Court Oath, agreed not to disband until France had a constitution. France got its constitution but also a bloody revolution which replaced the traditional hierarchical authority of the ancien régime with a reign of terror and egalitarian anarchy which was only saved from chaos by the autocratic bureaucracy of Napoleon Bonaparte.

Modern lawn tennis had been a gentlemanly amateur game for almost a century when, on March 30, 1968, the members of the International Lawn Tennis Federation met at the Automobile Club, in Paris, to consider the All-England Club's proposal to hold an open tournament in June. The ILTF had nominally governed the leisurely world of amateur tennis since its founding in 1913. After hours of discussion, the Paris meeting ended in a confusing compromise which nevertheless allowed Great Britain to hold the world's first open tournament in April, at the West Hants Club at Bournemouth, and the first open Wimbledon in June. "After years of hypocrisy and increasingly flagrant breaches of the unworkable amateur rules," wrote a jubilant British tennis journalist, "the game at last became honest."

But just as the idealistic spirit of the Tennis Court Oath eventually degenerated into a reign of terror and anarchy, so the petty hypocrisies of the ancient amateur regime in tennis have now been replaced, especially during the Connors-McEnroe decade, 1974–84, by a ruthless moneyed game played by adolescent dropouts who are apparently ungovernable in spite of an ever-increasing number of bureaucratic regulations backed by a fearful and divided authority. And if the anarchy and cynical rowdiness of this new tennis regime goes much further, the game may have to call on some autocratic czar. "Before Nastase and Jimmy Connors and John McEnroe, players were under the thumbs of strict national associations, many of them ruled by pompous fools," wrote Barry Lorge in *World Tennis* (1983). "There was no 'Code of Conduct,' but there was an unspoken code of honor passed from generation to generation, as it still is in golf."

One wonders if the gutless moneymakers who run the modern game really are an improvement on the "pompous fools" of the ancien régime. In this chapter we shall take a look at the brave new world of professional tennis since its inception in 1968, and especially since 1978, when vulgarity and rowdiness were given a boost in America by the dehumanizing conditions of the new National Tennis Center at Flushing Meadow.

===

In hindsight, it was probably inevitable that open tennis should have come about in the late sixties or early seventies.* In the early sixties, for example, three important things pointed to the eventual revolution in tennis. First, the American game was at a very low ebb at the time; no American had won at Forest Hills since Tony Trabert beat Kenneth Rosewall in 1954; our Davis Cup teams had done poorly, especially in 1965, 1966, and 1967 when we were beaten in early rounds by Spain, Brazil, and little Ecuador. Second, the world became a global village after 1960 when for the first time, five jet trunk lines circled the globe (see Figure 25).

Third, along with the increasing affluence of the 1950s and 1960s, the "under-the-table" support of the top amateur players got scandalously out of hand. The last World Champion as an amateur, John Newcombe, made some $15,000 in 1967. Twenty years later, Newcombe explained to Richard Evans, a British tennis journalist, how a New Orleans promoter named David Dixon persuaded him and his doubles partner, Tony

---

*I prefer to think of the open era as actually the pro or professional era. Only the first two U.S. Open Championships included amateurs and professionals. There are no Harvard Phi Beta Kappas, like Barry Wood, or mathematics professors, like Gil Hunt, playing at Flushing Meadow today. At any rate the best book on the subject is Richard Evans, *Open Tennis: The First Twenty Years (1988)*. In a brilliant move back in the summer of 1962, Gladys Heldman anticipated that the jet airplane would play a vital role in any world tennis tour in the future. Before the Nationals at Forest Hills that year, she and nine friends put up seventeen hundred dollars apiece and chartered a jet to fly some seventy foreign players from Amsterdam to New York. Joe Cullman was the first to send in his check. I happened to go out to Forest Hills on opening day that year and incredulously watched the first truly international tennis tournament I had ever seen. I of course had no idea how it came about. Not even Gladys could have imagined that a dozen years later, in the tennis year 1973–74, a black tennis champion would have played on five continents, made 129 airplane trips, slept in 71 different beds, and flown 165,000 miles, as Arthur Ashe recorded in his diary of that year.

FIGURE 25

Dates of Jet Aircraft Debuts on Ten Major Trunk Air Routes

Route	Airline	Dates
1. North Atlantic	Pan American	26 Oct 1958
2. U.S. Domestic	National	10 Dec 1958
3. U.S. Transcontinental	American	25 Jan 1959
4. Europe–East Asia	Pan American	10 Oct 1959
5. South Atlantic	Air France	16 Aug 1960
6. North–South America	Pan American	20 Jul 1959
7. Pacific	Qantas	29 Jul 1959
8. Polar	Pan American	27 Aug 1959
9. Europe–Australia	Qantas	15 Oct 1959
10. Europe–Africa	T.A.I./U.A.T.	10 Sep 1960
11. Central Atlantic	Air France	20 Jun 1960

Source: R. E. G. Davies, *A History of the World's Air Lines* (London, 1964) p. 486.

Roche, to finally turn pro: "I was staying at the Roosevelt in New York just prior to playing Forest Hills," Newcombe told Evans.

> It was 1967 and I had just won Wimbledon. One morning Rochey calls me from his room and says, "How'd you like to make a million dollars?"
>
> Well, I was clearing about $15,000 a year as the No. 1 amateur in the world at the time so it sounded pretty good. I was getting $500 to play Forest Hills, and that was supposed to cover two weeks of expenses in New York for my wife and myself. I used to have brown toast and beans for breakfast and at night Angie and I would often eat at the Horn & Hardardt cafeteria. So when Rochey said two guys called Dave Dixon and Bob Briner wanted to meet us, I said "When?"

When the two eager Aussies first met with Dixon, they were taken across Madison Avenue to Brooks Brothers where they were both outfitted with tailor-made suits. When they eventually signed up as professionals, they were taking a gamble that they would never play at Wimbledon again. Fortunately, within a few weeks, the chairman of the All-England Club, Herman David, publicly denounced the amateur game as "a living lie" and clearly stated that in 1968 Wimbledon would be open to all players, whether amateur or professional. At that first open Wimbledon, Rod Laver beat Tony Roche in the singles final and Newcombe and Roche won the doubles.

During the first quarter-century of open tennis, five American men were World Champions for ten years, or 40 percent of the time (see Figure 26). In terms of gentlemanly behavior and education, these five men can be broken down into three distinct generations: in the first generation, Arthur Ashe and Stan Smith were both college graduates reared in the gentlemanly traditions of amateur tennis; in the second generation, Jimmy Connors and John McEnroe, both college dropouts whose entire tennis careers were spent during the open era, were supreme symbols of the roughneck era of American tennis which brought the game to the lowest level of mannerly civility in its history. Jim Courier's becoming World Champion in 1992 symbolized the establishment of the third American generation; he and his three peers— Andre Agassi, Michael Chang, and Pete Sampras—never went to college, or even had normal high school educations; the development of their tennis games, at considerable professional cost, was provided for by their ambitious parents. They marked the final triumph of the computerized one-dimensional man in the deadly serious tennis business.

—————

Arthur Ashe knew how important it was that the first generation of pros, having been reared in the amateur era, still knew how to have fun when he described an evening out on the town in Paris with two Romanian friends, Ion Tiriac and Ilie Nastase. It was the night before Nastase was to play a big match: "Tiriac was especially good company in those days," Ashe wrote. "With a few drinks, he would eat glasses (preferably fine crystal) and bang foreheads with whoever dared to take him on. And, as I remember, the only reason we bothered to call it quits at four that morning was because that was when Nastase threw up all over his date. . . . But nobody stays up till four anymore drinking before a big match, because it's not a big match anymore—it's big money."[1] I was reminded of Bill Talbert's story of one of his big matches when he stayed up till dawn before beating Bobby Riggs one of the few times in his career: "I had to change directly from my dinner clothes into my white flannels," wrote Talbert in his autobiography. "I had got back from the party only a couple of hours before, with just about time for a long cold shower in between. That, plus my usual morning insulin and breakfast, was the extent of my training for my thirty-third match against the leading amateur tennis player in the United States."[2]

FIGURE 26
World-Class Tennis in Three Eras

World Champions by Year 1920–1992

American Golden Age 1920–1949 11 Men 24 Years		Australian Golden Age 1950–1967 11 Men 18 Years		Open Era 1968–1992 13 Men 25 Years	
Tilden 20–25	(6)	Sedgman 50–52	(3)	Laver 68, 69	(2)
Lacoste 26, 27	(2)	Trabert 53, 55	(2)	Newcombe 70, 71	(2)
Cochet 28–31	(4)	Drobny 54	(1)	Smith 72	(1)
Vines 32	(1)	Hoad 56	(1)	Nastase 73	(1)
Crawford 33	(1)	Cooper 57, 58	(2)	Connors 74, 76, 78, 82	(4)
Perry 34–36	(3)	Fraser 59, 60	(2)	Ashe 75	(1)
Budge 37, 38	(2)	Laver 61, 62	(2)	Borg 77, 79, 80	(3)
Riggs 39	(1)	Osuna 63	(1)	McEnroe 81, 83, 84	(3)
Kramer 46, 47	(2)	Emerson 64, 65	(2)	Lendl 85–87	(3)
Parker 48	(1)	Santana 66	(1)	Wilander 88	(1)
Gonzales 49	(1)	Newcombe 67	(1)	Becker 89	(1)
				Edberg 90, 91	(2)
				Courier 92	(1)

World Champions by Nationality

US	(7)	14–60%	Aus	(7)	13–72%	US	(5)	10–40%
Fr	(2)	6–25%	US	(1)	2–11%	Sweden	(3)	6–24%
GB	(1)	3–12%	Czech	(1)	1	Aus	(2)	4–16%
Aus	(1)	1– 3%	Mex	(1)	1–17%	Czech	(1)	3–12%
Total	(11)	24–100%	Spain	(1)	1	Romania	(1)	1– 4%
			Total	(11)	18–100%	Germany	(1)	1– 4%
						Total	(13)	25–100%

Grand Slams by Era

Donald Budge 1938	Rodney Laver 1962	Rodney Laver 1969

10 All-Time Champions by Era

Tilden, Cochet, Perry, Budge, Kramer, Gonzales	Laver, Newcombe	(Laver, Newcombe) Borg, McEnroe

10 Classic Matches by Era and Place Played

At WIMBLEDON
Davis Cup 1937
Budge d. von Cramm
6–8, 5–7, 6–4, 6–2, 8–6
Semifinals 1927
Cochet d. Tilden
2–6, 4–6, 7–5, 6–4, 6–3
Finals 1933
Crawford d. Vines
4–6, 11–9, 6–2, 2–6, 6–4

At FOREST HILLS
Finals 1927
Lacoste d. Tilden
11–9, 6–3, 11–9
Finals 1933
Perry d. Crawford
6–3, 11–13, 4–6, 6–0, 6–1
Finals 1949
Gonzales d. Schroeder
16–18, 2–6, 6–1, 6–2, 6–4

At ROLAND GARROS
Davis Cup 1928
Tilden d. Lacoste
1–6, 6–4, 6–4, 2–6, 6–3

At ROLAND GARROS
French Final 1962
Laver d. Emerson
3–6, 2–6, 6–3, 9–7, 6–2

At WIMBLEDON
Finals 1975
Ashe d. Connors
6–1, 6–1, 5–7, 6–4

Finals 1980
Borg d. McEnroe
1–6, 7–5, 6–3, 6–7, 8–6

"So, what the hell," Ashe concluded, "we gave up fun for the money. The last of us who knew, who *lived* all those Paleolithic shamateurism days will be phased out in another five or six years. By then, I guess the whole tour will be made up of guys like Brian Gottfried, practicing twelve hours a day and sleeping the other twelve."

Ashe was more prophetic than he ever could have imagined: today's well-behaved automatons, in the third pro generation, have apparently had little education or fun in the process of their being programmed, almost from their cradles, to make money out of tennis. Pete Sampras, for example, had his first date after winning his first major tournament at the Philadelphia Spectrum in 1990. As he told John Feinstein, "I never went to a dance, to my prom, to my formal, to anything when I was in high school."[3]

Pete's good friend, Jim Courier, who helped to dress him for that first date, had more or less the same deprived childhood. Courier's home was in Dade City, Florida, about an hour and a half's drive from the Bollettieri tennis camp in Bradenton. He was taken there every week where he lived and played tennis. "There's no question I gave up my childhood to become a tennis player," he told Feinstein. "I think it was worth it. I mean you can't have everything in life. I wanted to play tennis. That doesn't mean there weren't times I hated it. The first year, every Sunday night when my parents dropped me off, I would go off by myself and cry. But I got through it." Millionaires in their teens, none of the one-dimensional boys in the third pro generation—Courier and Sampras, good friends and Agassi and Chang, loners—could possibly imagine the following scene at the Newport Casino in 1938, described by Billy Talbert in his autobiography:

> Bushman and I checked in at the big attic dormitory above the Casino, where about 40 players were being lodged on cots. The place was alive with the kind of steady pandemonium you'd expect of any large pair of rooms in which several dozen young fellows had been thrown together. It was like an army barracks with the sergeant called away. A pillow fight and a wrestling match were already in progress. One small guy had been hoisted bodily onto a huge chandelier by a group of playful colleagues, and was being swung gently back and forth while he clung to his perch like a frightened parrot, screaming useless protests. Another group was huddled together conspiratorially, drawing up a scheme to plant a live lobster in the bed of a keeper of late hours.[4]

The last gentlemanly generation to play championship tennis in the open era included eight Australians—Roy Emerson, John Newcombe, Rod Laver, Fred Stolle, Ken Rosewall, Tony Roche, Bob Hewitt, and Owen Davidson—and one South African, Frew McMillan; all were winners of ten or more Grand Slam tournament titles, and all save McMillan won two or more of these titles during the amateur era; McMillan and his older partner, Bob Hewitt, won thirty-nine straight doubles matches in 1967 including the Wimbledon doubles (see Figure 27).

Rod Laver and John Newcombe, among the ten best tennis players in

FIGURE 27

Men's All-Time Champions: Grand Slam Winners in Singles, Doubles, and Mixed Doubles, 1880–1989

	Aus.	Fr.	Wim.	U.S.	Overall S-D-M	T
Roy Emerson, 1959-71	6-3-0	2-6-0	2-3-0	2-4-0	12-16-0	28
John Newcombe, 1965-76	2-5-0	0-3-0	3-6-0	2-3-1	7-17-1	25
Frank Sedgman, 1949-52	2-2-2	0-2-2	1-3-2	2-2-2	5-9-8	22
Bill Tilden, 1913-30	*	0-0-1	3-1-0	7-5-4	10-6-5	21
Rod Laver, 1959-71	3-4-0	2-1-1	4-1-2	2-0-0	11-6-3	20
John Bromwich, 1938-50	2-8-1	0-0-0	0-2-2	0-3-1	2-13-4	19
Jean Borotra, 1925-36	1-1-1	1-5-2	2-3-1	0-0-1	4-9-5	18
Fred Stolle, 1962-69	0-3-1	1-2-0	0-2-3	1-3-2	2-10-6	18
Ken Rosewall, 1953-72	4-3-0	2-2-0	0-2-0	2-2-1	8-9-1	18
Neale Fraser, 1957-62	0-3-1	0-3-0	1-2-0	2-3-3	3-11-4	18
Adrian Quist, 1936-50	3-10-0	0-1-0	0-2-0	0-1-0	3-14-0	17
John McEnroe 1977-89	0-0-0	0-0-1	3-5-0	4-4-0	7-9-1	17
Jack Crawford, 1929-35	4-4-3	1-1-1	1-1-1	0-0-0	6-6-5	17
H.L. Doherty, 1897-06	*	*	5-8-0	1-2-0	6-10-0	16
Henri Cochet, 1922-32	*	4-3-2	2-2-0	1-0-1	7-5-3	15
Vic Seixas, 1952-56	0-1-0	0-2-1	1-0-4	1-2-3	2-5-8	15
Bob Hewitt, 1961-79	0-2-1	0-1-2	0-5-2	0-1-1	0-9-6	15
Reggie Doherty 1897-05	*	*	4-8-0	0-2-0	4-10-0	14
Fred Perry, 1933-36	1-1-0	1-1-1	3-0-2	3-0-1	8-2-4	14
Don Budge, 1936-38	1-0-0	1-0-0	2-2-2	2-2-2	6-4-4	14
Tony Roche, 1965-76	0-3-1	1-2-0	0-5-1	0-1-0	1-11-2	14
Willie Renshaw, 1880-1889	*	*	7-7-0	*	7-7-0	14
Lew Hoad, 1953-57	1-3-0	1-1-1	2-3-0	0-1-0	4-8-1	13
Jacques Brugnon, 1925-34	0-1-0	0-5-2	0-4-0	0-0-0	0-10-2	12
George Lott, 1928-34	0-0-0	0-1-0	0-2-1	0-5-3	0-8-4	12
Owen Davidson, 1966-74	0-1-1	0-0-1	0-0-4	0-1-4	0-2-10	12
Tony Wilding, 1906-14	2-1-0	*	4-4-0	*	6-5-0	11
Bjorn Borg, 1975-81	0-0-0	6-0-0	5-0-0	0-0-0	11-0-0	11
Jimmy Connors, 1973-83	1-0-0	0-0-0	2-1-0	5-1-0	8-2-0	10
Rene Lacoste, 1925-29	*	3-2-0	2-1-0	2-0-0	7-3-0	10
Jack Kramer, 1940-47	*	*	1-2-0	2-4-1	3-6-1	10
Tony Trabert, 1950-55	0-1-0	2-3-0	1-0-0	2-1-0	5-5-0	10
Frew McMillan, 1968-81	0-0-0	0-1-1	0-3-2	0-1-2	0-5-5	10

Source: The Official USTA Yearbook, 1992.

history according to many experts, were surely the two leaders of this gentlemanly generation. Laver won the first open Wimbledon in 1968 and the next year completed his second Grand Slam (1962 and 1969), the only man to attain this distinction both as an amateur and as a professional. No other man completed even one Grand Slam during the rest of the pro era. Newcombe won the next two Wimbledons (he also won the last Wimbledon in the amateur era). Both these great Aussies were among the top five all-time winners of the Big Four or Grand Slam tournament titles, in singles, doubles, and mixed doubles, Newcombe winning twenty-five such titles and Laver twenty (see Figure 27). Laver and Newcombe were also longtime members of the Australian Davis Cup teams. Both won many doubles titles. Both loved to play the game in the amateur spirit which they of course carried into the pro era.

While their tennis records were not on a par with those of Laver and Newcombe, Arthur Ashe and Stan Smith were the best Americans in this last gentlemanly generation of pros. Ashe won the Intercollegiates for UCLA in 1965 and Smith won it for USC in 1968; Ashe won our National Championships in 1968 and Smith in 1969 and 1971; both won Wimbledon, Smith in 1972 and Ashe in 1975, both were ranked Number One in the World in the years of their Wimbledon victories (see Figure 19). Both were patriotic Americans who had solid Davis Cup records.

Stan Smith was born of a comfortable family in Pasadena, California. His father was a physical education teacher. Young Stan, at six feet four inches, excelled in both basketball and tennis. A good but not exceptionally gifted athlete, he made himself a champion by hard work and great tenacity of purpose. All through his active tennis career, and since, he has been highly respected for his stolid moral stance and deeply felt Christian convictions. In his heyday in the 1970s, he was considered by many to be the "Jack Nicklaus" of tennis. As the last WASP to win our National Championship, he was surely in the sporting and moral tradition of Frank Merriwell. Arthur Ashe considered him one of his best friends and always trusted him completely down to the tragic end of his (Ashe's) life.

═══

The reign of rampant rudeness in top tennis circles began in 1972, when Arthur Ashe lost in the U.S. Open finals to Ilie Nastase of Romania, one of the most gifted and stylish of world-class players. Upon accepting his runner-up check, Ashe forthrightly told the officials and the crowd that Nastase would be an even better player if and when he improved his court manners. Unfortunately, Nastase did not take Arthur's advice and his manners and his tennis game steadily deteriorated, especially after 1973 when he was ranked Number One in the World.

Nastase absorbed his bad manners from his mentor and Davis Cup partner, Ion Tiriac, eight times Romanian Champion and a great bear of a man who is the only top tennis player to have also played Olympic ice hockey (in the roughneck style of our Dave Shultz). Tiriac was and still is an utterly charming and clever man of great integrity. His sense of humor was suggested when he once described himself as the "best player in the world who can't play tennis." On the tennis court, as in all games, on the other hand, Tiriac simply had no sense of that alien, Anglo-Saxon ethic of sportsmanship. Instead, he seemed to have the attitude that one must do anything and pay any price to win. After defeating Ashe in the U.S. Open in 1972, Nastase and his partner Tiriac almost won the Davis Cup from the Americans in a notoriously unsportsmanlike final round played at Bucharest in October. In one of the finest and most courageous sporting feats in tennis history, Stan Smith, almost single-handedly, came to the rescue and led the American team to victory.

Back in 1971 the U.S. Davis Cup team had beaten the Romanians 3–2 in the challenge round, Stan Smith winning both his singles matches against Tiriac and Nastase. For complicated political reasons, America agreed that the 1972 Final Round (title changed that year) was to be played in Romania. Stan Smith was the best player in the world when he came there to play in the Davis Cup that October. He had defeated Nastase in a brilliant five-setter in the Wimbledon final. The American team, captained by Dennis Ralston, included Smith, Tom Gorman, Eric van Dillen, Harold Solomon, and Brian Gottfried. The whole city of Bucharest was in the grip of this unprecedented Davis Cup event. The atmosphere was quite panicky, as many remembered the assassinations of members of the Israeli Olympic Team at Munich the previous August. "Because of rumors that Black September terrorists would make Bucharest their next target," wrote Curry Kirkpatrick for *Sports Illustrated*, "extraordinary security was set up around the American team and its two Jewish members, Harold Solomon and Brian Gottfried. Romanian President Ceausescu let it be known that heads would roll if there was a hint of an incident. As a result, the U.S. players walked, talked, rode in private limousines, took meals and practiced while surrounded by 20 unsmiling secret police, officially known as 'translators.'"

"The American team lived in isolation on the 17th floor of the sparkling new Intercontinental Hotel," Kirkpatrick continued. "They were watched by monitored cameras. They rode a private elevator. They were not allowed near windows, and they disappeared nightly upstairs to eat meals with their guards and watch movies sent over by the U.S. Embassy. When they did go out it was only to practice at the Progresul Club [where the Davis Cup was to be played]. They left and returned by different routes each time. It seemed silly, but after Munich who is to say?"[5]

It was in this conspiratorial, if not totalitarian, atmosphere that the Davis Cup matches were played over a fine October weekend. In many ways the American players found their experience on the courts during the matches just as harrowing as their days cooped up in the Intercontinental Hotel. On opening day, Smith and Nastase played the first match which Smith won in three straight sets. In the second match, Gorman, who had been chosen over Solomon at the last minute, played Tiriac. He ran through the first two sets easily. Then Tiriac, realizing the Cup would be lost if he didn't win the match, pulled out his full bag of tricks—sitting down, appealing to linesman, orchestrating the crowd in booing and whistling and so forth—and completely turned the match around. When he finished the slaughter 4–6, 2–6, 6–4, 6–3, 6–2, Gorman was in tears, according to Kirkpatrick, and Ralston was furious: "Tiriac should be thrown out of tennis for life," he said. "This is the most disgraceful day in the history of the Davis Cup." Ralston hadn't seen anything yet.

On Saturday, Tiriac was sure he and Nastase would easily beat Smith and van Dillen in the doubles, as they had done the year before in the Davis Cup challenge round. But van Dillen played the match of his life as he and Smith won in three easy sets 6–2, 6–0, 6–3. Tiriac and Nastase were so upset that they never spoke to each other throughout most of the match.

On Sunday, Smith's job was to clinch the tie by beating Tiriac in the first match of the day, which he did in five sets, consuming two hours and fifty minutes of the most harrowing gamesmanship on Tiriac's part ever seen by the members of the American team. Smith was always the perfect gentleman. Tiriac's conspiratorial gamesmanship in the Smith match made his behavior in the Gorman match pale by comparison. "At one point," Smith later said, "I started to believe they weren't going to let me win no matter how well I played." At the end of the match, he gravely shook Tiriac's hand and said: "Ion, I must tell you that I will always respect you as a player. But I will never again respect you as a man." Probably for the first time in his life, Tiriac was speechless.

Herbert Warren Wind watched those three wild days of play in Bucharest and wrote about them in his annual *New Yorker* article (1972). In spite of himself, he was both attracted and repelled by Tiriac whom he deftly described as follows:

> He is a tenacious fighter and, depending on how you look at it, one of the most resourceful or one of the most disgraceful gamesman in all sport. He has the look of a 'heavy' all right. His hair is a mass of Brillo that droops in a sort of Transylvanian Prince Valiant style. Beneath beetle brows, his eyes slant downward, giving him a mien both dolorous and forbidding. The rest of his face is overpowered by a thick black Fu Manchu mustache. Tiriac comes from Brasov, northwest of Bucharest, where his father was a clerk in the mayor's office. He himself, one hears from time to time, is a member of the secret police. Anyway, he speaks eight languages and is straight out of Eric Ambler. . . . Looking back on that five-set battle—and what a battle it was!—I find myself torn between admiration for Tiriac's fighting spirit and disdain for his ruthless contempt for fair play.[6]

Wind concluded his *New Yorker* article as follows: "The ethics of sport may not be the most important thing in the world, but the final at Progresul, for all its color and thrills, was a travesty of a kind that no game can afford. Some tennis people have suggested that, beginning as soon as possible, all Davis Cup matches, from the round of sixteen on, be held at *one* venue, with the conduct of the matches entirely in the hands of neutral officials. That seems right on the mark to me." At any rate, as Nastase's game deteriorated after 1973, he "began to resort to every possible crudity, including abusing of officials in order to disconcert an opponent and extricate a match he was in danger of losing," wrote Wind in the *New Yorker* in 1983.

After playing the match of his life at the age of 33 against Smith in Bucharest, Tiriac went on to become a major force in open tennis as coach and manager of such famous tennis players as Guillermo Vilas,

Henri Leconte, and Boris Becker. Vilas, an Argentinian aristocrat who speaks four languages, published two volumes of poetry while winning the French and U.S. Open titles in 1977 and the Australian titles in 1978 and 1979. Leconte, a brilliant but inconsistent French star, played an important role in France's winning the Davis Cup in 1991, for the first time since the days of the Four Musketeers in the 1920s. Becker, ever since winning Wimbledon at the age of 17 in 1985, has been a major star in pro tennis in the third generation. All the while Tiriac has become a multimillionaire through tennis and crafty investment elsewhere, which he has put to good use in becoming an important behind-the-scenes architect of a new social order in Romania.

Twenty years after the Bucharest affair, Tiriac was interviewed by *Tennis* magazine's senior staff writer, Peter Bodo. When asked whether the game today is better or worse than it was in 1972, Tiriac replied as follows:

> Economically, there is no comparison to my time. It is a thousand time better. No more. On the other side, the industry has kicked out the human factor. It is not in doubt. The money, the [computer rankings] points, the travel, the industry in general. . . there are too many responsibilities. In my time, we had a job to do and we had a life. Now, players just have a job to do, and hope they have a life later.[7]

━━

In 1974, James Scott Connors, with two brilliant victories over Rosewall at Wimbledon (6–1, 6–1, 6–4) and Forest Hills (6–1, 6–0, 6–1), came to the top of the tennis world. Born in a rapidly deteriorating neighborhood in East St. Louis in 1952, after high school Connors was taken out to the West Coast by his adoring and domineering, tennis-teaching mother to study at the Beverly Hills Tennis Club, under Segura and Pancho Gonzales. For some reason, he also enrolled at UCLA but eventually dropped out. As his biographer put it:

> He cut most of his classes. But he had money to spend, and paid a graduate student to turn out a term paper for him. Unfortunately, Jimmy's critical faculties were underdeveloped. The paper was too good to have come from him, but he handed in a mimeographed copy of it anyway. When he got to

class, the instructor is said to have taken him by the shirt front, thrown him against the wall, and ordered him to address the class on the meaning of the paper. His performance was unworthy of his hireling's efforts.[8]

While still at UCLA, he became the first freshman in history to win the National Collegiate Athletic Association (NCAA) Tennis Championship, held that year at Notre Dame.

From the beginning of his professional career, Connors was defiantly opposed to the tennis establishment, refusing to play on the United States Davis Cup team,* refusing to join the Association of Tennis Professionals, and refusing to join the World Championship Tennis Circuit. His adolescent attitude was most clearly revealed at the Centenary Wimbledon Championships in 1977 when he refused to join the parade of former champions before the Queen on the Center Court, thus absenting himself from the greatest group of tennis talent ever assembled in one place at one time. While Connors's continual clowning, use of obscene language and obscene body gestures, and his general rudeness have alienated most traditional tennis devotees, they have pleased the bored and boisterous new fans who have always been more interested in incidents and confrontations than in the fine points of tennis.

Finally, we have Connors to blame for originating two of the most annoying aspects of pro tennis today: he was the first tennis player to use the "grunt" and the first to bounce the ball interminably before serving. The latter annoyance has been limited by the so-called sominex rule (a stop watch now allows only thirty seconds of such nonsense).†

Over the years, Connors quite naturally became good friends with Nastase. But unfortunately friendship as well as friendly relations between players before, during, and especially after matches, has fallen victim to the no-holds-barred competitive atmosphere which sheer greed has imposed on modern pro tennis. It would be almost impossible, for example, for a Connors or a McEnroe to understand how Roy Emerson

---

*In February 1975, the United States lost an early-round Davis Cup competition to Mexico on the same weekend that Jimmy Connors was playing a $100,000 television exhibition match against Rod Laver in Las Vegas.

†A witty member of the tour tested the rule for himself and found that, if he bounced the ball eighteen times, all was well; the nineteenth bounce broke the rule. Such are the ways of mechanistic bureaucracies.

and Fred Stolle, in the amateur days of 1964 and 1965 when both were finalists at Wimbledon, could have roomed together, cooked each other breakfast each morning, fought each other desperately to win on the court, and still remained friends after their matches.

The Nastase-Connors friendship suffered a severe rupture in the spring of 1977 when they met in two highly publicized exhibition matches at the Cerro Mar Hotel in Puerto Rico and, a few weeks later, at Caesars Palace in Las Vegas. On March 4, Romania and Bucharest suffered the worst earthquake in their history. The next morning, a former Davis Cup player and longtime friend of the Nastase family telephoned Nastase's manager in Puerto Rico from Brussels, and informed him of the disaster; as all telephone lines to Bucharest were down, no one knew whether Nastase's parents were safe or his beloved house was still standing. As the match was to go on that afternoon, his wife, Dominique, kept the bad news from Nastase. When the two players appeared for a pre-match warm-up, however, Connors shouted across to Nastase: "Hey, buddy, you'd better call Bucharest. You might not have a house anymore." Nastase's biographer, Richard Evans, wrote of the incident:

> One could be charitable and simply dismiss it as the most tactless crack of the year. . . . If indeed it was a deliberate, premeditated act of psychological warfare a couple of hours before the two were due to play a match involving some $650,000, there can hardly have been a more unpleasant example of dirty pool in the history of professional sport.[9]

Although Nastase, who had been shielded from news of the earthquake by his wife and his manager, probably felt this was just another one of his buddy's crude jokes, he suffered from the sun and heat and was rather easily defeated. After the match, Connors laid it on the line when he "remarked that it was difficult to maintain a sufficiently tough winning attitude in big matches if you are constantly playing against a great friend." (As of 1980, Nastase was the only man to have a winning record over Connors 16–10).

Things were turned around a few weeks later at Caesars Palace: Nastase won and their friendship took another blow. In Las Vegas, Connors was rude and uncooperative from the beginning, refusing to show up at press conferences or promotional functions and generally enraging the management at Caesars Palace. Nastase, for some reason, was extremely cooperative. But he nearly blew all this goodwill when he showed up on the court late. He had not been warned of a time change and his lateness was not deliberate, but Connors thought it was one of his usual stalling acts, and as Nastase walked on to the court, according to Richard Evans, "the No. 1 tennis player in the world was standing at the net, lashing it with his racket and shouting, 'Fuck you, Nastase, fuck you.'" The crowd (not the national TV audience) soon got its money's worth in the verbal showdown which followed Connors's winning of the first set. It all happened during a commercial break and Evans described it as follows:

Nastase had just won a game with a backhand passing shot to go 2–1 up. As they walked back to their seats by the umpire's chair, Connors said something about "that fucking backhand."

"What you mean? You think I was lucky or what?" asked Nastase, unable to ignore his opponent's taunts any longer.

At that Connors leaped out of his chair and confronting Ilie face to face, let rip a stream of abuse that kept the courtside spectators agog for almost a minute.

Finally, for the first time since it all started back in Puerto Rico, Nasty lived up to his name and went for the jugular.

"Why don't you get your bloody mother down here on the court," he said, looking Connors firmly in the eyes. "You know you can't win anything without her."

Jimmy reacted as if he had taken a punch in the mouth. Reeling back, he sat down with a thump in his chair and never said another word for the rest of the match.[10]

———

Soon after these two ugly incidents between Nastase and Connors in Puerto Rico and Las Vegas, John Patrick McEnroe, Jr., burst upon the world tennis scene at Wimbledon. While still a student at the Trinity School in Manhattan, in 1977 he went abroad and, at the age of 17, qualified for Wimbledon and became the youngest player and first qualifier to reach the semifinal round where he was beaten by Jimmy Connors.

John Patrick McEnroe, Jr., was born in the U.S. Air Force Hospital at Wiesbaden, West Germany, in 1959, making him seven years younger than Jimmy Connors and sixteen years younger than Arthur Ashe. He was brought to the

United States as soon as his father got out of the Air Force, in 1960. The family settled into a high-rise apartment in Flushing while John Senior went to law school. Appropriately enough their apartment was five minutes away from the Louis Armstrong Stadium, the site of the U.S. Open eighteen years later, in 1978. The future "Super-brat" of American tennis was weaned in the shadow of Fitzgerald's "Valley of Ashes" and today's vulgar National Tennis Center. Within three years the family moved to the solid middle-class suburb of Douglaston, not far geographically from Flushing but many steps up the social ladder. John Senior was now working for a top-rated Wall Street law firm where he was doing well enough to support (when John Junior was eight), another upward move to the exclusive Douglas Manor not far from the Douglaston Tennis Club, which the family soon joined.

John McEnroe Senior's story was right out of Horatio Alger. Both his parents had come to America from Ireland, his father finishing his life as a security guard at the Chase Manhattan Bank and his mother as a switchboard operator in a New York brokerage house. By the time John Junior was fifteen, his father was made a partner in the highly prestigious Wall Street law firm of Paul, Weiss, Rifkind, Wharton and Garrison. John's mother, Kay McEnroe, was half Irish and half English. It was she rather than her husband, who was concentrating on his own career, who did the most to push her eldest son, especially in school where he received high grades.

In his teens, John McEnroe was definitely reared in privileged circumstances. In addition to living in a small and exclusive neighborhood, he was sent into Manhattan each day where he attended Trinity School, the oldest private school in Manhattan, founded in 1709 by Trinity Church (Episcopal) at the head of Wall Street. Though Trinity School is located on the Upper West Side today, John's graduation ceremonies were held at Trinity Church. He was a very good and hardworking student and one of the better all-around athletes in the school.

John was a model child and a model student at Trinity, according to both the Headmaster and his favorite master, an Englishman who taught him the classics. He had the equivalent of a British public school education. In his many hour-long trips from Douglaston to Trinity School by train and subway, he had an opportunity to observe what he called "the phoneyness" of the city. No wonder his adolescent hero was J. D. Salinger's Holden Caulfield, of Pency Prep, who hated "lousy phonies" with a passion.

After his astonishing success at his first Wimbledon in 1977, McEnroe went to Stanford where he dropped out after winning the NCAA Championship, like Connors, in his freshman year. In 1979, he followed Connors in winning the U.S. Open Championship at Flushing Meadow. Connors and McEnroe were the first Irish Catholics to win our National Championship; between them they won every Flushing Meadow final for the first several years—Connors in 1978, 1982, and 1983, and McEnroe in 1979, 1980, 1981, and 1984.

═══

The National Tennis Center, in Flushing Meadow Park, Long Island, is right next to Shea Stadium, home of the baseball Mets and the football Jets, and right under the flight path of an endless stream of fuming and booming jet airplanes taking off from nearby La Guardia Airport. If Wimbledon symbolizes a mannerly past still casting its shadow into an increasingly uncivil present, Flushing Meadow, having cast off any mannerly restraints which might have still remained at the West Side Tennis Club at Forest Hills, is surely a fitting symbol of the egalitarian and moneyed values of modern American tennis. While Wimbledon is doing its best to retain some semblance of the manners of an amateur game once played in white,* the Flushing Meadow Establishment has frankly recognized that the modern game is played for green. The snobbish values of the "400" at Newport have finally been totally replaced there by the moneyed values of the Fourth Estate, especially television. As a breezy biographer of James Scott Connors once put it:

> Tennis, descendant of a game invented at monasteries that became the sport of kings. Pastime of the rich, who needed more exercise than croquet

---

*The rules are more lenient now than in 1972 when Chris Evert noticed a sign in the Players Waiting Room at Wimbledon which stated that: "Clothing which displays any form of advertisement (other than one manufacturer's small logo) is not permitted to be worn on the courts. Players are also reminded that all clothing must be predominantly white."

In an early round at Wimbledon in 1984, McEnroe showed up on the Centre Court in dark blue shorts and was told to go back to the locker room and change to white. He did so. Later at Flushing Meadow, of course, he wore the same blue shorts with impunity in an atmosphere where anything goes.

offered. Less expensive than polo, it goes to show how clever capitalists can be with grass. (Incidentally, tennis was not played in Russia for many years after the revolution.) Originally a patball game, it became a power game. Finally, it is entertainment fodder for the boob tube. And it is controlled by the people who make money from it.[11]

Everyone has commented on the dehumanizing and disenchanting atmosphere at Flushing Meadow. In the anniversary issue of *Tennis* magazine, for instance, a writer contrasts the serenity of the Newport Casino with the frantic materialism of Flushing, where

> the atmosphere is distractingly untraditional. There freeway traffic screams by; graffiti-splattered subway trains clank in and out of the local station; jet aircraft shriek up, up and away from neighboring La Guardia Airport. There, inside the concrete and steel stadium complex, the steeper vantage points are eerily remote from the court; the spectators, who seem to be evenly divided between corporate expense-account revelers and long-lost refugees from the Ebbets Field bleachers, are raucously authentic.[12]

Why, I would like to know, is "raucous" behavior more *authentic* than "mannerly" behavior? No wonder, to paraphrase one of Ebbets Field's more famous personalities, "nice guys finish last at Flushing Meadow." Bjorn Borg, one of the more gentlemanly of modern tennis millionaires, won the French Open six times and Wimbledon five times in a row but, in nine attempts, could never win the U.S. Open. After his defeat by Jimmy Connors in the finals of the first Open at Flushing Meadow in 1978, his coach and confidant, Lennart Bergelin, was enraged at the whole affair: "How can you have a championship like this—these lights, so bright and far away, everybody running in and out, the airplanes—this is not a tournament, but a circus—a circus! To play at night, this is the worst."[13] In a calmer mood on another occasion, Bergelin of course saw that playing under lights was dictated by money: "There is no other sport where the athlete can finish at midnight and have to play the next afternoon at two o'clock. I understand the theory behind the two gates—it's a way of selling more tickets. I just don't think that's as important as fairness and the player's health." Bergelin failed to notice that an even more important reason for night playing is the need to please the television networks. In 1982, for instance, the men's final was put off until after four o'clock (and hence the possible need for lights at the end) because Sunday afternoon prime time that day was appropriated by the opening games of the National Football League.

Herbert Warren Wind, dean of American tennis writers, was disenchanted by the uncivil atmosphere at Flushing Meadow from its inception in 1978. He wrote in 1980:

> On the eve of the United States Open Tennis Championships, I spent some time in the company of a dozen or so deeply involved tennis fans, who surprised me by agreeing, almost unanimously, that they seriously doubted whether they would ever be able to adjust to the championship's new home. . . . They cannot understand why the U.S.T.A. selected such a questionable site in the first place, and they are bewildered that, having chosen Flushing Meadow Park, it has made no real effort to turn it into a fine, functioning tennis capital, and seems content to accept the cheap, carnival-midway milieu that has emerged. They do not buy the rationalization that Flushing Meadow Park represents the new, more egalitarian world of American tennis. "I think we are all aware that sports have become a big industry," one of the more outspoken members of the group declared. "At Flushing Meadow, however, the whole operation is geared so specifically to money making from tennis that I am reminded of an Australian friend's definition of a sheep as a machine that turns grass into quid. . . . Much as I like to watch the great players in action, going out to Flushing Meadow strikes me as an ordeal, when by rights it should be a treat, a delight."[14]

It is significant that Wind's annual *New Yorker* article in 1983 was entitled "Order on the Court." After a judicious analysis of the problems of order and authority in tennis today, he ends with a comment on the complete commercialization of tennis at Flushing Meadow:

> Tennis is likely to remain the multimillion dollar international business that television has made it. . . . However, increased commercial restraint in tennis is certainly necessary. For example, many patrons of our Open were offended when, after the final match of each of the separate championships was played, the chairman of the U.S.T.A.'s Championships Committee stepped to the microphone and, over the public-address system, introduced an officer from whichever of the Open's commercial sponsors—say, a shampoo company—had contributed a goodly sum to the prize money

awarded the players in that particular division. The sponsor's spokesman then took over the microphone and presented the checks to the runner-up and winner, who, in their speeches, thanked the sponsor as well as their fans and the U.S.T.A. There is already too much money and fragmentation in tennis without this nonsense.[15]

How differently things are still done at Wimbledon where the finalists are presented their trophies (no visible signs of checks being passed) by the Duchess of Kent with her Duke standing by. A few polite words pass between the players and the royals, but no sound goes out to the television audience; the sound tracks are turned off. But perhaps the dignity of Wimbledon will not last, as the Anglo-American critic and novelist, Wilfred Sheed, has suggested:

Thus, in Flushing Meadow—the very name is like a warning—the U.S. Open may have become the first of the great roughneck tournaments [he wrote in 1982]. And if it were the last, it might at least be quaint. But my guess is that instead of Wimbledon being the model for all other tournaments, Flushing may be the future model for Wimbledon and the rest. Because these same crazy players go everywhere, whipping up an uproar like tent-preachers. And Wimbledon sounds noisier, less housebroken, already. (If it keeps up, Borg may not be able to win there either.)[16]

The British author Anthony Burgess, whose book *A Clockwork Orange* was a prophetic portrait of a world run by roughnecks, finds Wimbledon to be increasingly irrelevant to our modern age. He writes:

At Wimbledon, players who do not wish to be also gentlemen, or ladies, are not greatly wanted. The players themselves are ceasing to care. . . . This ought to signify that, like the capitalist state in Karl Marx's program, it will wither away. Make no mistake about it: it will not wither away. . . . Wimbledon is going to survive forever, but it will have less and less to do with tennis.[17]

═══

Stanford White, who surely ranks among a handful of the greatest architects in American history, saw architecture as an expressive and pictorial symbol, as a permanent set, of an age. And his Newport Casino, which seated fewer than 4,000 ladies and gentlemen by the time of our last National Championships there in 1914 (1,000 new seats had been added only that year), remains a classic symbol of the founding era of lawn tennis. When Herbert Warren Wind visited the Casino for the first time in 1965, he surely caught the spirit of that era when he wrote: "One enters the interior quadrangle through an archway of dull-red brick and comes into a strange, vanished world that suggests Dick Williams and Maurice McLoughlin less than it does that eminent mixed-doubles team of Edith Wharton and William Dean Howells."[18] Similarly, one enters the concrete bowl at Flushing Meadow Park, its interior splashed with advertisements, with the shocking recognition of how faithfully the whole thing reflects the values of our own age. It suggests, following Wind, not only the bad manners of Connors and McEnroe, but also the money- and sex-obsessed heroes of the books by the eminent moneymaking mixed-doubles team of Jacqueline Susanne and Harold Robbins.

While the Newport Casino was created by an eminent architect, Flushing Meadow was built in one year under the expert direction of the late William Ewing (Slew) Hester, Jr., of Jackson, Mississippi, the scion of a family of Copiah County politicians and the first United States Tennis Association president from the Deep South. An excellent tennis player and administrator (heading the Mississippi Tennis Association and the Southern Tennis Association), he was a man of wide and varied business experience, having been successively a salesman, head of a trucking company, and from 1962 onward an independent oil producer, or wildcatter. Though sensitive souls may have disliked the crass materialism of Flushing Meadow, Hester apparently was thoroughly pleased with his creation, according to an interview with *World Tennis* during the sixth championship there in 1983:

> Actually, I'm a traditionalist at heart. I like players to wear white and dislike the antagonism between players and umpires and all that. But I could do without tradition to achieve an American perception of the game of tennis, which I think we have done at Flushing Meadow.
>
> I think the National Tennis Center is just as American as apple pie. It's not Wimbledon because we don't have royalty. It is American because we have all the people. Some of them, in my mind, are not ready for tennis, they're not entitled to be part of a tennis crowd because they're boisterous and they don't wear shirts, but this country is a melting pot and this tournament is strictly American in the same way.[19]

If one takes the leveling *down* view of our *defiant* democracy, as opposed to the leveling *up* and *deference* democracy symbolized by Wimbledon, one can hardly argue with Hester's point of view; and the anti-heroes of the age of rudeness in professional tennis agreed with him. Thus in the same issue of *World Tennis*, Jimmy Connors was reported as saying: "I enjoy playing in front of animalistic crowds in New York because that's when I play my best tennis. I enjoy playing more in front of a crowd that gives me an attitude from watching as I have an attitude towards my game."[20] (No wonder he once paid for a term paper at UCLA!) Connors's friend Nastase also felt right at home in Flushing Meadow: "I feel like the crowd is for me. New York fans watch hockey in the winter, they watch football in the fall. It's not really a tennis crowd, it's mixed with everything. The crowd is very wild, very noisy. I love it."[21] Not all players, of course, felt the same way as Connors and Nastase: "You're playing in a park with people screaming all the time," the Australian Mark Edmundson told *World Tennis*. "The crowds are badly supervised. Simply put, it's the most difficult place in the world to play."[22]

In our age of equality and anti-authority, of course, both American crowds and professional tennis players in general are badly supervised. As Herbert Warren Wind wrote as far back as 1976: "Sometimes it seems that everyone in tennis is preoccupied with making money and no one is bothering about running the game properly."[23] This is still so today, two decades later (1994).

———

On his way to winning his first U.S. Open in 1979, McEnroe met Nastase in the second round and participated in a match which has become the supreme symbol of the roughneck age of tennis at Flushing Meadow: "Ilie Nastase vs. John McEnroe," wrote Richard Evans, "was the kind of match-up that any fight promoter would have willingly put into Madison Square Garden. And that, of course, was part of the problem." According to Evans, one of the best descriptions of that infamous evening at Flushing Meadow, often referred to since as the "Thursday Night Massacre," was written by the then dean of British tennis writers, Rex Bellamy, who wrote in part as follows:

When the U.S. Championship was moved to a public facility at Flushing Meadow, the gates were flung open to a rowdier breed of sports fans—

more interested in a hot dressing than a cold salad. It seemed a good idea at the time. The game would reach a wider public who could inject it with a little more vitality and a lot more dollars. The concept briefly turned sour, though, round about the midnight that separated Thursday from Friday during the first week of this year's championships. What happened then was the threat of a mob take-over, even mob violence. The bottom line was that the disqualification of Ilie Nastase was rescinded not because of any procedural error by the umpire or the referee but because the fans were dangerously angry. The fans will remember that decision.

John McEnroe beat Nastase 6–4, 4–6, 6–3, 6–2 in a three-hour match that produced the loveliest singles play of the week. With versatile shot-making, they improvised some breathtaking rallies. But the fans wanted more than that from two antiheroes who are not renowned for their composure or dignity. It didn't help that this obviously combustible contest was scheduled for the second match in the evening—a time when the inhibitions of the 10,549 spectators had been loosened by alcoholic voices. It didn't help that the crowd decided that Nastase was their boy, that provocative anti-McEnroe barracking was part of the script. It didn't help that the fans were ignorant of the point penalty system and that no one explained it to them.

Frank Hammond . . . is a fine umpire and a warm, charming man. But the circus had come to town and the ringmaster was having a bad night. . . . What brought the pot to the boil was Hammond's ultimate application of the point penalty system. With McEnroe serving at 2–1 in the fourth set, he was controversially granted a point for a service Nastase said he was not ready to return. Nastase protested and so—more clamorously—did the crowd. Hammond then awarded McEnroe the game. Thus began a 17-minute interruption enforced by wildly angry scenes. The din was almost terrifying; chanting, cat-calls, boos, and the rest. The trash thrown on court included beer cans and cups. Fighting broke out in the crowd. An invasion of the court seemed imminent. Police and security men were summoned. Hammond—now reinforced by the referee Mike Blanchard—appealed to the players to get the show on the road because there seemed no other way of pacifying the public. But Nastase, 1–3 down, refused to serve. Finally, on Blanchard's instructions, Hammond "put the clock" on him. Having allowed Nastase 58 seconds instead of the official thirty, Hammond awarded the game, set, and match to McEnroe.

The tournament director, Bill Talbert, then decided that the threat of a riot was serious. He reckoned the only way to restore order was to overrule the Blanchard-Hammond decision, dismiss Hammond, and resume the match with Blanchard in the chair. Frank Smith, the Grand Prix Supervisor, agreed. Their judgment may or may not have been sound. Perhaps they—or even Blanchard—should have moved sooner by suspending the match or replacing Hammond. Perhaps so many things. . . .

As a last word on the whole unsavory business, it is possible to feel sympathy for everyone involved—except the minority of spectators who obviously came to see a brawl, even if they had to provoke it themselves.[24]

As an Englishman and a guest in America, Bellamy was too polite to do more than carefully document the rowdy behavior that night and early morning at Flushing Meadow. Richard Evans and Gene Scott, surely among the best tennis journalists, however, seemed to see the rowdy behavior as inevitable in a sport which they were pleased to see had become more and more successful and popular in the Flushing era. "Reality is no longer clothed in white flannels," wrote Evans in his discussion of rowdy behavior in his biography of McEnroe. "Gene Scott got it about right," he continued, "when he wrote in *Tennis Week*":

We have entered a new era of spectator tennis. And those who insist we return to the fans of yesteryear with jackets and ties and "excuse me's" after an audible cough are out of touch. Professional football, baseball, and ice hockey have had raucous scenes in the stands for years. Fighting and violence on and off the field are commonplace—however distasteful we find it.[25]

Evans apparently was even more pleased than Scott with the notoriety brought to their beloved game by the likes of Nastase and McEnroe and the Flushing atmosphere in general when he wrote:

But however much the purists and traditionalists want to keep it as a sport locked behind pristine doors for the exclusive use of ladies and gentlemen of a certain class, the hard facts of the matter remain that tennis desperately needs the wider appeal that characters like Nastase bring it. . . . During the twelve days of the 1979 U.S. Open only one person connected with the game had their photograph displayed on the *front* page of the New York *Post* on three different days. Needless to say that person was Ilie Nastase—and he had lost in the second round.[26]

In contrast to Evans, I should think that tennis lovers of all classes would *desperately* want to *discourage* the wider appeal that characters like Nastase brought to Flushing Meadow. And let us remember that, in those ancient amateur days when tennis was "locked behind pristine doors," tennis lovers and tennis players from all walks of life were welcome in the stands of all the better tournaments. Even in the most snobbish days of the "400" at Newport, when the very proper Philadelphia millionaire R. Norris Williams beat his good friend Maurice McLoughlin, who learned the game on the public courts at San Francisco, in the 1914 finals before some 4,000 spectators, there were a goodly number of "townies" and locals in the stands who had no monetary or social standing but nevertheless loved and appreciated the game. These same kind of people, in 1979, however, were and still are denied access to the 5,431 seats at Flushing Meadow with a decent view of the court. Such seats are permanently sold out to a handful of millionaires and a host of corporations (see Figure 28). The waiting list for these seats (which cost $500 to $550 each back then) was so long that the director of corporate promotions for the USTA instructed her staff not to add any more names to the list. "There's no point," she said. "Applicants won't live that long. No one gives them up. They leave them in their wills!" Such was the pure dollar democracy at egalitarian Flushing Meadow on that infamous Thursday night in 1979.

═══

After reaching the semifinals at his first Wimbledon in 1977, McEnroe had two bad years there, losing in the second round in 1978, and in the fourth round in 1979. Finally, in 1980, he reached the finals where he played the finest tennis of his career while losing to Bjorn Borg in a five-set match which was one of the best ever played in Wimbledon history.

Bjorn Borg was the best tennis player in the world (some said of all time) when he came to seek his fifth straight win at Wimbledon. He played on the Swedish Davis Cup team at the age of 15 in 1972, and he won the first of six French titles at the age of 17, in 1974. The next year he led the Swedish Davis Cup team to its first ever victory in the challenge round. In 1976, he won his first of five straight Wimbledons (including his last in 1980). In 1979, he became the first man to win over a million dollars in prize money in a single year; he was worth some five

FIGURE 28

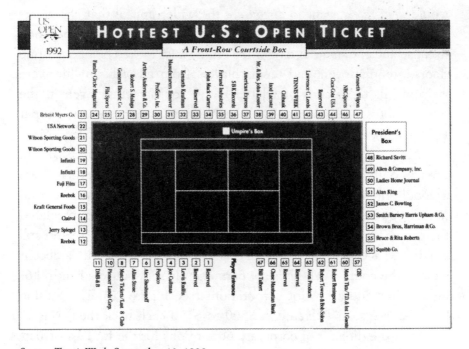

Source: Tennis Week, September 10, 1992.

million by the end of 1980. Perhaps most important of all, Borg was the first in a steady stream of first-rate, Swedish tennis players to reach world-class rankings, among them Mats Wilander, World Number One in 1988 and Stefan Edberg, World Number One in 1990–91 All of the Swedish players, from Borg through Edberg, have had impeccable court manners.

The dramatic classic between Borg and McEnroe in the 1980 Wimbledon final was best described by Richard Evans in Eugene Scott's *Tennis Week,* one of the more thoughtful tennis magazines. "For once," Evans wrote, "the statistics alone reveal something of the drama. Bjorn Borg became Wimbledon Champion for the fifth successive year by defeating John McEnroe 1–6, 7–5, 6–3, 6–7, 8–6 with the fourth-set tie-break stretching to eighteen points to sixteen. McEnroe eventually won that set on his seventh set point and Borg finally won the match on his eight match point. And if further evidence is needed for just how close this three-hour fifty-three-minute marathon really was, the total number of points and games won and lost will do. Borg won 190 points to McEnroe's 186 and 28 games to his opponent's 27."[27]

As the great final fades into history almost everyone who saw it will always remember the famous fourth set and lengthy tie break which Richard Evans described as follows:

> At 4–4 in the magnificent fourth set, Borg forced another breach in the New Yorker's armor. Again it was his ability to meet McEnroe's sizzling first serve, which flew at him off the apex of the service box, with a crushing cross-court return that earned him the break, and when he reached double match-point at 40–15 in the next game, we prepared for the end.
>
> It was then that the twenty-one year old American wrote himself into the folklore of the game, proving, for those who still doubted it, that his strength of character matched his skill. He hit Bjorn with a firm back-hand pass down the line on the first match-point and a forehand pass on the second, and the crowd realized the Swede was not the only player out there with nerves of steel.
>
> A great back-hand service return sealed the break back and soon we were into the historic tie-break. It stretched over twenty-two minutes and thirty-four points—more than would be needed to win an entire set 6–1—and was so finely balanced that match-points and set-points seemed to ricochet back and forth across the court with the blur of syncopated rhythm. The sequence built crisis by crisis with Borg reaching two match-points (his third and fourth of the match) at 6–5 and 7–6; then McEnroe with two set-points; then Borg back on the threshold again with three more match-points and then a run of four set-points for the American before he clinched it on the fifth with a heavily top-spun service return that was dipping too quickly for Borg to control as he tried an ambitious stop volley.
>
> The Centre Court erupted. John McEnroe Senior was out of his seat and Junior was clenching his fists and staring at the heavens. Two sets all; the greatest title in tennis still up for grabs. Could the implacable Swede—the Centre Court's immovable object for the past four years—hold onto his treasured crown? Once again the answer was yes.[28]

After this great Wimbledon triumph, Borg had high hopes of winning his first U.S. Open title at Flushing Meadow. But he lost once again, in a brilliant five-setter, to McEnroe in the finals. The battle at Flushing took four hours and thirteen minutes, or twenty minutes longer than the Wimbledon classic. Having won both at Roland Garros and at Wimbledon, however, Borg was ranked number one that year for the last time. The next year McEnroe won the number one ranking for the first time, beating Borg in the finals at Wimbledon and Flushing Meadow (both in four sets). After his second loss in a row to McEnroe in the finals at Flushing Meadow, Borg walked off the court before the presentation ceremonies. Not long afterwards, he announced his withdrawal from the pro tour.

====

"London has got to be the most civil, civilized city in the world," wrote Arthur Ashe, the thinking man's favorite American tennis player, in his diary during the Wimbledon Championships of 1973. And every thinking man knows that all the democracy and freedom in the world will never create civility, which, on the contrary, may well be the major prerequisite of both. During the 1980s, even Londoners were witnessing a steady decline in civility, highlighted in July of 1981 when gangs of white, black, and Asian youths roamed and rioted in its streets, as urban England in general was experiencing its worst riots in over a century.

That same summer, Arthur Ashe, an honorary member of the All-England Club and captain of the American Davis Cup team, was a spectator at Wimbledon when McEnroe won the Gentlemen's Championship for the first time. If McEnroe's uncivilized court manner was a disgrace to himself and his country, his failure to show up at the traditional champions' dinner and ball at the Savoy was unprecedented in its rudeness. Unlike Ashe and other champions before him, McEnroe was *not* made an honorary member of the All England Club: "I've never seen Wimbledon so mad, I mean burning," said Ashe, as reported in *Sports Illustrated*. "Not even when Connors insulted the Queen by not showing up for the centenary celebrations in 1977."[29]

All through the Wimbledon tournament that year, McEnroe displayed an adolescent sense of injustice untempered by any sense of adult civility: "Never in the history of the sport," wrote two Wimbledon historians, "was there so public a display—taken round the world by television—of bad court manners when temperament caused him to go beyond acceptability in his opening match on Court One against Tom Gullikson. His offensiveness to the officials—including the phrase 'You're the pits of the world' as a term of abuse—was established as an example of what sportsmanship should not be."[30] In an interminable and trying semifinal match against an unseeded Australian, he threw no less than thirteen tantrums, articulated in unprintable language. After one particularly crude outburst, Lady Diana Spencer left the royal box: "The wedding's off," a spectator was heard to say. "Her ears are no longer virgin." McEnroe even revealed his own special brand of racial justice when, in the course of a doubles match against the Amritraj brothers from India, he accused a dark-skinned linesman wearing a turban of "bias." No wonder Vijay Amritraj, an impeccable gentleman on the court and the Champion of India, once remarked that if he had to win Wimbledon by acting like McEnroe, he wouldn't want it. McEnroe's fellow countrymen have been ambivalent about his behavior from the beginning, as the following two letters to the editor of *World Tennis* (September 1981) suggest:

> Not only did John McEnroe insult his British hosts, disgrace himself, and degenerate the game of tennis; he betrayed his country. He reinforced the American image our enemies like to promote, the image of Americans as spoiled and domineering children. . . .
>
> Hooray for John McEnroe! After all the garbage he had to take from the British press and the All England Club he deserved to win Wimbledon. And I hope the Wimbledon Committee has nightmares remembering it.[31]

Richard Evans, after twenty-one years of reporting the Wimbledon Championships, was surprised and rather hurt when his admired friend, Dan Maskell, then the Voice of Wimbledon on the BBC, told him: "I found McEnroe's behavior so offensive that it completely ruined my enjoyment of this year's Wimbledon." In his excellent and sympathetic first biography of McEnroe, Evans devoted a whole chapter to an explanation of how and why the McEnroe family failed to attend the championship dinner at the Savoy; here I should only like to quote McEnroe's father, who ended his explanation of why he advised his son not to attend the affair on the following note: "But insisting that the champion sit through a formal two-hour dinner making small talk to people he barely knew was beyond my comprehension." It is surely hard to imagine how a partner in one of New York's more prestigious law firms could have failed to notice that the most honored leaders in any civilized profession spend countless hours at tedious testimonial dinners making small talk with their professional peers and their wives. On the other hand, he may only be reflecting the fact that his son is only a pro tennis player with no sense of the duties which the practice of any true profession demands. At any rate, McEnroe Senior's reasoning helps to explain why his son finds the civilizing rituals of life little more than hypocritical "bullshit" as he once implied on another occasion: "I was watching Prince Charles and Princess Diana on television this evening," McEnroe said to Evans some time after the royal wedding. "They were on tour of Wales or something. I really feel sorry for that girl. All day she has to smile and go through all that bullshit."[32]

John McEnroe had his last and greatest year at the top of world tennis in 1984. He reached the finals at Roland Garros for the first and only time in his career. After winning the first two sets, however, he lost to Ivan Lendl in five. He then went on to win Wimbledon and the U.S. Open with ease, beating Connors in England 6–1, 6–1, 6–2 and Lendl in America 6–3, 6–4, 6–1. As in 1980, his court triumphs were accompanied by sudden outbursts of rude and uncivil behavior. For one thing, he continued his previous year's rudeness in Paris where he called an official a "fucking French frog fag" and shouted at the fans, "I hate this country." While beating Jimmy Connors in the French semifinals in 1984, he was so rude and obnoxious that Connors yelled at him saying "Shut up. Grow up. I've got a son your age." After losing the final to Lendl, he swiped a French cameraman with his racquet and cracked his lens, cutting one of the cameraman's fingers in the process.

═══

The two leading American tennis journals of that day, *World Tennis*, "the magazine of the membership of the United States Tennis Association," and *Tennis*, which boasts "the largest circulation of any tennis publication," took somewhat contrasting views of the state of the art of American tennis as of the fall of 1984.*

World Tennis was almost euphoric about the virtues of Flushing Meadow in its "Special: U.S. Open Preview" issue. Eulogies of so-called democracy verged on the defensive. Neil Amdur, a distinguished tennis journalist and the newly appointed Editor-in-Chief, had only unrestrained praise for

---

*World Tennis has since ceased publication and *Tennis* is now the semiofficial organ of the USTA.

Flushing Meadow. "The U.S. Open," he wrote in the opening line of his September editorial, "is my favorite tournament. . . . More than any single tournament, the Open has soul." He was especially proud of the fact that, although "corporations now control an uncommonly high percentage of tickets, . . . the Open has remained a people's tournament." In the course of the editorial, he reflected the deadly fear of boredom which afflicts our aimlessly affluent democracy: "The Open is never dull," he wrote. "Pick out almost any year, and you will find a multitude of controversies—anti-apartheid demonstrations, a spectator getting shot in the stands, and fans chanting 'Hell no, we won't go,' when officials tried to evict them prematurely from an afternoon session." "I hope the Open never changes," he concludes. "Tennis is a sport in need of soul, and the Open's sweat, vitality, intensity and insanity is refreshing."[33]

In a more brassy article in the same issue of *World Tennis* on the "Do's and Don't's for the U.S. Open," a contributing editor, Mike Lupica, who once wrote of the beauties of Flushing Meadow in terms of its proximity to Manhattan nightlife, added a few hilarious hints on how to enjoy the tournament: "Okay, okay. So there are things in tennis I don't know." But, he continued, "I know the United States Open, the one played at the National Tennis Center, is the greatest tennis tournament in the world at the greatest site. And I know the site is just twenty minutes from Manhattan, the only civilized place left on earth. That's why I feel obligated to offer a humble list of Do's and Don't's for this year's Open."

Among Lupica's perceptive Do's were:

The No. 7 Train: Take the subway at least once to the national Tennis Center, especially if you're from out of town. You've heard of "the melting pot"? It's on the 7 Train. But I wouldn't do my Fila warm-up on the old 7, or go on and on about the *fabulous* crab meat quiche I had at the tournament the day before. Instead, I'd keep a close watch on my wallet.

Among the Don't's:

Airplanes: I don't want to hear one bitch from the players about airplanes flying over matches. I mean it. If the roar of the airplanes is too much for someone out there playing for zillions of American dollars, here's my advice: Don't come to the Open. Hey, this is New York. We got noise here.

Nostalgia: If you want to wax nostalgic about the Good Old Days at West Side Tennis Club, stay away. West Side was a closed club for snobs. It is from an American tennis era well left dead. The National Tennis Center is a joy, and it is for everyone.

Tickets: Don't ask me. I don't have any. . . .

In striking contrast to *World Tennis*'s defensive rationalizations of the rowdy tone at Flushing Meadow as merely a reflection of our Democratic Soul, the November issue of *Tennis* magazine courageously confronted the absence of civilized authority in modern American tennis in a beautifully written editorial by Arthur S. Hayes entitled "MAC THE MOUTH: Next Time Ban Him for a Year." Hayes carefully and objectively documented the long list of rude incidents which had marked McEnroe's seven-year career of increasingly more brilliant tennis combined with behavior which continually "shocks anyone with the slightest trace of civility." It is my impression that not a single one of the 48 gentlemen who have won the United States Singles Championship, from Richard Sears to Arthur Ashe, would disagree with the mature tone of the editorial. Even that impish master-gamesman, Bobby Riggs, probably chortled in agreement. At any rate, Hayes pointed out that most of McEnroe's peers were sick of his unsportsmanlike gamesmanship and adolescent behavior.

At the end of the editorial, there followed a brief psychological profile of McEnroe by Allen Fox, a former world-class player and Ph.D. in psychology, who coached the tennis powerhouse at Pepperdine University. After a very sensitive and sympathetic character analysis, Allen concluded as follows:

McEnroe is trying to change. . . . It is a slow process because his desire to control himself is intellectual, and intellect and emotion mix about as well as oil and water. . . . Errant children are controlled more quickly by fear of punishment than they are by reasoning. The tennis authorities could help McEnroe reform sooner if they were willing and able to impose penalties that are severe enough to scare him.[34]

It is no accident that this *Tennis* editorial came out about the same time as a *Time* magazine cover story (November 5, 1984) entitled: "Mind Your Manners: The New Concern for Civility." Ever since 1978 (the first Flushing Year) when the editors of the *Washington Post* reluctantly allowed her to write an etiquette column as *Miss Manners*, the subject of the *Time* story, Judith Martin, had been an increasing success. Americans were yearning for a return of manners, and most of her flood of mail came from young people. "One of the biggest sorrows in America is that people want to retaliate against rudeness," she wrote. "One of my main missions is to say, no, there is no excuse for rudeness." Judith Martin was not only a popular success, she was also increasingly respected in the academic community. Thus she was invited to give one of the John M. Olin Distinguished Lectures in Philosophy and Free Institutions, at Harvard. She might well have been answering those who praise the *authenticity* of bad manners at Flushing Meadow, when she told the Harvard audience that "The belief that natural behavior is beautiful and that civilization and its manners spoil the essential goodness inherent in all of us noble savages is, of course, the Jean-Jacques Rousseau school of etiquette . . . which survives in the child-rearing philosophy that has given us so many little—savages." It is finally interesting that President Reagan was referred to several times in the *Time* cover story. Among the numerous professors of etiquette springing up all over the modern landscape, Marjabelle Stewart was quoted as saying: "One of the greatest things this President has brought is good manners. He shows you can be nice to your wife and comfortable with her admiring you. It's a fabulous example of American manners." At one time, Stewart had almost five hundred apostles around the country who were teaching "White Gloves and Party Manners" at $15 an hour; enrollment tripled in the first two years.

In its failure to properly discipline McEnroe, the American tennis establishment was still living in an Age of Aquarius which even a goodly majority of youthful voters repudiated in November 1984. In this new climate of manners-seeking opinion then, it came as no surprise that the "MAC THE MOUTH" editorial drew the greatest response in *Tennis* magazine's history: "In nearly twenty years of publication," the editors wrote in the January issue," no article in *Tennis* magazine has provoked anything close to the reaction stirred up by our November editorial. . . . We called upon the sport's authorities simply to do what pro tennis' rules say they can. Suspend a player for a year when his pattern of misconduct violates established guidelines." Although it is rare for readers to phone a writer about an article, Hayes began to receive calls as soon as the issue appeared. Of course, any publication always hears more from those who are *against* what they write. What surprised the editors was the number of readers who wrote and phoned in *support* of the editorial: "McEnroe has riled up enough fans sufficiently so that the mail is running only slightly in his favor." It is hard to imagine even a handful of tennis lovers before 1968 supporting McEnroe's behavior.

After printing some two dozen letters from its readers, the editors inserted a brief editorial in a box at the bottom of the page: "A week after the November 1984 issue of *Tennis* magazine hit the newsstands," they wrote, "McEnroe unleashed a vintage temper tantrum during the semifinals of the Stockholm Open." After describing his boorish behavior, which I myself and millions of other Americans saw over and over again on the evening news programs at the time, the editorial noted that he was fined a mere $2,100 and suspended for twenty-one days because he had gone over the yearly $7,500 limit. "Clearly," they concluded, "McEnroe has established 'a pattern of conduct.' . . . The council had a chance to act upon *Tennis'* call for a one-year suspension of McEnroe. But it didn't, and the game is the worse for its timidity."

John McEnroe, along with his Davis Cup partner, James Connors (whom he actively disliked), returned to Sweden soon after his suspension ran out. The United States lost the first three matches in a row in the Davis Cup finals held in Göteborg. Connors was almost disqualified for rude and crude behavior on the first day. On the second day, McEnroe and Peter Fleming lost their first Davis Cup doubles match ever. Though McEnroe salvaged one point on the third day, the supposedly greatest imperial power in the world was humiliated by little Sweden in a 4–1 loss.

The remaining years of the 1980s were dominated by Europeans; no American won either Wimbledon or Flushing Meadow for the rest of the decade. McEnroe never again won a Grand Slam title and his world ranking dropped to third in 1985, ninth in 1986, tenth in 1987, and out of the First Ten in 1988. In 1989, he made a big effort and brought himself up to a number four ranking; he was optimistic about his tennis when he took his family out to Australia at Christmastime, expecting to play in the Australian Open in January.

═══

The supreme symbolic end of the roughneck era came on the seventh day of the Australian Open when McEnroe was defaulted in a fourth-round match against Michael Pernfors, a low-ranking Swede educated at the University of Georgia. For the first three rounds, according to John Feinstein, McEnroe had been the talk of the tournament. He won his three matches with ease and seemed to have regained his old, and incomparable, touch. Then, at 5:30 on Sunday afternoon, January 21, 1990, the ax fell. In the fourth set, McEnroe was first given a warning for glaring menacingly at a lineswoman and then a point penalty for abusing his racket or, in nonjargon English, smashing his racquet on the court. McEnroe then put up what he knew was a hopeless argument. The supervising official of all Grand Slam tournaments, Ken Farrar, was called in on the dispute. Just as he was walking off the court, McEnroe, enraged at having lost the argument, yelled at him in a loud voice: "Go fuck your mother." Farrar turned around, saying that "no player has ever spoken to me that way," and walked over to the umpire, an ex-British footballer, who had also been enraged by the filthy remark. They conferred a moment and then the umpire made the unprecedented announcement: "Verbal abuse, audible obscenity, Mr. McEnroe. Default, Game, set, and match, Pernfors." The next day the story was on the front page of almost every newspaper in the world.

Several things should be said about McEnroe's tragic default in Australia. In the first place, the default should have come far earlier in his career. As Denis Ralston, a leading coach in the open era who, as an amateur, had been suspended by the USLTA just before Forest Hills in the early sixties, told Richard Evans as they were milling around after the match in a small group discussing the incredible McEnroe default: "I was mad as hell at the time. But I have no doubt at all that it did me good. I needed straightening out and I am sure John would have benefited from a much stricter discipline right at the start of his career." He should have been suspended by the wimpy American authorities during that disgraceful match with Nastase, at Flushing Meadow in 1979, the year he won his first Open Championship. He should have been defaulted in an early round at Wimbledon, in 1984, the year he played in the greatest final of the open era. Second, it is important to note that American officialdom would never have had the guts to defy the fans and television officialdom by defaulting McEnroe at Flushing Meadow.

Nineteen-ninety was the second great watershed year in the history of open tennis: just as Jimmy Connors's defeat of Arthur Ashe in the 1972 finals at Forest Hills marked the beginning of the roughneck age of American tennis, so 1990, when Pete Sampras became the first American to win the U.S. Open since McEnroe's win in 1984, marked the end of the roughneck era and the coming to the fore of America's third generation, led at the moment by Sampras, Chang, Courier, and Agassi. It is too early to judge this third generation, but it can surely be said that "Sweet Pete" Sampras has nothing in common as a person with "Mac the Mouth" McEnroe; they both, however, have exciting, one-handed, serve-and-volley, all-court games, quite in contrast to the, to me, thoroughly boring two-handed base-line bangers of the Bollettieri school, Andre Agassi and Jim Courier; the acrobatic retriever, Michael Chang, is also a two-handed baseliner who, nevertheless, is always a pleasure to watch for his gutsy persistence alone.

The preoccupation with making money, especially in America as symbolized by the whole atmosphere at Flushing Meadow, lies at the very root of the corruption of discipline and all right use of authority in American professional tennis today. And it is my impression that the whoring after money both among officials and players is increasing in the third generation. Thus, Peter Sampras went on from his victory at Flushing Meadow to take part in a new moneymaking event, the Grand Slam Cup, held in Munich, Germany, in December. He took home two million dollars after defeating Brad Gilbert, (a money-hungry American if there ever was one), in three easy sets. When John McEnroe heard of this event, he was enraged and said: "They are trying to turn us into money whores. It's obscene. None of us should play unless a large percentage of the prize money is donated to charity."[35]

How right McEnroe was on this one; and how right he has almost always been when discussing a wide variety of issues having to do with professional tennis. I have always been painfully ambivalent about the "super-brat," hating his foul language and unforgivable behavior on the court while admiring his sane and sound comments on the state of the game.

Ever since I taught one of John's Trinity School classmates and a fellow tennis player there, I have felt that McEnroe behaved so badly because of a deep-down resentment of the *phoney* values of pro tennis. For, as my student said of their school days, John was forever calling his opponent's bad shots good and never arguing over bad calls by his opponents. I therefore was delighted to read the following paragraph in Richard Evans's second book on McEnroe:

Then and now John McEnroe is at heart the true amateur sportsman. I realize how preposterous that may sound to anyone who has only observed the millionaire athlete screaming his head off at some underpaid linesman. But that is McEnroe all wound up in the competitive arena. In a sense, he becomes a different human being the moment he walks on court to play a match. But there is an equally real side to him that, in an earlier, calmer age, would have fitted perfectly into the world of amateur sports as it was played—and still is played for that matter—at Oxford and Cambridge and the Queen's Club on a Saturday afternoon. One can just see him wandering around Queen's with his socks round his ankles, clad in the same pair of wrinkled shorts that he had worn to whip some bemused opponent the week before, his school scarf trailing from his neck. Once on court the same intensity would have been evident. But generally, both on court and off, I suspect that McEnroe would have been much happier amidst the camaraderie of the amateur sporting world with its code of honor than the code of conduct he faces on today's cut-throat professional circuit.[36]

Never has the bitter truth been better said.

Looking back at the careers of John Patrick McEnroe, Jr., and William Tatum Tilden, Jr., I am impressed with the fact that, in the 1980s, McEnroe dominated the imaginations of tennis lovers and sports fans in general to almost the same extent as Tilden did in the 1920s. Although both men were original, sui generis geniuses, they nevertheless had much in common: both were the sons of very successful, self-made men; both were momma's boys, both graduated from fine old private schools, both dropped out of college; both were tennis artists who loved their art in an amateur way; both had broader interests than most of their tennis peers; both loved music and were appreciators of the fine arts in general; both were brilliant spoilers on the court, not only because of their irritating temperaments but largely because their wide variety of shots, used with the touch of genius, always kept their opponent off balance. Finally, if Tilden was a gentleman possessed by genius, McEnroe was a genius obsessed by the ungentlemanly phoniness of so much of the pro tour. While Tilden played a number of memorable classic tennis matches, McEnroe played only one of lasting memory (which he lost to Borg at Wimbledon). But this, I think, was due to the differences between the amateur and professional games: while the fine arts speak to the ages, commercial art, made for money at the moment, has little of lasting value (see Figure 26).

In May of that watershed year of 1990, Ted Tinling, six-foot-seven guru of modern tennis, died within a month of his eightieth year and the beginning of the Championships at his beloved Wimbledon. From the age of 17, in 1927, he had lived in the inner circles of the tennis world; he had known most of the great players from Suzanne Lenglen and Tilden to McEnroe and Steffi Graf, many of them his good friends. Before he died, according to John Feinstein, he had come to the pessimistic conclusion that the players on the pro tour were destined to follow in the footsteps of the tragic heroes in Richard Wagner's *Ring* operas: in *Götterdämmerung*, the fourth and final opera, all the Gods perished, destroyed by their own greed and selfishness: "Great and Godlike as all these players are," Tinling reluctantly concluded, "the sport will have to be destroyed—and then completely rebuilt again—before it will ever be sane. Ever since the game's been professional, there's been nothing but chaos. Now, they all smack their lips and count their money. It won't last, though. It can't."[37]

John McEnroe would undoubtedly agree with the Ring theory of his sport, as would his young German friend, Boris Becker.

FIGURE 29

Tennis Hall of Fame Enshrinees

	Year Enshrined		Year Enshrined
Pauline Betz Addie	1965	Art Larsen	1969
George Adee	1964	Rod Laver	1981
Fred Alexander	1961	Suzanne Lenglen	1978
Wilmer Allison	1963	George Lott	1964
Manuel Alonso	1977	Gene Mako	1973
Arthur Ashe	1985	Molla Bjurstedt Mallory	1958
Juliette Atkinson	1974	Alice Marble	1964
Tracy Austin	1992	Alastair Martin	1973
Lawrence A. Baker, Sr.	1975	William McC. Martin	1982
Maud Barger-Wallach	1958	Kathleen McKane Godfree	1978
Karl Behr	1969	Chuck McKinley	1986
Bjorn Borg	1987	Maurice McLoughlin	1957
Jean Borotra	1976	Frew McMillan	1992
Maureen Connolly Brinker	1968	Don McNeill	1965
John Bromwich	1984	Elisabeth Moore	1971
Norman E. Brookes	1977	Gardnar Mulloy	1972
May Sutton Bundy	1956	R. Lindley Murray	1958
Louise Brough Clapp	1967	Julian S. Myrick	1963
Mary K. Browne	1957	Ilie Nastase	1991
Jacques Brugnon	1976	John Newcombe	1986
Don Budge	1964	Arthur C. Nielsen, Sr.	1971
Maria Bueno	1978	Betty Nuthall Shoemaker	1977
Mabel Cahill	1976	Alex Olmedo	1987
Oliver S. Campbell	1955	Margaret Osborne duPont	1967
Malcolm Chace	1961	Rafael Osuna	1979
Philippe Chatrier	1992	Mary E. Outerbridge	1981
Clarence M. Clark	1983	Sarah Palfrey Danzig	1963
Joseph S. Clark	1955	Frank Parker	1966
William J. Clothier	1956	Budge Patty	1977
Henri Cochet	1976	Theodore R. Pell	1966
Ashley Cooper	1991	Fred Perry	1975
Gottfried von Cramm	1977	Tom Pettitt	1982
John H. Crawford	1979	Nicola Pietrangeli	1986
Joseph F. Cullman 3rd	1990	Adrian Quist	1984
Allison Danzig	1968	Dennis Ralson	1987
Dwight Davis	1956	Ernest Renshaw	1983
Lottie Dod	1983	William Renshaw	1983
John Doeg	1962	Vincent Richards	1961
Lawrence Doherty	1980	Bobby Riggs	1967
Reginald Doherty	1980	Tony Roche	1986
Jaroslav Drobny	1983	Ellen C. Roosevelt	1975
James Dwight	1955	Ken Rosewall	1980
Roy Emerson	1982	Dorothy Round Little	1986
Pierre Etchebaster	1978	Elizabeth "Bunny" Ryan	1972
Bob Falkenburg	1974	Manuel Santana	1984
Neale Fraser	1984	Dick Savitt	1976
Shirley Fry-Irvin	1970	Ted Schroeder	1966
Charles S. Garland	1969	Eleonora R. Sears	1968
Althea Gibson	1971	Richard D. Sears	1955
Pancho Gonzales	1968	Frank Sedgman	1979
Evonne Goolagong Cawley	1988	"Pancho" Segura	1984
Bryan M. "Bitsy" Grant	1972	Vic Seixas	1971
David Gray	1985	Frank Shields	1964
Clarence Griffin	1970	Henry W. Slocum, Jr.	1955
Gustaf V, King of Sweden	1980	Margaret Smith Court	1979
Harold H. Hackett	1961	Stan Smith	1987
Ellen Hansell	1965	Fred Stolle	1985
Darlene Hard	1973	Bill Talbert	1967
Doris Hart	1969	Bill Tilden	1959
Ann Haydon Jones	1985	Lance Tingay	1982
Gladys Heldman	1979	Ted Tinling	1986
William E. "Slew" Hester, Jr.	1981	Bertha Townsend Toulmin	1974
Bob Hewitt	1992	Tony Trabert	1970
Lew Hoad	1980	James Van Alen	1965
Hazel Hothkiss Wightman	1957	John Van Ryn	1963
Harry Hopman	1978	Guillermo Vilas	1991
Fred Hovey	1974	Ellsworth Vines	1962
Joseph R. Hunt	1966	Virginia Wade	1989
Francis T. Hunter	1961	Marie Wagner	1969
Helen Hull Jacobs	1962	Holcombe Ward	1965
William M. Johnston	1958	Watson Washburn	1965
Perry Jones	1970	Malcolm D. Whitman	1955
Billie Jean King	1987	Anthony F. Wilding	1978
Jan Kodes	1990	Richard N. Williams, 2nd	1957
Jack Kramer	1968	Helen Wills Moody Roark	1959
Rene Lacoste	1976	Sidney Wood	1964
Dorothea Lambert Chambers	1981	Robert D. Wrenn	1955
Al Laney	1979	Beals C. Wright	1956
William A. Larned	1956		

EPILOGUE

The subjects of Constantine were incapable of discerning the decline of genius and manly virtue, which so far degraded them below the dignity of their ancestors; but they could feel and lament the rage of tyranny, the relaxation of discipline, and the increase of taxes.
>   —Edward Gibbon

BETWEEN 1588, WHEN A FLEET OF AMATEUR ADVENTURERS LED BY DARING Francis Drake defeated the Spanish Armada, the greatest professional navy of that day, and 1914, when thousands of volunteers from the public schools of England as well as Oxford and Cambridge gave their lives on the Western Front, the British gentleman became a model of civilized man, respected and envied throughout the world. At the Great War's close, a transatlantic class of Anglo-American, amateur gentlemen still stood for an authority at home and abroad which gradually declined in the postwar decades. As I write, in our increasingly classless and bureaucratic world, the gentleman's descendants in America and in England have abdicated authority, not only over their wives and children but also over their nations and the world.

———

Throughout this book, especially in the last chapter, I have had a lot to say about the decline of the gentlemanly ideal in modern America, as symbolized by Flushing Meadow. At the same time, I have tended to uphold Wimbledon as the last bastion of this Anglo-American ideal, which Anthony Burgess so beautifully described in an article written for *World Tennis* in 1983:

> Wimbledon, mecca of tennis, is also the mecca of the British upper-class sports theology. . . . Both cricket and tennis, to the British ruling class, symbolized a system of conduct and decorum that, like the British Constitution, had better not be exactly formulated and certainly must not be written down. We all know what is meant by the phrase, "It's not cricket." The Nazis were not cricketers, and they took war seriously. The Charge of the Light Brigade was not war, but it showed a sporting attitude fit to be commemorated by Alfred Lord Tennyson, whom James Joyce called Alfred Lawn Tennison, gentleman poet. Wimbledon . . . is for ladies and gentlemen.[1]

But Burgess was writing of a fading ruling class, for, ever since the revolutionary year of 1968, the British, especially the children of the ruling class, have been engaged in an egalitarian crusade against most of the values the English gentleman once stood for. Two examples come to mind: in the first place, a witty Scotsman possessed of a persuasive pen, George MacDonald Fraser, published no less than ten best-selling (in both England and America) historical novels, between 1969 and 1990, slyly ridiculing Thomas Arnold's ideal of the Christian Gentleman, as popularized in Thomas Hughes's *Tom Brown's School Days* (1857). Fraser's fictional hero was Harry Paget Flashman, Tom Brown's Rugby classmate, who was booted out of the school for "ungentlemanly conduct." The mood of England's anti-gentleman generation is nicely suggested by the blurbs on the back of the American paperback edition of the first book in the Flashman series (see Figure 30).

In the Flashman era, as one might expect, barely a handful of English tennis players have earned computer rankings of less than 100; the only two English Wimbledon Champions were women—Ann Jones in 1969, and Virginia Wade in 1977—who was born in Bournemouth, raised in South Africa, and now lives in America. The gentleman's game of cricket is also in a bad way, according to a recent issue of the London *Economist*:

> Supporters of English cricket have come to accept a certain disarray as a normal condition of the game, but lately their casual exasperation has quickened into a sense of crisis. Victory in a test series is a distant memory, and the national side has just lost to the Australians, following last winter's comprehensive defeats by India and Sri Lanka. . . .
>
> Consider the spectacle variously afforded by the recent season and indignantly reported in the press: slanging matches between players, vicious bouncers aimed by bowlers to intimidate (or decapitate) batsmen and a general air of surly bad humor. Just as unseemly was the appalling standard of grooming, with cricket's traditional clean-cut look giving way to designer stubble, flapping shirt-tails and tacky furnishing such as wrap-around sunglasses
>
> Some also find modern cricket's rampant commercialism alarming. Even at Lord's, the conservative home of English cricket, the white perimeter wall is lined with garish adverts. Throughout the test series against Australia, the grass behind the wicket was emblazoned with the sponsor's logo, in letters easily visible on television. And the players themselves displayed the brand names and symbols of Australian and English beers conspicuously on their shirts.[2]

The gentlemanly ideal, with its ancient roots in feudal chivalry, has always had more in common with the military virtues of honor than with the money-making virtues of business. The Vietnam War was a major cause of the 1960s'

FIGURE 30

Tom Brown's Rugby Classmate, Harry Paget Flashman

SOLDIER, LOVER, ADVENTURER, HE FOUGHT AND
WENCHED HIS WAY TO GLORY (AND LECHERY AND
SKULLDUGGERY AND CONDUCT UNBECOMING A
GENTLEMAN)..."SPLENDIDLY ENTERTAINING!"
—TIME

CAN A MAN

—who is expelled from school as a drunken bully*

—who seduces his father's mistress to begin a secret life that leads
from the boudoirs and bordellos of
Victorian England to the erotic frontiers of her exotic Empire

—who lies, cheats, steals, fights fixed duels,
betrays his country, and proves a coward on the battlefield

BE ALL BAD?

FLASHMAN

"DEMOLISHES BOWDLERIZED HISTORY...A VIEW OF OUR NOBLE
ANCESTORS BOTTOM UP, SO TO SPEAK, WHICH IS A VIEW
NO CIVILIZED PEOPLE OUGHT TO NEGLECT. BRAVO FLASHMAN!"
—Washington Post Book World

"THE REFRESHINGLY FUNNY AND RIBALD ADVENTURE STORY
TOLD BY A ROGUE WHO IS A CROSS
BETWEEN BYRON'S DON JUAN AND FIELDING'S TOM JONES."
—Best Sellers

*In *Tom Brown's School Days,* a wretched bully
was expelled from Rugby for ungentlemanly conduct (i.e., being drunk).
That wretched bully was none other than our hero, Harry Flashman.

Source: George MacDonald Fraser, *Flashman* (New York, 1969).

revolt of the younger generation not only in America, but also in England and
on the Continent. And for the first time in the twentieth century, the most
privileged youths in America used their affluence and educational elite status
to avoid the duties of military service. While all of Theodore Roosevelt's four
sons graduated from Groton and Harvard and afterwards died in uniform
while serving their country, only a handful of Groton (1) and Harvard (20)

men gave their lives in the tragic Vietnam War. But Groton and Harvard, class schools for birthright and aspiring young gentlemen in the days of Teddy, Kermit, Archie, and Quentin Roosevelt, have become, since World War II, academic meritocracies with no common moral standards or codes of gentlemanly honor.* The majority of these meritorious students were bred, since kindergarten, on rights rather than duties: "We have the right to choose," many of them would have agreed, "whether or not to support our country in an evil war." And Cambridge, Massachusetts, became a leading center for the study and encouragement of draft evasion. A fine journalist on the staff of the *Atlantic Monthly*, James Fallows, a *magna cum laude* graduate of Harvard (1970) and a Rhodes Scholar, has written with touching honesty and some regret of his own clever defeat of the Cambridge draft board as an undergraduate, all the while watching the naive boys from working-class Somerville joining up with enthusiasm.

The Vietnam War was of course a tragic blunder. But was this not also true of the blundering Charge of the Light Brigade in the Crimean War, of the charge up Cemetery Ridge by Pickett's Virginians at Gettysburg, of the Churchillian blunders at Gallipoli, and of all the pointless slaughter in the muddy fields of Flanders?† The difference is that the generation of Teddy Roosevelt's sons, including Dick Williams and other tennis greats of his time, took seriously, while all too many members of their grandsons' generation would have derisively dismissed, the famous lines by Tennyson, gentleman poet:

> Someone had blundered:
> Theirs not to make reply,
> Theirs not to reason why,
> Theirs but to do and die . . .

In contrast to the boys from the posh boarding schools and prestige colleges were the 129 boys from the parochial and public schools in

---

*Teddy, or General Theodore Roosevelt, Jr., 57 at the time, went ashore with the first wave at Utah Beach on D-Day and earned a Congressional Medal of Honor in the process.

†In the battle of the Somme in 1916, in one day, July 1, the British army suffered 60,000 casualties, 20,000 officers and 40,000 men. Old Etonians carried much more than their share in making the ultimate sacrifice on that terrible summer day (equal to 40 percent of all Americans killed in the eight years of the Vietnam War).

Levittown, Pennsylvania, a small lower-middle-class suburb up the Delaware River from Philadelphia, who made the ultimate sacrifice. Among the boys from Levittown was an authentic hero, David Christian, brought up close to poverty by his welfare mother who had served as a WAC under MacArthur in the South Pacific. Wounded by guns, knives, grenades, bombs, and land mines, he had been given last rites on the battlefield twice before he was 19. At 21, he was a retired Captain with seven Purple Hearts, two Distinguished Service Crosses, two Silver Stars, two Bronze Stars, the Air Medal, and more. In Theodore Roosevelt's or Lord Tennyson's terms, David had more real class than his age peers from Groton School or Harvard College.

Like David Christian, Arthur Ashe had little in common with the anti-ROTC and draft-evading values of his preppy peers at posh colleges. He had taken ROTC at UCLA and was in uniform when he won the U.S. Championship, in 1968: "I view my escape from the war as one of the great omissions of my life," he wrote in his autobiography. "It may sound barbaric and inhumane, but I've always wanted to be in a war. Perhaps it is a death wish of sorts. I think every man wishes secretly that he would have an opportunity to fight, win a lot of medals, and come out with only minor injuries. War is the ultimate symbol of Western masculinity. Unfortunately." The Ashes have had a fine tradition of serving their country in time of war. Ashe's brother, Johnny, had two tours of duty as a Marine officer in Vietnam and was wounded each time.

Service in the armed forces in time of war and peace, of course, has always been one of the privileges and duties of all citizens in free and democratic societies. Is it any wonder that today, for the *first time in our history*, we are relying on an all-professional or mercenary army? Maybe money is the major motivator of men left in America?

When rights and privileges are divorced from duty and honor, traditional upper-class authority has had its day. Most meritocratic youth has never been taught that the gentleman always has placed duty above rights. Groton, a school for turning out Christian gentlemen in Endicott Peabody's day, is now a co-ed school for good grade getters who know their rights rather than their duties to a now-extinct class.

═══

This book has been about the decline of traditional class authority in our increasingly bureaucratic era of atomized professional elites and increasingly impotent leadership. In this connection, I have been concerned with the fact that, ever since the close of World War II, and especially since the unmannerly sixties, unwritten class codes of honor, decency, and deference democracy have steadily been replaced by a defiant democracy endlessly wrangling over bureaucratic rules written and rewritten by professional bores in evermore tedious detail.

While growing up in the 1920s and 1930s, for instance, I never heard of dress codes for school or club tennis courts (one wore white as a matter of course). Nor did I ever encounter a book of written rules of court behavior. Ever since the professionalization of world-class tennis in 1968, however, written rules have replaced traditional manners in both professional and amateur tennis. Thus, at the height of the roughneck age of American tennis, the late Colonel Nick Powell, who "flew a desk" during World War II, as he once put it, was appointed chairman of the USTA Tennis Rules Committee, where he served from the late seventies to the end of the eighties. Powell produced a set of no less than *forty-three* precisely defined rules of court behavior which in turn became the official "Code" of both the professional and amateur game. Perhaps even more revealing of the decline of traditional class authority in America was a little book entitled *Tennis Disputes* which had, according to its author, "answers to over 400 on-court arguments." First published in 1982, the book was so popular that a second edition was published in 1984, "officially recommended by Nick Powell." At the end of the book there is a list of "Twenty Most Commonly Disputed Issues"; insight into the bureaucratic mind at work is suggested by Issue 18—"*Toilet Visit*: A bona fide toilet visit is permitted. [Rule 30, Case 2, Code 41.1 (Dispute Subject 303).]"

From what I have heard and observed of schoolboy and college tennis these days, I would not be too surprised to hear of a young man's being defaulted for a non-*bona fide* visit to the toilet. It is now a possibility, at least.

═══

As an educator, I am also concerned with how the professionalization and bureaucratization of college life today is burying the life of the mind and the search for meaning under ever-rising piles of specialized knowledge taught by increasingly one-dimensional academics who value the techniques of research above the art of teaching. Up until the Second World War or the middle 1960s, for example, the best undergraduate colleges were concerned with producing amateur gentlemen with certain qualities of mind and manners; the training of specialized elites was left to the professional and graduate schools. At Harvard College, for instance, when undergraduates received formal letters from the administration, their surnames were followed with an "Esquire." This ancient tradition was of course discontinued in the 1960s and the undergraduates, no longer honored as gentlemen, are now caught up in the pre-professional treadmills, the honorable "Gentleman-C" being replaced by the more marketable "Pre-Professional-A." While the undergraduates at Harvard and the rest of the Ivy League institutions have probably never been so affluent and formally well educated, hardly any of them are thinking about being, or becoming, gentlemen; and ladies are a dying breed, appropriately dismissed by the avidly pre-professional feminists. Pre-professionalism, moreover, is now corrupting larger and larger areas of college sports. The Ivy League, with its anachronistic amateur concept of the scholar-athlete, is doing its best to buck the trend. In the meantime, as mild pre-professionalism is taking much of the fun out of even Ivy League athletics, more and more undergraduates, many of whom have had older brothers or friends at Oxford or Cambridge, are turning to rugby and cricket, forming their own teams, without paid coaches, and playing the game for fun and fellowship. And these new, sporting gentlemen join their opponents for postgame beer parties.

It is important to remember that the word "amateur" derives from the Latin *amare*, meaning to love. The amateur plays the game for the love of the process and not for the prize. To make love for money is the sad lot of the prostitute who has not only been looked down on, and pitied, throughout history but so often comes in time to despise sex and even herself. In a very real sense, although we should hate to admit it, are not more and more of us, not only in the tennis, baseball or football businesses, but also in the law, medicine, and education businesses, becoming more and more like the members of the oldest profession in making more and more of our lives into means to money rather than ends in themselves? The Christian concept of the soul once made all men equally *priceless*; in our moneyed age the self-made success is generally *worth* at least several millions, while most of us are *worth less*. The more our greatest and most talented athletes sell themselves to the entertainment business, the more they lose the sense of fun and joy in competing. And we Americans have never been so over-entertained, and never so bored and joyless.

Many years ago, when asked by a reporter why he always turned to the sports pages before reading the more serious political news, Chief Justice Earl Warren replied: "Because the sport pages record man's aspirations and triumphs, while politics is a record of man's failures." In a world where decency, self-discipline, character, trustworthiness, self-denial, and lasting love were becoming more and more rare, and politics increasingly corrupt, the sports pages used to be oases of joy and spiritual renewal, as Chief Justice Warren implied. But the sports world is now becoming not only joyless but increasingly unheroic and corrupt, as Peter Pascarelli, a sportswriter in my local paper *The Philadelphia Inquirer*, said so well, several years ago:

> You leaf through the sports pages to read about baseball and find news about drug probes and urine tests.
>
> In search of box scores, you read about $350,000 [million today] a year players threatening to strike and [multi-] millionaire owners pleading poverty. . . .
>
> And you quickly realize that these are times that try baseball's soul. You quickly realize that heroes are hard to find . . .

Like the unwritten British Constitution, the Anglo American amateur sporting mores were deeply rooted in unwritten class codes of honor and decency, originating in England and brought to America during the half-century leading up to the First World War. In every healthy and free society, the so-called *majesty* of the law has always depended on the support of a *nobility* of unwritten class customs.

I do not wish to imply that all amateur athletes lived up to the sporting code all of the time before 1968. Of course they didn't. The sportsman's code was, and always is, an ideal and not a description of actual behavior. It is only in caste or tribal societies that behavior usually mirrors norms or ideals; in all dynamic and changing societies there are always breaches of honor, decency, and so forth. Theodore Roosevelt stepped in to quell the brutalities of football in the days when the genteel tradition was still in vogue. At the same time, many of the leading colleges in the nation were breaking with rivals who, so they thought, were violating the codes of honor and gentlemanly behavior: thus Army and Navy broke between 1893 and 1899; Harvard and Yale between 1894 and 1897; Penn and Lafayette between 1900 and 1903. And of course the gentlemen of Princeton were forever breaking with their "less gentlemanly" rivals, with Harvard between 1897 and 1912, and again between 1926 and 1934; with Penn from 1894, in what was called the Second Battle of Trenton (selected as a neutral location) up until 1935.

The point to be made here is that class ideals once did exist and they were most often enforced informally by threats of class ostracism (perhaps classless ostracism is a contradiction in terms); that is to say that breaches of honor, honesty, or decency were taken far more seriously on the football fields and tennis courts, or on the campuses, than they are apparently today. Men like Dick Williams in his day, as well as Bill Bradley or Stan Smith or Arthur Ashe in theirs, were admired and looked up to as much for their honorable characters as for their skill in the game. They still had a sense of class or style which campus authorities should be cultivating today more than ever. Or as Reginald E. Selnick, writing in the socialist *Dissent*, put it in 1966:

> When I was an undergraduate at Princeton ten years ago, things were just the opposite. Then the University subtly demanded of its students that they be like *it*, fashioning themselves in its image. The style of Princeton and many of its professors drew the students like a magnet. The "multiversity" of the 1960's, on the other hand, finds it impossible to play this kind of role. To be a mediator among the conflicting interests of the community is no goal of idealistic youth, and arguments that such a role is essential for the functioning of the university within the body politic are unpersuasive.[3]

Idealistic youths of today are given no ideals to live by, either by the authorities at Princeton or the officials of the United States Tennis Association that built and run the tennis game at Flushing Meadow. All the while, the written rules are multiplying, most of them now made on college campuses, in accord with the values of Victim Political Correctness.

I remain pessimistic about the direction American tennis and American society as a whole have taken since 1968, fearing, following Gibbon, the "decline of genius and manly virtue" in modern America. The trouble in tennis largely lies in the radical change from a provincial amateur game dominated by the ideals of an Anglo-American upper class and its British Commonwealth counterparts to a new world tennis game with no common sporting ideals held together by the common pursuit of money. An inspection of Figure 31 is instructive here. Thus English-speaking nations won 90 percent of the Davis Cup challenge rounds between 1900 and the end of the amateur era in 1967. Since 1968, on the other hand, only 64 percent of the winners were English-speaking. Whereas only four nations (France the first non-English) won the Davis Cup in over fifty amateur years, eight, or twice as many, nations won the Davis Cup in the first twenty-five years of the pro era.

In our global village, made possible by the jet plane and television, in other words, the bureaucratic, classless, and professional form of tennis is here to stay. There is no possibility of a return to amateurism at the top levels of the international game. All this is for the good in opening up new opportunities for youths in the some hundred nations now entering Davis Cup competition.

Not only has the new world of professional tennis brought many new nations into the game; here at home ethnic and racial prejudices no longer mark the professional game.

The United States is still, some seven decades after Tilden was the first American to win the Wimbledon Gentleman's Singles Championship, the leading tennis nation in the world. We must take the lead in exerting some new and effective authority over the pro game I of course do not presume to know in detail how this will be done. In my judgment, however, the United States Tennis Association will fail to gain real respect from the world tennis community unless it learns from Flushing Meadow (voted the *worst* of the Grand Slam venues in every modern poll of player opinion; see Figure 32) and comes up with a new tennis complex of real *quality* rather than just something bigger to draw more ticket-buyers and make more money.

Biggest is rarely the best and usually the worst. I am convinced that the American tennis establishment must concentrate on remaking tennis into an elite and quality game by increasing the quality of the audience by decreasing the stadium size and the money take. Rather than the

FIGURE 31
Davis Cup Winning Nations: Amateur and Professional Eras

Nation	Number of Wins	Year First Win	Percent Wins	
Amateur Era 1900–1967 (56 years of competition)				
USA	19	(1900)	34%	
England	9	(1903)	16%	
Australia*	22	(1907)	40%	English-Speaking 90%
France	6	(1927)	10%	
	56		100%	
Professional Era 1968–1992 (25 years of competition)				
USA	11	(1968)	44%	
Australia	4	(1973)	16%	English-Speaking 64%
S. Africa	1	(1974)	4%	
Sweden	4	(1975)	16%	
Italy	1	(1976)	4%	
Czechoslovakia	1	(1980)	4%	
Germany	2	(1988)	8%	
France	1	(1991)	4%	
	25		100%	

Runner-Up Nations: Romania (1969), Germany (1970), India (1974),** Czech.
(1975), Argentina (1981), Switzerland (1992)
Number of Nations Competing: 1900 (2); 1920 (5); 1927 (23); 1939 (25); 1967 (47);
1992 (93)

* The cup was first taken down under by Australasia in 1907. Actually, Australia's first win was in 1939; the Australasia teams were largely made up of Australians after Norman Brookes and Tony Wilding first won it in 1907.
** India defaulted to S. Africa in 1974 as a protest at their racial policies.

biggest stadium in tennis, we need the smallest of the four Grand Slam stadiums. Perhaps I am too unrealistic, as Americans will always value quantity and size above quality and excellence.

———

This book has been primarily concerned with the "gentlemanly" ideal in America. But what about the ladies?

In the first place, and above all, it should be said that there has been a far greater deterioration in the behavior of men than of women during the professional era, a far greater difference between gentlemen ama-

FIGURE 32

Grand Slam Rankings

Wimbledon's Rated Most Prestigious Slam

Wimbledon is the most prestigious Grand Slam tournament and also has the "best" audience, according to *Tennis* magazine of France (June 1989), which surveyed 89 of the top men and women pros regarding their thoughts about the four Grand Slam events. Among the respondents were Stefan Edberg, Ivan Lendl, John McEnroe, Yannick Noah, Arantxa Sanchez and brothers Javier and Emilio, Pam Shriver, Helena Sukova and Mats Wilander.

A roster of the participants reveals the following nationalities: United States (16); Sweden (11); France (10); Italy and Czechoslovakia (6); Spain (5); Argentina and Australia (4); Austria, Belgium and Switzerland (3); West Germany, Great Britain, the Netherlands and Yugoslavia (2), and South Africa, Denmark, India, Iran, Haiti, Hungary, Mexico, Peru, the Soviet Union and Uruguay with 1 each. Below, the results of ranking the creature comforts and

day-to-day workings of the Grand Slams:

MOST PRESTIGIOUS
1. Wimbledon
2. French Open
3. U.S. Open
4. Australian Open

BEST ORGANIZATION
1. French Open
2. Australian Open
3. Wimbledon
4. U.S. Open

BEST AUDIENCE
1. Wimbledon
2. French Open
3. Australian Open
4. U.S. Open

BEST PLAYERS' FACILITIES
1. French Open
2. Australian Open
3. Wimbledon
4. U.S. Open

BEST TRANSPORTATION
1. French Open
2. Australian Open
3. Wimbledon
4. U.S. Open

MOST BEAUTIFUL STADIUM
1. Australian Open
2. Wimbledon
3. French Open
4. U.S. Open

BEST OFFICIATING
1. French Open
2. Wimbledon
3. U.S. Open
4. Australian Open

BEST WELCOME
1. French Open
2. Australian Open
3. Wimbledon
4. U.S. Open

BEST FOOD
1. French Open
2. Australian Open
3. Wimbledon
4. U.S. Open

BEST TROPHY CEREMONY
1. Wimbledon
2. French Open
3. Australian Open
4. U.S. Open

BEST TRAINING CONDITIONS
1. French Open
2. Australian Open
3. U.S. Open
4. Wimbledon

MOST PATRIOTIC PUBLIC
1. French Open
2. Australian Open
3. U.S. Open
4. Wimbledon

TOUGHEST PHYSICALLY
1. French Open
2. U.S. Open
3. Australian Open
4. Wimbledon

BEST SCHEDULING
1. French Open
2. Wimbledon
3. Australian Open
4. U.S. Open

FAVORITE CITY
1. Paris
2. New York
3. London
4. Melbourne

Source: Tennis Week, July 6, 1989.

teurs and professional men than between amateur ladies and professional women. In the quarter-century since 1968, for instance, no American
women have produced such vulgar and inexcusable behavior on the
courts as Jimmy Connors and John McEnroe. Moreover, while all too
many modern fans have found the vulgarities of Jimmy and John far
more exciting than the mannerly styles of the two most cultivated gentlemen on the tour, Arthur Ashe and Ivan Lendl, few fans have favored the
often rude and hard-edged feminist, Billie Jean King, over the feminine
and always ladylike Chrissie Evert. In spite of the modern feminist
dream of making women more like men (and men more like women)
through cultural conditioning, biological human nature will probably always lurk just beneath the surface of cultural and social control, maleness
implying aggressive and often antisocial behavior, and femaleness implying a more passive and placating nature. All of which suggests that men
are far more in need of societal and cultural restraints than women. Thus
in periods of rapid social change when cultural restraints are loosening
and society disintegrating, men suffer far more than women: witness the
plight of males in modern African American society, or the Margaret
Thatcher phenomenon in Flashman's Britain.

Almost exactly a century ago, a French sociologist, Emile Durkheim,
noted this difference between men and women in his classic work, *Le
Suicide* (1897). He found that in times of societal disintegration or societal anarchy (he used the French term *anomie*), the restrictions on
divorce are loosened; contrary to conventional wisdom, however,
Durkheim noted that strict divorce codes were more necessary for the
mental health of men than for women: as the divorce rate increased, the
rate of suicide among men *increased* while that of women *decreased*. All
this is to say that the gentlemanly code among men is far more necessary
for societal stability than the ladylike code is for women. It also follows
that women are by nature more emotionally stable and stronger (in a sur-
vival, rather than simple brute strength, sense) than men.

The incredible careers of Hazel Hotchkiss Wightman, May Sutton
and her three older sisters, and Elizabeth Ryan—all Californians of the
first aristocratic generation—as well as Billie Jean King, a Californian of
the first generation of the open era, are splendid and convincing examples of the great staying power and stability of American women tennis
players: Wightman died at the age of 88, in 1974, May Sutton died the

following year at 89, and Elizabeth Ryan at the age of 88, in 1979. Billie Jean King, at 50 in 1993, has been a leader in women's tennis since winning Wimbledon in 1966 and the U.S. Open the following year. Their stories, and the stories of the other great women tennis players, could fill a whole other book, but its conclusions would be far different from those presented here.

===

I will conclude with three incidents which clearly show how far we have come in terms of sportsmanship from the heyday of amateurism.

By 1985, I had been watching the University of Pennsylvania tennis team for almost half a century (ever since I had captained the freshman team in 1936). That spring of 1985, for the first time I left a match in disgust after watching a member of the Penn team constantly call his opponent's good shots out, both the doubtful and the clearly in.

That same summer I watched the disgraceful doubles final at Flushing Meadow between Ken Flach and Robert Seguso, of the United States, and Henri Leconte and Yannick Noah, of France. The tennis was brilliant, the teams splitting the first two sets 7–6, 6–7; the French had set point in the third-set tiebreaker (5–4) when Leconte hit a ball which many thought hit Flach before landing out of court; the umpire hesitated; Flach said nothing; the ball was ruled out; the Americans took the third set; the French gave away (tanked) the fourth set 6–0 and lost the match 7–6, 6–7, 7–6, 6–0. Though Flach later admitted that the ball *might have* touched him, he also argued that it was up to the umpire to make the call. Contrary to Flach, McEnroe, who rarely followed Tilden's rule when bad calls were made in his favor, felt this was the one call a player must make himself: "If the ball hits me, I always say so."

McEnroe's biographer, Richard Evans, wrote of the incident as follows: "In my 20 years of covering this game, Ken Flach is the only player I have ever heard use the phrase 'might have' when discussing this kind of situation. . . . It really is a *question of honor and that is a word people who deal with pro sports have become afraid of. It is thought ridiculous for professional athletes to operate under an honor code when there is so much at stake. This is a view, I am afraid, that is particularly prevalent in America"* (italics mine).[4] Apparently, honor has a price in modern America's classless society: it used to be priceless. In a press conference after the match, Yannick Noah, a popular African French tennis star, said: "For me, tennis is still a game and I like to enjoy playing it. I cannot enjoy it if my opponent is being deprived of points he has earned. That is the way I am. Mats Wilander is that way, too. Personally, I would not like to feel the way Ken Flach feels now. He knows the ball hit his shoulder and yet he took the point. He cannot feel happy."

My third experience with dishonorable behavior among our tennis youth today was particularly personal and painful. In the spring term of 1992, I became good friends with one of my "A" students, Nicos Hecht, who turned out to be the grandson of Ladislav Hecht, Czechoslovakian Davis Cup star who was the number one foreign seed at the Men's Championships at Forest Hills in 1941. Nicos, a perfect gentleman whose hero and model was his grandfather, played number one on Penn's tennis team. As I watched him play his final match for Penn against another Ivy League team, his opponent, at a critical point in the second set, let loose a powerful serve which Nicos called out (the opposing coach saw the serve and afterwards agreed that Nicos had made the right call). Two points later, Nicos returned a rather soft shot which clearly landed well within his opponent's court.* I was sitting less than five yards away and carefully watching Nicos's opponent who, after hesitating for a moment, called the ball out. The incident was upsetting to say the least, and Nicos lost the match. Never had I seen such blatant cheating in a lifetime of playing tennis. Even worse, however, was the fact that Nicos and others on the Penn team informed me that this sort of behavior was becoming more and more frequent in college tennis, even in the Ivy League. As retaliatory gamesmanship increases, moreover, it will become harder and harder to *trust* one's opponent.

=====

Not long ago, I spent a chilly September evening at Flushing Meadow in one of the seats made available to middle-income tennis-lovers like myself. The players were too far away to see in any human sense (many of the surrounding spectators used binoculars); the glare of the lights pro-

---

*Six inches or more inside the baseline and five inches inside the sideline nearest me.

duced two shadows chasing each of the contestants around the court and the public address system endlessly and continuously repeated "please remain seated while play is in progress, thank you . . .; clear the aisles, thank you . . .; please, please, please . . .; thank you, thank you, thank you . . ." Unable from my bird's-eye view to enjoy the finer points of the game, I turned to watching the privileged and beautiful people, including well-fed, middle-aged men with youthful, fur-decorated companions, move in and out of their seats, and wondered how many of them were there because of the in-status of the event and their prestigious seats, rather than any real knowledge or love of the game. Did any of their kind, I asked myself, participate in the rowdiness of that Thursday night massacre in 1979? For, surely, the rest of the fans that night, I calculated, were too far away to pose any real threat to order on the court.

"People want excitement," Richard Evans concluded in his discussions of that Thursday massacre in 1979, "and if they can't find it at a tennis stadium they will go off and seek it in less savory places." Let them go, for goodness sake!

Notes

Chapter 1. Introduction

1. This and the quotations from James which follow are taken from C. L. R. James, *Beyond a Boundary* (1963).
2. John McPhee, *Levels of the Game* (1969). The discussion of Arthur Ashe which follows (including all quotations) are taken from this book.
3. Arthur Ashe (with Frank Deford), *Portrait in Motion* (1975); Arthur Ashe (with Neil Amdur), *Off the Court* (1981); Arthur Ashe and Arnold Rampersad, *Days of Grace, A Memoir* (1993).
4. Ted Tinling (with Rod Humphries), *Love and Faults* (1979).
5. See "Glory Days: Memorable Moments from the U.S. Championship," *Racquet,* Fall 1991.

Chapter 2. The Anglo-American Amateur Tradition, the Making of a National Upper Class, and a Gentlemanly Code of Honor in America, 1880–1914

1. See Asa Briggs, *Victorian People,* Chapter 4 (1955).
2. Thomas Hughes, *Tom Brown's School Days* (1856).
3. Samuel Eliot Morison, *The Founding of Harvard College* (1935).
4. Anthony Wilding, *On and Off the Court* (1913).
5. R. W. B. Lewis, *Edith Wharton* (1975).
6. Stewart H. Holbrook, "Frank Merriwell at Yale—and Again and Again," *American Heritage,* June 1961.

7. Frank D. Ashburn, *Peabody of Groton* (1944).
8. *Ibid.*
9. Owen Wister, *Roosevelt: The Story of a Friendship* (1930).
10. John R. Tunis, *The American Way of Sport* (1958).
11. *The Letters of Theodore Roosevelt,* selected and edited by Elting Morison, Volume 3 (1952).
12. Tunis, *op. cit.*
13. Perry Anderson, "The Origins of the Present Crisis," in the *New Left Review,* January–February 1964.
14. Max Weber, *The Protestant Ethic and the Spirit of Capitalism* (1958).
15. Ernest Earnest, *S. Weir Mitchell* (1950).

Chapter 3. The Rise of Lawn Tennis

1. "The Origins of Lawn Tennis," in *The Encyclopedia of Tennis,* edited by Max Robertson (advisory editor, Jack Kramer) (1974).
2. *Ibid.*
3. Herbert Warren Wind, "The First Hundred Years," *New Yorker,* 1973.
4. Mark Girouard, *The Victorian Country House* (1985).
5. Edward C. Potter, Jr., *Kings of the Court* (1963).
6. Joseph Sill Clark, typewritten letter, undated.
7. *Dictionary of American Biography,* Volume 2 (1928).
8. Richard O'Connor, *The Scandalous Mr. Bennett* (1962).
9. *Fifty Years of Lawn Tennis in the United States* (1931).
10. See Anthony Bailey, "Promenade Des Anglais," *New Yorker,* July 12, 1982.
11 Frank B Copley *Frederick W. Taylor, Father of Scientific Management* (1923).
12. *Fifty Years of Lawn Tennis in the United States.*
13. *Ibid.*

Chapter 4. The Expansion of Lawn Tennis in an Age of Innocence, 1887–1912

1. Henry W. Slocum, "Early Days in Newport," in *Fifty Years of Lawn Tennis in the United States* (1931).

2. Edward C. Potter, Jr., *Kings of the Court* (1963).
3. Dwight F. Davis, "The Establishment of an International Trophy," in *Fifty Years of Lawn Tennis in the United States.*
4. *Ibid.*
5. A. Wallis Myers, *The Complete Lawn Tennis Player* (1905).
6. Potter, *op. cit.*
7. Dame Mabel Brookes, *Crowded Galleries* (1956).
8. *Ibid.*
9. Anthony Wilding, *On and Off the Court* (1913).
10. *Ibid.*

Chapter 5. Class Complacency Challenged in 1912

1. Walter Lord, *A Night to Remember* (1955).
2. Wyn Craig Wade, *The Titanic* (1979). This and the following quotations are taken from Wade's book, far and away the best on the sociology of the *Titanic* disaster.
3. *Ibid.*
4. *Ibid.*
5. Herbert Warren Wind, "The Story of Hazel Hotchkiss Wightman," *New Yorker,* 1952.
6. *American Lawn Tennis,* December 15, 1909.
7. Wind, *op. cit.*
8. Gail Baxter, *The Berkeley Tennis Club: A History* (1976).
9. *Ibid.*
10. Wind, *op. cit.*
11. *American Lawn Tennis,* December 15, 1910.
12. Wind, *op. cit.*

Chapter 6. The Old Order Changes

1. *American Lawn Tennis,* January 1913.
2. *Ibid.,* February 1913.
3. *Ibid.,* March 1913.
4. Edward C. Potter, Jr., *Kings of the Court* (1963).
5. Dame Mabel Brookes, *Crowded Galleries* (1956).

6. *American Lawn Tennis,* February 1913.
7. *American Lawn Tennis,* February 1915.
8. *Ibid.*
9. *Ibid.*
10. *Ibid.*

Chapter 7. Two Philadelphia Gentlemen

1. Alfred Lief, *Family Business: A Century in the Life and Times of Strawbridge & Clothier* (1968). I have relied on this book for family background and so forth. A great deal of the material in this chapter, however, has come from talking to young Bill Clothier during a friendship of over half a century, especially during the decade of writing this book, which began after several weeks one summer spent in browsing through Bill's excellent tennis library at "Valley Hill Farm."
2. James A. Michener, "Swat'more Collich," in *Swarthmore Remembered,* edited by Maralyn Orbison Gillispie '49 (1964).
3. Three members of the Porter family, Andrew (1743–1813), David Rittenhouse (1788–1867), and Horace (1837–1921), were distinguished enough to be listed in the *Dictionary of American Biography,* Volume 15 (1935).
4. *Harvard College Class of 1904:* Twenty-Fifth Anniversary (1929).
5. August Heckscher, *St. Paul's: The Life of a New England School* (1980).
6. Walter Isaacson and Evan Thomas, *The Wise Men* (1986).
7. Axel Kaufmann, "William J. Clothier II, Top Tennis Administrator, Wins Marlboro Award," *World Tennis* May (1960).

Chapter 8. Racism and Anti-Semitism

1. Arthur M. Schlesinger, Jr., *The Crisis of the Old Order, 1919–1933* (1957).
2. Francis Biddle, *A Casual Past* (1961).
3. Arthur Schlesinger, Jr., *The Coming of the New Deal* (1959).
4. E. Digby Baltzell, *The Protestant Establishment: Aristocracy & Caste in America* (1964).
5. Cleveland Amory, *Who Killed Society?* (1960).
6. Richard L. Zweigenhaft and G. William Domhoff, *Jews in the Protestant Establishment* (1982).

7. David Gray, "Gray's Anatomy of How It Happened," *World Tennis* (June 1978).
8. Robert Minton, *Forest Hills: An Illustrated History* (1975).
9. *New York Times,* August 8, 1968.
10. Amory, *op. cit.*

Chapter 9. William Tatum Tilden II

1. William T. Tilden II, *My Story: A Champion's Memoir* (1948).
2. Quoted in Frank Deford, *Big Bill Tilden: The Triumphs and the Tragedy* (1975).
3. *Ibid.*
4. William T. Tilden II, *Me—The Handicap* (1929).
5. *Ibid.*
6. Tilden, *My Story* (1948).
7. Frank Deford, *Big Bill Tilden: The Triumphs and the Tragedy* (1976).
8. William T. Tilden II, *Match Play and the Spin of the Ball,* edited by Stephen Wallis Merrihew (1925).
9. Tilden, *My Story.*
10. *Fred Perry: An Autobiography* (1984).
11. Tilden, *My Story.*
12. Ted Tinling (with Rod Humphries), *Love and Faults* (1979).
13. Tilden, *My Story.*
14. The fine description of this match and the quotations as well are taken from Deford, *op. cit.*

Chapter 10. The Finest Five Years in Tennis History

1. Al Laney, *Covering the Court: A 50-Year Love Affair with the Game of Tennis* (1968).
2. William T. Tilden II, *My Story: A Champion's Memoirs* (1948).
3. *Ibid.*
4. Laney, *op. cit.*
5. Frank Deford, *Big Bill Tilden: The Triumphs and the Tragedy* (1976).
6. Don Budge, *A Tennis Memoir* (1969).
7. Tilden, *My Story.*

8. Budge, *op. cit.*
9. *Ibid.*

Chapter 11. Big Bill Tilden

1. Frank Deford, *Big Bill Tilden: The Triumphs and the Tragedy* (1976).
2. Al Laney, *Covering the Court: A 50-Year Love Affair with the Game of Tennis* (1968).
3. Deford, *op. cit.* Deford refers to *The Art of Tennis* (1921) only once and gives no date. The book was Tilden's first.
4. Quoted in Deford, *op. cit.*
5. Jean René Lacoste, *Lacoste on Tennis* (1928).
6. *Fred Perry: An Autobiography* (1984).
7. Quotations are from Deford, *op. cit.*
8. Jack Kramer (with Frank Deford), *The Game: My 40 Years in Tennis* (1979).
9. Deford, *op. cit.*

Chapter 12. The Grass-Court Circuit Becomes a Melting Pot, and Perry Jones Leads a Second California Invasion of the Eastern Establishment

1. Allison Danzig, "Doeg Defeats Shields for U.S. Championship" (1930), in *The Fireside Book of Tennis,* edited by Allison Danzig and Peter Schwed (1972).
2. *Fred Perry: An Autobiography* (1984).
3. Stan Hart, *Once a Champion: Legendary Tennis Stars Revisited* (1984).
4. William F. Talbert (with John Sharnik), *Playing for Life* (1958).
5. *Ibid.*
6. Richard Evans, *Open Tennis: The First Twenty Years* (1988).
7. Arthur Ashe (with Frank Deford), *Portrait in Motion* (1975).
8. Throughout this chapter I am gratefully indebted to Patricia Henry Yeomans, *Southern California Tennis Champions Centennial 1887–1987: Documents and Anecdotes* (1987).
9. Ted Tinling (with Rod Humphries), *Love and Faults* (1979).
10. Jack Kramer (with Frank Deford), *The Game: My 40 Years in Tennis* (1979).

11. Bobby Riggs (with George McGann), *Court Hustler* (1973).

12. Allison Danzig, "Sidney Wood," in *The Fireside Book of Tennis.*

13. Allison Danzig, "Bryan (Bitsy) Grant," in *The Fireside Book of Tennis.*

14. George Lott, "The Great Doubles Teams," in *The Fireside Book of Tennis.*

Chapter 13. Gentleman Jack Crawford of Australia, and Fred Perry, the Last Great Englishman

1. I am much indebted to Alan Trengove's fine book, *The Story of the Davis Cup* (1985), especially in my discussions of the years 1932 and 1933.

2. *Fred Perry: An Autobiography* (1984).

3. *Ibid.*

4. *Ibid.*

5. *Ibid.*

6. *Ibid.*

7. *Ibid.*

8. See Paul Metzler, *Great Players of Australian Tennis* (1979), for a fine discussion of Crawford's place in the history of tennis in Australia.

9. Quoted by A. Wallis Myers, "Crawford Defeats Vines," in *The Fireside Book of Tennis,* edited by Allison Danzig and Peter Schwed (1972).

10. Stan Hart in an unpublished interview with Crawford.

11. Perry, *op. cit.*

12. *Ibid.*

13. Ted Tinling with Rod Humphries, *Love and Faults* (1979).

14. Perry, *op. cit.*

Chapter 14. Budge and the Baron

1. C. David Heymann, *Poor Little Rich Girl: The Life and Legend of Barbara Hutton* (1983).

2. J. Donald Budge, *A Tennis Memoir* (1969).

3. *Ibid.*

4. Stan Hart, *Once a Champion* (1985).

5. Budge, *op. cit.*

6. *Ibid.*

7. Alan Trengove, *The Story of the Davis Cup* (1985).

8. Budge, *op. cit.*
9. *Ibid.*
10. *Ibid.*

Chapter 15. Indian Summer of a Golden Age

1. Bobby Riggs (with George McGann), *Court Hustler* (1973).
2. Stan Hart, *Once a Champion* (1985); interview with Don McNeill.
3. *Ibid.;* interview with Frank Parker.
4. *Ibid.*
5. Jack Kramer (with Frank Deford), *The Game: My 40 Years in Tennis* (1979).
6. *Ibid.*
7. *Man with a Racket: The Autobiography of Pancho Gonzales,* as told to Cy Rice (1959).
8. *Ibid.*
9. Kramer, *The Game.*

Chapter 16. Lean Years in American Tennis and the Reign of Harry Hopman's Australians

1. Tony Trabert with Gerald Couzens, *Trabert on Tennis: The View from the Center Court* (1988)
2. Jeane Hoffman, "Art Larsen," in *The Fireside Book of Tennis,* edited by Allison Danzig and Peter Schwed (1972).
3. Bill Talbert (with Pete Axthelm), *Tennis Observed: The USLTA Men's Singles Champions, 1881–1966* (1967). As in the case with Larsen, Talbert wrote wise and knowing notes on all the U.S. champions from Richard Sears through Frederick Stolle, the Australian star who won in 1966. Even more important, the book contains the official draws (including the scores of each match) of every championship 1881–1966.
4. Kramer, *The Game.*
5. John Sharnik, *Remembrance of Games Past: On Tour with the Tennis Grand Masters* (1986).
6. Kramer, *The Game.*

Chapter 17. The Great Revolution, 1968–1992: The Rise of Open (Pro) Tennis and the Decline of Civility

1. Arthur Ashe (with Frank Deford), *Arthur Ashe: Portrait in Motion* (1975).
2. William F. Talbert, with John Sharnik, *Playing for Life* (1958).
3. John Feinstein, *Hard Courts* (1991). See also in Sampras and Courier: Eliot Berry, *Tough Draw: The Path to Tennis Glory* (1992).
4. Talbert, *op. cit.*
5. Curry Kirkpatrick, "Mr. Smith Goes to Bucharest," *Sports Illustrated,* October 1972.
6. "Cupa Davis" (originally a *New Yorker* article) in Herbert Warren Wind, *Game, Set, and Match: The Tennis Boom of the 1960s and 70s* (1979).
7. Peter Bodo, "Ion's World," *Tennis,* September 1992.
8. Jim Burke, *The World of Jimmy Connors* (1976).
9. Richard Evans, *Nasty: Ilie Nastase vs. Tennis* (1981).
10. *Ibid.*
11. Jim Burke, *op. cit.*
12. *Tennis,* September 1981.
13. Bjorn Borg, *My Life and Game,* as told to Eugene L. Scott (1980).
14. Herbert Warren Wind, "West of Mayfair, East of Manhattan," *New Yorker,* October 6, 1980.
15. Herbert Warren Wind, "Order on the Court," *New Yorker,* October 24, 1983.
16. Wilfred Sheed, "It's a Knockout," *World Tennis,* September 1982.
17. Anthony Burgess, "Whither Wimbledon?" *World Tennis,* July 1983.
18. Herbert Warren Wind, "Horseshoe Piazza, Horseshoe Stadium" in *Game, Set, and Match* (1979).
19. *World Tennis,* September 1983.
20. *Ibid.*
21. *Ibid.*
22. *Ibid.*
23. Wind, "Horseshoe Piazza, Horseshoe Stadium."
24. Quoted in Richard Evans, *op. cit.*
25. *Ibid.*
26. Evans, *op. cit.*
27. Richard Evans, "King Borg Reigns for Fifth Year at Wimbledon, Appoints McEnroe His Worthy Successor." *Tennis Week,* July 17, 1980.

28. *Ibid.*
29. Curry Kirkpatrick, "His Earth, His Realm, His England," *Sports Illustrated,* July 13, 1981.
30. Alan Little and Lance Tingay, *Wimbledon Men: A Hundred Championships 1877–1986* (1986).
31. *World Tennis,* September 1981.
32. All the above quotations are taken from Richard Evans, *McEnroe: A Rage for Perfection* (1982).
33. All the above quotations are from *World Tennis,* September 1984.
34. *Tennis,* November 1984.
35. Richard Evans, *McEnroe: Taming the Talent* (1990).
36. *Ibid.*
37. John Feinstein, *Hard Courts* (1991).

Epilogue

1. Anthony Burgess, "Whither Wimbledon?" *World Tennis,* July 1983.
2. *Economist,* September 25, 1993.
3. Reginald E. Zelnick, "Prodigal Fathers and Existential Sons," *Dissent,* May–June 1966.
4. *Tennis Week,* September 19, 1985.

Index